Self-Support

C. H. Carpenter

ESPRIOS DIGITAL PUBLISHING

Self-support,
Illustrated in the History of the Bassein Karen Mission
from 1840 to 1880

by

C H Carpenter

With an Introduction by Alvah Hovey, D.D., LL.D.

1883.

PROFITS OF PUBLICATION DEVOTED TO THE BASSEIN N. AND
I. INSTITUTE.

"In majorem *DEI* Gloriam."

PORTRAIT OF REV. E. L. ABBOTT

TO
THE PRECIOUS MEMORY OF
THE FATHERS OF MODERN MISSIONS,
INTO WHOSE LABORS WE HAVE ENTERED,
AND TO THOSE LABORERS IN OTHER FIELDS
WHO PATIENTLY AND HOPEFULLY WORK ON IN THE
FACE OF HARDNESS WHICH WE OF THE KAREN MISSION
HAVE
NEVER KNOWN, AND TO THOSE HIGH-BORN SOULS WHO
DARE TO LEAVE AN EASY PATH FOR A ROUGH ONE,
IN SIMPLE LOYALTY TO A LAW OF DEVELOPMENT
IN CHRIST'S KINGDOM, (IS IT UNWRITTEN?)
THIS VOLUME IS INSCRIBED,
WITH REVERENCE AND SYMPATHY,
BY THE AUTHOR.

INTRODUCTION

Three questions, to which the supporters of foreign missions at home and abroad will readily give their earnest consideration, are partly, if not fully, answered by this volume. *First*, Does the Christian religion, as understood and embraced in these latter days, ever kindle a deep and holy enthusiasm in the souls of men, so that, in times of distress, they prove to be heroes and martyrs? *Second*, Does it produce in them the impulses of a noble manhood, that cares little for self, and much for others, so that, in times of peace, they are willing to give liberally, out of their deep poverty, for the support of Christian institutions among themselves, and for the conversion of men who are still in darkness? *Third*, Does the method of help adopted by their foreign teachers always cultivate as effectually as possible this noble and strenuous type of Christian manhood, so that converts from heathenism are rapidly prepared for self-support, and even for aggressive work, in the regions beyond?

To the *first* question, several chapters of this history furnish a decisive answer; not, indeed, the only decisive answer, but one of the most thrilling and convincing. For, while it would be easy to select from the list of Protestant missionaries belonging to the present century many names that might be confidently added to the roll of believing "witnesses" in the eleventh chapter of Hebrews, they would be names of exceptional men, who had inherited force of character with their blood, and had been trained to reverence for God and his truth under the best Christian influences. But the Karen martyrs of Bassein were members of a broken and timid race, were born of parents, who, through fear of their oppressors, had been all their lifetime subject to bondage, and were themselves recent converts to the Christian religion, having little knowledge of divine truth, and brief experience of the Saviour's grace. Yet that grace was sufficient for them; and, sustained by it, they passed with extraordinary firmness through the terrific ordeal of religious persecution waged by a relentless people. The story of their fortitude under suffering, and their victory over death, is here told in sympathetic language, but without exaggeration; and every

Christian who reads it will bless God for the power of faith in these humble disciples during their prolonged and fiery trial, and will feel his heart bounding with joy when he comes to the record of their deliverance from persecution, and of their continued progress in the good way under the banner of peace. Such a narrative refreshes our confidence in Christian faith as still and always the victory that overcometh the world. By virtue of it, these Karens, who were for a time literally "destitute, afflicted, tormented," "wrought righteousness, obtained promises, escaped the edge of the sword, out of weakness were made strong, waxed valiant in fight, turned to flight the armies of the aliens." In other mission-fields similar illustrations of the power of Christ to keep and strengthen "his own" have been given in these latter days, but none more remarkable or encouraging than these.

To the *second* question, also, many chapters of this history furnish a satisfactory answer; for they prove beyond reasonable doubt, that the Christian religion as understood and received by the Karens of Bassein has produced in them a new and true life,—a type of manhood that cares little for self, and much for the common weal; a spirit that is subject to the law of love, and prompt to manifest itself in deeds of benevolence. By united effort, continued through a long period, they have given "out of their deep poverty" large sums for the support of Christian preachers and teachers, for the building of chapels and schoolhouses, and for the evangelization of other tribes in Burma. Their career verifies in a signal manner the truth of Christ's saying, "It is more blessed to give than to receive." If, under persecution, they showed how "sublime a thing it is to suffer and be strong," they have also, when living unmolested and without fear, shown how wise and beautiful a thing it is to bear one another's burden, and so fulfil the law of Christ.

But it is not our purpose to represent the Bassein Christians as faultless. They themselves would be the first to condemn such a representation. None of their missionaries or pastors would approve it. The instructive reports of Mr. Abbott and Mr. Beecher show that they saw many faults in the life of these disciples. And the history of Mr. Carpenter, composed chiefly of the letters and reports of these two missionaries, is no studied eulogy of the Bassein churches. From it we learn not only that many of their early pastors were deficient in Christian knowledge, but also that a few of them had grave defects of character, and that some in later times have lacked steadfastness or humility. Moreover, it is evident that the standard of discipline in certain churches has sometimes been lower than the word of God requires. But, in spite of these abatements, it remains true that the Karen disciples of Bassein have, on the whole, borne themselves as men, being "steadfast, immovable, always abounding in the work of the Lord."

To the *third*, a more delicate and practical question than either of the preceding, many chapters of this history contribute materials for an answer, if they do not rather, for all ordinary cases, absolutely decide what that answer must be. Of this we are confident: the facts here recited will convince every unbiased reader of the essential wisdom of the course pursued by the leading missionaries to the Sgau Karens of the Bassein field. "By their fruits ye shall know them;" and the fruits of this field bear witness, not only to the grace of God, but also to the excellent method of spiritual culture early adopted, and faithfully continued, by those in charge of it. The method thus commended is that of laying upon the native disciples the support of Christian worship and education among themselves, with little or no help from the mission treasury. "Self-help," as the duty of all Christian converts, and the best means of producing in them a worthy character, is the lesson of this remarkable story.

"This book is a history, but it is also an argument. It is, however, almost wholly an argument made by the facts themselves. Mr. Carpenter lets documents and events tell their own story in the main, with just enough of narrative to connect them, and of comment to make them intelligible. In the concluding chapters he adds a strong and convincing plea, based on the history he has recited, in favor of the self-supporting policy in all our missions." These sentences, from the pen of Dr. Bright, editor of "The Examiner," describe with perfect fairness the character and aim of this volume. We are not sanguine enough to expect that the policy here advocated will be approved by all the missionaries in the foreign field, or even by all the friends of missions at home; but we believe it to be thoroughly wise, and certain to prevail in the end, and we expect that this history will draw to it far closer attention than it has yet received.

Mr. Carpenter's history will be read by not a few persons whose memory of mission-work does not go back to the first half of the period which it reviews; and to them we cannot offer a more useful paragraph than the following, from a notice of "Self-Support in Bassein" by Dr. Bright: "This is a book of thrilling interest and of great value. The first twenty years covered by it constitute one of the most important periods in the history of our Asiatic missions, — years in which there were heart-burning differences between the missionaries and the officers of the Missionary Union, as well as between the missionaries themselves, — years in which the very existence of the missions seemed at times to be threatened, and yet years in which some of the brightest victories were gained that have been known in missionary annals. To tell this story interestingly, faithfully, justly, without uncovering the smouldering embers of old controversies; to give an account of all that it is necessary for the present generation of Baptists to know, and leave in their grave things that had better not be brought to light, — this was no easy task. Mr. Carpenter has achieved it with an unfailing tact, and with a sweet and charitable Christian spirit."

ALVAH HOVEY.
NEWTON CENTRE, Feb. 8, 1884.

PREFACE.

"I sometimes think there is not wisdom enough in the whole Baptist denomination of America to manage their foreign missions one day, and, if the Head of the Church does not do it, I do not know who will." —Rev. Dr. J. G. WARREN, *Corresponding Secretary*, Nov. 11, 1868.

IF this sketch fails to show the hand of Christ guiding his servants, sustaining them in weakness, overruling their mistakes, and defending them from their foes, it will miserably fail of its true end. Surely no Christian reader will fail to see that omnipotent and sovereign power was necessary to choose out one of the smallest and most degraded of peoples, and to make of them so shortly a fruitful branch of his own redeemed people. By divine grace alone a devil-worshipper may become an heir of heaven.

Another end ought to be furthered by the philosophy which underlies this piece of history. Christian missions conducted on opposite principles have existed side by side in various lands for nearly fifty years. The one principle, followed still in the great majority of missions, is that of depending principally upon pecuniary support drawn from Christian countries: the other — followed by the Moravian missions, by Bassein and a few others — is that of self-help from the outset, with an early arrival at local support for all native preachers and all primary education whatsoever. It would seem that time enough has elapsed for the fruit of these two systems to appear, —enough time for results and conclusions, for lessons so plain and emphatic that the blindest might learn, and that thus the uniformity of management so sorely needed might be secured. In the interests of important truth we might without arrogance, perhaps, challenge comparison between the results, present and prospective, of the Bassein Karen mission and those of any mission conducted on the opposite principle. But, alas for our weak human nature! comparisons are odious. And yet bare argument without practical illustration is of little avail. Abuses there are in all missions, home as well as foreign, —abuses common to all charities, unless the latest patented "wood-yard" charity be an exception. They come chiefly from the tendency of the weak everywhere to throw themselves full length upon the strong, to the encumbrance of the latter and to their own perpetual and self-perpetuating weakness. The tendency has been oftener pointed out than successfully grappled with.

Meanwhile, the wasteful, debilitating evil spreads and grows, and it is becoming more and more a serious question how the armies that God is raising up for himself, through our preaching in foreign lands, are to be transformed, out of the tattered regimentals of Falstaff's hundred and fifty, into the full uniform of Christ,—from weak-kneed dependence, into the steady discipline, the organization, the patient service, the self-sacrifice and self-respect which should mark all the battalions of King Jesus. If the way to this transformation has not been rediscovered in Bassein, we know not where to look for it outside of the New Testament; and, if the transformation itself be not speedily accomplished throughout our missions, we may too soon find ourselves swamped by a rapid but superficial success.

It is high time, we believe, for the dead to speak, and for the living, both in America and Burma, to give ear. The powerful letters and appeals of E. L. Abbott have waited thirty-five long years to gain the public attention. The good hand of our God upon his associate Beecher and their successors has demonstrated the truth of his positions and the wisdom of his counsel. It is for the Christians of America to say whether the men whom our fathers sent forth to lay down their lives for the establishment of Christ's kingdom in Burma, on Christ's own principles, shall now have an attentive hearing or not. *"Thy God hath commanded thy strength: strengthen, O God, that which thou hast wrought for us."*

The work of preparing this book for the press has been one of compilation, rather than of authorship. As far as practicable, the workmen have been allowed to speak for themselves. Not a little valuable information has been secured from the earliest Bassein converts, who are fast passing away. Their posterity, perhaps, will be more grateful than readers in Christian lands for the rather minute record of the beginning of their Christian history. Their history prior to the advent of the missionaries is lost beyond retrieval in unlettered, pagan night.

Acknowledgments are due to Rev. Dr. J. N. Murdock, Corresponding Secretary of the A.B.M. Union, for free access to the correspondence of the Sandoway and Bassein missions; also to the same, to Rev. Dr. Alvah Hovey, late Chairman of the Executive Committee of the Union, to Rev. Dr. J. G. Warren, late Corresponding Secretary, and to Rev. O. W. Gates especially, for valuable advice following a patient perusal of the manuscript.

NEWTON CENTRE, MASS., NOV. 1, 1883.

CONTENTS:

INTRODUCTION

PREFACE

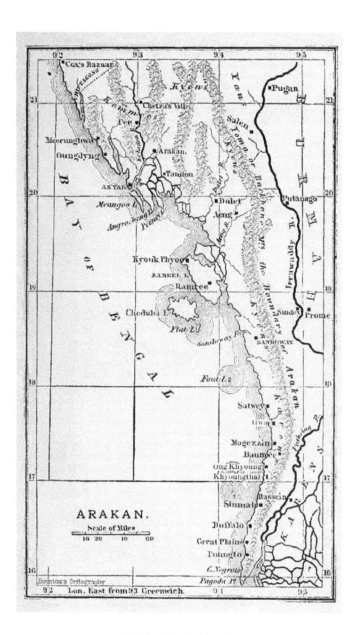

MAP OF ARAKAN

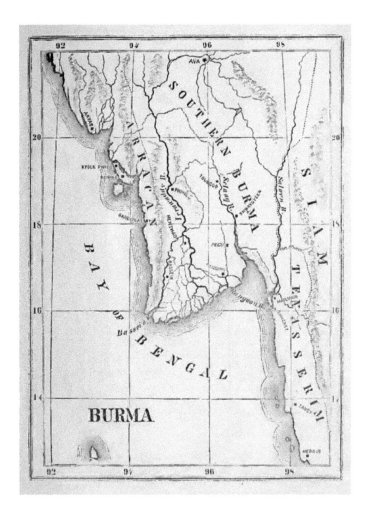

MAP OF BRITISH BURM

ILLUSTRATIONS:

PORTRAIT OF REV. E. L. ABBOTT (Frontispiece.)
MAP OF ARAKAN
MAP OF BRITISH BURMA
BOAT-TRAVEL IN BURMA
PORTRAIT OF REV. J. S. BEECHER
FACSIMILE OF MR. ABBOTT'S HANDWRITING
PORTRAIT OF PASTOR MAU YAY OF KYOOTOO
GRADUATES OF THE BASSEIN KAREN GIRLS' SCHOOL
FACSIMILE OF MR. BEECHER'S HANDWRITING
MISSION-HOUSE BUILT BY MR. BEECHER, 1858
GIRLS' SCHOOLHOUSE, BASSEIN, BUILT 1875
KO THAHBYU MEMORIAL HALL, DEDICATED MAY 16, 1878
BASSEIN KAREN MISSIONARIES TO THE KAKHYENS

CHAPTER I.

1835-1837.

"If I had to choose for my dearest friend on earth a position where there is afforded a full field for the exercise of a man's powers and influence, and where the truest happiness may he secured, I should say to him, 'If you love Jesus Christ, [and can accomplish it], become a missionary.'"— *Anonymous.*

Although blistered now with the heat of a tropical sun, and now drenched in tropical rain and steam, British Burma is a fair and fruitful land. The most prosperous of the British provinces in India already, the agricultural possibilities of its future are grand indeed. Under the fostering care of a Christian government, the population is increasing at the rate of nearly fifty per cent each decade; while the foreign trade, stimulated by British capital, is increasing in a still more rapid ratio.

Into the history of this land we cannot enter fully. Suffice it to say, that British Burma comprises within its present bounds three divisions,—Arakan, Pegu, and Tenasserim. At the close of the first Burmese war, in 1824, the first and the last of these divisions, or provinces, were annexed to "The Honorable East India Company's" dominions; viz., Arakan, a narrow strip of coast on the east of the Bay of Bengal, stretching from Chittagong on the north, by the western Yoma range, to Maudin Point, near the mouth of the Bassein River, on the south; and Tenasserim, another narrow territory on the east of the Gulf of Martaban, extending from a point on the Salween River, not many miles north of Maulmain, southward to the Isthmus of Kraw. The central province, Pegu, which was by far the most valuable portion of the old Burman Empire, was annexed by Lord Dalhousie in 1852, at the close of the second and last war with Burma. By this annexation, the great English trading-company united under its control the entire seaboard of India, Ceylon, and Burma, from Kurrachee in the north-west to the Isthmus of Kraw in the south-east,—a coastline of more than five thousand miles. Thus the king of Burma at the same time lost the great rice-granary of his kingdom, Pegu, and was cut off from all independent access to the sea.

Bassein is the south-western district of the Pegu division. The present area of the district is 7,047 square miles, about equal to that of Massachusetts, or the principality of Wales. Of this area, 5,996 square miles are officially returned as culturable, of which only 536 miles are under cultivation. Of rich lowland, adapted to rice, it is estimated that Bassein has twice as much as any other district in Burma. Indeed, it may be said that in natural fertility of soil, in the regularity and abundance of the rainfall, and in general adaptation to the growth of a grain which constitutes the staple food of a majority of the human race, and is becoming more and more a necessity in the economy of European life, Bassein is hardly excelled by any district in the world. According to the census of 1881, the population is 389,419 (Karens 96,008), which is barely 55 to the square mile. At the same time, the demand for the chief product of the district seems to be constant and increasing at well maintained prices. So far, then, as room for growth and a chance for a livelihood go, the native Christians of Bassein have a goodly heritage.

The district headquarters are in Bassein, a municipality containing 28,147 inhabitants,—about one-fifth of the population of Rangoon, or one-third that of Maulmain. The town is situated on the east bank of the Ngawoon, or Bassein River, about eighty miles from its mouth. The largest ships and steamers come up to the town without difficulty. The facilities for milling and loading the grain are excellent; so that Bassein now stands second to Rangoon only, in the amount of rice exported annually.

To trace the beginnings of missionary effort in Bassein, it will be necessary to go back to Burman times, seventeen years before the conquest of Pegu by the British arms. In April, 1835, Rev. Thomas Simons, returning from a visit to Arakan, determined to travel overland, through the Burmese territory of Bassein, to Rangoon. Armed with a pass from the English commissioner, he proceeded by boat from Comstock's house in Kyouk Pyoo, *viâ* Sandoway to Khyoungthah, where he arrived April 20, late in the evening. From this point, Bassein missionaries of the present day can trace with interest every step of his way to the residence of Rev. Messrs. Webb and Howard in Rangoon. Mr. Simons writes: —

"At nine o'clock, P.M., the island,[1] which is at the entrance of the creek we wished to enter, was in sight; and we were soon inside, and anchored for the night."

{ Footnote: [1] On this gem of an island, fifty feet above the sea, the Bassein mission now has a healthful place of rest for the hot season. In 1876 the British Government kindly granted to the American Baptist Missionary Union two acres of land on the most eligible part of the bluff. A clearing has been made, and a cheap bungalow erected, without expense to the society. The island is within the limits of the Bassein district, — about thirty miles due west from the town. }

"*April* 21. — This morning, before leaving the boat, the villagers came to me for some tracts, and were supplied. The head man had my baggage carried to his house, where I am now reclining on a bamboo couch, surrounded by Burmans and fourteen Karens, — six men and eight women. The Karen women look well, and are very well dressed. Their village[2] is near by, and contains fifteen houses. I gave them the Catechism, and requested them to get a Burman to read it to them; and they must hearken, for it would tell them good things. I informed them that the Karens near Tavoy, Maulmain, and Rangoon, had the same word, and liked it very much. Several Burmans came for books, and the house was full nearly all day. At night I bargained with six men to carry my baggage over the mountains, and we are to leave before sunrise."

{ Footnote: [2] These Karens who surrounded the couch of the weary traveller, undoubtedly came from Kangyee, a hamlet less than two miles distant on the south side of the river. Within seven years after this passing visit, they were worshipping the true God. With their children, and probably with some of the younger members of that very party, the compiler of this sketch is well acquainted. For him they built with their own hands the first mission sanitarium on the island. He has eaten their rice, and slept in their houses. They have guided him in long journeys up and down that picturesque coast. He has communed with them by the way, and he knows that they are children of God. To our deceased brother belongs the honor of communicating to that little community the first gleam of light from the Father of lights, and from the ever radiant cross. }

At four o'clock the next morning the traveller's luggage was put into two of the little canoes peculiar to that locality; and a party of nine men, including an armed policeman, escorted him up the river by the brilliant light of the tropical moon. The mangrove-trees, with their aerial roots growing close down to the water's edge; the wild "sea-cocoanut" trees overlooking them; rare orchids, that would bring a fortune in the conservatories of England, clinging to tree-trunks and branches in every direction; the hoot of the night-owl, giving place, as the day dawns, to a great variety of tropical birds; families of monkeys looking for a breakfast of crabs on the muddy banks; beautiful jelly-fish, pink and white, lazily floating with the tide; the weird songs and cries of his own boatmen, — all tell the venturesome young missionary that he is in a strange land far from kindred and friends, exposed, perhaps, to dangers at which he can only guess. At seven o'clock they reach the landing at the head of the stream. Crossing the British boundary, and breakfasting by the way, the difficulties of the nine-miles' walk through tangled forests, over the low mountain pass, are surmounted by one, P.M., when they emerge at the head waters of the Kyouk Khyoung-gyee Creek, on the border of the great deltaic plain, which stretches away eastward for two hundred miles without a hill. Wading occasionally, they go down the shallow brook, passing a score or more of men cutting bamboos, where they still cut them for use in the city and many of the eastern villages. With the quick eye of an observer, he marks their sleeping-places high up in the tree-tops, out of the reach of prowling tigers and wild elephants. He writes: —

"They soon collected around us, and had many questions to ask. I opened my budget of books, and gave the Catechism to each one, and, in addition, the 'Golden Balance' and 'Ship of Grace' to the owner of the borrowed boat. For some time they sat talking together, admiring the books,—first, the whiteness of the paper, then the writing, as they supposed it to be, and, last of all, the subject. Hired a boat from one of them for a rupee, and at two, P.M., embarked to descend the creek, taking three of the [Khyoungthah] men with me, the rest returning with the head man and guard. Overtook several rafts of bamboos floating down the creek, with three or four men on each. Gave tracts to them, also to the people whom I met in their canoes, and to the inhabitants who live on the banks of the creek. Passed a Karen settlement of three or four houses; but, seeing no one out, I placed a Catechism at the end of a canoe, in hopes that when they came out to their boat they would see it, and get some Burman to read it to them."

This, again, is historic. That little Karen hamlet was Thaupo, a branch of Kaukau Pgah, the banner church of Bassein, and probably the most enterprising and benevolent church in all Burma (see chap. xix.). How would our brother's heart have leaped with joy if he could have foreseen the future! What prompted him to leave a Burmese Catechism in a crack of that wretched little Karen canoe? And, having done it, what led him to write to America about it? And why should Dr. Bolles print it? And why, on this twenty-first day of April, 1881, just forty-six long years after, should this man light upon it, and, knowing all the wonderful sequences, seize upon it as treasure-trove? Was it not that American Christians might again be reminded that such leaflets and bits of Scripture are potent? that God's word cannot return unto him void? But if the doubter prefers to believe that the Karens never found the little book; or, finding it, never employed a Burman to read it to them; or, having found an interpreter, that they received not the truth into their hearts,—then we seize upon the incident all the same, and pronounce it a prophecy. The simple faith and the love in the heart of my father's Newton classmate, Simons, led him to do what he did. He believed, that, come what would to himself or his book, God had a chosen people in those jungles and in that very village at his side; and so he left a fragment of God's truth on the empty boat, as Jacob set up his rock-pillow for a pillar, anointing it with oil, and saying, "This shall be God's house!" Nor has the God of Jacob ever failed to honor and richly bless such faith in his servants.

At sunset of the same day our pioneer reached the large Burman village of Kyouk Khyoung-gyee, on the Bassein River, seven or eight miles above the town. Here, after reporting his arrival to the head man, Simons busied himself in preaching, and distributing tracts, until ten, P.M. At four, A.M., the government men came, when, damp and cold from the heavy dew, he got into their canoe, and two hours later was landed in Bassein. In due course he visited the principal officials, and was kindly received, but as a traveller, not as a religious teacher. The night after his arrival he was taken quite ill, owing, doubtless, to fatigue and exposure. Still, from the 23d to the 25th he managed to do considerable religious work.

At two, P.M., on the 25th, he left Bassein in a Burman boat for Pantanau, by the usual route. At dark, he says, they left the river, and entered a creek, now called the Rangoon Creek. "Came to a small village [Kanyna, undoubtedly] about nine o'clock, where the boat was made fast with other's, and I went to sleep. Started very early on the 26th, and stopped at a village[1] about eight, A.M." Here, as usual, he went ashore, and distributed tracts. He adds, "As I passed along to-day, I heard the Karens singing in their villages." How familiar is this ground to the missionary now! The songs which Simons then heard were plaintive enough, but intensely demoniacal. For forty years now, those same villages have resounded with the songs of Zion. Passing through one of the three narrow *yay-gyaus*, or cross-cuts, which lead to Rangoon, he reached Shwayloung on the 29th, Pantanau on the 1st of May, and thence, by the Panlang Creek, to Kemendine and Rangoon, on the 3d, arriving at the house of his missionary brethren after dark. He adds, that on this trip he gave away more than eight hundred tracts, mostly in places where neither missionary nor tracts had been before.

{ Footnote: [1] Probably Myoungmya, where there is now a court, two or three English officials, and a Roman-Catholic mission. At this point he was within four or five miles of Kyootoo, the village of the "young chief," where Abbott first preached the gospel, and the first

Christian Karen church was formed, within the present limits of the Bassein district. }

Prompted, perhaps, by Mr. Simons's successful journey, Mr. Webb writes on the 31st of December, 1835, "We are preparing to go in a few days on a tour to Bassein, and may possibly go over to Arakan." This plan was partially carried out by Mr. Howard alone in the following October.

In April, 1836, Mr. and Mrs. (Marcia D.) Ingalls, newly arrived missionaries, on their way from Maulmain to settle in Arakan, were stopped at Cape Negrais by a violent storm, and went up the river to Bassein for refuge. As storm-bound travellers, they were kindly received by the officials. Permission to remain until the close of the rains was granted to them, but on condition that they would not circulate Christian books. As they could not give such a pledge, and as the season seemed to be too far advanced to proceed to Arakan in safety, they reluctantly returned to Maulmain.

Oct. 2, 1836, Rev. Mr. Howard reached Bassein from Rangoon, *viâ* Pantanau and Shwayloung. He staid three days in the town, and distributed many tracts among the Burmans. Going and coming, he met many Karens, mostly Pwos. He learned that the Bassein Karens could speak Burmese more generally than those of other districts. He also adds his opinion, that "these Karens are much less filthy in their personal appearance than any others I have seen."

Our space is too limited for even a brief consideration of the remarkable but well-known traditions of the Karens. The Bassein branch of the race, reputed to be of somewhat ignoble origin, shared fully in these traditions; and the day of their redemption is now ready to dawn. Rumors of the great work begun among their brethren in the eastern districts have reached them. The spirit of God has already begun to sway the hearts of not a few towards himself, inclining them, not only to receive the message of salvation when it shall be brought to them, but to go long distances, through an enemy's country, in search of "the white book," and the white brothers who have come from the distant West to teach them.

Christ's chosen vessel to bear his name to them—the wise master-builder, who is appointed and prepared to lay the foundation-stones of a divine building among them—is at hand.

Elisha Litchfield Abbott, the spiritual father of the Bassein Karen Baptists, and one of the most striking characters in the history of modern missions, was a descendant of a Yorkshire family, a native of Cazenovia, N.Y., and a son of the seminary at Hamilton. Arriving in Maulmain Feb. 20, 1836, at the age of twenty-six, he was met on the threshold of his career by a well-nigh fatal attack of jungle-fever. Establishing himself temporarily at a new station on Balu Island, after his recovery, he applied himself diligently and most successfully to the study of Karen. In September of the same year he accompanied Rev. Messrs. Vinton and Howard on a long tour in the Rangoon district. In the vicinity of Maubee, about thirty miles north of the town of Rangoon, they baptized a hundred and seventy-three Karens who had become Christians, chiefly, Mr. Howard says, through the instrumentality of Ko Thahbyu. United in marriage to Miss Gardner, in Tavoy, April 2, 1837, he proceeded with his wife to Rangoon, for the purpose of laboring among the Karens of that region, arriving on the 20th. The Karens received them with great joy. Only one of the large number baptized the previous year had apostatized.

On the 25th of May Mr. Abbott baptized three Karens, and wrote that many others were waiting for the ordinance, most of whom had been converted for several years. A number of young men and boys who had previously learned to read came in to study,—the first of a long succession of youth who resorted to him with ever increasing delight for instruction in the word of God. The Burman authorities had forbidden the Karens to have books, or to learn to read. What could have been better adapted to provoke them to the pursuit of knowledge than the disapproval and prohibition of their savage oppressors? Hence Abbott is able to record, "Although there have been no regular schools established, yet there are several hundreds who have learned to read at their own homes, when no Burman was near to report them to the rulers." Several young men besides Ko

Thahbyu had been sent out to preach from village to village, who generally came in once a month to report.

The hostility of the Burmans, and rumors of war, made it advisable for the Abbotts to leave for Maulmain on the 10th of August. They were absent, however, less than three months, returning at the opening of the dry season. Nov. 10 Abbott writes, that three men called from the vicinity of Pantanau in the Bassein district. One professed to have worshipped God for three years; another, for some months. Others came with them the next day, "very stupid, and indifferent to the subject," he says. But he did not know Karens at that time as well as afterwards. The very fact that they would venture to visit the white teacher, as they did repeatedly, in opposition to the well-known will of their cruel masters, was enough to prove that they were far from being "indifferent," however stupid they may have been in appearance or reality. On the 13th the party returned to their homes, with a good supply of books, and two of Mr. Abbott's assistants to teach and preach in their vicinity. In the letter announcing this, he says, "No teacher has ever yet visited that region." This, then, is the first reference in the annals of our missions to direct gospel-work in behalf of the Karens of Bassein.

Meanwhile, for the encouragement of the inquirers in Bassein, the Rangoon Christians are grievously oppressed. They are taxed so heavily, that some parents are obliged to sell their children as slaves to the Burmans. De Poh, one of the best preachers, is threatened with death if he does not renounce Christianity. The Karens are divided among themselves; one party embracing the new religion, another as earnestly opposing it. Me Poh, an old Karen chief, does his utmost to incite and to help the viceroy put down the Christians. Never was a young missionary in more trying circumstances, but his faith and courage were equal to the occasion. Dec. 14 Mr. Abbott left Rangoon to make his first visit to Bassein. He shall tell the story in his own language.

"*Dec. 16.*—About ten this morning, arrived at the point where the Rangoon branch [Panlang Creek] separates from the main body of the river. The Irrawaddy was before us in all its grandeur and majesty...Crossed the river, and came to a Karen village.[1] The first house we entered was a house of prayer. We found several Christians, some of whom I had previously seen in Rangoon. Very soon an old man came in, and almost his first words were, 'Teacher, I want to be baptized.' Upon inquiry, I learned the following story. Two years ago a Barman came along, and wanted to sell the old man two little books. As he could read Burmese, he purchased them for two large bunches of plantains. They proved to be 'The Ship of Grace' and 'The Golden Balance,' which the Burman probably received from a missionary. He read the books, and they told him about the great God. He was not satisfied. He had heard that the Karens in Maubee had received a 'new religion.' The old man made his way thither, through the wilderness, exposed to wild beasts and robbers, obtained light, gave up all his former customs, embraced the gospel with all his heart, and for one year has been a faithful and consistent Christian, *with all his house*. He has been the means of the conversion of several of his neighbors."

{ Footnote: [1] Undoubtedly Sekkau, just within the old limits of the Bassein district, and still a Christian village connected with the Rangoon association. }

BOAT-TRAVEL IN BURMA

"*17th, Sabbath.*—Had worship in the morning and evening with the Christians. But few others came in. Towards evening, went out into the village, and gathered a little group; but they all with one consent began to make excuse. The Karens are a peculiar people. They are either for or against, and that altogether. There are no neutrals. Were it not for an almighty Agency accompanying the truth, I would close the book of God, and retire in despair. I cannot but remark the difference between Christian and heathen families of children. In the former, all is quiet and order. No fears are manifested at my approach, as in other families: on the contrary, the children cluster around, lay hold of my hands, sit at my feet, and receive lessons in reading.

"*18th.*—Left these good people this morning, and arrived at Pantanau[1] at four, P.M., four days north-west from Rangoon. Here, again, I was joyfully received by the friends of the missionary's God. At evening the people assembled, and listened to the parable, 'Behold, a sower went forth to sow.' There are but three individuals who are decided Christians; although many others have abandoned all their old customs, love the truth, keep the sabbath, etc., but still think they have not new hearts. The people of the village are all anxious to learn to read. If I had a good assistant to leave here, no doubt many would embrace the truth."

{ Footnote: [1] Not the large Burman town of that name, but a Karen village some distance below,—Khateeyah perhaps, where pastor Nahkee has long resided. Both this church and Pgoo Khyoung retained their connection with the Bassein association until 1875, when they united with Rangoon. }

"*19th.*—The village which I especially designed to visit being one day farther on, I left the people where I stopped last night, and arrived at this village[2] towards evening. The people flocked together, old and young, to express their joy at my arrival. After some conversation, I asked them how many had embraced the Christian religion. 'All,' 'All.' 'Every one of us,' was answered by forty voices. We sung a hymn of praise to God. What cause of devout gratitude to the Saviour, that he is raising up in these wilds a people to serve him, and to perpetuate his glory on the earth! At evening the people assembled in the most convenient house in the village, and listened to the words of Christ to Nicodemus: 'Ye must be born again.' After prayer and singing, several came forward, and asked for baptism. On inquiry, I learned that the first they heard of the gospel was four years ago, from Burmese tracts, which they obtained from the Burmans. Some began to worship God from that time; but, not having sufficient light, they still practised some of their former customs. Two years ago some of the old men visited Maubee, obtained further instruction, and became more consistent in their religious life. Eight or nine months since, another deputation was sent to visit the Maubee church, learned to read, obtained books, and, returning, became missionaries to their neighbors. I have seen several of the old men in Rangoon; and two of the assistants have spent a few of the last months in these villages. For the last six months there has been a general turning to the Lord, so that, at present, there are very few who are willing to acknowledge themselves heathen. After I had stated to them the prerequisites of baptism, many of them hesitated, saying, 'We are not yet worthy.' They dispersed at a late hour, with a promise of assembling early to-morrow morning."

{ Footnote: [2] Exact location uncertain, probably on the main river, below Shway Loung. Was it Ko Dau's village? }

"*20th.*—Spent the day in the examination of those who had asked for baptism.[1] At the setting of the sun we assembled on the banks of the river, where I baptized thirty-four, in obedience to the command of my divine Master. The scene was deeply solemn. The banks were lined with an attentive group, who beheld in silence the observance of this ordinance for the first time. These mighty waters, which have hitherto only echoed the heathen's prayer and the songs of devils, have at length witnessed the baptismal vows of converted Pagans. God Almighty grant that such scenes may follow in quick succession, till not a cottage shall be found, where there may not be seen an altar to the living God, till every canoe floating on the broad bosom of the Irrawaddy shall bear disciples of King Jesus, and until the songs of demons shall be hushed to silence by the sweeter melody of Prince Immanuel's praise! After the baptism, the people assembled for worship; and I repeated to them the words of the Saviour: 'He that followeth me shall not walk in darkness but shall have the light of life.' At a late hour of the night I heard the voice of prayer and praise from many families in the village, till I fell asleep."

{ Footnote: [1] Mark the carefulness and deliberation with which these first Bassein converts are received. }

"21st.—I had intended to make this village the extent of my present tour, not knowing but that the long-talked-of war may come before my return to Rangoon; but trusting in that good Providence which has hitherto been as a cloudy pillar by day, and a pillar of fire by night, I will venture on. At a large village three days west, there lives a Karen chief, who is the head of all the tribes in this region. He has heard something of the gospel, but is still a heathen in practice. Having heard that I intended to come this way, he left word with the people, that, if I came, I must certainly visit him at his own village. Perhaps he wishes to see me to gratify his curiosity; perhaps, if I visit him, the word of God will enlighten his dark soul, and guide him to heaven. I consequently left this morning, and am passing quietly down the river, the banks of which are lined with Pwo Karen[1] villages, which have hitherto heard nothing of the gospel. I intend to send to Tavoy for a Pwo assistant and books, and try to do something for that people."

{ Footnote: [1] The Karens of Pegu and Tenasserim are divided into two tribes,—the Sgaus and the Pwos, who speak somewhat different dialects. }

"23d.—Arrived at the Karen chief's this evening, after three days' travel through the wilderness, with only here and there a Burman village, especially the last two days. The chief (Myat Oung by name) is an old man of seventy-five, full of strength and of years, and hardened in sin. His eldest wife exhibits only the last glimmerings of reason, but few removes from idiocy. At evening a few who had heard of my arrival came in, but were as wild as the mountain deer."

13

Mr. Abbott was now well within the present narrower borders of the Bassein district. Careful inquiry of old men who were present at this visit of their revered teacher makes it certain that the location of the village reached by Mr. Abbott on this occasion was much lower down the Kyunton Creek than the present Christian village of Kyootoo. Rev. Mau Yay, the pastor of that mother-church, and from the first one of the ablest and most devoted Christian leaders in the whole district (one of the two "Moung Yés" of Abbott's journals), informs me that the old village was on the east bank of the stream, only two bends, or two bends and a half above its mouth. It was below Sittabeng, and four or five miles north from Myoungmya (p. 7). The spot where the gospel was first preached in Bassein to an attentive, believing congregation might well be marked by a monument; and Christmas Day, 1887, the semicentennial anniversary of this historic visit, might well be celebrated throughout Bassein by solemn assemblies for praise and worship. Of the reception of the missionary's message on the morrow, of the arrival of company after company all day long, of the breaking-down of the house, and of the remarkable meeting Christmas Eve, prolonged under the open sky until long past midnight, we leave Mr. Abbott to tell in his own graphic language:—

"*Dec. 24, Sabbath.*—By ten o'clock this morning seventy or eighty had assembled for worship. Very good attention was given, and some appeared to be pricked in the heart. At one o'clock the morning assembly dispersed; and another company of about the same number, who were detained in the morning, came. These listened till sunset. After these had left, other companies came flocking in from distant villages, many of whom had travelled all day without eating, fearing they should not arrive in time to see me. We had commenced singing a hymn, the people still flocking in, when the cry was heard, 'The house is falling.' It was not very strong, but I should think would contain two hundred with safety. The people hastened out, spread a mat on the ground in the open field, upon which I sat, and themselves gathered around, and sat upon the ground. A few old men sat near, who would question when they did not understand. All around was the darkness and stillness of night. Not a cloud obscured the heavens, which were spread out over our heads as a beautifully bespangled curtain. In one hand I held a dimly burning taper; in the other, the word of God. The firmament on high showed God's handiwork in the creation of the world: the Bible in my hand taught the wonderful story of its redemption by Jesus Christ. Midnight had long passed away ere the assembly dispersed, and then they withdrew reluctantly. May the good Lord of the harvest pour out his Spirit, and gather in many of these poor souls, and may they shine eternally in glory, the trophies of victorious grace!"

On the following morning, Dec. 25, the missionary started on his return to Rangoon, leaving a young man, Mau Mway by name, to teach the people to read, and to exhort them to take heed to the things which they had heard. On his way back, he stopped two nights at the Christian village of "Pantanau," where he baptized nine more; making a church in that place of forty-three members. Friday night he spent at a Karen village, where there were a few Christians. Saturday evening he arrived at Sekkau, where he spent Sunday, and baptized the old man who bought the tracts from a Burman, his wife, his son, and three others; making in all forty-nine baptized on this trip,—the first-fruits of the gospel in Bassein. New-Year's Day, 1838, he spent in his boat, "ruminating on the past, with now and then a glance to the future, surveying the field of the Saviour's future triumph." The man of faith and works adds, in conclusion, "The work of the Lord is going on among the Karens, and will go on, in spite of the Burmans and the Devil."

CHAPTER II.

1838-1839.

"The truth in my heart was like a stake, slightly driven into soft ground, easily swayed, and in danger of falling before the wind; but, by the sledge-hammer of persecution, God drove it in by successive blows, till it became immovable." — AMOOJAH, *North Armenian Mission.*

The circumstances under which the Karens of Rangoon and Bassein first came into the kingdom of Christ were adapted to test their sincerity and faith to the utmost. They were still absolutely in the power of the Burmans. The degree of despotism which prevailed around them, the fines and fiendish tortures which Burmese ingenuity was accustomed to inflict, they well understood. That any communication with the white man, any disposition to adopt his religion, any aspiration after learning that was not Burmese and Boodhistic, would provoke the wrath of their masters, and bring them into direful straits, they were well aware. They knew, moreover, that, of their own kindred and language, there were not a few of the baser sort who would gladly betray them. Widely different are the circumstances under which the native subjects of Victoria now profess Christianity. These, exposed at most to family trials, to some inconvenience, perhaps to loss and popular odium, are sure of protection as to life, property, and the exercise of all natural rights: reasonably sure, also, are they of help in times of famine or other trouble. Those, on the other hand, were exposed to the loss of all things, to tortures and death itself; their teachers being powerless to help or relieve them. Still, sustained by the true martyr-spirit, thousands of them did not falter, "of whom," it may be said, as of the ancient worthies, "the world was not worthy."

Mr. Abbott continued in charge of the Karen work in the Rangoon district. On the 24th of March, 1838, he writes: —

"On the 15th I left Ponau at five, A.M., and travelled over the plain west, eight miles, to the village of Raytho, the most central of the Maubee cluster. The brethren, notified of my coming, came together, with many who were asking for baptism. Spent the day in examining candidates. At evening a large concourse from the adjacent villages. Finished the examination at ten, P.M., when we repaired to a small lake. The multitude assembled on its beautiful banks. The full moon rose in a cloudless sky; nature was silent; we bowed and prayed, and God was there. I then baptized thirty-seven who had been received by the church. After this, I administered the sacrament of the Supper to more than a hundred of my Master's disciples. At half-past twelve o'clock I lay down on the ground, and slept until four, A.M.

"On the 16th I returned to Ponau, and sent word to all near to come in at evening. The people began to collect at sunset, in such numbers that no house in the village would contain them. We assembled, therefore, in the open field, as on the preceding evening. The examination of candidates continued till eleven o'clock; after which I baptized thirty, and administered the Lord's Supper to a hundred and fifty. Half an hour past midnight I bade adieu to these precious disciples of Christ, and started for Rangoon, where I arrived at six, P.M.

"I had but two objects in visiting these people at this perilous time. One was to give some instructions as to discipline; the other, to administer the Lord's Supper. I well knew, that, if the Burmans were apprised of any large gathering at the present time, it would excite persecution: I therefore moved cautiously, and even forbade the people to meet in large congregations in the daytime. But they came flocking around, and pleaded so earnestly for baptism, giving withal such evidence of a change of heart and life, that I could not repel them. Most of those whom I baptized have been consistent Christians for five years. A few had embraced the gospel within the last year. I have since heard, that, after I left, a multitude came in from different villages to see me, many of whom wished to be baptized. The work of the Lord is certainly going forward in the jungles, through the instrumentality of the native assistants. I have heard of several villages where the people have mostly forsaken their former customs, and embraced the Christian faith. But it will not do for me to visit them at present...All the threats and oppression of the Burmans have not turned aside a single individual from his integrity."

Close communication is still kept up with the infant churches in Bassein. On the 25th of January Mr. Simons wrote that three young Karen Christians had returned from the villages near Pantanau, where brother Abbott had left them to teach the Karens to read, etc. He gave them three Testaments, and some tracts to distribute. On the 2d of February these same young men called, on their way back to Pantanau; and Mr. Simons gave them a supply of Karen tracts, which Mr. Abbott had left for distribution among the heads of families; also six Burman Testaments, and a number of Burman tracts and Scripture Digests, to be given to Karens and Burmans. On the 10th of March Mr. Abbott again sends two young Karen disciples into the Bassein district, with a good supply of books, to teach the people to read and pray. Again, on the 5th of April, he sends some assistants to Pantanau to teach school, and preach in that vicinity.

May 7 he writes: "Assistants returned from Pantanau. The church-members there, as yet, enjoy their liberty, and appear to be moving onward steadily and joyfully in the Christian course. Since my visit very many have turned unto the Lord, and are now asking for baptism. Nearer Bassein, they are repeating their calls for books and another visit." May 13, Sunday: several Karens came in from the Pantanau church. "Had worship with them morning and evening in Karen. Thank the Lord," he writes, "for another quiet sabbath with the dear Karen disciples!" In view of the persecutions and dangers to which they were subjected, he thought it wise to defer exclusions for delinquency; e.g., the Burman *woondouk* of Rangoon now threatens to thrust hollow sticks filled with gunpowder down the throats of the Karen Christians, and blow them to atoms.

On the 8th of June several Christians from Bassein and Pantanau arrived in Rangoon, "to visit the teacher." They brought a letter to Mr. Abbott from Shway Weing, "the young chief" of Kyootoo,—a man of superior talents and extensive influence, who first heard the gospel from Mr. Abbott during his memorable visit at Kyootoo the previous Christmas. Since that time he had learned to read and write his own language well, had renounced heathenism, and embraced the religion of the Bible. Mr. Abbott translates the letter as follows:—

SHWAY WEING'S LETTER TO HIS BROTHER.

O TEACHER,—My brethren at the villages of Pahpay, Kaunee, Kahkau, and Kyouk Khyoung-gyee, and on towards the setting sun, all worship God, every one. But we have no books. That we may have books and instruction, will you not come and bring them? There is not an individual, among all who worship God, who can teach us. O teacher! that we may fully understand the word of the eternal God, and keep it, and be enabled to distinguish between right and wrong, we are very anxious that you come again. If you cannot come yourself, send teacher De Poh with books. O brother teacher! although we worship God, we do not know any thing yet. If you come, do not forget to bring a great many books. O brother! your brethren, Shway Weing, Mau Yay, and Moung Shway, request you to come. I have therefore written this letter. When it arrives, and you look at it, you will understand, O brother!

June 10 Mr. Abbott began school with a class of fourteen young men, most of whom were from Bassein, and unbaptized. They were very urgent to be baptized immediately, but their teacher thought it more prudent not to baptize them in the city. On the 20th Shway Weing himself arrived with nine other young men, who had been converted under his instrumentality, (query: was it not, more likely, under the instrumentality of Mau Yay?) and had now come to study with the teacher. We quote from Mr. Abbott:—

"He says, that, for several weeks past, his house has been thronged with visitors from distant villages, who have come expressly to learn from him concerning this new religion. Many of these stay with him several days, learn to read a little, get a book, and return to tell their neighbors what they have heard, and to read to them. His object in coming to me now is to be baptized, and carry back books on his return. On learning that I had but very few Karen books just now, he said that he must have five hundred, one for each house; if not so many, by all means thirty, one for each village.

"*21st.*—The young chief says he cannot return to his village unless he is baptized. I spent yesterday and last evening with him, and a more interesting converted heathen I never saw. When I first saw him, in December last, he was a most ungovernable, wicked, and reckless heathen. He is now 'clothed, and in his right mind, sitting at the feet of Jesus,'—a praying, humble, consistent Christian.

"*22d.*—Very early this morning repaired to a small lake away from the city, in a retired spot, where I baptized Shway Weing, after which he left us for his native wilds. Eight of the young men who came with him remain with me, making my class twenty-two, more than I intended to allow to remain in the city at one time. I know not but we shall draw down upon ourselves the wrath of the Burman officers."

Through the remainder of this month and July the school was carried on, but under great difficulties, and with most serious risk to health and life. The rains were at their heaviest. The living-rooms of the mission family, the schoolroom, the Karen sleeping and cooking rooms, were all under one narrow roof. Several of the pupils came down with fever. Abbott himself had a violent attack, and was so reduced, that his physician urged a sea-voyage: but he felt that he could not leave his class. At last, being convinced that all could not remain in so close quarters with safety to life, he sends six or eight of the young men away to study with an assistant in the jungle. At the beginning of August he has fourteen students doing well in their studies, and several begging for baptism. But there is a dark cloud in the horizon, which will shortly break upon them, and try the souls of the missionary and his young converts severely. We condense Mr. Abbott's account in the Magazine:—

"*Aug. 5, Sabbath.*—Thirty Karens at worship, among whom are the young chief from Bassein, and several from Pantanau, who have come for books, and to ask for baptism. Four have died in Bassein within the last few weeks, all of whom first heard the gospel last

December. They had all renounced their superstitions, and embraced the truth. One has died in the Pantanau church, — an old woman one hundred and twenty years of age. After groping in the dark for more than a century, at the close of her hundred and twentieth year she heard of salvation by a crucified Saviour. A ray of light divine pierced her poor, dark soul. She believed and was baptized, and died in the faith. She had been unable to walk, and quite blind from old age, for the last thirty years. When I baptized her, her son brought her in his arms to the waterside. I took her in my arms, and immersed her; then her son took her again, and carried her to the house. Shway Weing says he wants a thousand books, — one for each of those who worship God, and have learned to read.

"6th. — Four of the Karens are under arrest, and will probably be cast into prison. The circumstances are these: fourteen Karens were to return to Bassein and Pantanau; some this evening, and others in the morning. Six of them, taking several books in a small covered basket, left the city, and went to sleep in their boat, which is off some distance. Others, also, took their basket of books, and started to carry it out of the city-gates, designing to return, and spend the night here, and take their books as they passed along in the morning. But, as one of them was passing out, the gate-keeper asked him what he had in his basket. 'Sugar,' was the reply; which was evasive, for he had more books than sugar. The gate-keeper, suspecting him, insisted on seeing what he had in his basket. On finding Karen books, he took him before an officer for examination. Some of the other Karens, who had escaped, came in great terror, and informed us of what had happened. I knew that it would not do for me to meddle with the affair; but a Bengali Christian, to whose house the Karen was going with his books, offered to go and testify to the character of the Karen, etc., believing that the officer would release him. Two young students who knew where the officer lived, accordingly started off to guide him. The officer's attendants, on seeing them, knowing them to be Karens, seized them also. The Bengali returned, but did not tell me of the apprehension of the two students. He said that the Burman official knew that there was a Karen chief at my house, and that he told him, that, if the chief would come, and claim his follower, he would release him. Shway Weing, with intense anxiety depicted in

21

his face, said, 'Teacher, what shall I do?' I unhesitatingly told him to go and demand his follower. He went, and was at once seized; so that now four of them are in custody, and the Burmans would have caught the rest if I had not kept them concealed in my house.

"*7th.*—The four Karens were taken before some of the principal officers to-day, and questioned as to where they live, what they are in this city for, their names, the names of their relatives, how many have learned to read Karen, and how many have been baptized and become the disciples of a 'foreigner.' In short, every thing relating to the kingdom of Christ, and my efforts among the Karens, was laid open before the officers, and recorded in 'the black book.' The Karens, after their ankles had been fastened in double irons, were thrust into the common prison with thieves and murderers. Their clothing was taken away, and a bit of old cloth given them to tie about their loins.

"*8th.*—Early this morning the affair was formally laid before the *woondouk*. 'Where are they now?' demanded the *woondouk*. 'In prison,' was the reply. 'There let them remain.' I sent Taunah to the prison to make inquiries. As he is a British subject, the Burmans dare not meddle with him. The poor prisoners told him how they had spent the night,—their ankles loaded with fetters, their feet elevated about two feet, and made fast in the stocks; their hands, drawn back over the head and upward, were made fast also, their hips alone resting on the floor. They told Taunah, however, that they should have cared little for this, comparatively, but for the swarms of mosquitoes which preyed all night upon their naked bodies. In the course of the day a Burman, connected in some way with the officers, who pretends to be friendly to us, came with a sad countenance, and said that the order had been given for them to be executed, as an example to the Karens and all others, that they are to receive no more Christian books. Although I do not credit his story, it is indicative of the disposition of the government. They have sent out this report, no doubt to frighten the people, and especially to induce the friends of the Karens in prison, or some one, to offer a large ransom. It is evidently the intention of the court to put a stop to the progress of Christianity among the Karens, as they have done among the Burmans; and they will not be scrupulous as to measures. The poor prisoners may have to suffer death for their religion, at least a long imprisonment, or be ransomed only at great cost. But what if they do suffer death? Is it recorded that persecution ever stopped the progress of the gospel of Christ? There are hundreds of Karens in these wilds, who would die, too, before they would renounce their faith in Jesus. Moreover, the work of conversion is going on at a rate hitherto unparalleled, and I believe, in God, is destined still to go on—

"'Though earth and hell oppose.'

"At evening, sent Taunah again to the prison to offer a present to the jailer, if, perchance, he will allow the prisoners a little rest.

"9th.—The present was accepted, and one foot and one hand of each of the prisoners were liberated. The Karen students all passed out of the city-gates this morning unobserved, and went to the jungles. There are now six others who came with Shway Weing, and who are hesitating whether to return, and leave him in prison. One of the six, a younger brother of the chief [Was it Kangyee?—ED.], says he cannot leave his brother in irons, and carry the news to his brother's wife and babes, and their poor old father and mother. Indeed, it is doubtful whether they will be able to return at all, as Burman officers have been hanging about our house all day, looking in at the doors and windows to see if they can lay hold of another Karen.

"10th.—Taunah visited the prisoners as usual to-day, carrying such things as would make them a little comfortable, as all prisoners in this country have to beg or starve. They told him to tell the teacher that he need have no more anxiety on their account, that they had been praying ever since they had been in prison; and that, although they were very fearful and sad when first taken, they are now happy. I have some hope to-day that their deliverance will arise from an unexpected quarter. Mr. Edwards,[1] the writer and interpreter to the British Resident at Amarapoora, while transacting business with the *woondouk* to-day, mentioned the case of the Karen Christians in prison, at which an attendant was ordered to bring the basket which was seized with them. There were in it several small tracts, Catechisms, and copies of Matthew and John,—in all sixty books. 'This is the way you do,' said the *woondouk*, smiling, 'is it? You come and fight us, and get away part of our country, and now you wish to turn away the hearts of the poor, ignorant Karens.' And then, with a pompous air which no one but a Barman could imitate, he proceeded to say, 'If you gave these books to the Burmans, who know too much to be carried away with their nonsense, it would be no matter; but what do the poor, ignorant Karens know?' Mr. Edwards at length extorted a promise that they shall be released. But it is the promise of a Burman."

{ Footnote: [1] This gentleman was of African descent, a man of education and ability. He afterwards served the English Government as collector of customs in Rangoon for many years. He was always a good friend of the missionaries, as well as his superior, Col. Burney, the Resident. }

"*11th.*—To-day the prisoners were sent to the great pagoda, two miles from the city, and offered to the gods. The 'young chief,' and the youth first apprehended, were in two huge pairs of iron fetters; the boys, in one each. Their labor will be to pull up the grass on the plat around the pagoda,—a task sometimes done by Burmans voluntarily as a kind of penance. They will also be compelled to beg their rice from day to day. But their condition is much better than when in prison, as they now have pure air and exercise, and are not confined in the stocks at night. Pagoda slaves are a class of about the same standing as lepers were in ancient Israel. In fact, these Karens are now under the charge of a keeper, who is called 'the leper-governor.' The thousands who flock to Shway Dagon on worship-days will suppose them to have committed some dreadful crime; and, when they learn that the crime consisted in becoming the disciples of Jesus Christ, they will wish to know what that religion is.

"*14th.*—I visited the pagoda again, and, as there were very few persons near, ventured to converse a moment with the slaves. One of the boys remarked to me, 'Teacher, the officers say, if we are released, we must never worship the foreigner's God again.'—'Well, what did you answer?'—'That we should worship with more zeal than ever.' Mr. Edwards mentioned to the *woondouk* this morning the fact of the Karens having been sent to the pagoda. He endeavored to evade it; said that his wife was the means of their going there, and that they could not be liberated, unless a petition were presented. The truth is, he is now sorry that he promised to release them. If he now removes his offering, he will commit sacrilege: if he do not, he will break his promise, which he would make Mr. Edwards believe he considers sacred.

"*15th.*—The *woondouk* publicly declared, that, if any man mentioned the affair of those Karens in his hearing, he would cut off his head. Of course he durst not include a British subject in that threat. Mr. Edwards has to-day extorted another promise that the Karens shall be liberated before the Resident leaves for the capital, which will be in six or eight days. The *woondouk* declares that he releases them solely as a personal favor to Mr. Edwards, and that he is the only person who can obtain their liberation.

"*20th.*—For the last few days I have occasionally visited the slaves at the pagoda, and have uniformly found them rejoicing in God, although it is still deemed doubtful by them whether they are ever liberated, notwithstanding the promises of the *woondouk*. I one day slipped a piece of money into Shway Weing's hands, as they found themselves rather straitened for food. But they did not show it, as they had heard it whispered that a foreigner was giving the slaves money; and they told Taunah that they hoped I would give them no more. I have been obliged to send word to the Christian chiefs to stay in the jungles for the present. They were about coming to present a petition to the *woondouk,* and endeavor to redeem their brethren. But the object cannot now be effected with money. I have made one fruitless attempt myself."

After many delays, with a view to extortion, and alternations of hope with darkest fear, the poor fellows were at last released, and sent to Mr. Edwards's house, on the 24th. Their teacher took them home, had them bathe, and gave them suits of clean clothing. Then they praised God together. While they were at the pagoda, some of the

Burman devotees reviled them on account of their religion. One said, "If you worship Jesus Christ, why does he not come and take care of you?" To which the Karen replied, "We are not the first among the disciples of Jesus who have suffered persecution." But the great majority of the people expressed sympathy for them. The missionary's journal continues:—

"*25th.*—Succeeded, after a good deal of trouble, in procuring a pass for Shway Weing, and in getting him ready to leave the city; for, the sooner he leaves, the better. He urged me to allow him to take as many books as he could conceal on his person; but I refused to give him one, and remarked, 'But yesterday those heavy fetters fell from your ankles: should you now be found with books in your possession, you would certainly lose your head.'—'Should so much sooner get to heaven,' was his reply. Having secured a promise from me that I will visit Bassein after the rains, the Karens departed, repeating their usual request, 'Pray for us.'

"*Sept. 9.*—Five Karens at worship, three of them students from Bassein, who fled to the Christians in Maubee when the others were imprisoned. As they return to-morrow morning, they urged me to allow them to carry a few small tracts. I told them I feared, on their account, to let a book go out of the city-gates. At sunset they were missing. I inquired anxiously, but could learn nothing of them. I had cautioned them to keep quiet, as the Burman officers were on the watch for them. Late in the evening, however, they returned with smiling faces. They had taken a quantity of books, passed out of the gates undetected, and had concealed them at 'John's house,' intending to take them as they pass along in the morning."

The young men succeeded in getting off with their treasures on the 10th, without molestation. Mr. Abbott writes in an unpublished letter:—

"What effect this affair will have finally on the cause of Christ will depend on future circumstances. The Karens are not a timid race; and they embrace the gospel with a full knowledge of the views, the designs, and the power of the Burman Government, and of what they are consequently to expect. There is a decision of character among this people which cannot be found among the Burmans."

From this time, by order of the *woondouk*, Mr. Abbott was closely watched. He could not travel in Burman territory without a pass. Nor could a pass be obtained without submitting to the closest questions, the answers to which would seriously endanger the Karens whom he so much wished to visit. It became more and more apparent that the government was in earnest in its efforts to put down Christianity everywhere in its dominions. We quote again from Mr. Abbott. The preacher to whom he refers is Maukoh, a good old man, still living, and well known to Bassein missionaries. One of his companions in suffering was Rev. Myat Keh, the noble pastor of the Kohsoo church.

"For a few weeks after Shway Weing and his associates were released, but few Karens ventured to call on me; yet more came than I wished. About the first of October three men came from Bassein to ask a question which was to me the precursor of evil,—'Teacher, what shall we do? Four of our brethren are in the stocks.' They informed me that an assistant whom I sent to that region, and three young men who joined him there, were out on a preaching-tour, and stopped one evening at a large Karen village near to the village of a Burman officer. As their custom is, they called the people together, and preached to them. They were warned that their course might awaken the wrath of the officers. But, as it seems, they deemed it advisable to obey God rather than man, and continued their meeting till a late hour. The next morning, before they had time to get away, the four were apprehended and beaten, with several who had listened to them the night before. The preachers were then put into the stocks, and reserved for torture. In ten days I heard again. The four had been liberated, but the officers had extorted a hundred and fifty rupees from the Christians. This sum had been promptly made up by voluntary contribution; some giving one anna, some two, and some a rupee. Yet not a Karen in all that region has been baptized, except 'the young chief.'

"On the 20th of November the assistant mentioned above came to me in Rangoon, pale and emaciated from disease. I asked him how he felt while they were beating him. 'Prayed for them.'—'But were you not a little angry?'—'No. I told them they might beat me to death, if they wished, but they would not make me angry, and that I should live again at the resurrection. At this they laughed, and, after beating me a little more, stopped.' Since that time he has been preaching in villages more remote from the Burmans, and has not been molested. The account he brings of the work of the Lord in those regions surpasses every thing I have heard of among heathen nations in modern days; and, if it be of God, it will stand."

On Sunday, Nov. 18, in Rangoon, Mr. Simons was an eye-witness of the dreadful scene which he describes below. It illustrates Boodhism, as well as the nature of Burmese government, and proves that the worst fears of the missionaries and the native converts were by no means groundless. The charge of rebellion was continually brought against the Karens, and it was on such a charge that these poor wretches (Burmans, probably) were put to death.

"The three men who are to be crucified to-day passed our house to the place of execution about ten, A.M. A number of officers and jail-keepers, with their large knives and spears, were in attendance; and a large concourse of people followed. Towards evening passed the place. Two of the men were still alive on their crosses, writhing in dreadful agony. Besides being nailed to the cross, each had a pointed thick stick, about two feet long, hammered down his throat. The man who was dead, I was informed, died instantly after the stick was hammered into his throat, and thus an end was put to his pains. I never had the idea of the agonies endured by persons nailed to the cross which I have had since I saw these two men with the nails in their feet and hands, saying, as well as they could to the bystanders. 'I thirst: give water.'"

Six days after this piece of savage cruelty Messrs. Abbott and Simons deemed it advisable to return for a season to the protection of the British flag in Maulmain. Their families had been sent thither three weeks before. The attempt to visit the poor sheep in the Bassein jungles must be indefinitely postponed. At the close of 1838 Abbott writes from Maulmain:—

"Notwithstanding my apprehensions and anxieties for what the Karen Christians have suffered, and are likely still to suffer, I experience a chastened joy, and would devoutly praise Him who is the head of the church for the manifestations of his presence and his power. Under circumstances the most alarming, we have witnessed the exhibition of all that is consistent and lovely in Christian character. Before magistrates and rulers, in prisons and in chains, have we seen bright evidence of the power of the gospel of Christ, and cheering promise of the triumph of the truth. In the great contest between the sons of Belial, cruel and blood-thirsty on the one hand, and the sons of God, meek and in chains on the other,—thanks be to God!—that truth has not faltered, and that the enemies of God have been amazed.

> "'O Jesus! ride on:
>   Thy kingdom is glorious.
> O'er sin, death, and hell
>   Thou wilt make us victorious.'"

"Rangoon, the only mission-station in Burma Proper at that time, was thus abandoned. The churches that had been gathered, and thousands of interesting inquirers, were now left emphatically, "as sheep without a shepherd,—to be scattered and destroyed, or to be preserved by a gracious and almighty Redeemer, to witness to the truth of his declarations, that his power is infinite, and his presence with his disciples constant to the end." The wrath of the enemy was aroused, and he seemed ready to destroy the scattered flock to the uttermost. If any thing would appease that wrath, it would seem to be the cessation, for a season, of direct efforts by foreign teachers for the extension of their faith in Burman territory. The step taken by the two brethren, therefore, of withdrawing to Maulmain, was undoubtedly a wise one. We quote a few lines from Mr. Abbott's letter of April 2, 1839:—

"The country around Rangoon has been in a dreadful state of excitement since we left. A spirit of rebellion is abroad in the land. The *woondouk* has slaughtered his countrymen, whom he calls rebels, with a merciless hand, seeking the most inhuman instruments of torture and death. Oh, when will the reign of blood be succeeded by the mild reign of the Prince of peace! I received a letter, a few days since, from one of the Karen assistants at Maubee, saying that the Christians were suffering no more than others. Persecution for the gospel's sake has been succeeded by oppression and plunder, in which all Karens suffer alike. He says that he has no hope that the country will be quiet for a long time to come, requests me to come and visit them if possible, and concludes with, 'Pray for us.' My heart bleeds at every recollection of the sorrows and wrongs of that ill-fated and long-oppressed people. Our consolation is, that Christ, the good Shepherd, knoweth his own, and will heal all their sorrows, and guide them safe home to glory."

It will be remembered that one Bassein man only, Shway Weing, "the young chief," had at this time put on Christ by baptism. Much had been done, however, in the way of publishing the gospel; and the good work begun was still spreading like wildfire. Among the earliest men sent over by Abbott to Bassein to preach, and teach the Karens to read God's word, we would rescue from oblivion the names of Mau Mway, Maukoh, and Shway Sah. To them, and others like them, Mau Yay, Myat Keh, and other natives of Bassein, joined themselves as disciples, and, soon learning all that their teachers had to impart, became, in turn, most zealous and useful preachers of the Word. So great was the desire for more teachers, that a formal call was sent at this time by the unbaptized Christians of Bassein to Oung Bau, one of the trusted Rangoon preachers, to come and live with them, and break unto them the bread of life. If he had gone, doubtless he would have lived on the fat of the land. Even in advance of these heralds of the cross, the Karens began to worship in many places. Shway Bau, pastor of the church in Nyomau, gives a dramatic description of the first attempts of these sincere but grossly ignorant people to worship like Christians: —

"The first that we heard about the new religion was, that Shway Weing had begun to worship God. Then we heard that he had a little book that told about God and the way to worship him; and straightway we had so strong a desire to see the book, that we could hardly stay at home, and we were talking about it, and wishing to see it, all the time. By and by we got a book, and one looked at it, and another looked at it, and said it was very nice; and then we looked at it again, one after another; and then we held it up between our hands, and worshipped it, and said to the book, 'O Lord! O Lord!' for we thought that God was in the book. It was a long time ago, teacher, when we did not know any thing at all.

"After a while, some of us learned to read the book; and it said that we must not worship idols. Then some were much afraid, and said, 'What shall we do? If we cannot worship idols, the Burmans will persecute and destroy us.' —'It is no matter,' answered others. 'If they do kill our bodies, they cannot hurt the soul, for God will take care of that.' The little book said that we must worship God continually: so, after we learned that God was not in the book, but in heaven, we used to meet together, and worship in this way: we all pulled off our turbans, and piled them in a heap in the centre, and then pulled our hair down over our faces [Karen men wear long hair]; and then one would pray, and another would pray, till all had prayed three times. We also thought, that, if we prayed till the tears dropped, there was great merit in it: so sometimes one would pray a while, and look up to another, and ask, 'Do you see the tears starting?' And if he said, 'No,' then he would pray again very hard; and, when one or two drops had fallen, he would say to another, 'Now you pray, for I am happy a little.' It was a long time ago, teacher, when we did not know any thing at all.

"And, if the mosquitoes bit us while we were praying, we thought there was merit in permitting them to bite us, and so we did not brush them off. They would bite until we writhed this way and that, and our bodies were covered with blotches. It was a long time ago, teacher, when we did not know any thing at all.

"We were taught by the book that we must not make feasts to the *nats*; but we thought we ought to make feasts to God: so this one and that one would make a great feast, and invite his friends and neighbors to come, and eat to the honor of God. And, when the guests had eaten all they could, the host would give portions to each, as they returned, saying, 'We make sacrifice to the Lord God' [P'mah boo K'sah Ywah]; and we thought there was great merit in doing so.

"Then we heard that Christ would come again soon, and that, when he came, he would give to his disciples great treasures and power. So one would say to another, 'Throw away your brass and tin ornaments and your cotton waist-cloths; for, when Christ comes, he will give us an abundance of silver and gold, and fine silk clothing.' This they said everywhere when we first began to worship God. But in some villages they did another thing: they said among themselves, 'These rice-pots and eating-dishes we used when we worshipped nats: they must be defiled.' So they broke them in pieces, and bought new ones, that they might retain nothing which was connected with nat and idol worship. It was twelve years ago, teacher, when we did not know any thing at all. But since the teacher came, and told us what the customs of Christ's disciples are, and gave us the Holy Book to read for ourselves, we have worshipped God correctly."

During this period of painful suspense, Mr. Abbott was not idle. He travelled among the Karens of Maulmain: and, between April and September, he relieved Messrs. Howard and Vinton alternately of the charge of the Burman and Karen boarding-schools. Meanwhile, through the extreme forbearance of the English, the threatened war was averted for a time. The Burmans, as always, attributing this forbearance to conscious weakness, increased in their *hauteur* and overbearing insolence. It seems to have occurred to the viceroy of Rangoon, however, that, under the circumstances, it might be as well for him to cultivate more friendly relations with the Americans. He therefore went so far as to send an urgent invitation to Messrs. Kincaid and Abbott to come back to his city. Accordingly, on the 4th of November, almost a year after the departure of the missionaries, these brethren arrived in Rangoon. The governor gave them a courteous and even friendly reception, and pressed them again to settle in their old quarters with their families. During their stay of about forty days, many of the Karen Christians found their way to them, of whom Kincaid writes:—

"They would come by twenties if we had not sent them word that it would be imprudent, and expose them to fines and imprisonment, and possibly to death. Some who had been bound with cords, and beaten till nearly senseless, for preaching Christ and the resurrection, came to see us. Often, when we returned from an evening walk, we would find four or five, or seven or eight, in our room, nearly worn out with their long march through the heat of the sun. Still they would sit up till after midnight, asking questions about Christian doctrines and duties, and difficult passages of Scripture. Even at that time of night it was not easy to get away to sleep, they were so eager to have every thing obscure made plain. Some of these are assistants, who have from twenty to sixty families each under their care. They are pastors, as well as preachers; each one, in his own parish, visiting from house to house, reading the Scriptures, and praying with the sick, conducting public worship on the sabbath, preaching to the unevangelized, and performing the rite of marriage according to Christian usage. They are not ordained, and therefore do not administer the ordinances. But they are God's anointed ones; and we have no doubt, that, in time, they will become efficient pastors and evangelists. It would be imprudent now to intrust them with power to baptize. They must have more instruction in 'the mysteries of the kingdom,' more experience, and more knowledge of character, or there would be danger of their filling up the church with mere nominal Christians. Two of the young men who were in irons and the stocks last year are now sitting near me, reading the New Testament. Both of them are fine, active young men."

Of the work in Bassein, Abbott writes thus:—

"Shortly after my arrival in Rangoon several assistants came in to see me from Pantanau and Bassein, where they had spent several months. The reports they brought were of the most cheering character. The Pantanau church is walking in the fear of the Lord and in the comfort of the Holy Ghost, and very many in the

33

surrounding villages have turned to the Lord during the year. In Bassein, Shway Weing continues to be as actively engaged in doing good as ever. His house is a great bethel, a temple of God, whither the people resort, from villages far and near, to learn to read, and how to worship God. He is the only baptized person in that region, and consequently the only one who can be reckoned a church-member. How many there are who would be considered proper subjects of baptism, it is impossible to say. The assistants think there are from six hundred to a thousand decided Christians. Although but one has been baptized, still the line of demarcation between those who serve God and those who serve him not is distinctly drawn; and generally there exists on the part of those who reject the gospel a bitter hatred towards the Christians. In fact, the Karen converts fear their own countrymen who are enemies to the gospel more than Burman officers. Sometimes, even in families, there exists deadly opposition; and not only are 'a man's foes they of his own household,' but they are often his bitterest foes. Notwithstanding, I know of several villages where the people are all decidedly Christian; and, although it has been denied [by Malcom] that there are whole villages which have turned to God, yet, if he will take a trip with me into the Karen jungles, I will show him several such."

The missionaries went back to Maulmain with the intention of returning shortly, with their families, to live and labor for their Master, under the nominal protection of their newly found friend in Rangoon. Meantime, however, the viceroy himself experienced one of those sudden vicissitudes of fortune to which the favorites of a tyrant are always exposed. He was summoned to go, in disgrace, to Ava, and perhaps to the death-prison. A most brutal and ignorant foe to foreigners was appointed to his place. From this time the relations of the two governments were more strained than ever. War might be declared any day or hour. Despairing of obtaining a place to do Christian work in Burman territory, Abbott, at the close of 1839, is turning his thoughts to Arakan. With the quick eye and prompt decision of a leader, he determines upon "a change of base."

While the record of 1839 is brief, owing to the scanty efforts of man in the field under review, who can measure the deepening and ever-widening work wrought that year by the unaided Spirit of Omnipotence on thousands of plastic hearts in the unexplored jungles of Bassein? In how many remote corners of the "Dark Continent" to-day, may a similar work of preparation be progressing, to be revealed only when the preacher shall find them peoples "prepared for the Lord"?

CHAPTER III.

1840, 1841.

"Not many wise after the flesh, not many mighty, not many noble, are called." —PAUL.

The history of the Bassein mission, beginning from this time, maybe divided into three periods: *first*, from 1840 to 1852, the period of ingathering by native agents, from a remote base in British territory; *second*, 1852-69, the period of home-mission work, in which the churches were multiplied, and instructed in the way of God more perfectly, from Bassein itself, the natural centre; *third*, 1869-80, the period of school-building, and the beginning of systematic effort for foreign missions. We now enter upon the first of these periods, a time in which God wrought mightily through Abbott and his faithful Karen assistants, as well as by his own angel of death and by the Pharaohs of that time and country.

The eastern or Arakan coast of the Bay of Bengal has long had an evil name, second only to the corresponding west coast of Africa. From 1824 to 1852, however, this narrow strip of hot, marshy territory, became an asylum, a land of promise to the oppressed Karens of Burma Proper. The British flag that waved over it tempered the heat, and so palliated the fever and other ills, that they became endurable, if not welcome. Sandoway was probably the least unhealthy of the towns on that coast; but, between it and the Karens of Bassein, there lay many long marches through a sickly, weary land. Four passes over the coast-hills are still used, to some extent, by the missionaries and the people of Bassein, to reach the former "cities of refuge" by the sea; viz., the Baumee Pass, on the north, by which Mr. Abbott made the journey detailed in Chap. vi.; the Khyoungthah Pass, easiest of all, and most travelled by the Karens; the Ng'Kwat, most difficult of all, as the author can testify from hard experience; and the Poloung Pass, in the south. When the oppression became unendurable, the Karens would flee, over these and other hill-roads, to the protection of Christian England. At length the Burman rulers would become loath to lose subjects so industrious and peaceable as the Karens. It would not enhance their reputation at Ava to have it known that thousands of the best tax-payers in the country were running over the border, to the hated foreigner. And thus it came to pass, in time, that the mere fact that such an asylum was open became a powerful check upon the oppressor. But for the time there was an exodus; and fever and cholera were to do their terrible work among the poor fugitives, and the heart of their teacher was to be often wrung with anguish, before those days of woe and spiritual purification should be overpast.

The Abbotts left Maulmain on the 11th of February, 1840, in the Company's steamer *Ganges*. With them were the Kincaids, bound for Akyab, Ko Thahbyu, already the aged "Karen apostle," and two of Abbott's old Rangoon students, Hton Byu and Mau Yay,[1] who fell into prison, and became pagoda slaves, with Shway Weing in 1838. Arriving at Sandoway on the 17th of March, Mr. Abbott writes as follows, under date of April 1: —

{ Footnote: [1] This Mau Yay (not to be confounded with the equally excellent pastor of Kyootoo, Bassein) was ordained in May, 1853, and lived to become a pillar of strength among the Rangoon Karen churches. On the evening of the last day of the year (1863), as we were at worship in his chapel at Raytho (p. 17), a messenger came in breathless, with the tidings that the pastor had been accidentally shot. The writer hastened out to meet the litter; but the good man's spirit had already gone to God. Only the evening before, he had read for singing Mrs. Vinton's beautiful imitation of "The day is past and gone." So soon for him had come the night of death, and rest in the bosom of divine love. }

"As I wrote you, it was my intention to return to Rangoon with my family, in the hope of doing something among the Karens in a quiet way; but, the British Resident having retired from the country altogether, I became more fully convinced than ever of the impossibility of doing any thing for the Karens, under the present government, without involving them in suffering more serious than they have yet experienced. Missionaries and all other foreigners can *remain* there with perfect safety to their persons and property. They always could, indeed, except in case of war; and then all foreigners are imprisoned and maltreated alike, without reference to character or profession. Very soon after the removal of the Resident, I received a letter from a British merchant still there, stating that all intercourse between foreigners and the natives was strictly prohibited. Such being the case, a missionary might as well be in Boston, as not an individual would dare to call at his house...

"I hesitated for some time between two courses. The one was to go into the country, itinerate and preach among the people, and leave the consequences. If persecution and death followed in my train, be it so; submit all to the Lord. I did not forget, however, that there is but one step between a 'zeal according to knowledge' and the most palpable presumption. The other course was to try to effect the same object by sending native assistants with letters of encouragement and love; men who could travel among their countrymen, and preach the gospel, without being suspected of political designs; men who, understanding the rudiments of Christianity, and their hearts set on the work, should be capable of instructing and building up the converts in the faith of the gospel. I have chosen this latter course, as affording greater promise of usefulness, with the least hazard and difficulty.

"Having adopted this plan, it only remained for me to select the most eligible location for its accomplishment. To think of reaching the Karens in the Burman Empire from Tenasserim is out of the question. Arakan, from its extensive frontiers adjoining Burma, seemed to be the only place where I could hope to enjoy the facilities I desired...Sandoway is a small Burman town fifty miles south of Ramree, on a small river, about fourteen miles from the sea as the river runs, or five in a direct course. The town is reputed healthy, and, from its location, I should judge would sustain its reputation. It has about four thousand inhabitants. From all I can gather on the spot, the Karens in Arakan itself are about equal in number to those in Tavoy and Mergui; [They are much fewer now.—ED.] and the facility of reaching them is about the same. There is this weighty consideration, however, the Arakan fever, which renders it hazardous to travel in the jungles at all. I have been admonished that I must not think of travelling here with the impunity that one might in Tenasserim.

"There is a Karen village, five or six miles from this town, where Ko Thahbyu has been preaching since our first arrival; but the people are surprisingly stupid and indifferent...I have sent Mau Yay and Hton Byu to Bassein and Rangoon with letters to the disciples. They will go from this place to Gwa, a small town on the coast, five days south. Three days thence, across the mountains which form the boundary, will bring them into the Burman Empire and into the vicinity of Christian villages. They will endeavor to persuade some of the young men who commenced studying with me in Rangoon, and were scattered by the persecution, to come over, and study with me, during the rains, in this place. Although the passes are strictly guarded by Burman officers, to prevent emigration, I hope that a few at least of those young men will escape their vigilance, and make their way into this land of liberty, where they may enjoy the benefits of Christian instruction without having to pay for it the price of imprisonment and chains. If, however, my messengers should be suspected themselves, and even thrown into prison, it would be nothing new to them, as they were of the four who were sent to the pagoda as slaves, two years ago in Rangoon. I shall feel a good deal of anxiety about them till their return."

The journal which follows will be read with interest: —

"*March 30.* — Visited a small Karen village a few miles from town. The people treated us with contempt, not only refusing to listen to any thing we had to say, but even denying us admission to their houses. To get out of the scorching sun, I ventured to enter the only house in the village which had any thing like a seat. It was occupied by a lazy-looking fellow, who, on being requested by my assistant, refused to rise, or to give us any accommodation. We made our way to another house, and took a seat on the floor, i.e., on a few bamboos laid across each other, with openings very convenient for falling through. During the day I tried in vain to get a hearing. How dark and stupid is the heathen mind!

"April 10.—Moung Koo (Maukoh, pp. 26, 27), a Karen assistant from Maubee, made his appearance to-day with other Karens, who have come eight days' journey. They had heard of my arrival from the two messengers. Several are to remain and study: others come to be baptized, and are to return in a few days. A few of them live in this province, but most of them in Burma. We had begun to despair of seeing any of our Bassein friends at Sandoway, but joy and hope have succeeded. The mountain passes afford a highway for the Christians on the other side, which I hope they will not be slow to improve. It is a long and arduous journey; but the anxiety of the Karens to get books, to learn to read, and to be baptized, will induce them to surmount every obstacle, so that I still hope to get a class of young men for the rains. No women, of course, can come such a distance.

"11th, Sabbath.—Sixteen Karens at worship, several of whom are asking for baptism; but, as they are to remain a week, I prefer to delay a little.

"12th.—Commenced school with a class of eight young men. More are on their way, and will be here in a few days.

"13th.—Seventeen more Karens arrived to-day, from a village one day this side of Bassein, several of whom I saw during my visit to that region two years ago. They were ten days on the way.

"14th.—Thirty-four Karens at worship, four others having just come in. One of them is a member of the Pantanau church. His accounts of the Christians there are very satisfactory. Not a case of backsliding, not one of discipline, in the church since we left. The Burman rulers seem disposed to let them alone.

"18th, Sabbath.—Sixty Karens to-day; Mau Yay having just returned with thirty-one others, whom he gathered in the jungles. Some are asking for baptism: others will remain and study. At the close of the day I baptized twelve, who came first, all of whom have professed to be Christians for more than a year. They all gave good evidence of a

change of heart and life; and their coming so far to obey the command of Christ is indicative of their zeal.

"Among the number baptized was a young man named Bleh Po, whose history and experience are of unusual interest. He first heard the gospel during my visit to Bassein in December, 1837. Shortly after, I saw him in Rangoon, gave him books, and he learned to read. He immediately embraced the truth, and, to appearance, with all his heart. His wife and relatives, however, used all manner of devices to turn him from the faith. Not long after his conversion his little child, two years old, was taken very ill, and, as a matter of course, his relatives charged him with being the cause;[1] that is, he had forsaken their religion, and the child's guardian demon was taking vengeance. As the custom is in such cases, they besought him to offer a sacrifice to this devil to appease his wrath. Bleh Po steadily refused, saying that he trusted in God, and had renounced the worship of devils. In a few days his child died. His friends then entered a complaint against him to the Burman ruler. He was apprehended, and arraigned in open court, in the presence of a crowd who were waiting to see the end. Among other charges was this: 'Bleh Po has a foreigner's book, and has embraced a foreign religion.' The judge, among other questions, asked what was in the book. Bleh Po thereupon gave an outline of the doctrines of the gospel, at the same time exposing the folly of idolatry and all heathen superstitions. The magistrate remarked that what he had said was good, but, if he did not take notice of the case, it would come to the ears of the king, and he himself would lose his life. Bleh Po replied, 'Don't you fear: send *me* up to the king, and let me answer for myself, or suffer.' He was released without fine, imprisonment, or stripes, and returned to his family; but it was to meet their execrations, rendered more malignant by defeat. They cursed him, charging him with the murder of his own child, and threatening to kill him. To this, the only answer he deigned to give was, 'If you do not kill me, I shall die myself soon.' To all their revilings he opposed a spirit of humility and patience, admonishing them on fit occasions, continuing firm in his profession, and showing the majesty of a meek and quiet spirit. Thus he triumphed. His wife and several of his relatives are now praying, consistent Christians, and his enemies are speechless.

{ Footnote: [1] A case exactly parallel to this occurred among the first Kakhyen converts in 1882. }

"That magistrate has ever since favored the Christians. He has heard the gospel more fully from Bleh Po, and has received Christian books. A short time since, an officer of high rank came down from the capital, and ordered him to put three or four Karen Christians to death, that, by that means, they might be brought back to the customs of their fathers. 'No,' says this man: 'they are our slaves, indeed, but they are quiet and peaceable, and pay their taxes; and, if they wish to worship *their* God, let them do so.'

"There are several other petty officers in those regions who are friendly to the Christians, who have Christian books, and have listened to the gospel from Bleh Po. The Karens think that some of them are real Christians. One of the governors of Bassein, who left for the capital a short time since, is a baptized Christian, the Karens say.[1] He was of good moral character, just, and universally beloved. Every Sunday he used to retire to his private apartments, and shut his door, allowing no court business on that day. He never worshipped idols, or celebrated the rites of Boodhism. I believe that he is a member of the Ava church. All these facts indicate the steady advance of truth, and its final triumph.

{ Footnote: [1] Moung Shway Moung, baptized in Ava the latter part of 1835, and sent down to Bassein from the capital, in 1837. See Dr. Kincaid's letter, Missionary Magazine, March, 1841, p. 62. Of. Magazine, 1838, p. 222, and 1840, p. 70. }

"*19th.*—This morning nineteen of my Karens left for their distant homes. They took all the books I had, and were anxious for more. It is astonishing how fast readers multiply. Some of them buy books of the Burmans. One man gave a rupee for a Burmese Testament; another, a day's work for a tract. Mr. Howard hardly supposed, when he was distributing Burman books in Bassein, that he was doing it for Karen Christians. Number of students to-day thirty-six.

"*24th.*—Three individuals arrived to-day from the Burman side, bringing letters from Hton Byu, one of the two whom I sent over. The poor man is very ill, and unable to return. The 'young chief' wrote, also, that he was staying at home to take care of Hton Byu, and that he would come and see me directly on his recovery. In the mean time he wished me to 'lay aside ten or fifteen hundred books' for his Christian friends. He will be disappointed in this.

"*25th, Sabbath.*—At worship a company of Burmans came in, to whom I directed my discourse in their own language (though in a broken manner), and gave them books, which they promised to read. But a Burman's promise is not much to be relied upon. A good many from the villages around call, and receive books; and Mrs. Abbott has almost daily visits from the women of the town, who come in and sit for hours, listening to the truth. Here is a promising field for a Burman missionary.

"*27th.*—Eight of our number left us, among whom was Maukoh, the assistant from Rangoon. He was travelling and preaching among the villages in Bassein, when he heard of my arrival at Sandoway, and immediately came to see me.

"*28th.*—Followed to the tomb the remains of a poor old man. He was one of the first company who came to be baptized. The long and difficult journey and the extreme heat were too much for him: he was taken sick, and sunk quietly away. It would have been a satisfaction to his relatives could he have been baptized. But, instead of following the footsteps of the Son of man into the watery grave, he has found a resting-place beneath 'the clods of the valley.' His spirit, I trust, has ascended up on high, and now enjoys the full measure of that 'glory laid up,' of which he but lived to get a glimpse on earth. He had been a Christian about a year. Three of my students also are suffering from dysentery, and thirteen are prostrated with fever, all under our own roof.

"It is singular that Karens coming from the interior jungles to the seashore are nearly every one attacked with some malignant disease. More than half of the students have already been down with fever: some are convalescent, others very ill. I attribute it to the change from Burma to Arakan. They all live in the delta of the Irrawaddy, — a country, I believe, much more healthy than this. Their long journey in this hot season, with the exposure and privations, has doubtless contributed to produce so many cases of fever. I have the services of the hospital physician, a native, who also supplies me with medicine. Otherwise, what should I do?

"*30th.*—Another company of six arrived from Burma. They met those who left on the 19th, at a Christian village near the mountains. Several of them sunk down by the way, through the intense heat, and were carried to that village on the shoulders of the strong. They will remain there until recruited, before crossing the mountains. Four of those who came to-day wish to remain and study, but my schoolroom is a hospital. My buildings are not sufficient for so large a boarding-school: the rains are upon us, and it is too late to build.

"*May 5.*—Four of the six who last arrived set out on their return this morning, one of whom I baptized yesterday. More than two years ago this man was called before an officer, and beaten, for holding religious meetings at his house. Two small books also were taken from him. Very soon after, said officer was taken ill. It came to him at once, that the Karen whom he had beaten had bewitched him; and he immediately sent back his books. But it did not avail: the poor man died. Of course, it was clear that the Karen had killed him by some wicked enchantment. The officer's relations believe it to this day, and not a few of the Karen Christians think that he died so suddenly because he had abused a Christian. The Burmans since then have let that Christian alone. He is a firm, intelligent man, conducts public worship in his village, and itinerates occasionally. As he promises to be useful, I have admitted him among the number of the assistants.

"*8th.*—Hton Byu and Shway Weing arrived to-day, having thirty in their train. They were twelve days on the way, sometimes without food, travelling through the heat of the day, and sleeping on the ground. Some of them were taken with fever: some fainted from exhaustion, and were left in the rear, to come on as they are able. Fifty or sixty started, but nearly one-half gave out. Several came to study. I really cannot send them back, and yet I see not how I can accommodate them.

"*10th, Sabbath.*—Baptized eleven of those who came in last. Twenty of them will return to-morrow, leaving twelve. This will make my class fifty, as I anticipated. Six are boys under sixteen, the remaining forty-four between that age and thirty. I pray the God of Israel, that we may all enjoy health and the light of his countenance, and that these young men may be taught the knowledge of the Lord, and established in the gospel.

"*13th.*—From a small village near by, a company of men and boys, and a few young girls, came in, seeking admission to the school. They cannot be received. I send them back, and a student with them to establish a day-school in their own village. These first heard the gospel since our arrival here. Their coming to school is a strong evidence of their interest, as no Karen would take such a course, were he not disposed to become a Christian. Some of them are now asking for baptism."

Dr. Kincaid, with his warm heart always enlisted in behalf of the Karens, writes at this time, of the work begun in Bassein, as follows:—

"All the men who have come over the hills represent the work as still going on, spreading from village to village in every direction...The full extent of this revival we do not know, but enough has been learned to convince us that it is an extraordinary display of divine grace. Probably more than two thousand souls are turned from the worship of demons to the service of the living God. This, too, has taken place under the jealous and intolerant reign of the new King. It is God's glorious work."

May 19 Mr. Abbott, in writing of the expenses of his school, and of his design to employ eighteen assistants in Burma and Sandoway, whom he had already selected, and was about locating, says, —

"Nearly all these assistants are at the head of large Christian congregations, and are, in fact, pastors, except in administering the ordinances...As to how many Christians there are, I dare not tell what I think. There are *baptized*, near Maubee three hundred and twenty-three, at Pantanau forty-eight, and in Bassein twenty-seven. The last are widely scattered, and are principally heads of villages, and leaders of Christian congregations. As to the entire number of *nominal* Christians, some of the assistants think there are four thousand; but, as I have no data on which to found a satisfactory estimate, I can give no opinion."

In the same letter, after asking for the very moderate appropriation of Rs. 1,921,[1] for the support of his theological school and eighteen assistants through the year, he adds, "I hope, in time, to succeed in introducing the system of each congregation supporting its own pastor; but this will require time and the fostering care of a beneficent Providence." Thus early had this New-Testament principle fastened itself in the brain of the founder of the Bassein mission, but the expression of it was not allowed. The sentence was put in brackets, and then in a pigeon-hole forty-three years, — why, we cannot imagine.

{ Footnote: [1] The *rupee*, at par of exchange, is about forty-five cents; an *anna*, nearly three cents. }

Again Mr. Abbot found himself, as in Rangoon, dangerously cramped for room for his school of fifty pupils. He writes: —

"As I arrived too late in the season to make suitable preparations for so large a boarding-school, we are very much straitened for room, and are compelled to convert our dwelling into a schoolroom, sleeping-room, and chapel for nearly all our students. In consequence of being so crowded, we have already had a good many cases of fever. Still I hope to be able to keep all my students this season."

At the same time, in view of their freedom from Burman oppression, he writes exultingly:—

"Thanks be to God, we have no such fears here. Under the British flag we are safe. The students can show themselves in the streets here, without apprehension or alarm. No self-conceited barbarian parades here with a band of minions at his heels ready to do his bidding. Here is no spy, gazing around to detect a 'foreigner's disciple.' Here no chains, no prison, for the followers of the Lord Jesus. How sweet are the blessings of civil and religious liberty! Who can appreciate them, but those who have dwelt in a land of relentless despotism? In the Burman Empire, my class of young men could not be kept together three days."

His hopes of a prosperous term were doomed to a sad disappointment. Dysentery followed the fever, and then cholera with all its terrors; the result being the death of five young men in quick succession. To diminish the danger, thirty were dismissed, to return to their distant homes, in the height of the rains. Those who remained made rapid progress in their studies, and gave evidence of their being sincere followers of Jesus. From the time of Mr. Abbott's arrival, until the close of school (the first week in September), he had baptized fifty-one. In two Karen villages near Sandoway, where there had been indifference and opposition, signs of good were beginning to appear. In closing his letter on the 10th of September, he writes:—

"Ko Thahbyu, our native assistant, died yesterday. He has been one of the most laborious and successful preachers in the Karen mission. His work is done, and he has gone to his rest."

The year 1841 opens with threatenings of the enemy, and with the exaction of heavy fines, far beyond the ability of the poor Christians to pay. Before its close, King Tharrawady leaves his capital, and proceeds in barbaric state to Rangoon. He was attended by an army of a hundred thousand men. The public prints of that time state that a fleet of from fifteen thousand to eighteen thousand boats was required to convey his retinue and soldiers with their *impedimenta*. Whether his purpose was war or peace could only be conjectured. The whole country was again full of warlike rumors and excitement. Although nothing came of it, the Governor General deemed it prudent to despatch armed vessels and additional troops to Maulmain. Amid all, the work of God goes on in the hearts of the rude men and women of Bassein. In a private letter, written in April, Mr. Abbott remarks: —

"We labor under difficulties and privations at Sandoway, arising from climate and location; and the constant exposure of the Karens in Burma to persecution adds to our sorrows; but, when we see the 'stately steppings of the God of hosts,' our light afflictions are swallowed up in joy."

His journal accompanying this letter follows: —

"*Dec. 24, 1840.* — Commending my wife and son to the care of that God whom we serve, left Sandoway at ten, P.M., yesterday, for a visit to the Karens on the eastern frontier of this province. Am indebted to the kindness of Dr. Morton, assistant commissioner, for the use of his schooner free of expense. As the sailors required none of my aid or advice, I enjoyed a quiet night in my berth. Awoke at daylight to find myself far from land.

"The coast presents a succession of broken hills, covered with jungle, apparently one vast wilderness; the Arakan mountains rearing their majestic heads, in the distance, above the dense clouds which hang around their base. There are villages along the coast; but they are few. Situated on the streams which flow from the mountains, and surrounded by trees, they cannot be seen from the sea. In many places, the hills extend down to the shore; and, not unfrequently, high rocky points project into the sea for a mile or more, making navigation dangerous. Where the coast is level, it is mostly covered with mangrove-trees, and at high tides with salt water. From these marshes, which cover a great part of the level lands of Arakan, a miasma arises, which is impregnated with fever, cholera, and death.

"*25th.*—During the night the wind was high, and the schooner rolled so, that it was somewhat difficult to keep in my berth. Weighed anchor at daylight; and, the wind being still favorable, our little bark bounded over the waves in grand style, till two, P.M., when we anchored in the mouth of the river, off Gwa. The little town is on the north bank of the river, near the sea, and, being surrounded with cocoanut-trees and shrubbery, is altogether a charming spot. Here are, perhaps, a hundred families, all Burmese. A plain extends back to the hills a mile or more, and up the coast ten or twelve miles, which is dotted with hamlets. The land is good, and affords an inviting field for cultivation and pasturage. I lodge in a small *zayat* erected on the beach for the Commissioner of Arakan, who is expected here soon. There is great excitement in Bassein, from the Karens learning to read 'the white book,' which the Burmans consider quite equal to open rebellion...I find here books and tracts which came from missionaries in Rangoon. Many of them are read; and, away in this wilderness, many persons are acquiring a knowledge of the Lord. In Bassein the officers lately made search, both among Karens and Burmans; and a large number of [our] books were collected, and publicly burned. Still, there are many dispersed through the country, where they will remain safely concealed, I trust.

"*27th, Sabbath.*—'This is the day the Lord hath made;' but oh, how different are the scenes here witnessed from those in Christian lands! One Karen Christian only with me during the day, who sits in a corner of the *zayat,* reading his Bible. A few people call at the door, and cautiously look in to gaze at the stranger. A Karen came in at evening, from a small village near, and asked for baptism. He and his wife are the only Christians in the village, all the others being decided opposers. As I remain near here for a few days, I deferred his baptism, so as to inquire further into his character.

"*28th.*—As the larger Karen villages are still farther south, left Gwa early this morning, and, with a good breeze, anchored in the creek by the small Burman village Magezzin, at evening. [Map, *Magyee syee.*] The Karen villages up the stream are known by the same name. It is too late to go to them to-night.

"*29th.* — At sunrise took a canoe, and in three hours reached a Karen village of fifteen families. The people immediately assembled in the house of the chief, which is used for worship. The gospel was first preached here about two years ago. There are Christians in every family. A few I have baptized at Sandoway: others have been waiting impatiently for me to visit them. An old chief from one of the nearest villages on the Burman side informs me that the Karens in that section have been fined a large sum for learning to read 'the white book.' His share amounted to eighty-three rupees. He has come over to select a place, hoping to escape, with his people, from oppression. At evening, forty at worship: seventeen asked for baptism.

"*31st.* — Baptized ten yesterday, and thirteen to-day. All live in this village. After the strictest inquiry, both in public and private, relative to their moral character, the evidences of their change of life were fully established. All have been Christians more than a year, and they have acquired an amount of Christian knowledge almost incredible. Myat Kyau, one of my best assistants, lives here, and is pastor of the church. He is a good man; studied with me last rains, and is prepared to guide the people in the way of life.

"Bleh Po came in from Burma during the day, with a company. He gives a more detailed account of the oppression near Bassein. Eleven Christian chiefs, whose names he mentions, have been arraigned, imprisoned, and fined for embracing our religion, and learning to read. These chiefs are the magistrates, in petty matters, of their respective villages, under higher Burman officers, and are the patriarchs of their people. Some of them have sixty or eighty families; others, only eight or ten, under their jurisdiction. Although they were fined in all Rs. 1,181, they deem it light, as most of their people are Christians, and contributed cheerfully to make up the amount. A question arises, whether they can consistently pay such fines. They have their choice, — to pay, or suffer. A refusal would be construed into open rebellion; and woe to the man, in that land of despotism, on whom that accusation falls! They are not required to give any pledge to worship the priests or pagodas, or to renounce their faith. When they were called before the governor, they were asked if they worshipped the foreigner's God, and read 'the white book.' 'Yes,' replied one; 'and many of the Burmans also, your own people, read "the white book."' After a few similar questions, the governor told them that they were fined so much, and committed them to prison till the sum should be paid. They were treated with a good deal of kindness for prisoners in Burma. Tortures and death would probably have been the result, had they refused to pay the fine. Did the officers require them to renounce their religion, I think many among the thousands of nominal Christians would equivocate to save their lives; but a great many, I am confident, would suffer martyrdom with unwavering fortitude.

"*Jan. 1, 1841.*—This first day of the new year has been one of painful interest to me. Several assistants arrived in the morning from Bassein, having eluded the pursuers sent by the governor to apprehend them. They left their homes in the night, and made their way through the jungles to this place, where I had appointed a meeting four months ago. If they should be caught, new trials and sufferings await them. Preached at evening, to a large and intensely solemn congregation, from 'Christ the good shepherd.'

"*2d.*—Baptized eleven in the morning. In the afternoon, lectured to the assistants from Tit. i. 6-12. At sunset, held a meeting; and nineteen asked for baptism. In the evening, expounded the parable of the tares. After the service my old companion, 'great heaviness of heart,' appeared. Not the first time I have invited such visits by attempting to pierce the gloomy cloud that overhangs the disciples of Jesus.

"*3d, Sabbath.*—After morning service, baptized nineteen. A more solemn company of Karens I never saw together. Never did I enjoy such freedom in preaching to them the gospel.

"*4th.*—In the morning Shway Weing arrived with several associates. He has been wandering in the jungles eleven days to reach this place, when it is only four days in a direct course. A friendly Burman officer informed him some time since, that he must keep himself quiet, as the governor of Bassein had his eye particularly upon him as a leader of the Christians. As affairs became more threatening, he told Shway Weing, that, if he would save his life, he had better renounce his religion at once. Being assured that Shway Weing would never deny his Lord, come what would, he told him that he must flee. Soon after, learning that men were in pursuit of him, he left his family with a brother, and retreated to the back villages. His friends pulled down his house at once; and when the officers arrived, finding not even a habitation, they gave up the pursuit.

"In conversing with Shway Weing, I asked him why he presumed to come to English territory to see me at this juncture, knowing, as he did, that the fact, if known, would aggravate his sufferings, in case of his apprehension. He replied, 'I wished to come and see the teacher's face, hear his voice, and go home and die.'

"Baptized nine at noon, most of them from the Burman side. One is a brother of Bleh Po. During his examination, I asked him whether he would endure persecution, and, if necessary, suffer death, rather than deny his Lord. He hesitated, and rather thought that he should not do as Peter did. I asked him if he dare testify, before God and that congregation, that he would endure unto death. 'I am afraid, teacher: I dare not.' I needed not so solemn a declaration to convince me of the genuineness of his conversion, but had other reasons for wishing to elicit a direct answer. A large congregation were waiting in breathless silence and expectation; so that it was impossible for me to recede. I asked him the third time. He still hesitated. I pressed him for a reply. He bowed his face to the floor, and wept. The stillness of the grave pervaded the assembly. He raised his head, the tears rolling down his sable cheeks, and said, 'I think,—teacher,—I shall *not* deny the Lord,—if he gives me grace. I can say no more.'

"It has fallen to my lot to baptize more than four hundred Karens since I have been in Burma; but never have I enjoyed such delightful seasons as during the last few days—our Jordan, a small stream running down from the mountains, overlooked by wild and beautiful scenery; the congregations attentive, solemn, and joyful; the dense forests resounding with songs of praise from a hundred happy converts plighting to Heaven their vows; an emblematical grave, giving up its dead to 'newness of life;' the presence of the Lamb of God hallowing the scene, and setting upon his own ordinance the seal of divine love. God Almighty bless these converts, and preserve them blameless to the coming of the Lord with all his holy angels!

"At evening, after a farewell charge to the disciples, I entered a small canoe to return, all my assistants and many others 'accompanying me to the ship.' The hour had arrived when I was to part with those beloved men, and it was an hour of sadness. Most of them were to return to Bassein, 'not knowing the things that shall befall them there,' but assured 'that persecution and afflictions abide them.' They reluctantly shook my hand, one by one, saying, 'Pray for us,' and departed. My own feelings were indescribable.

"*5th.*—After the assistants and people had left us last evening, I retired to my berth exhausted. A few minutes past nine we heard Karen voices on the shore. I went on deck, and found they had come a long distance to see me and be baptized. The vessel was anchored in the middle of the stream, without a boat. There was not a house, or a canoe even, on their side; and the Burman village opposite was some distance inland. The Karens called many times to the villagers to come and take them across, but in vain. With flint and steel, they struck a fire, concluding to sleep on the sand, and return in the morning, unbaptized, after all their efforts, and after coming within the sound of the teacher's voice. Mothers and infant children were in the company. But Providence favored them. After an hour or more two women were seen on the opposite shore, to whom we called for aid. They launched a canoe, and finally ferried the Karens all over, two or three at a load; then they took me ashore. We walked two miles to a Karen village, and found the assistants engaged in a prayer-meeting. I made inquiry relative to the applicants; and as several of the assistants could vouch for them, and all agreed, I baptized fifteen in a small stream near by. As there was a full moon and clear sky, we needed not the light of the sun. After commending them all to God, I left them, some time past midnight, and returned to my vessel. Awoke this morning at daylight, after a few hours' sleep, 'out to sea.' A severe headache reminded me of the exposure and fatigue of the previous evening, and I feared an attack of fever. A powerful dose of medicine has relieved my head, but prostrated my strength, so that, for the first time in my life, I have been really seasick.

"*6th.*—Arrived at Gwa at two, P.M. Was glad to find Capt. Bogle, the Commissioner of Arakan. He has come down the coast to inquire into the condition of his people, hear complaints, and redress grievances. He invited me to dine with him, a privilege I gladly availed myself of, as I am rather short of provisions. Another applicant for baptism at evening. As he intends to see me soon at Sandoway, I deferred his request.

"*8th.*—Sailed for home yesterday morning, accompanied by seven Karen boys who go to Sandoway to study. Wind changed at evening, and increased to such a degree, that, to human view, we were in peril of our lives. At sunset it blew with such violence directly against us, that we were obliged to 'go about,' and let our vessel drive. The boys were very seasick. The night continued very tempestuous, and we were emphatically 'in the deep.' The waves broke over us at a fearful rate. I ascribe our preservation to God's mercy. We were driven down the coast past Gwa, and found ourselves this morning where we were day before yesterday. The wind abating, we were able to use the oars, and at evening anchored at Gwa. I now return to Sandoway by land, my Karen boys preferring *terra firma* to the sea.

"*9th.*—Left Gwa mounted on a lame pony, which will hinder more than aid me, I fear. My saddle is something like my old grandmother's 'pillion;' my bridle, a very good string. The Karen boys and the old Bengali cook follow in single file. In a civilized land we should present a somewhat grotesque appearance. Travelled over a fertile plain till eleven o'clock, when we came to half a dozen Karen houses, only one of which has a Christian family. Nearly all the people attended evening worship.

"*10th, Sabbath.* — After morning service, examined and baptized three persons, — one from Bassein. Most of the villagers have become attached to Boodhism, and are decidedly opposed to the gospel. 'The kingdom of heaven has come nigh unto them.'

"*11th.* — Started on our way at three, A.M. The light of the moon was soon obscured by overhanging branches and foliage; and we made but slow progress over the rocks, roots, and logs. At daylight, came out upon the beach, and found good travelling till nine o'clock, when we came to a small Burman village, and breakfasted. During the day, passed two or three hamlets only, around which are small fields; otherwise it is an impenetrable jungle, uninhabited, except by wild beasts. Were it not possible to travel on the beach, I see not how a path could be made from village to village.

"*12th.* — Told the cook to call me at three, A.M. After a refreshing sleep, I heard, '*Sar, Sar,*' and, on looking at my watch, found it only half-past one o'clock. Drank a cup of tea, ate a dry biscuit, and started. With a bright moon, it is more pleasant travelling on the beach by night than in the heat of the day. Passed a small village at five, A.M., where we struck a passable track through the jungle. With the exception of one other hamlet, we saw not a sign of a human being or habitation all day. The trees are larger to-day; and, the boughs meeting overhead, we travel through the heat of the day with comfort.

"*13th.* — Slept at a small village called Mee-gyoung-yeh, or the 'Ferocious Alligator.' Started at three, A.M., as usual, taking the precaution to provide lights for the dense jungle through which we have to pass. At nine, A.M., all the Karen boys gave out; and the old cook said that he could not keep up. I hired a Burman guide, determined, if possible, to reach home in the evening. At three, P.M., ate my dinner of dry bread, three weeks old, and told my guide I must reach Sandoway before I slept. He tried to dissuade me; said we should have to lie out in the jungle among the tigers; but, for a fair reward, he ventured to go along, and point out the way. Reached home at seven o'clock. The schooner which left Gwa when we did arrived two hours before me; the Karen boys and the cook, a day later, two or three of them threatened with fever.

"*28th.*—Mau Mway, one of the Rangoon assistants, and pastor at Ponau (p. 17), arrived to-day. I have not heard direct from Rangoon for several months, and am rejoiced to learn that the disciples are enjoying rest from persecution. There are several cases of discipline. Some who appeared well are halting; others, again, are coming out on the Lord's side, and are desirous of baptism.

"*Feb. 1.*—Hton Byu and Mau Yay returned to-day, after an absence of five months. They went to Bassein, Pantanau, and Rangoon, and spent several weeks with their friends at Maubee. On their way back, they preached through the villages north of Maubee, crossed the Irrawaddy five days above Rangoon, came on across the country to the north of Bassein, crossed the mountains, and reached the Bay, three days south of Sandoway. They relate the success which attended their efforts with a smile of joy.

"*7th, Sabbath.*—Baptized twelve. They have all been with me a week, affording sufficient time for examination. Among the number is a little lad who ran away from his father's house to avoid being 'pressed' into the service of the devil; his parents being confirmed 'devil-eaters.'

"*9th.*—Fourteen Christians left us for their distant homes in Bassein and Rangoon. I sent letters and circulars to the assistants. They took six hundred and fifty books to scatter among the reading people of the jungles. I left more than four thousand at Magezzin, which are all distributed, the greater number in Burma.

"*16th.*—Myat Kyau and Oung Bau came in from Rangoon. About forty-five days ago I sent the former on a tour to the east, to inquire into the state of the churches. He spent several days at Pantanau, visited Ko Thah-ay, the Burman pastor in Rangoon, and thence went to Maubee. Oung Bau, the pastor of the Karen-river church, one day north of the city, accompanied him on his return. They brought several letters, one from the Rangoon pastor. The old man enjoys tolerable health, preaches quietly, and encourages the few disciples there in the way of life. He speaks of excitement arising from the expectation and fears of the people relative to the visit of the king; thinks it by no means desirable that a missionary visit Rangoon at present. It is the prevailing opinion there, that if the king, or his son, does come down to the lower country, the end will be a war with the English.

"*23d.*—Assistants returned to Rangoon. Have endeavored to impress it upon their minds that *they are to lead* the host of God in Burma; that they must not lean upon missionaries, but upon God. I am looking forward to the time when some of them will be deemed worthy of ordination, that they may fully discharge the duties of pastors. My meetings, intercourse, and parting with these dear young men, have been most solemn and interesting. The prosperity and perpetuity of Christ's kingdom in Burma is dependent, under God, on their fidelity and zeal.

"*March 15.*—Baptized three from Rangoon yesterday. As small-pox is in the place, dispersed our class of ten Karen boys, who are studying English under Mrs. Abbott's tuition. They had just begun to make perceptible progress. But not one of them has had the disease; and we think it best to send them away, although they would have remained and taken the risk, had I consented. I baptize three promising candidates to-morrow.

"*28th, Sabbath.*—Nine Karens from Bassein and Rangoon asked for baptism; were received, and baptized at sunset.

"*31st.*—Sent a circular to the Rangoon assistants, advising them to communicate with Maulmain. I have corresponded with brother Vinton on the subject. As he is nearer Rangoon than I, he can take charge of them, if Karens can pass and repass the eastern frontier. They will meet with obstacles; still I hope a good many from Rangoon will be able to go and study a part of the year at Maulmain.

"*April 1.*—How invaluable are the privileges and enjoyments of Christian society! Yesterday we were cheered by the arrival of our beloved brother and sister Stilson from Ramree. Shut out as we are from the Christian world, we count such visits among the most precious of earthly blessings. Our friends come to spend a few days here for their health. Two Burman assistants accompany them; and the poor idolaters around us will hear the gospel of peace from their own countrymen.

"*12th.*—Brother Stilson baptized three Karens to-day. His address being in Burmese, the Burman congregation on the banks of the river were enabled to understand the nature and design of baptism. During his prayer all was quiet, and I witnessed the administration of the ordinance with peculiar satisfaction...We have been in Sandoway one year, and have experienced much of the goodness of our heavenly Father. Surrounded by disease and death, we have enjoyed good health. Eight Karens have died on our compound during the year, and the cholera has swept away one-eighth of the inhabitants of the land in three months. 'Eastern Golgotha' is a term not inaptly applied to Arakan.[1] More than six thousand gospels, tracts, hymn-books, etc., have been distributed among the Karen Christians; and these books have cost the disciples in Bassein nearly Rs. 1,200,[2] or $545. I have seen all the assistants in Burma but one, and given them such counsel as their trying circumstances seemed to demand. A hundred and eighty-four have been baptized in the likeness of the Saviour's death. At Magezzin, south of Sandoway, is a church of forty-four members; at Baumee, one of thirty. Three of the baptized live at Sandoway, and five near Rangoon. The remaining one hundred and two reside in thirty-six small villages in Bassein. They are principally the leading men in their respective villages. Several other villages are decidedly Christian, but the exact number I cannot give. There are, probably, about twelve families in a village, on an average.

{ Footnote: [1] One-third of the European residents of Arakan died that season from fever and cholera, among them a most worthy physician, Dr. Claributt, to whose devotion and skill Dr. Kincaid felt that he owed his life, when near succumbing to a sharp attack of cholera.

[2] In most other missions these books would have been given away, or sold at a merely nominal price; e.g., Dr. Mason, writing from Tavoy, says (Missionary Magazine, July, 1843, p. 181), "At one time we commenced selling the Karens books; but it was 'no go.'" }

"Before the persecution, they had sabbath worship in some convenient place, where all the village assembled, listened to the reading of the Scriptures, singing, prayer, and exhortations. Since the jealousy of the government has been aroused, they have assembled in small companies of two or three families; and in some places, where 'informers' are stationed, they meet to worship God only at night, when their enemies are asleep. My last accounts from Bassein are more cheering. The principal officers are divided in counsel as to the course to be pursued with the Christians. Some are for severe measures: others incline to toleration, fearing, I apprehend, that the Karens will emigrate to this province in a body,—an event which I should deprecate at present, as it would involve fearful consequences. Our consolation is, 'the Lord reigneth.'"

Before the time for beginning his rainy-season school, Mr. Abbott had prepared temporary buildings for a school of assistants only. For want of funds, he was obliged to send away, imperatively, several who were very anxious to study. This year the term of four mouths passed away without interruption from sickness, and most profitably. As only nineteen assistants came in, enough select youth were received from neighboring villages to bring up the number to thirty. In the cold season, also, Mrs. Abbott, as usual, taught a class of boys, partly in English studies, making the whole number under instruction about forty. Of his own work he writes:—

"My time was exclusively devoted to the assistants, considering it of the highest importance that they clearly understand the first great principles of the gospel which they preach. Besides lessons in arithmetic and geography, I established a course of morning lectures on Paul's Epistles to Timothy, in the course of which I endeavored to bring out to their view, distinctly and explicitly, the organization of a Christian church, the qualifications, call, appointment, and duties of bishops and deacons, and to impress upon their minds the directions given in those epistles for the guidance of ministers. In the afternoon their attention was directed entirely to the Gospels. We had preaching and religious exercises every evening.

"They all enjoyed good health, and were enabled to pursue their studies uninterruptedly. Their growth in grace and in divine knowledge was perceptible and highly gratifying. The season passed away pleasantly and profitably, and I now look back upon it with joy and devout gratitude. They left us for their distant homes Sept. 1. Karens seldom weep; but some of them, when we parted, turned away to conceal their tears. A part of them are to be stationed in this province, in Bassein and Pantanau, as pastors; and others are to itinerate, and preach the gospel to their people, who have never yet heard the joyful sound. I have agreed to meet them at Magezzin, near the frontier, on the 1st of January next, as that will be as early as I can venture into the jungle with safety."

So far as is known to the writer, E. L. Abbott was far in advance of all contemporary foreign missionaries, boards, and secretaries, in his views as to the necessity of bringing up the congregations of converted heathen to the practice of self-support. He found himself at this time, however, in circumstances of great difficulty. The Karens of Bassein were then the poorest of the poor. Their unhusked rice, when they were allowed to sell it, would bring them only five rupees a hundred bushels; they were loaded with fines; though not baptized, they were struggling to build chapels for the worship of God, never dreaming of outside assistance. All that their missionary had asked for towards the support of native preachers, the school, *including buildings*, and his own travelling expenses, was Rs. 1,500; yet from the straitened state of the treasury, and from some extraordinary views as to equality in the distribution of mission-funds, the Board had allowed him only Rs. 1,000. Under these circumstances the overburdened missionary writes:—

"Will the children of God in America send me money for the support of these beloved men in their self-denying, perilous labors for our Master? or must I, at the coming meeting, tell them to return to their paddy-fields, and labor with their hands to keep their families from starvation? The last letter from the foreign secretary says, 'Reduce your expenditures in *any* way...Reduction *must be made.'* Are the days of the Karen mission numbered? Are the four thousand poor, persecuted, bleeding lambs of Jesus, scattered through the wilds of Burma, to be left to famish for the bread of life for want of a few paltry dollars?...In many new places the people are calling for preachers; but, owing to the secretary's orders, all such calls must pass unheeded. Ministers of the gospel in the Karen jungles cannot travel, and spend all their time, laboring in the vineyard of the Lord, and support themselves and their families on air, any more than it can be done by ministers of the gospel in America."

In a letter just then received, the Board had offered, rather tardily, to remunerate Mr. Abbott for a loss by fire of live hundred rupees. While acknowledging their generosity, he declines this personal assistance, as no longer needed. He proposes, however, to draw on them for a part of the sum, to eke out the assistance absolutely required for his preachers.

"Instead of a thousand rupees, I had expected fifteen hundred at least: in fact, I must have that sum to meet my engagements the present year. If Ramree, with two or three assistants, and Akyab, with the same number, receive each one thousand, I had supposed that Sandoway, Bassein and Pantanau, with *twenty* assistants under engagement, would receive a larger sum. Of course the Board can dispense only what they receive...Until I hear from the Board, I shall keep within the thousand rupees, hoping at the same time to prevail on Mr. Kincaid to let me have a few hundred from Akyab. The Ramree brethren say they cannot spare a rupee...I have told the assistants distinctly, that they must not expect to be supported by foreigners always. When I send my detailed accounts, the secretary can observe that many of them receive but a few rupees. Were it not for the [Burman] government, under which most of the Christians live, they would not care about receiving any foreign aid at all to support their own pastors. They have aided the assistants (by feeding them and by gifts of clothing) to the amount of several hundred rupees, besides paying their enormous fines to government, in addition to their usual taxation. I have received from a few of them twenty rupees for the cause. They are also now engaged in this province in building chapels, which will require all their means."

He closes thus:—

"The secretary will perceive that this is dated at Ramree. I am here in pursuit of that fleeting goddess, Health. I am happy to say that her ladyship appears to be approachable. I fear that I have an inflammation of the liver, which is the cause of weakness, and pain at the stomach, owing, probably, to close confinement during the rains. After the school closed, my very good friend Dr. Morton furnished me with a vessel free of expense; and, with my family, I came to this place, and intend to remain here till the season arrives for jungle travelling. I did think I should be obliged to go to sea: but the secretary's letter will induce me to defer it; or, if it still seems to be necessary, I shall endeavor to pay the cost myself. Travel and change, with the blessing of Him whom we serve, will, I trust, restore me again. I am admonished, however, that what I do must be done quickly."

CHAPTER IV.

1842, 1843.

"Truly, merchants themselves shall rise in judgment against the princes and nobles of Europe; for the merchants have made a great path in the seas, unto the ends of the world, and sent forth ships and fleets of Spanish, English, and Dutch, enough to make China tremble: and all this for pearl and stone and spices. But for the pearl of the kingdom of heaven, or the stone of the heavenly Jerusalem, or the spices of the Spouse's Garden, not a mast has been set up." —LORD BACON.

This chapter is the record of two years' further progress in the Bassein mission, so far as that progress has been reported by the principal actor. Some condensation has been necessary; but we are sure that no "editing" can improve the graphic descriptions penned by Mr. Abbott amid the very scenes which he portrays, nor would our readers wish the account materially abridged. It must be remembered, however, that by far the greater part of the work now going on throughout the extensive plains of Bassein was wrought by obscure men, whose deeds and sufferings were unseen and unrecorded, save by the angelic chroniclers above. Abbott's own praise of these humble men was never stinted. In January, 1842, he wrote: —

"My confidence in the assistants is more and more confirmed. They are a faithful, laborious, successful, worthy set of men; and, through *their* instrumentality, the gospel is certainly triumphing in many parts of Burma."

The work of the year 1842 begins, as usual, with the annual cold season visit of the missionary to the Christian Karen communities down the coast. As his coming was widely advertised, he was met at the several villages by considerable numbers of unbaptized Christians from distant places beyond the frontier. During his absence of thirty-one days, Mr. Abbott baptized two hundred and seventy-five persons, most of whom were from the Burman province of Bassein, and the fruits of the ministry of Karen assistants. We leave him to tell the story in his own language.

"*Jan. 7, 1842.*—Arrived at Gwa this evening. Five assistants from Burma met me on the shore, accompanied by some twenty men, who have come over 'to see the teacher,' and ask for baptism. Three of them live on the Irrawaddy, north of Rangoon. Accounts from the Christians in Burma are, on the whole, satisfactory. Near Rangoon they are obliged to submit to annoyances, but to no severe oppression. At Pantanau, and thence on this way to Bassein, all is quiet, and they wish me to come over and visit them.

"*8th.*—Left Gwa at daylight, and anchored in Magezzin River at noon. At five, P.M., reached the Christian village in a small boat. The first object that attracted my notice was the new chapel, just erected by the church, and dedicated to the service of God. It is one of the best buildings I have ever seen in the Karen jungle, and does honor to the pastor, Myat Kyau, under whose direction it was erected. In Burma it is reported that this chapel is a palace for the Karen king! Found assistants here from Burma, waiting my arrival, letters from Maubee and Rangoon, and a good many persons who have come over for baptism.

"*9th, Sabbath.*—Preaching at nine, A.M., and a covenant meeting at noon, preparatory to the communion in the evening. At four, P.M., assembled again for the examination of candidates. All these applicants came over with their teachers, under whose instructions they have embraced the gospel. For want of time, I ask the assistants, in whom I have perfect confidence, whether they are acquainted with the candidates, and can vouch for their good moral and Christian character since they believed. I propose certain questions to each one, but admit them mainly on the testimony of the assistants. Just before sunset we assembled near the chapel, on the banks of the stream, hallowed in our affections by scenes which we have here formerly witnessed. I baptized twenty-four men from villages in Burma. In the evening, administered the Lord's Supper to more than a hundred communicants. This has been one of those happy days, a day of ingathering, which abundantly compensate us for months of anxiety and toil.

"*10th.*—Left Magezzin this morning, and returned to the mouth of the river. Fifty men followed me to procure books. At evening they left me for their homes over the mountains.

"*11th.*—Headache and fever during the night. I pray I may not be stopped in my labors now. God is my protector, and to him I commit my ways. Started at sunrise, notwithstanding my indisposition, and walked two hours on the beach, to the mouth of the Baumee, which must be a mile wide. Waited here for my boat, which was obliged to go a long distance out to sea to get around a ledge of rocks and shoals. Ascended the river till noon, and arrived at a Christian village of five families, a branch of the Baumee church. After evening worship, inquired into the standing of the church-members.

"*12th.*—A meeting to settle a difficulty between two brethren, which gave me an opportunity to instruct the disciples on the subject of discipline.

"*13th.*—Went on up the river till nearly noon, to the largest and most central Karen village on the river. As there were several applicants for baptism, I lectured on the qualifications requisite for admission, marking also disqualifications. Thirty-one were received, and baptized according to apostolic precept and example.

"*14th.*—Administered the communion this morning. The church now numbers seventy-four members; one death having occurred during the year, but no case of discipline. Moung Bo is stationed here; but as he is going into a destitute region in Burma, away towards the northern mountains, I have appointed Shway Bay to conduct services, and exercise a general supervision over the Christians, having reference to me at Sandoway.

"*15th.*—During the night my men rowed down to the mouth of the river. At daylight, proceeded down the coast till four, P.M., when we ran into a small bay, and anchored. One hour's walk brought me to a Karen village called Ong Khyoung [i.e., Cocoanut Creek]. The Christians have erected a neat chapel upon a little hill a short distance from the village, which contains a pulpit withal,—a wonderful improvement for the jungle, and quite in advance of the age.

"*16th, Sabbath.*—The people fired a gun last evening to notify those at a distance of my arrival: so they came flocking together at an early hour,—men, women, and children. The principal man of the village and others with him were baptized at Sandoway a year ago. As there is no assistant here, I was obliged to move cautiously in the examination of candidates. None were admitted who had not borne a good character for several months. Near the close of the day, thirty-six publicly professed their faith by baptism. In the evening, constituted them into a church of thirty-nine members, who will be able to support a pastor, at least in part.

"*17th.*—Continued down the coast until near evening, and ran in for the night behind a small island called Khyoungthah (p. 3). Went on shore with tracts, but scarcely an individual would receive one. An old priest took a bound volume, but returned it again, fearing lest he should commit himself by its reception.

"*18th.*—Started, as usual, at daylight, and ran into a bay in the afternoon, on the shore of which stands a Karen village called Sinmah [Female Elephant]. The Christians have a small chapel in a beautiful grove twenty or thirty yards from the beach. Met them at evening worship, after which several applied for baptism. But, as I intend to return here for the sabbath, they were willing to wait.

"*19th.*—Walked on the shore till nine o'clock, and waited for my boat to come around a rocky peninsula. Rowed all day, as usual. Arrived at a Karen village at evening, called 'The broken-legged Buffalo.' Nearly all the people here are emigrants from Burma, who have fled from persecution. They have erected a convenient chapel, and have a worthy and efficient man for their teacher. Here, under the British dominion, they enjoy that most precious of blessings, religious liberty—Ay, and

'Freedom to worship God.'

"*20th.*—After a season of prayer with the people at an early hour, I lectured those who were to come forward for baptism. When I gave the opportunity, a large company presented themselves. They have been under Tway Po's instruction two years or more, and they are all well aware of the qualifications requisite for baptism. I had also made particular inquiry of the assistant relative to their character. A few who would have come forward were deterred by the assistant, as he was not perfectly satisfied of their fitness: consequently, all who did present themselves were quite certain to be admitted. After a short intermission, again assembled, and, in addition to those accepted in the morning, several little girls, ten or twelve years old, came before the congregation, and asked to be baptized. On inquiring why they did not come forward in the morning, I was told they were afraid of being rejected; that some of them went home weeping, and one little girl induced her parents to ask for them. Another went to her parents weeping, because 'the teacher had not written her name in the big book, among those who were to be baptized.' Another told the assistant that she might die before another year, unbaptized, and asked him to present her case to me. I inquired particularly of their parents and of Tway Po, and on hearing their testimony, and on questioning them individually, I became satisfied of the genuineness of their faith, and, as all the baptized approved, they were received. After singing and prayer beside a small river, seventy-five converts were baptized into the name of the Father, Son, and Holy Ghost. These are precious seasons. The time occupied in baptizing the whole was about an hour. In the evening, organized a church, and gave them a lecture relative to their new relations, particularly the obligations they are under to their pastor. Tway Po is a worthy man, and possesses the entire confidence of the people. He has spent several months in study with me, and I see not why he may not be ordained another season. Married a couple after evening service.

"*21st.* —Spent the day with the people. Preaching morning and evening. At the close of the evening service, at eight, P.M., we sang the parting hymn [by Dr. Mason], —

'According to the will of God,
Brethren, we must part.'

The congregation then, one after the other, came and shook my hand. I retired to my boat to sleep, and ordered the men to turn the prow towards Sandoway, distant at least ten days. This is [at present] the most southern station in the province of Arakan, distant, as we travel in a small boat, about two days from Cape Negrais, and about the same distance from Bassein by land.

"*22d.* —Found myself in sight of Sinmah at sunrise. At evening the few Karens here assembled for worship, and several requested baptism. The assistant, Dah Po, was baptized last year at Sandoway. Although a young man, not receiving support from the mission, he appears worthy and faithful. Inquired into the character of the candidates.

"*23d, Sabbath.* —Twenty were examined and baptized to-day, in the open sea, in front of the chapel. Here is now a small church of twenty-one members; but as they are emigrants from Burma, recently arrived, it is doubtful whether they will remain here, or remove to some other Christian village. In the evening, instructed them as to the mutual duties and obligations of church-members, and commended them to the great Shepherd of Israel.

"*27th.* —After three days' detention at Sinmah by adverse winds, were able to put out to sea with safety. Arrived at Khyoungthah at mid-day, and there remained till the sea-breeze died away, late in the night.

"*28th.* —Stopped at eleven, A.M., in the lee of a large rock, on an uninhabited coast. The wild elephant and tiger are seldom disturbed here. Just before sunset, walked on the shore with my gun, and shot a peacock. Returning to my boat, near a thicket, heard the fearful growl and crashing of an elephant. The two natives with me ran away, of course, and, not relishing the idea of being crushed under the feet of the huge creature, I ran too.

"*29th.*—Went on at ten, P.M., and reached Magezzin River at noon. Saw a company of Karens on the shore, waiting with a canoe to take me up to their village. At five, P.M., arrived, and found a hundred and fifty men from Burma, waiting my arrival. As I was detained at Sinmah, they have been kept waiting here an equal time. Assembled immediately for worship. The large and beautiful chapel was filled with attentive listeners, many from a distance of hundreds of miles. After a hymn of praise, I preached on repentance. As several of those who came from Burma had hired a boat on the Baumee River, and agreed to return it to-night, they asked to be baptized immediately. I inquired of the assistant, and, being satisfied, baptized twenty forthwith, who then shook hands, and departed.

"*30th, Sabbath.*—After morning worship, sixty-nine candidates were admitted. They all came over with the assistants, and were recommended by them. The assistants have such clear views, and the qualifications of a candidate for baptism are so distinctly marked, that an unworthy character seldom presents himself. Among the applicants to-day were six women from Burma,—the first who have come over the mountains. Old mothers in Israel with their daughters have come through the wilderness, a journey of four days, on foot, to be baptized. What an example of the constraining influence of the love of Christ! Assembled again after the afternoon service, and those admitted in the morning were baptized. May all these beloved disciples who have here witnessed a good profession before rejoicing angels endure to the end as good soldiers of Jesus Christ! I commend them to the Good Shepherd. May they be shielded from the persecutor's rage and from the wiles of the great adversary!

"After preaching in the evening, had a long conversation with the assistants, on various points where they are in doubt or have experienced difficulty. Among other matters, a letter was handed me, which contained a request that Bleh Po might be ordained. It was signed by several old men, and was concurred in by all the

69

assistants; which not only indicated his standing, but a good degree of right feeling among the assistants. However, Bleh Po himself wished the subject to be dropped for the present, as he intends to study with me another season at least.

"Several of the assistants understand Pwo, and preach in it: others have a Pwo interpreter travelling with them. So the truth is spreading among that people. They are calling for books, and for a man to teach them; for both of which I have written to Tavoy and Mergui, but can get neither. How many Pwos have been baptized I cannot say exactly. There are, however, more than forty Christian families among that people in [Bassein]. I have appointed an assistant among them, who was baptized to-day. [Probably S'rah Shway Bo, now for many years pastor at Engma.—ED.] Another man, baptized to-day, has agreed to come and study with me, if I will get a Pwo book. I intend to study that dialect as soon as I get one.

"*31st.*—Had a season of prayer this morning with the Christians; gave them a short lecture and a few parting words of admonition. We then separated, in companies of from half a dozen to twenty, and started for our distant homes. I came down to the mouth of the river, to my boat; but the sea-breeze had already set in. We must remain here, therefore, till it lulls during the night.

"*Feb. 5, Sandoway.*—Arrived here in five days from Magezzin, by rowing from midnight to ten or eleven, A.M., and lying by the rest of the time,—a mode of travelling not quite as agreeable or speedy as the car or steamer. Bowed down before the family altar with my dear wife and infant children, and offered up to God an oblation of thanksgiving for all his rich goodness.

"*13th.*—Baptized four who came over from Burma expecting to find me at Magezzin. As I had departed, they followed me on to Sandoway, where they arrived five days ago. They all gave very good satisfaction on their examination, and Shway Weing testified to their good character."

In a note which accompanies the above, Mr. Abbott gives somewhat later intelligence of a most cheering character: —

"Since I closed my journal, Myat Kyau, the pastor at Magezzin, has visited me with another assistant, and others who came from Burma to be baptized. As I send this away by the present mail, I cannot give the number of those who will probably be baptized tomorrow. The report they bring from Burma gladdens my heart. The Christians meet in large congregations. Burmese officers frequently come in while they are at worship. The assistants travel and preach in the most public manner, and the government looks on in silence. I feared that the great numbers who are coming over, and returning with books, would excite persecution; but no one has been annoyed. It is reported that the king, during his late visit to Rangoon, inquired concerning the Karens who had embraced a foreign religion. On being told that they were a quiet people, and paid their taxes, his Majesty replied, 'Then let them alone.' This may be true: still, no dependence is to be placed on the promise of a Burman official of any rank."

During the rains of 1842 about thirty of the assistants assembled in Sandoway for study. To them, as always, Mr. Abbott devoted his time and best energies. After their departure, early in September, he sent to press a skeleton of his lectures on the following topics, — God, Creation, Redemption, Resurrection, Eternity, Bishop, Deacon, Church, Baptism, Lord's Supper, etc. Dec. 14 the missionary wrote: "In a day or two we (Mrs. Abbott and babes accompanying) are to be off to the jungles for the season. What will be our success who can say? A multitude, without figure of speech, are waiting for baptism. God's name be praised!" He did not know the dark cloud of trial which was even then resting upon the churches in Bassein. Again the poor Christians are under the ruthless hand of Burman extortioners; and cholera, chiefest in the retinue of death, is sweeping hundreds into eternity. Among them, the mission suffers a grievous loss in the death of Bleh Po, whose name is familiar to our readers. As his death occurred before the close of the year, we insert Mr. Abbott's tribute to his memory at this point: —

"He was one of the first and most noted of the Karen converts in Bassein. The opposition he encountered was well calculated to test the genuineness of his conversion, and to induce that steadfastness which was so essential in his after-life. He silenced the clamor of his relatives by his meekness and wisdom, and finally became instrumental in the conversion of most of them. Still, he was obliged to sacrifice some property in becoming a Christian. He soon encountered the opposition of petty officers, who apprehended and threatened him, in order to compel him to cease preaching. But Bleh Po always disarmed them of their hatred, and converted them, either into friends or harmless enemies. No other Karen could preach to this class of men as he could, without getting a beating; and no other preacher suffered less. It is believed that a few of them are now Christians at heart.

"Bleh Po's knowledge of the Bible was necessarily limited, as only the Gospels and the Acts were translated before his death; but, being a man of thought and studious habits, he treasured up in his heart whatever came within his reach, so that he had committed to memory the greater part of the Gospels. While with me, he studied the principal doctrines, and listened to my lectures with deep attention. These fundamental truths were not lost upon him. He was apt to teach, and knew when to speak and when to be silent. In cases of difficulty and discipline beyond the control of others, Bleh Po was sent for; and his voice would generally still the troubled waters. His weight of character, also, gave him almost unbounded influence over the Christian community. A man of unwavering integrity, of guileless simplicity, his entire being was as transparent as the light. Discreet withal, and of sterling good sense, his word was law to his converts, and commanded the respect of his bitterest foes. His consistent piety added greatly to his influence. He kept the even tenor of his way. From the first hour of his embracing the gospel, to the gates of the grave, his path was emphatically 'the path of the just.' Prayer was with him a fixed habit, essential to his existence. Many a time, at the dead of night, when the rest of the world were wrapped in slumber, he was awake, pouring out his soul to his God. While a student, he very frequently would get away into some secluded place, and spend a day in fasting and prayer.

"A self-sacrificing spirit was characteristic of his piety. The idea of *self* never seemed to awaken the least anxiety. In 1842 he received from the mission thirty-six rupees, not one *pice* of which, I believe, he ever appropriated to his own use. He said that it was God's money, and, seeking out poor Christians, gave it all away, trusting in Providence for the support of his family. Nor in temporal matters alone did he exhibit this quality. When apprehended and threatened, not knowing but a cruel death would be his portion, he did not seem to have one anxious thought. This spirit manifested itself in all his course, and in his preaching assumed the character of active benevolence, zeal for God. He preached the gospel from Bassein down to the seacoast, along the mountains to the north, and away east towards Rangoon. From village to village, and from house to house, his voice was heard, like that of John in the wilderness. And he counted it no sacrifice: he labored cheerfully and with joy.

"During the last few days of his life this spirit was more conspicuous than ever. The cholera appeared in his village, and he was one of the first attacked. He soon recovered, but could not rest. Although his strength was prostrated, and his friends, fearing a relapse, advised him to keep quiet, he forgot himself; and, wherever one was attacked, there was Bleh To, exhorting them to trust in God, and consoling the dying with the promises of the gospel. But he could not endure it. In three days the relapse came. His friends gathered around him: still Bleh Po manifested the same self-forgetfulness. In the dreadful pains of that most fearful of diseases, he exhorted his friends to be steadfast, and never to desert the cause of Christ. He was told that he was dying, knew that he was dying; but he heeded it not. He spent his last breath in exhorting and comforting his friends. He died Dec. 20, aged thirty years.

"As will be supposed, Bleh Po was beloved. Since his death I have seen hundreds from his own and the neighboring villages, and they all speak of him with affection and grief. I did not see his relatives till several weeks after his death; and then the first word they would say to me would generally be, 'Teacher, Bleh Po is dead! What shall we do now?' A great many of the aged women from his village came to the Baumee chapel. They all loved to talk about Bleh Po, to dwell on his sayings, his goodness, his humility, his faithfulness; and, with tears running down their old cheeks, they would say, 'Teacher, what shall we do now?' There is an intensity and depth of feeling manifested in their grief which I have never seen exhibited by Karens before. '*Pga hau dau kauh nyah*' ('The whole country is in tears'), an assistant told me who had travelled widely. Take him all in all, I have never seen his equal in Burma. When I think of his death, a kind of awful sadness comes over me, and my heart melts within me."

Along with increased ingatherings and the continued impossibility of a missionary visiting the Christians beyond the frontier in person, a practical question of great importance comes up in 1843 for final settlement. To us who have seen the happy result of the "experiment" of ordaining a native ministry, it is difficult to understand the shrinking felt by most missionaries of that period at taking this necessary and entirely scriptural step. In Bassein alone, including those deceased, more than fifty Karen ministers have assumed the solemn responsibilities which follow ordination. Of the entire number, not one, within the writer's knowledge, has disgraced his profession, or failed to perform its duties with a fair degree of credit. Still there was opposition. So good and wise a man as Francis Mason could write this very year, with reference, perhaps, to the step which Abbott was contemplating: —

"In my early years of missionary labor, before I was fully acquainted with native character, I was decidedly in favor of ordaining the prominent assistants; but of late I have been so fully persuaded of their general unfitness for the ministerial office, that I could not in conscience consent to the ordination of a single one with whom I have ever been acquainted." —*Miss. Mag.*, July, 1843, p. 178.

Fortunately, Mr. Abbott was not accustomed to take counsel of timid fear. He had a large measure of sound common sense, and that happy combination of self-reliance with reliance upon a higher power, which is needful for the exigencies of a pioneer missionary's life. He was now rapidly making history of the best kind. With thanksgiving to the Author of the rich blessings recorded, we insert the journal of his annual tour, substantially as he wrote it: —

"*Dec. 21, 1842.*—Left Sandoway with my family last evening, in a government boat which Mr. Phayre, the senior assistant commissioner, gives us for the trip. Put to sea at daylight, and with a favoring breeze have been sailing down the coast through the day. Many thanks to Mr. Phayre for his kindness. We are much more comfortably situated than we could be in a native boat.

"*22d.*—Arrived at Gwa this evening. Came on shore, and are stopping in a small government bungalow. The native officer and people of the place came crowding around to get a sight of the white woman and children. Old people say Mrs. Abbott is the first Englishwoman they have ever seen. If we walk through the bazaar, there is such a running, and gazing, and staring! Groups will stand and gaze till we pass, and then run on ahead to get another front view.

"*24th.*—Left Gwa at two, A.M., in a native boat, and, after sis hours' rowing southward, entered the Kalah River. There is a small Christian village in the vicinity.

"*25th.*—Christmas, and, though not a 'merry,' a very happy, and, I trust, a profitable day. Preached through the day, and at evening baptized three. One is from Gwa; one lives near Bassein; and the other, several days up the Irrawaddy from Rangoon. I have known them for more than a year.

"*27th.*—Left Kalah River at three, A.M., and entered the Baumee about eight. Breakfasted, and then onward, up the river with the tide, arriving at Baumee chapel about sunset. This house of God, erected by the Christians here, marks another step in advance. It is finished better than any of those built last year, and will seat eight hundred comfortably, I think. It does great credit to Shway Bay. In this vicinity are more than forty Christian families, who, although they live in hamlets a little distant, are near enough to come to worship on the sabbath. In this house may the Lord our God take up his abode, and magnify the riches of his saving mercy!

"*28th.* — As it was late when we arrived last evening, but few came in to see us. But, while we were at breakfast, they came around in scores, particularly interested to get a sight of the *mama* and the children, 'with such beautiful white faces.' One among the many benefits arising from such visits is, that the native Christians may be taught by example. We eat in public, and they see that our table and its furniture are kept clean, and arranged in an orderly manner. They see the family come from their private apartment with clean garments and *clean faces*, and sit down to their table, and eat their food with expressions of thanksgiving to God. We do not wish, of course, that Karens should adopt all American customs; but it does them good to see the order of a civilized Christian family.

"Several assistants and others arrived to-day from Burma. There is a very good path from here over the hills; and the distance to the first [Christian] village on the other side cannot exceed fifteen miles. Sad tidings again are brought from the disciples in Burma. Not only are they subject to the common oppression, but, as Christians, they are especially liable to suffer from relentless extortion. The population of whole villages, after suffering to the last point of endurance, — their all, even to their supply of food, wrung from them, — have fled hither and thither, obliged to conceal themselves, and to borrow or beg till they can make another harvest.

"The following case is but one of the kind: one of the assistants, while preaching on Sunday, was interrupted by a petty officer, who entered, seized the book from his hand, and ordered him to interpret its contents into Burmese. The preacher did so; and the officer, in a rage, struck him on the face with the book, fined him fifty rupees, and, as security, took the assistant's wife, and walked away with her to his own house. The only alternatives for the injured man were to let his wife remain a slave, or pay the fine. His Christian brethren made up the sum, several hundred giving each a few annas, and in two or three days his wife was at liberty. There is no help in such a case. Had the man appealed to higher authorities, he would probably have been beaten and imprisoned, and fined fifty rupees more.

"This chapel is believed at Bassein to be a palace for a Karen general who is going to invade Burma at the head of a large army, and is to make this his headquarters. It is said the palace has so many hundred posts, and, most ominous of all, a kind of 'royal cupola,' which, on any building except a royal palace or religious monastery, would in Burma be an aggravated insult. The small vessel in which we came down to Gwa becomes at Bassein a dozen ships-of-war. All the Christian villages have been searched, and every thing in the shape of a musket has been taken away. The officers say the Christians are to join the invading army. The poor disciples know not what to do. They see that the jealousy of the government is awakened, and they know that it is as 'cruel as the grave.' They are in a state of fearful apprehension, and many of them are beginning to waver, and I fear may apostatize. In such seasons the poor missionary hardly knows where to turn. Cholera, also, is sweeping off multitudes in Burma. Some Christian villages have been nearly depopulated. In one case, a whole family died, and their bodies were left to feed the dogs. The pestilence passed over the mountains from us to the east some months ago.

"*30th.*—Baptized nineteen this morning, all residing within the bounds of this church. One man we were obliged to exclude. He had been admonished time and again, and committees had visited him, but in vain. There was but one alternative. The Baumee church numbers over a hundred members. Shway Bay is young, but appears to exert a good influence. He is a man of promise.

"*Jan. 1, 1843, Sabbath.*—This New-Year's Day has been one of joy and hope, one of those days which I have longed to see,—an emblem of the eternal day, prefiguring the rest of the people of God. I awoke a few minutes past midnight, breathing a prayer for the conversion of the world. I thought of the millions of Christians in other lands, whose intercessions will come up to-day before the throne of God. May their prayers be heard! May this be a year of wonders and of the manifestation of God's saving mercy among the nations! At morning service this fine chapel was filled by a multitude who came up to listen to the gospel, and pay their devotions to the living God. Towards evening sixteen converts witnessed a good confession. May they go on their way rejoicing! In the evening the church partook of the emblems of that body slain, and of that precious blood which cleanseth from all sin.

"2*d.*—But few Karens have come over from Burma. The officers near the frontier are on the alert. Have been consulting with the assistants and principal men relative to ordaining an evangelist to send into Burma, and as to a pastor for this church, but have come to no conclusion.

"4*th.*—Walked with my family from the mouth of the Baumee to the mouth of Magezzin River: our boat, going round the point meantime, came near being swamped. Stopped in a small zayat during the day. At evening the head man of the district came in, and very gravely informed me that he had just received news from Burma to the effect that an army of several hundred men were coming over to seize the 'Karen teacher,' and take him to the king of Ava. He advised me to flee towards Sandoway; felt it his duty to inform me of the report, and considered he should not be blameworthy should such an event now occur. This report will doubtless end like all others of the kind. They tend, however, to keep the poor people in a state of alarm.

"An event has just occurred which increases the rancor of the Burman Government. The only son of the Mayahwaddy prince, the elder brother of the present king, who was killed, I think, near Toungoo, during the war with the English, has just escaped into British territory. This young prince is, of course, near the throne. Consequently, when the present king began to slaughter his rivals, he very wisely fled. He has been three or four years making his way from the capital to Bassein, begging his food, and dressed mostly in Karen style, to avoid detection. A few days since, he crossed the frontier, with his family and some thirty followers. He will doubtless be protected, and treated with honor."

Even the foreign secretary, Dr. Peck, regarded the ordination of native ministers as a hazardous step. In printing this journal in the "Magazine," he refers to the subject thus:—

"The subject introduced in the next paragraph is one of extreme delicacy and difficulty. Were baptism *essential* to salvation, it would be less questionable whether any of the native converts should be empowered to administer it. Yet, if their character be like that ascribed to Bleh Po, the danger of improper admissions would not seem to be greatly increased, although placed beyond the personal observation of the missionary. And the privileges of the church of Christ ought not to be unnecessarily withheld from any who are entitled to them, nor the appointed instrumentalities for its edification set aside. The case involves, on either hand, a fearful responsibility."

Mr. Abbott proceeds as follows:—

"*8th.*—The ordination of native pastors over the Karen churches has been a subject of deep anxiety to me. Obliged as I am to be absent from them most of the year, and never able to visit them in Burma, the care of all the congregations is, of necessity, committed to men chosen from among themselves. No one is ever recognized by me as an 'assistant,' except upon the testimony and by the request of the people of his own village, nor until I have become satisfied that he possesses the necessary character and qualifications. It is also upon the condition always, that each one thus recognized is to come and study with me a part of each year. I have appointed a number somewhat in the character of Methodist 'class-leaders.' They receive no pay from the mission, are not reckoned among the assistants, do not itinerate and preach, but simply lead religious services in their own villages. The 'assistants' are, in fact, pastors, or evangelists, except that they are unordained. If they are competent to preach, to lead and instruct Christian congregations, why not recognize them as also competent to administer the ordinances? I have discouraged the idea of Karens coming ten or fifteen days' journey to be baptized by me. Why not ordain their own pastors, under whose preaching they were converted, and under whose guidance they are to live?

Why not allow their pastors to baptize them at their own homes? There are hundreds of Christians in Burma who have never seen a missionary, and, unless a revolution sweep down the present monarchy, never will. They wish, of course, to be baptized; and why not ordain them pastors? If God has called these men to preach the gospel, has he not also called them to administer its ordinances?

"Bleh Po was the man whom I had selected as the first to be ordained. The great Head of the church had selected him as a ministering spirit to wait around the throne. There are others whom I had thought of ordaining. Among them is Myat Kyau, a man of experience and influence, of sober judgment, and one who has the confidence of all the assistants. He has been much blessed as a preacher; and, after the strictest inquiry among his people, I am satisfied as to his moral character. I have been endeavoring to ascertain the wishes of the church-members, but it is not an easy matter. They would consent to any thing 'the teacher' proposes, but I try to make them see that the ordination of a pastor particularly concerns *them*. Of course, the subject is all new to them; and they can only do as they have been taught, so far as form is concerned, which is just what people do all over the world. The members understand that they are to testify as to the candidate's character; that they are to receive, honor, and support him; also that I impart ordination at their request.

"A meeting was called to-day. Many of the assistants and members from other churches were present, enough to constitute a council; and although we did not adopt the usual method of electing a moderator (which office I filled myself), etc., the business was conducted with a good degree of decorum. I examined Myat Kyau at great length; not for my own satisfaction, but by way of precedent. He has studied with me three rains, and I know his intellectual qualifications. Then all the assistants, male members of the church, and visitors spoke, each according to his own views. I next proceeded to ordain Myat Kyau by the imposition of hands and prayer. Then, with the 'right hand of fellowship' and a solemn 'charge,' I recognized him as an ordained minister of the gospel. I have never experienced greater satisfaction than in the performance of this deeply interesting service. May He in whose cause we labor bless the young pastor in the discharge of his fearful responsibilities, and guide him safely through!

"At sunset I baptized the pastor's wife. She was a Pwo Karen Christian, though unbaptized, and is an intelligent, amiable person. At evening, assisted by the pastor, I administered the Lord's Supper. Myat Kyau discharged his part with great propriety. The Magezzin church has nearly a hundred members, and will probably soon double that number, being often augmented by emigrants from Burma. A Burman living near is asking for baptism, and wishes to unite himself to the Karen church. Several Karen families who have been decided opposers show signs of a change. Some of them wish to be baptized, but the old patriarch does not yet consent."

Returning to Gwa on the 10th, Mr. Abbott next proceeded to fulfil his appointments at Baumee and Ong Khyoung, not without a struggle; for he was compelled to leave his "youngest child sick with jungle-fever, and Mrs. Abbott without a medical adviser or any earthly friend, alone in a little hut on the sea-beach."

"*14th.*—Arrived at the Baumee chapel this morning. The first man I met was a Pwo assistant, who immediately asked if I had brought Pwo books. He said the Pwos were looking for books with much anxiety. As I walked up towards the chapel, a multitude of men, women, and children, met me, among whom were many strangers from Burma.

"*15th, Sunday.*—Another blessed day, fraught with joy and hope, yet not without many forebodings. The spacious chapel was filled with a congregation who listened with *intense* interest. I preached from those 'words' to which the apostle referred when he said, 'Comfort one another with *these words.*' Precious words, and full of comfort, indeed; and the occasion demanded their application. The poor Christians from Burma are all mourning the loss of friends. The cholera is making fearful ravages. Scarcely a family where the destroyer has not entered. Moreover, the bearing of the government is alarming. God Almighty, save thy heritage from reproach! After preaching, candidates came pressing around, asking for baptism. I questioned them but little, simply to elicit from each a testimony, and confession of faith in Christ. My chief reliance is on the testimony of the assistants, who have conducted them to me as fit subjects for baptism. They have all studied with me, and this subject has been dwelt upon *minutely* and *repeatedly*. Moreover, all have seen my example. Were the reception of candidates left to my judgment alone, I should often be at a loss what to do. Those who pass the best examination do not always make the best Christians. After reception, seventy-six candidates witnessed a good profession. Myat Kyau and I went down into the water alternately.

"16th.—Myat Kyau baptized four this morning. They appeared to have no choice as to the administrator. After prayer and a word of admonition to the people, I sent them away to their homes, with much apprehension. I fear their coming hither in such numbers will excite the jealousy of government. Left about noon, and came down to the mouth of the river, where I hoped to find news from our sick child. Have been waiting till late at night, but no letter.

"17th.—Long before daylight I sent a man to a village on the way to Gwa to inquire. He returned about eight, A.M., bringing a letter, which would have come last night but for the indolence and stupidity of the bearer. The poor child is suffering under a dreadful fever: still Mrs. Abbott is willing I should fulfil my appointments. I had agreed to meet the Ong Khyoung church to-morrow. It is a long walk for one day, and will keep me from my family at least five days longer. I decide to go on, having but little hope of finding the babe alive on my return. After a very hard day's walk, over rocks and mountains, and through swamps, arrived at Ong Khyoung. The people soon assembled in their new and commodious chapel; and, after singing a hymn, I forgot the fatigues of the day.

"18th.—A covenant meeting and preparatory lecture in the morning. In the afternoon, ordained Tway Po. I examined him, and offered the consecrating prayer, laying on hands with Myat Kyau. Myat Kyau gave the charge, and hand of fellowship. His address was fraught with piety and good sense, and adapted to the wants of the new pastor. Perhaps, were it written, it would not attract much attention as a literary production. It was not remarkably brilliant, but just what we should expect a pious, godly Karen would say to his brother under such circumstances. After these services we assembled at the water-side, and the two pastors baptized fifteen converts. I stood on the shore, a spectator, and repeated the loud 'amen.' During the evening the pastors administered the Lord's Supper, and gave each a short lecture to the Christians. And now my work here is done for the present; and my thoughts are turned towards Gwa, the sick child, and the lonely mother. The distance cannot be more than fifty miles; and, with a good path, I might hope to reach them in one day and night. But such a road! It is impossible to give any just conception of it."

At one o'clock the next morning Mr. Abbott left Ong Khyoung for Gwa, where he arrived early on the 20th. The child was yet alive, though greatly reduced by the fever. The following week Mr. Abbott returned to Ong Khyoung, visiting the place again in April, from Sandoway.

"*Gwa, Jan. 22, 1843.*—My fears for the people who came to the meeting at Baumee were not unfounded. A letter has just arrived, which states that several families, men, women, and children, were taken by the officers before they reached their homes. The parents and other relatives of Bleh Po were included. The men were dreadfully beaten, and bound with iron fetters; the women were put into a boat, anchored in the middle of a river; the young children, left crying on the shore, within hearing of their mothers. Poor creatures! they are beyond the help of mortal arm, and need to exercise great faith and patience. The men exhibited a noble fortitude under their beatings. Some of them, even while being beaten, prayed to God with a loud voice, much to the astonishment of their persecutors. One of them, Shan Byu by name, was asked by an officer, among other things, if he worshipped Jesus Christ. 'Yes,' was the prompt reply.—'Well, you must worship no more.'—'I shall worship him though you kill me,' returned the fearless disciple. The officer said, 'These Karen Christians are *teh ket the* (a very hard case).' Shan Byu is a specimen of a class who would doubtless die rather than equivocate. There are others, who, when asked whether they were disciples, have answered, 'No;' and afterwards we hear of their repentance and confession. It is not for man to judge.

"*25th.*—News again from the prisoners. Several have been liberated by an officer in whose district they were taken. Some think him to be a Christian. However that may be, he has certainly favored the converts now. As Bleh Po's relatives, including women and children, were apprehended by officers from Bassein, and spies who hope for a reward, they are taken to Bassein. Walking from the boats to the prison, through a dense crowd, the women were chained together, two and two, the chain around an ankle of each. Their sufferings will be inconceivable to any one who has never seen a Burman prison, and knows nothing of its discipline. They will be dependent on the pittance doled out by the most compassionate of their ruthless foes. There are several children but a few months old. These and their poor mothers excite the deepest sympathy. As to the men, they are nearly all 'substantial men,' and a few weeks' imprisonment may be only salutary. My own feelings can hardly be appreciated.

"*27th.*—Nearly all who accompanied us to the jungle, are prostrated with fever. Our son is a little better. God is merciful. At a late hour last evening, there were Karens sitting about the room, some from Rangoon, others from Bassein and the hills, conversing as to the sufferings of their brethren now in prison,—what would probably be their fate; how they would endure; and, if killed, whether they would meet death joyfully. While speaking on this point, one of the assistants gave an account of the death of an old woman, a few days since, at Baumee,—one of the happiest deaths of which I have heard among the Karens. I have seen many of them pass away, and generally they have no ecstasies and no fears: they die resigned to the will of God. 'God will take care of me,' is generally the answer to questions as to their exercises. This old woman had been a Christian several years, and was much given to prayer. She was sensible of the approach of death for several days, and rejoiced at the prospect. 'I have been looking for the coming of Christ to judgment, but shall die and not see the day; but,' she continued, 'I shall go to see him.' She exhibited that divine joy, that brightening of the powers of the soul, that foretaste of glory, which sometimes precede the death-hour. After this story another of the assistants said, 'Such happy deaths are becoming more frequent;' and then he gave the particulars of several such cases which had fallen under his observation. After he had ceased another went on to tell of the happy deaths *he* had witnessed; and then another, and another still, till a very late hour. I listened to their narrations with delighted surprise. Such resignation, such unshaken confidence in God, such bright and sure hopes of heavenly joy, light from eternity beaming down upon souls just emerged from midnight darkness, — it was one of the happiest evenings of my life."

As nearly forty years have elapsed since the writing of this journal, the following hitherto unpublished reference to the distinguished Gen. Sir A. P. Phayre, afterwards the first chief commissioner of British Burma, governor of Mauritius, etc., will be pardoned. All of the earlier missionaries in Burma experienced his kindness, and could heartily indorse the expressions of Mr. Abbott.

"*Ong Khyoung, Jan. 30.*—I have come down to meet the senior assistant commissioner of Sandoway, Mr. Phayre, who is making a tour through his district, to hear the complaints of the poor, and look after the interests of government. He is a generous-hearted, amiable man, as well as a scholar and gentleman; and he renders the mission essential aid. We are making arrangements relative to Karen villages, in anticipation of the arrival of emigrants from Burma. We could do nothing without his assistance.

"*Feb. 2.*—Mr. Phayre arrived. A head man is appointed over the Christian village. Complaints are heard, and grievances redressed.

"*5th.*—Arrived at Baumee chapel with Mr. Phayre. Heard from the prisoners. Gloomy prospects. Poor creatures are starving. One of the assistants, a young man just beginning to preach, on being asked by an officer if he worshipped Jesus, replied 'No.' I have not seen him since. Notwithstanding his denial, he may be a real Christian.

"*Gwa, 7th.*—Arrived here this morning, a little past sunrise; and, at evening, came on board a beautiful new government schooner, bound for Sandoway. Mr. Phayre returns by land, and very kindly offered to Mrs. Abbott and family the use of his vessel. As I have no object in going by land, I prefer the sea."

To this great kindness Mr. Phayre soon after added a personal donation of two hundred rupees, for the benefit of the mission. The journal continues:—

"*Sandoway, 14th.*—Arrived after a very unpleasant voyage of seven days. The small-pox is sweeping off the people here in large numbers. An old Karen woman died on our compound but two days ago. She was one of the brightest specimens of the triumphs of the gospel that I have ever seen. 'Died praying, praying.' Vaccine being unattainable, we must inoculate our children.

"*25th.*—Heard from the prisoners. Their sufferings are not severe, except from hunger. Bleh Po's aged mother was allowed by the jailer to go out to the Karen villages to beg rice. She returned with all she durst bring; and the jailer took it almost all away from her, leaving the Karens nearly as hungry as before. They are set to servile labor, but complain of nothing but hunger. They will probably be liberated, as the rulers disagree on their case. There is the *myo-woon*, who holds 'three swords;' the *myo-thoo-gyee*, who holds two; and the *akouk-woon*, who holds two. Then there are others, who hold but 'one sword.' Their relative rank and power are thus indicated. The first is the governor of Bassein district, so called; i.e., he is at the head; the second is governor of the city; and the third is the custom-house officer. These are all appointed by the king, are afraid of each other, and always quarrelling. The Karens who are in prison live in the *myo-thoo-gyee's* district. The custom-house officer, wishing to bring him into disgrace, sent spies into his district, and apprehended the Karens. They are suffering in prison, while the officers are quarrelling over the subject. Shan Byu, one of the prisoners, said to the *myo-woon* in public, 'Kill us at once: we cannot bear starving with our wives and children.' In consequence of these acts, the Christians are emigrating to Arakan.

"*March 8.*—Our children have been mercifully preserved through the small-pox. Our eldest son, five years old, had it severely for inoculation,—more than two hundred pustules on his face, one on his eyeball, and his mouth filled with them. Most of those inoculated had but few pustules, and those small.

"*11th.*—The poor captives are liberated, but it cost them five or six hundred rupees. After the *myo-woon's* order for their liberation was issued, the jailer had his claims to prefer, and the prison subordinates came up for a reward for *their* services. The Karens were told that they were to make the compensation required in such cases. It was several days before they came to a settlement. The jailer withheld their pittance of food, and starved them into submission. They were not required to give a pledge, and no orders were given them relative to their religion. The officers had tried to force a concession and had failed, and very wisely shunned another defeat. In fact, the government wished to release them; but a pledge was required of the *myo-thoo-gyee* in whose district they lived, to the effect that they were to worship the 'foreigners' God' no more. *He* becomes surety to the government that the new religion shall be extirpated. He will probably tell the Karens privately, as many of the petty district officials do, 'Worship as you like, but do it secretly, or *we* shall have to suffer for it;' and the Karens will worship as they please, in peace, till informers bring the subject before the authorities publicly, when they must pay attention to it. The same scenes are liable to be enacted yearly.

"But what will the end of all these things be? The noble, fearless testimony which those prisoners bear to the truth has given their cause notoriety and character. The common people throughout the country generally look upon the new religion with interest, and whisper their sympathy with its suffering votaries. In conversation the assistants speak from time to time of Burman Christians. Eternity will reveal them if there are any.

"*April 16.*—Have just returned from Ong Khyoung. Mr. Phayre took me with himself in the government schooner, eight days ago, to make arrangements relative to the location, etc., of emigrants. Made the voyage down in thirty-six hours. Spent the sabbath with the people. One hundred and twenty Christian families have come over to that place since I was there two months ago, bringing with them more than two hundred buffaloes. The chapel would not contain more than one-fourth of the assembly on Sunday. They built booths around within hearing. Mr. Phayre is to supply them with [rice], and wait a year for the pay, without interest. They had just gathered their harvest in Burma; but the acts of government so alarmed them, that they left all their paddy and fled hither, on the assurance that food would be supplied them for a year. They will not find such fruitful fields, and rivers abounding in fish, this side the mountains; but they find religious freedom. Here they may worship God in the open face of day, and not a dog move his tongue.

"On Monday morning I staked out a new street at Ong Khyoung, and a location for a new and larger chapel. On that plot of ground, when the brushwood and grass had been cleared away, we all kneeled down, men, women, and children, and consecrated it to God. After all arrangements had been made, I gave them the parting hand, went on board ship, and in five days reached home.

"*22d.*—Karens asking for baptism, I sent them back with a letter to the Magezzin pastor. An assistant arrived from Baumee. Emigrants are still coming over with their buffaloes. What will become of the Redeemer's kingdom in Burma if these persecutions continue? Myat Kyau has baptized seventy or more, and Tway Po more than forty, since I left them. Both are sent for from distant places, and they have remained with their own people scarcely two days in succession since they were ordained. May the number of converts be multiplied as the drops of the morning!

"*28th.*—Shway Bo, one of the assistants from Burma, arrived. [Not the Pwo Karen of that name (?) .—ED.] I last saw him at Gwa, a few days after others had been seized, and taken to Bassein. He arrived at Gwa just at dark; said he had come to see me once more; that the officers were on his track, and that on his return he should give himself up, and go to prison with his brethren, and probably to death; said, if he fled, the Christians in his village would suffer, but if he gave himself up no others of his village would be molested. He left me early the next morning, with a sad heart; shook my hand, but said not a word. My own emotions were too deep for utterance. He returned, was arrested as he had anticipated, was taken before an officer and bound, but not beaten nor cruelly abused, as others were. He was confined over night, and the next day examined at great length. He was asked how many seasons he had been to study with me, what he studied, who and how many went with him, etc. All his answers were written down. He was told that he must not worship in this way any more. 'I must,' was his reply. The officer did not threaten him, but said finally, 'Well, if you must follow this new religion yourself, you must not get great congregations together, and make a great noise preaching.' To this Shway Bo made no reply; and, very much to his surprise and joy, he was dismissed. It cost him four rupees,—the 'costs of suit,' as we should say in a civilized land.

"He is a noted man, and, I fear, will have no rest. Three years ago he came to me at Sandoway, a wild, green boy. He wished to stay and study. I thought he had better follow the plough, but finally allowed him to remain. He began to improve at once, manifested an intense eagerness to learn, went home, and came again the next year. I began to hear a good report of his zeal and piety, and gave him liberty to preach. He came and studied again last rains, and I recognized him as an assistant. Unless I am greatly deceived, he is now a successful preacher, and an eminent Christian. Other such cases might be enumerated. Again, many who appeared very well at first, we have been obliged, after a trial, to dismiss.

"Had news to-day from Tway Po. He had just returned from a tour to the south, whither I went last year. He baptized nearly a hundred, all of whom had been Christians for a number of months, and with whom he was well acquainted. Emigrants are still coming over, the number of families having increased to over two hundred. The comet which has appeared so suddenly and splendidly for a few weeks has sent consternation through the land. Many of the Christians partake of the alarm, and the most dreadful calamities are prognosticated."

In a letter accompanying the preceding journal, dated May 2, Mr. Abbott says, —

"My journal should be rewritten and corrected, as it is now only written from dates and rough notes; but I cannot rewrite it. My students will soon be in; and I have their studies to prepare, lectures to originate, and their board, lodgings, etc., to attend to. My hands are full of labor, and my heart full of care, sometimes of anguish, — nearly a thousand baptized converts, many of them suffering under an iron despotism; over two hundred families of emigrants, fugitives from persecution, who look to me for food till they can reap a harvest; thirty native preachers to teach, guide, and govern; two ordained pastors to watch and tremble over; elementary books to write and translate, — add to this a sick family, and not a good night's rest for many months. I have had thoughts of calling for a colleague in the Karen department, but hardly know what to say. The uncertainty which is constantly present with me renders it impossible for me to be explicit in regard to it, connected also, as it is more or less, with the possibility of my return to Burma [Proper]. I am hoping for some indications of the Divine Will; still, as things are, I can do much more for the Karens *here* than I could under the inspection, jealousy, and hatred of the Burman government. My coming to Arakan has been attended with blessed results, beyond my most sanguine hopes: still, I am not clear as to my future course. Had it not been for my family, I *think* I should have been in Bassein during the persecution; and yet any interference on my part would have added to the sufferings of the converts, and increased the difficulties attending their liberation. Are we then to give up Burma? This is a question that thrills my soul at times, and occasions intense anxiety. I can only commit my way to God. May He guide us all in the way of truth and duty!"

He closes his letter on the 14th of May thus: —

"Have just heard of the death of Mrs. Comstock, — that dear sister, amiable and devoted friend, efficient missionary, lovely child of God. What a loss to her family, to the mission circle, to Arakan! I don't know what poor Comstock will do."

In July the afflicted missionary from Ramree visited his sympathizing friends. Within one year from the death of Mrs. Comstock, two children and the thrice stricken father had followed her gentle spirit to the better land. Our last letter from Mr. Abbott this year, dated Sept. 15, contains heavy tidings.

"In my letter of May last I gave an account of the emigration of Christian families from Burma to this province, and of the prospect of their becoming permanently located, and dwelling in peace. At Ong Khyoung they had erected a large and beautiful chapel. Eighty dwelling-houses were also completed; and the people were beginning to plough and sow, when the cholera broke out, and one hundred and thirteen persons died in a few weeks. A panic seized the poor people. Parents caught up their little ones in their arms, and fled to the jungles. Some of them crossed the mountains to their old homes in Burma: others halted at villages where the cholera had not yet appeared, and waited for the pestilence to pass away; but a great many died in the forests. Within two months after my last visit, Ong Khyoung was desolate, and their chapel had become a habitation of owls.

"Forty families had settled at Magezzin. The cholera appeared there also. Fewer died, in proportion to their number, than in Ong Khyoung; but the village is quite broken up. The small villages around Baumee chapel are dispersed; and that spot, rendered sacred by so many tokens of God's presence, is deserted and silent. Shway Bay was the first victim of the pestilence, a young man, who, I had hoped, would become a strong pillar. I had hoped to see those Christian villages settled, having schools, chapels, and pastors, enjoying the means of grace and religious liberty beyond the reach of cruel tyrants. I had hoped for permanency and perpetuity to the institutions of the gospel among that long oppressed people. 'My thoughts are not as your thoughts, saith the Lord;' and though dark clouds gather over the visions of the righteous, the bow of promise appears, and the soul takes fast hold on 'the true sayings of God.' We still labor in hope. He who cometh will come, and His kingdom will triumph."

In addition to the losses on the Arakan side, Mr. Abbott estimated that more than five hundred Karen Christians were swept off by cholera this year in Burma.

It should here be noted, that, from the beginning of 1843, Rev. Mr. Vinton of Maulmain assumed charge of the Karen churches of Rangoon. The distance to Sandoway was found to be too great, and nearly all who attempted the journey thither from Rangoon were stricken by disease.

It is worth while to record Mr. Abbott's list of assistants, and the payments to them for the year 1843. It is the earliest list that we have been able to find.

"Paid Rev. Tway Po, Rs. 66; Rev. Myat Kyau, Rs. 60; Ong Sah, Rs. 42; Kah Gaing, Rs. 10; Shway Bo, Rs. 48; Bogalo, Rs. 40; Tongoo, Rs. 36; Nahkee, Rs. 40; Min Gyau, Rs. 36; Ong Thah (dead), Rs. 5; Wah Dee, Rs. 40; Rehthay, Rs. 36; Sau Bo, Rs. 48; Shway Bay (dead), Rs. 20; Mau Yay, Rs. 20; Nahyah, Rs. 36; Pah Yeh (reader), Rs. 5; Shway Too, (ditto) Rs. 17; two copyists (at Rs. 4), Rs. 44. Total for twenty Karen assistants, Rs. 649."

In the accounts of the Arakan mission for this year, the society is credited with a donation of Rs. 94 from the Karen Christians by E. L. Abbott. His total expenditures for the year, for assistants, Karen and Burman school, and buildings, including a house for the Burman assistant at Sandoway, were Rs. 1,293.

CHAPTER V.

1844-1847.

"All our evangelistic efforts are to aim, *first*, at the conversion of individual souls, and *secondly*, though contemporaneously, at the organization of the permanent native Christian Church, self-supporting, self-governing, self-extending." —*Principles of the Church Missionary Society.*

It is seldom that the hand of a sovereign God is more clearly seen, both in judgment and in mercy, than in the history of the Bassein mission at this period. Karens in their native state are the slaves of fear. As they themselves express it, "our bellies are full of fear." They fear human enemies, but, most of all, those unseen powers of earth and air which produce disease and death. In instances without number, a heathen almost persuaded to become a follower of Christ has been turned from his purpose by an outbreak of cholera, or some other misfortune. "The spirits surely are angry at our leaving their worship. They are powerful and malignant. The Christian's God may, or may not, be as powerful; but he is good, —too good to do us evil. It were better for us to follow the way of our ancestors. If they went to hell, we, too, will go to hell." This has been the avowed reasoning and conclusion of hundreds of Karen inquirers, since the great ingatherings here recorded. It is plain that nothing but a mighty outpouring of the Divine Spirit could have kept those weak and superstitious souls from wavering and fall, whether under the stress of the sea of afflictions which befell them in 1843, or in the long-continued absence of their beloved teacher, which so soon followed.

To the omnipotent and ever blessed Name be the glory and everlasting praises! Mr. Abbott writes: —

"*Magezzin, Dec. 12, 1843.*—A new chapel has been erected on the seashore, about four hours' walk from the old village. Many houses in sight are falling to decay, which gives the place a desolate appearance. During the outbreak of cholera many of the inhabitants died, mostly the heads of families. Others returned to Burma. Only twenty families are left. Of the twenty-five emigrant families, only six remain. This is not a good location for a large village, and I anticipate another removal before a permanent settlement is made. In the evening, preached from the words, 'In the world ye shall have tribulation; but be of good cheer.' Nearly every one is mourning the loss of friends.

"13th.—Preaching in the morning, and a church-meeting, preparatory to the Supper of the Lord. I preached from the text, 'I beseech you therefore, brethren, by the mercies of God, that ye present your bodies a living sacrifice,' etc. Several old men sat on the floor near my feet, and gazed up into my face, their countenances indicating the intensity of their feelings. On such occasions it is delightful to preach the glorious gospel of the blessed God. In the afternoon applicants for baptism were heard. Most of them have been Christians two or three years. They came from Burma a few months since, and have delayed asking for baptism until now. I preferred that the pastor should baptize them, but he insisted on my doing it. Seventy-five were received at evening, and were baptized; after which I assisted the pastor in administering the Lord's Supper. Two of the baptized, and thirty-one who had not been baptized, died of cholera. The church now numbers a hundred and seventy-seven members. They are so scattered, that they require the constant watch-care of a faithful pastor. A number of villages, from which but few have embraced the gospel, lie near. Myat Kyau has a large field before him, and he enters into the work like a man in earnest.

"Ong Khyoung, 18th.—Spent four days with the Magezzin church, very agreeably, and, I trust, not without profit to the people. A contrary wind with rain threatened to drive us out to sea, and kept us back, so that we did not reach this place till nine o'clock this morning. The first house that I came to on entering the new village was that of Tway Po, the pastor. He has in this shown his good sense, and a desire and capacity for social improvement. Perhaps a man's house and garden (his amount of wealth being considered), is not an unfair test of his relative position in the scale of civilization.

The next building was the chapel, large and commodious, all that I could wish. I looked through the village, and its desolate appearance filled me with sorrow. Of the hundred and forty families of emigrants, only twenty remained. I struck the gong: the people came together, and I preached a funeral sermon for a hundred and twenty souls. Towards evening, visited each family: in nearly every one are some ill, either of fever or measles, or of some one of the peculiar diseases to which Karens are subject. One family of fifteen persons, consisting of the grandfather and his descendants, were all prostrated with fever. Their harvest was not reaped, and has been destroyed by wild animals. The old man told the tale of his sufferings with tears. Many are disheartened, and wish to leave the place.

"Two months ago I sent a circular to the assistants to meet me here on an appointed day. They have all arrived but two. I preached to them this morning from the words of Paul to the pastors of Ephesus, Acts xx. 28. Endeavored to impress upon their minds a sense of their responsibilities as shepherds. Oh that they may be sanctified for their high calling, and strengthened to endure trials as good soldiers of Jesus Christ! Sixteen assistants are publicly recognized and employed by the mission. The two pastors and two assistants live in this province, the others in Burma. On an average, they do not receive from the mission one-half the amount requisite for their support. Some of them receive nothing, being supported entirely by their people. The Karens are a liberal, hospitable people, and in their poverty and oppression can do something for the support of their teachers. Several hundred rupees are annually contributed. The 'readers' are chosen and approved by the assistants in council, and receive no support from the mission, except when they spend all their time as school-teachers. But few of them are yet prepared for that important work.

"There has been a melancholy case of defection. A young man was approved two years ago as an assistant.[1] He maintained an unspotted character for a year, and gave promise of usefulness. A year ago his wife died. A few months after, he was guilty of lewdness with the sister of his deceased wife, and was dismissed from mission service. Still he maintained, in other respects, a fair Christian character; and the other assistants had hopes of his final restoration. But a few months since, he fell into the same sin again. The girl's mother reproached him in severe and bitter language. He became sad and melancholy. Five days afterwards an assistant went to his village to preach. At the evening meeting the transgressor was missing. Search was made, and he was found dead in a field. 'He went out and hanged himself.' His friends then recollected that he had said, a few days before, that his reputation was gone; that he could never again become like the other assistants. A sense of shame drove him to the fatal deed. But satanic cunning has overleaped itself. This event is as a flaming beacon, of which the other preachers, I trust, will not soon lose sight.

{ Footnote: [1] Mlah Wah, one of the earliest converts, and pastor of the church at Nau-peh-eh. }

"In the morning had a church-meeting. Cases of difficulty had occurred between brethren which required adjudication; not serious, but, e.g., a man's buffaloes had broken into his neighbor's field and destroyed his crops, the consequence being sharp words, repentance, and confession. There were no cases of immoral conduct, and the people live in peace. The remainder of the day was spent in prayer and self-examination, preparatory to partaking of the symbols of the Saviour's death. At evening a hundred and fifty assembled at the table of the Lord. With what solemn joy does the disciple of Christ think of those endearing words, 'Do this in remembrance of me!' Yes, precious Saviour, we remember thine atoning blood, thy dying love.

"A few months ago this church numbered a hundred and sixty-five. Forty-three have died, leaving a hundred and twenty-two. What desolation death has made in these families! An old man comes to me, and sitting down before me on the floor, with eyes downcast to conceal his tears, begins to tell of his afflictions. Six months ago he had a wife and six grown-up children around him. All are dead, and he left, a poor, old, feeble man. A little crying infant, eight months old, is pointed out to me, the relic of a large family. Parents, elder brothers and sisters, six months ago all in health,—now all gone but the infant. Tway Po has baptized in all three hundred and forty-four during the year. How melancholy must have been those days, when he followed a hundred and twenty of his own villagers to the grave in quick succession! He has won the affection and confidence of all who know him.

"*24th, Sunday.*—Arrived at Great Plains yesterday. After preaching, a church-meeting. At sunset the Ong Khyoung pastor baptized ten, and in the evening assisted in administering the communion. This church numbers a hundred and eighty-four. Several have arrived from Burma during the year. Two have died, and two have fallen away. An assistant and a 'reader' are stationed here. They have a large chapel on the seabeach, back of which is an extensive and beautiful plain, well cultivated, where the village is built. The place has hitherto been healthy. It escaped the dreadful scourge which passed through Ong Khyoung; and, with the blessing of God, there is a prospect of permanency. If the plan of building up Karen churches and villages under the English government be of God, it will succeed. But the experiment at Ong Khyoung has taught us that our most sanguine hopes are liable to be blasted in a day. I have no hope of seeing the Karen Christians settled permanently in large villages, except they have buffaloes and plough the soil, instead of cutting and burning new fields each year. In the latter case, but few families can live in one place, and it is quite certain that they will remove once in two or three years. A very few may remain for some years in one place; but, so far as my experience goes, it is not certain that a village will be found next year where it is this. A dozen families with buffaloes will form a centre, where the pastor will reside, and where the chapel and schoolhouse will be erected. Great Plains is such a village, and Ong Khyoung also; and others are forming.

"*Ong Khyoung, 30th.*—In returning from Great Plains, the men rowed from village to village during the night, which gave me all of the day and evening to spend in the villages. A few have died since I was here. The hand of affliction is heavy upon them. It is wholly owing to the influence of the pastor, and two or three other stable men, that they do not scatter to the four winds.

"In this church there is one of those 'widows indeed,' of whom Paul writes to Timothy. She formerly lived in Burma, and, by her zeal, won a reputation which threatened to involve her in serious consequences. The Burmans called her the 'woman preacher,' and she was marked for vengeance from the government. She wisely fled to Arakan, and has found here open houses and open hearts. Should a stranger pass through this place about one, P.M., on Saturday, he would hear a gong; and, should he go by the chapel, he would see the widow sitting on the floor, surrounded by a group of women and children; and, if he could understand Karen, he would hear from the widow's lips the truths of the gospel. Should he go to the sick-room, he would there see her administering the consolations of religion to the suffering and dying. She has no kindred, and lives on the charity of God's people. I bid her God speed with a hearty good will.

"*Baumee Chapel.*—The Christians come flocking in from the hamlets. Baptized eleven this morning [no date]. Twelve have died during the year, including their pastor, Shway Bay. The present number is a hundred and fourteen. They are so scattered that it is impossible to collect a large number of children in a day-school. An assistant and reader are stationed here. But few have come over from Burma to meet me here this year. I have discouraged their coming in large companies.

"*Jan. 7, Sabbath.*—Spent yesterday and to-day with the Christians at Magezzin; have this evening given them my parting counsel, and am now ready to start for Sandoway. Myat Kyau is going into Burma. The Christians have been calling him from a great many villages, especially from the region that I visited in 1837. The converts there have not been molested for some months. Burmese officers frequently go into their assemblies, look on, and say nothing,—a calm which to me is rather threatening.

"I took Myat Kyau away into the jungle, and sat down with him on a large stone, and gave him my last words of advice. He will probably be absent several months, and a great number will apply for baptism. I have confidence in his discretion and judgment: he has received the best instruction I am capable of giving him, re-iterated and enforced. He has seen my manner of procedure for years, and although he may be more liable to err than I, will be less liable to be deceived; for he is a Karen, can go from house to house, and can ascertain the character of individuals to better advantage than any foreign missionary. I shall follow him with my unceasing anxieties and fervent prayers. Could I make my voice heard through the American churches this evening, I would say, 'Pray for us.' Pray for these pastors, pray for the native preachers, pray for these churches, pray for the people of God in Burma, groaning in bondage, pray that a day of salvation and deliverance may dawn, — pray, pray, PRAY!

"I have long seen the importance of establishing day-schools in all the Christian villages. It is possible to collect but a small part of the children into boarding-schools: and, were it practicable, I would not deem it advisable; as, in my opinion, the plan of day-schools, well carried out, is better adapted to the end contemplated. In boarding-schools my object has been to instruct assistants and school-teachers. There are three day-schools in operation this season, taught by competent teachers, — one at Great Plains, one at Ong Khyoung, and one at Magezzin. There are other schools also, of from six to a dozen children each, in the smaller villages, conducted by men who will not do much more than teach reading and writing. I regard schools as one of our most efficient instrumentalities.

"*Sandoway, 14th.* — Arrived at home. My family had arrived from Akyab some time previous. The loving-kindness of the Lord has followed us, and his mercy endureth forever.

"*Feb. 23.* Returned yesterday, after an absence of a month. Went in company with Capt. Phayre. He put me on shore at Ong Khyoung, where I remained six or eight days, administering medicine to the sick. Went across country to Baumee chapel. The Christians in the nearer villages on the Burman side, having heard of my arrival, came over, a hundred or more, men and women. Held meetings there several days, and Tway Po baptized thirty-seven. Came down Baumee River; stopped at Magezzin several days, and baptized eleven. Captain Phayre came along from the south. I accompanied him to Gwa; and then he gave me his vessel to return to Sandoway, he returning by land.

"April 25. Received the following letter from Myat Kyau:—

"'Great is the grace of the eternal God! Thus by the great love of our Lord Jesus Christ, more than 1,550 have joined themselves to the Father, Son, and Holy Ghost.

"'I, Myat Kyau and Ong Sah,[1] we two went forth, God opened our way, and we went in peace and joy. O teacher! we think of what the teacher told us, that, if we always set God before us, he will open our way and sustain us.

{ Footnote: [1] This Ong Sah, or Oo Sah, was ordained, in 1856, as pastor of the large church in Mee-thway-dike, which he served till his death in 1868. He was a good man. On this memorable tour he followed Myat Kyau in a strictly subordinate relation. }

"'Moreover, we went to Bassein city, and there we met a Beringee teacher (a Roman-Catholic priest); and he talked to us, and said, "What you are doing is not proper." And we asked, "Why not?" And he said, "Why do you not baptize all, old men, and children, and infants?" And we answered and said, "Not so. The Lord Jesus Christ has said that whosoever does not repent cannot enter the kingdom of God." And that Beringee man disputed with us all day. O teacher! that we may be able to dispute, pray for us.'

"A laconic letter, but full of good news. Myat Kyau was absent four months. He went to the Irrawaddy north of Rangoon, spending several days, and baptizing in each Christian village. He was not molested in the least; and, since his return, I have heard of no persecution following his labors. That great multitude baptized are like sheep in the wilderness, but the Shepherd of Israel slumbereth not.

"*May* 3. Have just heard of the death of brother Comstock. He was with us, a few weeks since, in good health, and full of hope respecting the success of the gospel at Ramree. Certainly the signs of the times there were full of promise...Brother Comstock is dead. Who will take his place? Who will come over into Macedonia and help us? God of mercy, we put our trust in thee. May thy word, which hath been published at Ramree, not return to thee void!

"*June* 10.—My time is entirely devoted to my boarding-school.—the two pastors, fourteen native preachers, several young men preparing for school teachers, and others from new villages, to the number of fifty. I deemed it important that the pastors and assistants leave their people, and devote themselves to study another season under my instruction. A great number of Christian villages are destitute, except as some one from among themselves conducts public worship. More native preachers are needed, and more money, to aid, in part, towards their support. To educate a native ministry, I consider now the most important department of the Karen mission."

In a private letter to the secretary, accompanying his journal, Mr. Abbott writes:—

"Mrs. Abbott frequently says to me, 'My dear, do you not think there should be two Karen missionaries here? Supposing you should be taken away!' And I leave the question for the Board to answer. I endeavor to communicate facts; and as Maulmain and Tavoy are amply supplied (comparatively), I do not deem it necessary to say more."

The above journal, closing with the words, "to educate a native ministry," etc., and the thrilling news of fifteen hundred and fifty baptisms by Myat Kyau in cruel Burma, had not reached America at the time of the meeting of the Triennial Convention in Philadelphia, in April, 1844: Enough was known, however, of the magnitude and promise of Abbott's work, to excite the deepest interest and solicitude of that large representative assembly.

The commitee on Asiatic missions consisted of Rev. Messrs. Jeter, Kennard, J. W. Parker, Devan, and W. W. Everts. Their report contained the following:—

"Your committee are of opinion that the Karen mission should receive particular attention. The Karens are a people prepared for the Lord. An abundant harvest invites the reaper to thrust in his sickle. Several missionaries should be sent as early as possible to Arakan, to labor among the Karens. *It is worthy of serious consideration whether the school for Karens should not be located in Arakan, instead of Maulmain.* [Italics by the Ed.] In Arakan and the adjoining provinces, the Karen converts are more numerous than in the vicinity of Maulmain. And the missions in the former need, more than in the latter place, the encouragement and advantages which would be afforded by the contiguity of such an institution."

After some discussion, the report was adopted by the convention. Rev. Dr. Binney at that very time was arriving in Maulmain, with instructions from the Board to establish the Karen Theological Seminary in that vicinity. A special committee, therefore, was appointed, consisting of Rev. Messrs. Colver, Peck, Kincaid, Ives, and Bailey, to take into consideration the expediency of the establishment of the seminary at Maulmain. At the close of the meetings they "reported that they had not been able to prepare their report, and requested to be discharged." They were accordingly discharged. (See "Missionary Magazine," July, 1844, pp. 157, 158, 164, 165, and 173.)

Although the time had not then come for the transfer of the general Karen school westward, this intuitive judgment of the American Baptist Triennial Convention seems to have had much truth and wisdom behind it. Had Bassein itself then been open, the projected institution would have been unanimously established in that place, with great advantage to the entire Karen field. As it was, Abbott himself was not in favor of placing the general school at Sandoway; and the subject was allowed to rest for another decade.

The school of fifty native assistants, and others preparing for that service in Sandoway, was dismissed in August, after the prescribed course of study was completed. The excellent doctrinal catechism prepared by Mr. Abbott was now available, and in use in Tavoy and other places, as well as in his own school. He writes at this time:—

"The field and demand [for qualified laborers] is increasing very fast; and I am happy to say that the native preachers generally are doing as well as I could expect. The pastors give me no cause for uneasiness. May God preserve and guide them all, and save his heritage!"

All too soon, however, the exhausting marches, the sleepless nights, the preaching, the endless talk, the overwhelming cares and labors of the past three years, had done their sad work upon the body of the devoted missionary, as well as their blessed work upon his spirit. His health during the rains was so alarming, that a journey to Akyab to consult a skilful physician was determined upon. The first intimation of danger was given to the public in the "Magazine" for March, 1845:—

"ARAKAN.—Our last advices from Akyab are of Oct. 11. Missionaries in good health, except Mr. Abbott, who had been ill several months, but was apparently recovering. Mr. Abbott was at Akyab at the above date, but would return to Sandoway in a few days."

The number for April contained much graver intelligence:—

"ARAKAN.—It appears from a late letter of Mr. Abbott, that his sickness is of a more alarming nature than was intimated in our last, and the promise of recovery more faint. Will not the friends of missions remember his case in fervent prayer? and will they not also answer the appeal for help which comes to them as from the sides of the grave?"

Mr. Abbott himself writes, Oct. 26: —

"The Akyab physician tells me I have the *seeds* of consumption, forbids me to preach, and advises a voyage to Singapore. I had a cough throughout the rains, with bad pulmonary symptoms during the month of August. That exhausting process went on till September, when I had a fever; since which I have been a little better. My cough still continues, and my throat and lungs are so affected I cannot preach if I would. But I must meet my assistants at Ong Khyoung, Dec. 20. If I am able to get there in a boat, I *must go*. It will then be cold weather; in the jungles, moreover, as here in Sandoway also, I have always been obliged to preach in the open air, often during a great part of the night, in a cold, damp, foggy air, perhaps with a wind blowing into my face. I have had a sore throat after such times, but nothing like what I have now. I shall not be able, I fear, to preach to the Karens this season, even if I am able to go to their chapels. Were this certain, I should still go and meet the assistants, as preaching is but one of the things to be done at those annual meetings. A few weeks or months will determine my destiny.

"I suppose the Board will not now hesitate to send a man to this station, to fill my place, *immediately*. I may live some time, but fear I shall be worthless if I do. If this pulmonary affection goes on, what *can* I do, even if I live some time? And to leave the three thousand baptized, the thirty native preachers, and the two ordained pastors here, as sheep in the wilderness, — oh, how utterly vain to attempt to express the emotions of my soul! Can any finite being know? Never! Will the Board send a Karen missionary to Sandoway? That I may know what to tell the people, if I live to get an answer, I wish the secretary to write me *overland*, on the reception of this; and, if then alive, I shall wish to write to the man who will come here, so that the letter may reach him before he leaves Boston. Now that the weather is mild, I am gaining strength, and some of the fearful symptoms are disappearing. I am comfortable, and only want that perfect assurance to be resigned and happy. I hope and trust in Jesus, but sometimes have doubts; otherwise, all is well.

"On the 12th of August we consigned to the grave a son, fifteen months old, a hale, happy, beautiful boy, just the one we did not expect was going to die. Removed from us to the bosom of God!

How consoling! and we have nothing to say. Oh, how sweet is submission!"

Thus, in the very hour of victory, ere a tithe of the fruits of victory have been gathered, the leader of the host on those shores is laid low. So mysterious are God's dealings with the frail children of men. In answer to the prayers of a multitude, in rude Karen as well as in his native tongue, the much afflicted man rallies once more; but the disease will never relax its hold until the end is accomplished.

The expenses of the Sandoway mission, charged to the society for the year 1844, were Rs. 1,375-8. In this sum was included Rs. 961 for Karen assistants, thirty-six of whom received, on an average, twenty-six rupees and a fraction each. Ten Burman assistants in the Arakan mission received for the same time Rs. 804-7.

Notwithstanding the very grave condition of his throat and lungs, Mr. Abbott, as we have seen, could not give up a last meeting with the "beloved men" at Ong Khyoung. The self-forgetful, self-sacrificing wife and mother insists upon accompanying her loved one, to nurse and comfort, perchance to bury him on some desolate beach or woody hill. Capt. Phayre again does all in his power for the comfort of the family, and they depart on their errand of mercy to the Karens. During their absence, both of the children were quite ill of fever, and their mother suffered not a little from neuralgia. Mr. Abbott's health, so far from being injured by his labors in preaching, appeared, on the contrary, to improve. Mrs. Abbott, in her last letter to a friend, says, —

"You are aware that I went to take care of Mr. Abbott; but, strange to say, he became nurse, and I and the children patients, for a good part of the time." After giving an account of the very interesting meetings at Ong Khyoung, and then of the distressing illness of the children, she remarks of herself, "I am but just able to drag about, though I have no disease in particular. Ascending a short flight of stairs puts me so out of breath, that it is with difficulty that I can speak for a quarter of an hour afterwards."

At this time little did any one think that the faithful, loving woman would be the first to die. But let the stricken husband tell the story. Bassein Karens at least will be thankful to read the smallest details; for this was a part of the great price paid for their reclamation to Christ.

SANDOWAY, Feb. 7, 1845.
Rev. S. PECK, D.D., *Corresponding Secretary.*

Reverend and dear Sir,—Mrs. Abbott is no more! She expired on the evening of the 27th ult., after a painful illness of four days. Death has again entered my household; and, through the mysterious dispensations of God, the Arakan mission is again clad in mourning. May these repeated afflictions become the blessed instrumentalities of our entire sanctification, and be overruled to the promotion of the glorious cause in which so many faithful laborers are sacrificing their lives!

As a few particulars respecting the last illness of Mrs. Abbott may be desirable, I give a hasty sketch. In November we left Sandoway to visit the Karen villages down the coast. We had a government vessel with excellent accommodations. As my health was bad, and Mrs. Abbott feared I might die in the jungles, she insisted on accompanying me. We went down to Great Plains, calling at the villages on the coast; and, on our return, spent a month at Ong Khyoung, in a small house which the Karens had built on the beach for our reception. While there, Mrs. Abbott had an attack of jungle-fever, from which she recovered in a few days; and on our arrival at Sandoway, Jan. 19, she was as well as usual, expecting her confinement in five or six weeks. On the 24th, five days after our return, she had another attack of the same fever, during the first paroxysm of which she vomited violently, which caused her the most excruciating, indescribable pain at the heart. She said the pain was such as she had hitherto had no conception of, and that it produced a dreadful sensation,—a kind of breaking-up of the very fountain of life. She soon began to breathe with the utmost difficulty, every breath causing intense pain. It was evident that some of the vital organs had suffered a fatal injury. The painful gasping for breath continued through the day, with fever; and at evening she gave birth to a son. We then hoped that the fearful symptoms would abate, but not in the least. During the three succeeding days she suffered indescribable agony: her groans and cries, at every breath, could be heard at a long distance from the house. Fever continued, and a thirst that was impossible to quench. Nature could endure no longer; and, on the evening of the 27th, she fell asleep. Her sanctified spirit, emancipated, winged its way to the world of light and glory...Who, for one moment, would detain a child of God in this dark world, away from the beatific fruition of heaven, and the open visions of the Godhead! I sorrow not for the dead.

Mrs. Abbott said but little during her illness: indeed, except at short intervals, she could not utter a word. She was conscious that the time of her departure had come, was perfectly resigned, and, consequently, perfectly happy. She bore her dreadful sufferings with all that calm fortitude which was so prominent in her character, and which bore her up during so many years of privation, suffering, and toil. The infant is still alive, but is a poor, feeble creature...

My own health was better. During November and December, while at sea and in Ong Khyoung, I improved rapidly. I regained the use of my voice to a good degree; so that during the association of native preachers I preached all the time, day and night, for several days, and do not think it hurt me at all. Since my return, before and since Mrs. Abbott's death, I have been rather going down again. Am now using Jayne's Expectorant, and awaiting results. The gentlemen here say they never expected to see me return from my trip to the jungle. I really do not see cause for great alarm, and think that a sea-voyage of a few months, so far as human means are concerned, would bring me up again. But I cannot leave my children...I intend to go to Kyouk Pyoo, and see what the change and sea-air will effect. And then, indeed, what then? What can I do among the Karens, two hundred miles away on the hills, with my small family to nurse, and with my health? I must come to some conclusion soon. If I live, will write again from Kyouk Pyoo.

I have much to write to the Board. All my notes of the association at Ong Khyoung are in pencil, and no one can decipher them but myself. The events at that meeting and others give those solid grounds for encouragement which we all so much desire to see. All are to me of the most interesting character; but when I shall be able to give them to you, it is impossible to say. Where is brother Kincaid? I trust the Board will hear that distressing call from Ramree, and not detain him in America longer than is necessary...

Ever yours in the bonds of the gospel, E. L. ABBOTT.

Mr. Abbott's account of the most interesting meetings at Ong Khyoung was, we believe, never written. He also speaks in a previous letter of having in hand Myat Kyau's journal of the great mission to Burma, which he intended to translate for the Board. His time and strength, however, were not sufficient; and hence the particulars of that "triumphal tour," as it was called, will never be known by us upon earth. To what villages those fifteen hundred and fifty believers which he baptized belonged, what the history of their conversion and of the persecutions they had undergone, what the thousand scenes of thrilling interest in which this lowly man of God doubtless mingled, neither we may know, nor those more deeply interested, the descendants of those earliest Bassein converts. For two long years and more those poor sheep must be left alone in the wilderness, exposed to a thousand enemies, but safe with God for their protector.

Leaving the desolate home and the graves in Sandoway on the 26th of February, Mr. Abbott arrived in Kyouk Pyoo with his motherless children March 2. The poor infant died just after their arrival. The eldest boy, of seven, was very ill; and the physician said that the only hope of his life was in a sea-voyage. The missionary accordingly took passage for Calcutta, arriving on the 24th. From thence he secured passage in the first ship that offered, the *Clifton*, bound for London. He had but three days in which to prepare an outfit for himself and children; but he found time to write to the secretary:—

"I am miserable—cough, cough. Still, I do not think that I have consumption...I left Arakan with a sad heart. The Karens are so dependent. Brother Stilson has agreed to meet with the association at Ong Khyoung in January, 1846...If the Board have not sent me a colleague, I suppose they will wait till my arrival...As life is uncertain, this may be my last to the Board. Send a man to Sandoway...Christ is my only hope; and oh, how rich is his grace to such a poor sinner as I!"

Writing from Cape Town on the 23d of June, he says that his pulmonary symptoms had been really alarming, and, another disease setting in, left him doubtful, at one time, of living to reach England. The children were both still feeble. He hopes, if possible, to reach home and set out again on his return before winter, so as to reach Arakan, and "look after those twenty-six churches and their pastors before the rains of the coming summer." London was reached Sept. 17, all in improved health. "Were it not for my motherless children," he writes, "I would now set my face towards the Karen jungles, without a moment's hesitation." The people of his adoption were dearer to him than friends and native country. He landed in New York Nov. 14, just in time for the special meeting of the old Convention, which resulted in the formation of the new "Missionary Union." His remarks on that occasion, as well as those of the venerable Dr. Judson, are said to have been listened to with profound interest.

An excellent home for the children was found with an aunt in Fulton, N.Y.; and Mr. Abbott gave himself, even beyond his strength, to developing a missionary spirit among the churches. His labors were excessive, and his prostration at times was great. The effect of his visits and eloquent addresses was unusually deep and permanent. In Philadelphia he says, "Our meetings, night after night, resemble the best hours of the convention at New York." But, in the midst of his success, his throat became so much affected that he could only speak in a low voice. May 26, 1846, he is resting at Williamsburg, L.I., unable to attend public meetings in Boston. He was then intending to start, in five or six days, for Vermont, to attend "Brother Beecher's ordination." He was still determined to return to

Sandoway at the earliest day possible. Rev. Mr. Beecher, under appointment to Sandoway, sailed with Dr. Judson and others for Maulmain, *via* the Cape, July 11, 1846. Unable to go with this party, Abbott pleads most earnestly to be sent overland, Sept. 1, so as to reach Calcutta by the 1st of December:—

"A missionary is standing at the door of the Mission Rooms, begging that he may be sent out to India by the mail-route, in order that he may be there in time to secure a year's labor among some thirty native churches, of more than four thousand members, with their pastors, who are without a guide and counsellor in their weakness and ignorance; among whom Catholic priests are making desperate efforts to seduce them from their faith, and to subject them to the Romish ritual. And this is the only missionary to those churches, and the mail-route the only way to secure that year's labor and influence. Look at it a moment! The Board will never be called upon to deliberate on another such case, never; so that the precedent will be harmless."

But all his appeals were in vain. Owing to the precarious state of his health and to financial reasons, the Board did not deem it wise to send him out that year. Deeply disappointed, the missionary submits with Christian resignation.

Meanwhile, what of the Lord's little ones in Bassein? We have every reason to believe that the work went on, perhaps with undiminished power; but no connected account can be given of the welfare or progress of the Christians. Mr. Stilson probably failed to reach the association in Ong Khyoung at the beginning of 1846. We know that some communication was had with the Sandoway and Bassein assistants: for the Arakan mission accounts show Rs. 510, paid to 34 Karen assistants, and Rs. 884. paid to 10 Burman assistants,[1] for the year 1845; Rs. 233 paid to Karens, and Rs. 880 paid to Burmans, for the year 1846; and Rs. 169 paid to Karens, and Rs. 843 paid to Burmans, for the year 1847. This year, also, the Akyab treasurer credits the Missionary Union with a "donation from the Karen disciples of Bassein," Rs. 36-12 in Burman silver, which exchanged for Rs. 29-8 in English money.

{ Footnote: [1] To get the full force of these figures, it should be observed, that, notwithstanding the liberal expenditure of money, lives, and earnest, prayerful labor on the Burman Missions in Arakan, no permanent Christian communities were established. The small churches formed in Akyab, Ramree and Kyouk Pyoo long since lost their visibility.}

In 1846 Mr. Ingalls visited Sandoway, but we have no account of his reaching the Karen villages. Most of the communication was kept up, probably, by the Karens themselves making the long journey up the coast, from Sandoway to Akyab. We have met a few Karens, who, as lads, attended the mission-school in the latter town. Myat Kyau reported the baptism of a hundred and fifty Karens in one tour in 1845; still later, the baptism of six hundred not previously reported is announced. In 1846 either Myat Kyau or Tway Po passed over into Rangoon, and baptized a large number. Miss M. Vinton writes from Maulmain, April 3, as follows: —

"I have heard one item of intelligence which cannot fail to interest you. A large company of Karens arrived to-day from Rangoon, saying that one of the ordained preachers from Sandoway came over last month, and baptized three hundred and seventy-two Karens at one time, who had long been worshippers of the true God, and waiting for the ordinance. We have cause for rejoicing, and, at the same time, for weeping: for rejoicing, in that the converts to the truth are being multiplied; and for weeping, that there are so few to watch over and teach them the way of God more perfectly. May God teach them by his Spirit, and shield them from temptation! The number of Karens baptized within the present year, in the regions of Sandoway, Rangoon, Tavoy, Mergui, and Maulmain, is about twelve hundred."

Still later in the year Mr. Ingalls writes from Akyab of the proselyting efforts of the Roman Catholics: —

"I am much concerned for Sandoway, especially if brother Abbott does not return. Several Karens are now in school here, who arrived since I last wrote you. They say that the gospel is now spreading far and wide among the Karens in Burma. The two pastors were going in every direction, and baptizing. The Karens at Shwaydoung, near Prome, are receiving the truth. The Catholics from Bassein are making efforts to seduce the disciples. I will translate what the Karen letter says on the subject:—'I will inform you of the state of the Karen churches in Burma. A very great sickness prevails. Those that die, die; those who are sick, are sick. The number of deaths is from fifty to sixty. We do not feel concern on that account, but on another. The Catholics have entered Bassein. The Romish priests are wolves, and desire to devour the sheep; for when they find a dead one, i.e., one who has been turned out of the church, they seize him in a moment, and run off with him; for which reason, we know them to be wolves.[1] The preachers of the gospel are those who take care of the sheep: nevertheless, if those who are wolves get in, there is no stopping them; and, if the wolves can get in, as many as can will get in. Now, if there are not those who will carefully watch the fold, there is reason to fear all will be destroyed. The sheep are now being devoured. The wolves' words are, "The shepherd should live with the sheep." (This is said by the priests with reference to missionaries who have left their flocks, or are afraid to live in Burma.) 'These reproaches,' says the writer, 'we now have to bear; and the churches are like the stars, which cannot shine in the rainy season, or candles covered by a bushel. Wherefore, O teachers! pity the churches in the East, and pray much for us. O teachers! by exhibiting compassion, exalt God. We have no refuge in ourselves: God alone has strength.' Thus does this young disciple make his urgent appeal. They dread the Catholics: some have gone over, and others may follow."

{ Footnote: [1] The one celebrated case in Bassein, which justifies the imputation conveyed in the Karen letter above, is that of the preacher Ko Dau, who was baptized by Mr. Abbott among the first, and employed by him for a time as an assistant. He was afterwards convicted of fornication, and excluded. He then went over to the Romanists, with a considerable number of his relatives; and there they and their descendants have ever since remained. There was another preacher, Tongoo, or Too-oo, one of the earliest converts, employed by Mr. Abbott for a number of years, who was often admonished and finally disciplined, for beating his wife, and covetousness. At last he fell sick, and finding it difficult, our informants say, to support his family, went over to the Roman Catholics, who had the reputation at that time of being liberal under such circumstances. His wife and children went over with him; but, after his death, they returned to their old faith.

It is due to the missionaries of that ancient church, as well as to ourselves, to say, that, during the last twelve years, so far as the author is aware, there have been few or no attempts at proselyting by either side. The Karen Christians as a rule are firmly attached to their respective teachers; and, in the case of the Baptists at least, the more intelligent they become, the more attached they are to the principles of their faith. }

Writing from Akyab, Sept. 13, 1846, Mr. Ingalls says, —

"Two Karens who had attended school here from Bassein have returned home; and I have written to the destitute disciples that a teacher is on his way, and that I will endeavor to meet them at their general meeting in January. But how I can make such a tour I know not. The Lord may open a way for me."

Early in 1847 he reports "thirty-two hundred and forty members of churches connected with twenty-nine out-stations; Ko Myat Kyau and Ko Dway [Tway Po], baptized eight hundred and twelve in 1846, including one Burman; and fourteen hundred and twenty-seven are waiting for admission to the churches. There are five other stations from which no returns were made; at one of them, a church of some fifty members." And thus grew the "Stone cut out without hands," which shall yet become a great mountain, and fill the whole land.

CHAPTER VI.

1848, 1849.

"The Church must send her ablest, most highly educated, and best men to the heathen; for the work in the foreign field is more difficult than at home." —GRAUL.

In May, 1847, Mr. Abbott delivered "a most affecting address" at the annual meeting in Cincinnati, and was at last permitted to take passage by steamer on the 16th of August for Arakan, *via* England and Egypt. He returned to his work alone; for he contemplated an early settlement among the Karen villages in Burma Proper, and it did not seem to him that it would be right for him to subject one of his countrywomen to the hardships, the loneliness, and the risks of such a situation. The cost of travelling by the "overland" route was then about three times what it is at present by "canal steamers;" but, in his case, the greater expense was the truest economy. Reaching Calcutta as he did on the 4th of November, he was in good time to do a cold season's work among his beloved Karens. Writing to the secretary from Calcutta on the 6th, he says, —

"I am again permitted to renew my correspondence with you from a heathen land. How different are my relations to the world now from what they were in April, 1845, as I sat in this room, by this table, and wrote my last letter to the Board, announcing my departure for my native land! Then by my side were two puny little creatures, dependent for guidance and protection on a feeble father, who was looking to the grave for healing, while they might have to traverse wide oceans alone to find some one to take their father's place...Since that day, through what varied scenes have I passed, especially in my native land! 'Yes, my native land, I love thee,' —I love those churches and ministers of Christ in whose cordial welcome I detected that deep interest in the cause of missions which I received as a pledge, not only of future support, but also of the final triumph of the missionary enterprise. My native land! What a crowd of images are flashing across my soul! 'My boys,' too, are there."

He writes that on the voyage across the Atlantic, and in England, he had a severe attack of pleurisy, which ended in inflammation of the lungs and a troublesome cough. He insisted on embarking for India, an invalid, contrary to the advice of his physician and friends in London. He was warned that he might live to reach Egypt, but could never cross the desert alive. His own opinion proved correct. The trying ride of twenty-six hours from Alexandria to the steamer at Suez seemed to refresh, rather than enfeeble him; and he reached Calcutta in what he calls "a good state of health." He adds, "I am here in good time. A steamer leaves for Arakan in three days, in which I embark. Brother Ingalls heard of my coming by last mail; and the sound has gone out ere this through the Karen jungles, so that their gaze 'towards the setting sun' for their teacher will become more and more intense."

Rev. J. S. Beecher and wife arrived in Sandoway soon after Mr. Abbott, and just in season to accompany him on his first trip down the coast to Ong Khyoung. As Mr. Beecher will, from this point, hold a place of increasing importance in the narrative, a word of introduction is in order. A native of the Green-mountain State, John Sidney Beecher, like his senior, Abbott, was from Hamilton, that prolific mother of missionaries. Abbott, the father of the Bassein mission, the compiler of this volume never saw; but he counts a personal acquaintance with Beecher as one of the pleasantest memories of his missionary life. In 1866 he was tall and erect in person, rather spare, with a long beard and a piercing eye, evidently a man of affairs and accustomed to respect. There was, perhaps, a trace of austerity in his manner, but one soon discovered that his spirit was kind and true. He impressed the young missionary, then connected with the Seminary at Rangoon, as not a man of many words, but as a manly man, a man of convictions, and a man of Christian honor. From his arrival in Maulmain, Dec. 5, 1846, he had applied himself to the study of Karen. During the next rains he had given some assistance in the boarding-school of that station, teaching a class, and beginning to preach a little in the barbarous tongue which was to be the chief medium of his future labors. When he shall finally be called upon, by the prostration and departure of his distinguished predecessor and associate, to take up and carry forward the work in Bassein, he will be found well fitted, by his training, by his original powers, and by divine grace, for the heaviest of tasks.[1]

PORTRAIT OF REV. J. S. BEECHER

{ Footnote: [1] Rev. G. W. Anderson, D.D., a classmate of Mr. Beecher's, narrates the striking providence which sent him to Burma. Mr. Beecher was the president of the "Western Association," so called, and pledged, it was supposed, to home-mission work. Mr. Abbott had come to Hamilton in search of an associate. He had applied to Mr. Beecher, and must have a reply on the Saturday evening prior to his departure.

"About two, P.M., brother Beecher came to my room in great perplexity. 'I have never once thought of going to the Eastern field. I cannot decide to go without consulting Miss——, and I have not the slightest idea as to her views on the subject.' I suggested writing to her, but she was in Chicago, and it would take more than a week to get her answer. Finally he thought of a lady, a friend of his *fiancée*, who might have heard something that would help him to a just view of her feelings. He left very soon, and returned in about half an hour.

"'Did you see Miss——?' I inquired.—'No, I did not go there,' was his reply. 'Just look at this.' He then showed me a letter which he had just received from the lady in Chicago,—a letter which had come at an unusual time and by an unusual route. She had been invited by Miss Lyon, of Mount Holyoke Seminary, to assist her in teaching for a few weeks. Against opposing circumstances she had finally decided to go, and added to her letter these words substantially: 'I think we ought always to go where duty calls; and, if at any time you should come to think it your duty to go to an Eastern field, I should lay no difficulty in your way.'

"'There, Anderson,' he said, 'what do you think of that?'—'I think you have precisely the answer you wanted; and I think you may justly say, 'This is the finger of God.'

"That evening he called on Brother Abbott, and consented to go to Arakan. His decision was a surprise to many of his classmates and friends, but he never wavered. They could see that in choosing, he chose; and there he stood. He was ready for any work that the Lord had for him to do,—to break up all his old plans if the Lord pointed him to a new course. I think that he judged and decided aright." }

Unlike in many respects, so unlike, indeed, that perfect sympathy and accord were almost impossible between them, they yet attained substantial unanimity in their views as to the main lines of mission policy. Abbott's remarkable prescience and power are manifested especially in this: that he gave such shape to the work that for forty years the mission, passing through half a dozen different hands, never lost the impress he gave it, nor suffered a single break in its continuity. To this fact is to be attributed, under God, the rare success which has attended the work in Bassein. There has been no tearing down and attempted reconstruction of foundations and walls already well laid by those who wrought before; and thus much of the deplorable loss incident, and sometimes necessary no doubt, to the work in other missions has been avoided.

Under date of Sandoway, Feb. 12, 1848, Mr. Abbott gives the following account of the meeting at Ong Khyoung and the information there gathered: —

"We have just returned from a tour of six weeks. I had previously sent a circular to Bassein, fixing a day when I would meet the preachers at Ong Khyoung; but sufficient time had not elapsed to allow the most distant to reach the place in season, so that but twelve of them had assembled on our arrival. When I found myself standing among that group of Karen brethren, and witnessed their intense joy at seeing me again, I forgot, for a while, the sacrifices, the hazards and misgivings, of the past; and we rejoiced together, and offered to the Lord a song of grateful praise.

"I was highly gratified at the indications of stability and improvement which the village gave. The pastor, Tway Po, has more than fulfilled my most sanguine expectations. He has won a fair, high character, and acquired a commanding influence, which in meekness and love he consecrates unreservedly to the cause of truth. During my absence he baptized six hundred, making about sixteen hundred since his ordination. Over the churches thus established, he has appointed 'elders;' and in no case have I seen reason to question the wisdom of his course. He is about to remove from Ong Khyoung to a new village, farther south, where he hopes to build up another large church.

"Myat Kyau, the other ordained pastor, has baptized five hundred and fifty since I left, mostly in Burma. He has formed them into churches, and appointed a preacher in each. He is to succeed Tway Po at Ong Khyoung. He is different from Tway Po,—is terribly severe in his denunciations of the wicked. Of an indomitable will, he pursues his own course, irrespective of friends or foes, and is liable to make enemies. Tway Po is the mild and lovely John, and has not an enemy in the world. Both are excellent men in their way, and I have never regretted that I ordained them.

"Of the twenty-four preachers that I left, two have died, and one has been suspended. In the death of one of the two, Hton Byu (see pp. 21, 36, 38, 41, 53), the Karens have suffered a great loss, and I have been deeply afflicted. I picked him up in Rangoon, in 1837, a wild, mischievous boy from the jungles. He soon, with a few others, became a pet in my family, then a brilliant scholar, and a lovely Christian. While at Rangoon he was imprisoned for studying 'the white book,' but was allowed to go out every morning, under guard, to beg rice for the day, dragging on his ankles a pair of heavy iron fetters. I recollect meeting him once while thus begging. The guard cast a scornful glance at me, as though he would say, 'Speak at your peril.' Hton Byu, as we were passing, turned towards me his beautiful, laughing eyes, as though he wished to say, 'Never mind, teacher.' He accompanied us to Arakan, and was finally appointed a preacher, and had the care of a very large church near Bassein. He was the best educated, and the most talented, of our native preachers. He had just married a young and lovely wife, and we were discussing the question of his ordination when I left the country; but he is dead.

"Min Gyau, the other deceased preacher, was a young man of fair promise, and the pastor of a large church in Burma. When I think of those beloved disciples and faithful preachers who have died, and of the high hopes which they had awakened, my heart bleeds afresh; and I have but to turn my head, and look out of my window upon the rude little monument beside a larger pile of bricks, to see the emblems of death's handiwork [in my own family]. Yea, the last mail brought a letter with a black seal from America, saying, 'Your old and dear friend, P. B. Peck,[1] is no more.' We had been like David and Jonathan from infancy to the day I sailed for Burma. O Death!

how deadly and cruel are thy darts! Go on: the day of thy doom, though delayed, will come.

{ Footnote: [1] Rev. Philetus B. Peck, eldest son of Rev. John Peck, and for a long time pastor at Owego, N.Y. }

"The remaining twenty native preachers have continued steadfast and immovable, abounding in the work of the Lord. All these are tried men, appointed before I left for America; and most of them are pastors of churches in Burma. In many cases they have suffered during my absence, as they do not feel at liberty to engage in any secular employment. Moreover, I am sorry to be obliged to say that our appropriations are not sufficient to enable us to relieve their wants.

"Sixteen others, appointed by the ordained pastors, have each the care of a church and congregation by which they are sustained. They were appointed provisionally, to supply an immediate demand, but to wait the final decision of the missionary. They are all to leave their churches and study with us during the coming rains, and will, we hope, prove themselves worthy of recognition as preachers.

"Thus there are thirty-six preachers, besides the ordained pastors, to be counselled and guided, to be watched and prayed over, to awaken our anxieties and multiply our cares and labors, and to add to the expense of the mission. They have under their charge nearly five thousand church-members. (More than that number have been baptized west of Rangoon since 1837.) The two ordained pastors and eight of the thirty-six, with about a thousand of the converts, are in this province. The other twenty-eight preachers, with four thousand converts, are in Burma, between the Arakan mountains and Rangoon. The churches number from twenty to two hundred and fifty members each; and in many of those in Burma there are large numbers of candidates for baptism.

"Moreover, there are in Burma, away to the north of Bassein and Pantanau, at least eight destitute districts, where twelve hundred converts are waiting for baptism;[1] and for these eight districts, pastors are demanded immediately. A large number of school-teachers will be required, all of whom must be educated by us at considerable expense; and all the pastors must, of course, study with us before receiving a regular appointment. Will the churches of our native land supply the wants of these churches? is a question which we ask ourselves with anxiety. Shall we be sustained in the toilsome work of educating the pastors, school-teachers, and the young men of these churches? Many of the pastors will be located where the people cannot [fully] sustain them, increasing the demands upon the funds of the mission.

{ Footnote: [1] Undoubtedly in the region since occupied by the Henthada mission. Rev. B. C. Thomas writes in February, 1856: "On reaching Henthada, fifteen months ago, we thought we had come to a region where the gospel had not been preached; but we were mistaken. Karen evangelists had long since gone through both the Henthada and Tharrawaddi districts. Many of the assistants and private Christians of Bassein and Rangoon had yearly visited these districts. They had gone even to Prome, urging their relatives and others to accept the gospel. But the message was unheeded, [?] except in the south about Donabew, where some four hundred had become Christians in the days of Burman rule. There were a few also baptized at the same time near Prome. Hence we found that we had come to a region whose inhabitants had long rejected the gospel, while many of their brethren, both north and south, had accepted it with joy." Is it not more probable, that, at the time of Abbott's writing, the Karens of Henthada were really ready to welcome the good news of salvation; but, neglected then, or debarred by circumstances from the privileges which they coveted, they grew cold and hard, so that when Thomas arrived, eight years later, they had lost their desire? }

"A few days since a Catholic priest made his appearance in Sandoway. He was formerly in Ava, and recently in Rangoon and Maulmain. He understands the Karen language well, and came around here to act in concert with his friend in Bassein, in attempting to seduce the Karen Christians from us. He had heard of my leaving the country, but not of my return, and supposed he would find the

Christians without a counsellor. He is now going about among them, using the plausible misrepresentations which are characteristic of his order; but he is met and vanquished by the simple word of God. Half a dozen, only, from the multitudes of Christians in Bassein, have been seduced by them; and they had either been excommunicated, or were of doubtful character.

"My recent tour was made in company with Mr. and Mrs. Beecher. A good many were baptized, and our visits among the churches were full of interest to us all. The details will be given by Mr. Beecher. We are now repairing our dilapidated buildings, preparatory to the boarding-school during the rains. The great object I had proposed to myself while in America, with such solicitude, is accomplished. Thanks be to God! And I have but to glance back a little to mark signal Divine interpositions in rescuing me from the border of the grave, and in bearing me on through dangers and sufferings to the present moment...Now I am more at ease. I have Mr. and Mrs. Beecher at my side, whose knowledge of the language will soon enable them to prosecute their labors with facility — good friends, desirable companions, and faithful fellow-laborers."

In a postscript he adds: —

"My health is really quite good, although I still suffer from the effects of the attack which I had before I left Boston and in England. I was enabled, while among the churches, to preach two or three times a day, but not without some suffering. At home I should have been an invalid. I have a recipe for sore throats: — Preach fourteen times a week in the open air, and continue your sermons till midnight if you like."

As the mission-house left by Mr. Abbott early in 1845 had gone without re-roofing for three rains, it was in a state of utter decay. Some of the posts were still serviceable, but nearly every thing else must be renewed. In rebuilding, and making the house barely sufficient for two families, the usual economy of this mission was practised. It may amaze this more prodigal generation to learn that eight hundred rupees only were expended for this purpose. For chapel, schoolroom, dormitories, and outhouses, of a temporary character, but sufficient to accommodate a school of sixty boarders, three hundred rupees only of mission money were used.

March 21 Mr. Beecher was attending to the work of building, and also giving "a little attention to a very promising class of young men in arithmetic. If there is one station," he writes, "that has been more abundantly blessed, that is more promising, and more worthy of ample support, than any other, that station is Sandoway...We very much need a young man like brother——[a first-rate teacher]. He would be, perhaps, more useful than a first-rate preacher." Thus early did Mr. Beecher put on record his conviction of the need of greater facilities for education among the thousands of Bassein converts. Most unfortunately, his appeals, as well as those of his associates and the Karens themselves, brought little or no response for many years from the unresponsive West. April 20 Mr. Beecher writes again: —

"The Pwo Karens are renewing their request for books, and a teacher to preach to them in their own language. If Maulmain needs four Karen mission families, Sandoway needs eight, even upon the supposition that our preachers shall, in the future, be educated chiefly at Maulmain. They are needed, not so much for preaching in person, as for preparing young men for the theological school, and for preparing others to go throughout Arakan and Bassein, teaching the children of the thousands of converts who are now asking for education with an eagerness that excels any thing I ever knew in our native land. There are now only three or four young men who are at all qualified for teaching. They have done well, but they say that their pupils now know as much as themselves; and, with renewed zeal, they are asking for more instruction. With a little more instruction these men would rank among our best preachers, and they cannot much longer be spared from their appropriate sphere of labor...The old proverb, 'If parents do not educate their children, the devil will,' is applicable in this case. If the Board neglects to educate the children which God has given them in Arakan, we must expect that somebody else will, and who so likely to do it as the emissaries of Rome?"

June 17 he writes again to the secretary, in the vigorous, inquisitive style which young missionaries sometimes indulge in: —

"Will you kindly inform me as to the *principles* upon which the annual appropriations are made to the several missions and departments of missions? While there are six thousand Sgau disciples for one invalid fellow-laborer and myself to watch over and educate, and as many thousands more of Pwos, who are ready to upbraid us for not teaching them the religion of Jesus, instead of praying that 'a wide and effectual door' may be opened to us, please pray the Lord, and pray the churches, that more laborers may be *speedily* sent to this field. Our boarding-school now numbers sixty-six. It does not number five hundred because we strictly charged them not to come this year. But next year! May the Great Teacher incline more teachers to come, and the churches and the committee to send them! There is a deeply interesting state of feeling among the Pwos, in the region of Bassein, and an alarming action of the Jesuits among them. [Most of the strength of the Roman-Catholic Karen mission in Bassein to-day is among that branch of the Karen people. — ED.] Brother Abbott's health is such that he lectures two or three times a day."

The school was dismissed Aug. 8, to the great regret of the pupils and their teachers. Mr. Beecher again pleads the necessity of educational work, and for the pittance needful to maintain at least a normal class for eight or nine months in the year. The average attendance for the entire term of six months was thirty-four. A considerable number returned to teach what they had learned, in their own distant villages. Mainly as a matter of historical interest to the Karens, we give here a list of the assistants recognized, and, to a small extent, aided, by the mission, as written by Mr. Beecher at Ong Khyoung in December, 1847. We also add the villages to which they belonged, so far as we have been able to ascertain them: —

"*Old Assistants.* — Rev. Tway Po; Rev. Myat Kyau; Mau Yay, Kyootoo; Sau Bo, Lehkoo; Wah Dee, Great Plains; Bogalo, Sinmah (afterwards near Kaukau Pgah); Shway Bo, Meethwaydike; Nahyah, Kyootah; Nahkee, Pantanau; Ong Sah, Win-k'bah; Myat Oung, Hseat

Thah; Sah Gay, Great Plains; Sau Ng'Too, Kweng Yah; Poonyat, Kyoukadin (afterwards Lehkoo); Sah Meh, Henthada; Shway Pan.

"*New Assistants.* — Moung Bo, Mohgoo; Thway Pau (excluded); Myat Keh, Kohsoo; Mohlok, Too-p'loo and Layloo; Tway Gyau, Kangyee and Thahbubau; Shangalay, Tholee; Kyau Too, Naupeheh; Sau Kway, P'nahtheng; Shway Oo; Theh Kyoo, a Pwo pastor; Kroodee, Buffalo, Tindah; Shway Bwin, school-teacher; Shway Too, school-teacher; Tohlo, school-teacher, Ong Khyoung and Naupeheh; Shway Bau, Aumah, Nyomau; Shway Bay; Thah Gay, the martyr, Kyah-eng-gon; Tau Lau, Pwo; Shway Meh, Khyoungthah, Hohlot; Shahshu, Mohgoo. Total, 36."

The amount paid to these men for the year 1848 by Mr. Abbott was Rs. 223. Mr. Beecher also received and used Rs. 428-11, a part of which may have been spent upon the school. In the accounts of the Arakan mission for this year, we find Rs. 63 credited to the society as a donation from Karens, by E. L. Abbott. The Burman assistants, ten in number, received Rs. 767-8 for the same period. Mr. Abbott, writing July 30, says, —

"*We are endeavoring to educate our churches to support their own pastors.* Those which are not able to do so, we aid. But we have had it thrown in our faces by one or two 'cross-grained' native preachers, 'Why do you not give us as much as they give their native preachers in Maulmain?' More of this hereafter."

In order to come to an understanding with his brethren on this subject of vital importance, and also to familiarize himself somewhat with the system of schools in Maulmain, Mr. Abbott made a journey to that city in September. After his return he gave to the executive committee his views at length on the subject of education. He set forth powerfully the need of training a large number of jungle school-teachers, the need of thorough English education for a select class of Karens, who should begin the study in early youth. He also indorsed strongly Dr. Binney's methods of theological instruction, and Mrs. Binney's normal school. Of this visit, and of Mr. Abbott's power over a Karen audience, Mrs. Binney gives a charming picture, which we quote from the "Missionary Magazine" for August, 1874:—

"We met Mr. Abbott only twice. The first time was in 1848, soon after his return from America. He came to Maulmain to make the acquaintance of Mr. Binney and of the theological school. He had urged upon the Board the importance of this work, and he came to encourage its leader. He spent two weeks with us, and learned well the workings of both the theological and normal schools. He was to us, in our solitude, almost as an angel strengthening us. The Vintons were in America; and we were with Miss Vinton at a new and isolated station, teaching the very elements of knowledge during the rains, and, during the dry season, visiting the churches in the jungle. The Karen language, though sufficiently familiar to enable us to use it fluently, was yet too new to us to be other than a foreign tongue. Mr. Abbott had been eight years longer in Burma. He knew the people as well as their language. I was accustomed to listen to good, instructive preaching in Karen, but had supposed that the language itself, perhaps, did not admit of that thrilling eloquence by which I had seen American audiences held as if spell-bound; and it was generally supposed that Karens were apathetic, and not easily moved.

"Mr. Abbott gave us other and truer ideas of the power of the Karen tongue to produce deep emotion, and of the susceptibility of the Karen mind to receive such emotion. On the sabbath preceding the day of his departure he preached his farewell sermon. He had asked if it would do to preach in Maulmain the duty of self-support, and of carrying the gospel to those still in ignorance of it, as he would do in Bassein. He was told that these Christians needed the truth, and would listen to it, whatever it might be. Besides the pupils of the theological school, there was a large station-school of over one hundred mixed pupils of all ages, and the normal school of about thirty promising youths. The Karens from all parts of the district had heard of his visit, and he was a magnet which drew them to him. For several days they came flocking in, till, on Sunday morning, the largest chapel was too small for them. As he rose to speak, his heart was too full for immediate utterance; but he soon obtained the mastery, and brought before his hearers the most vivid panorama of their past, present, and hoped-for future: their past heathenish darkness, ignorance, oppression, sin; their present, the gospel light dawning upon them; in British Burma, at least, freedom to worship the God of whom they had learned; everywhere, the freedom which the gospel brings, and the hopes which it inspires, and with it the privilege, if need be, of suffering and dying for the love of Him, who, for our sakes, 'counted not his own life dear unto himself.' He told them of the great boon now offered of a special school for the training of preachers and teachers to carry forward this work; then pictured before them their future, if they were wise to know, and brave to perform, what the wonderful providence of God now required. He pointed to the Karens rising from their filth and degradation to the rank of an enlightened people, taking the lead in evangelizing the tribes and peoples around them, and appearing like a city on a hill, to which the people should gather. Finally, in view of the whole, he pressed upon them, in detail, the sacrifices required, the difficulties they would meet, the terrible consequences if they failed to meet these responsibilities, and their record, if they truly acted in the spirit of the Master who had called them to this service,—all in a manner inimitable, perhaps unparalleled. At the close of a sermon of nearly two hours, during which we 'took no note of time,' or of aught else save the thrilling thoughts presented and the occasional sobs which could not be wholly suppressed, he sat down entirely exhausted.

"We took him to the house and kept him quiet, but with difficulty; as the Karens filled the verandas, eager to get a few last words before he left them. We told them his state, and begged them to spare him. He arose the next morning refreshed, took a slight breakfast, and started for his boat, which was a mile or more down the river. He did not leave, however, till he had spoken a few words to the Karens, prayed with them, and shaken hands with every one of them, not overlooking the smallest child before him. The road between the house and the street was too muddy for a carriage to cross. When the Karens saw him preparing to walk to his carriage, they rushed for a chair, seated him in it, wrapped his old-fashioned cloak about him, and carried him, as if he had been a prince, he waving his adieus till out of sight.

"Almost his last words to us were, that he was a happier man for what he had seen, for the prospect of the glorious work among the Karens being made permanent and aggressive by the educational system so happily inaugurated in Maulmain. He repeatedly spoke of the pleasure it gave him to see the cheerfulness which prevailed among us. He did not like 'missionaries to seem as if they had been whipped into the traces.' When on his way to the boat he stopped to bid a mission family good-by, and was asked if he thought his trip and visit had done him good. 'Good? Why! I would have come all the way from Sandoway, in my little boat, in the rains, just to hear——laugh. It has done me good every way.'

"The next time we met was in 1853, at Newton Centre, Mass. He had 'come home to rest, probably to die.' He felt that his direct, personal work among the Karens was done; but he urged our speedy return...We never saw his face, now so pale and worn, again; but the mention of his name is still like precious ointment poured forth, and his example has ever been to us an inspiration." [1]

{ Footnote: [1] For a very interesting sketch from the same pen of Kyautoo and wife, Bassein pupils in Dr. Binney's school at Maulmain, see Missionary Magazine, 1848, pp. 107 sqq. The widow afterwards married Rev. Oo Sah of Meethwaydike, where she exerted a strong influence for good until her death a few years ago. }

It was believed at this time that the Burmese government, seeing the folly of repressive measures which only drove from its borders a most valuable class of subjects, was now ready to retrace its steps, and at least allow religious liberty to the Karens. In fact, Mr. Abbott himself had received more than one urgent invitation from Burman officials to go and reside near Bassein. One of these invitations he fully purposed to accept, early in 1849. Mr. Ingalls of Akyab was intending to join him in the expedition ("Missionary Magazine," January, 1849, p. 22), but was prevented. The Karens also who had left their ancient homes in Bassein to settle in British Arakan were getting restless. Beecher writes, Jan. 17: —

"They are turning their thoughts, and not a few of them their steps, towards the rising sun, and will not remain much longer in this sickly and unproductive land, either for love or liberty."

Mr. Abbott left Sandoway to make his first attempt to enter Bassein, Nov. 21, 1848. Before returning, he attended the association at Ong Khyoung, early in January. His account of the journey is as follows: —

"*Sandoway, Feb. 17, 1849.* — I have recently returned from a long tour. When I left, I hoped to be able to enter Burma. I had previously been invited to come by the governor of Myoungmya, who had promised to allow me to build a house and reside in his city. His district lies to the south and east of Bassein, towards Rangoon; and he is entirely independent of Bassein. The Karen Christians in his district, headed by Shway Weing, had made such representations as to persuade him to give me this permission. After twelve days at sea in a native boat, I entered the Bassein River, and was stopped at a watch-station near the mouth,[1] under the jurisdiction of the governor of Bassein, and was forbidden to enter the country until *his* permission could be obtained. I had hoped to be able in some way to pass by that station and enter Myoungmya, knowing that the governor of Bassein would oppose me; but I did not succeed. I was detained five days, while the officers sent a despatch to Bassein. As I feared, the answer came that I could not enter the country, but, if I would remain at the station three months, the governor would send to Ava, and learn the will of the king on the subject. The case has been sent up to the king, I believe, not only by the governor of Bassein, but by the governor of Myoungmya also, who is quite sure that he will secure the royal permission. I do not expect to hear the result for several weeks yet. If the Lord has need of me, he will set before me an open door.

{ Footnote: [1] On Heingyee Island. If Mr. Abbott had had the help of a good map, we believe that he could have avoided the jurisdiction of the Bassein governor altogether, by entering Myoungmya directly from the sea, through the mouth of a smaller river, a few miles to the eastward of the Bassein. Shway Myat, who attended Mr. Abbott on this expedition, told me that Shway Weing and other Christians met him at the island; that when summoned to go to the irresponsible officer of the Burman guard, the missionary took his double-barrelled gun on his shoulder, the consequence being that he was treated very respectfully. Tohlo and Thahree also accompanied him on the journey. }

"That the king has ordered all the governors to cease persecuting the Karen Christians, I have no doubt. Since 1844, the year after the great persecution and the year of the great emigration, the Christians have had rest, and are encouraged by Burman officers to build chapels, and worship God in their own way. The Christian communities are becoming so numerous that they exert a powerful influence upon the Burmans. Burmans are being converted and baptized by the pastors, uniting with Karen churches, and many are coming under Christian influence. The thought has arisen in my mind, whether the Lord will not convert Burma to Christianity by means of the Karens. Oh, how I have longed to enter that country! But Heaven has denied me the privilege. How different the scenes I should witness now from what I witnessed on my first tour in that region, in 1837!...

"I have since visited the eight Arakan churches scattered along the coast from Pagoda Point to Sandoway. I found many things to condemn, but more to approve. The pastors are willing to listen to my advice and submit to the control of truth. There are but few cases of discipline, less, perhaps, than among the same number of churches in America. Additions are being made by baptism. Day-schools are established in nearly every village; and the people are increasing in knowledge, and walking in the fear of the Lord.

"On the 10th of January we held our association at Ong Khyoung. Thirty-five preachers were present from all parts west of Rangoon. There has ever been to me more of intense interest connected with my intercourse with those men than with any other relations of my missionary life. I baptized them all. They have sat under my teachings month after month, while I have watched them growing up from infancy of knowledge to manhood in Christ. I have followed them as they have gone forth into their wild jungles preaching the gospel; have seen churches built up under their instructions, and thousands becoming obedient to the faith. Upon two of their number I have ventured to lay my hands, and to recognize them as bishops of the church of Christ. I have bowed with them on the seashore, and commended them to the grace of God, ready to depart for a distant land, wasted by disease; while each of us trembled under the unuttered foreboding that in this world we should meet no more. I have seen them again, standing firm like good soldiers of Jesus Christ, converts multiplying around them as the drops of the morning, as pastors of churches, magnifying their office and glorifying God. The affection we entertained towards each other years ago has not abated. It will, I trust, be perfected above and perpetuated through all eternity. Blessed be the name of God forever!

"I shall not be able to give the details of our last meeting. It would be impossible. Our statistics at the close of 1848 stand as follows: churches, 36; members, 4,341 reported, in Bassein and Arakan; baptized during the year, 373; native preachers, 44; scholars in day-schools, 421; died, 72; excluded, 24. Twelve chapels are completed, and do honor to the enterprise and spirit of the people. They are beautifully finished, and accommodate several hundred worshippers each. There are reported, also, 5,124 unbaptized Christians, who maintain as religious a life as the members of the church, only not baptized. Adding these and the nominal Christians to the church-members, and we have a population of not less than 12,000, who would bear comparison, as to moral character, with any Christian population in the world, and all enjoying the means of grace. The Executive Committee and the friends of missions will rejoice to hear that but *six hundred rupees*[1] were expended on these pastors, native preachers, and schools, during the year 1848.

{ Footnote: [1] Of course Rs. 600 from America is meant. The Karens themselves must have given several times that amount in cash and its equivalent. Abbott and Beecher had an appropriation that year of Rs. 1,500 for these very objects, of which they thought it wise to spend but Rs. 600. If they had paid their unexcelled assistants Rs. 80 each, the Maulmain Karen rate, they would have required Rs. 3,520 for preachers alone; or, if they had paid them at the Maulmain Burman rate, nearly Rs. 8,000 would have been consumed before beginning on schools. They were singular in their views, their assistants received a singular training at their hands, and God honored them with singular success. }

"At our recent meeting the native preachers unanimously and cheerfully gave up the relations they have hitherto sustained to the mission, and are in future to rely entirely on their churches for support. *Native pastors to be sustained by native churches* is the great principle by which they are to be governed. Churches are multiplying; and many are too poor to sustain their teachers, in which case we shall give aid. Schools also must be multiplied, so that the coming year will demand as much from us as the past; but the system of supporting the native ministry will be permanent. In this case the native brethren exhibited a spirit of self-denial, of true devotion to the cause of Christ, which I have not hitherto witnessed. Those men have made a noble sacrifice for the kingdom of heaven's sake, and verily they will have their reward. I believe their action is unparalleled in the history of modern missions."

Thirty-four years have elapsed since this stand was made. No backward step has been taken, and already Abbott's prophecy has been fulfilled. The Karen leaders have had the only reward they desired,—the steady advancement of their people, and the rapid upbuilding of Christian institutions among them on a firm, indigenous basis. Beecher, who was present when the resolution was adopted, says, however, that the preachers were not quite unanimous.[1] As a body they were noble men, and cheerfully acceded to what their beloved leader asked of them; but it was mainly Abbott's own principles and spirit infused into them, and his rare power exercised over them, that did the work. A weaker man might have failed. There have been fields equally promising in which the appointed leaders have followed on in the old ruts, attempting nothing like this, or, attempting, have failed through weakness. There have been yet other fields in which the work was started right; but, falling into the control of men whose wisdom and power were inadequate, they have lapsed into the state of mercenary dependence which is here deprecated.[2]

{ Footnote: [1] This is the account he gives in an unpublished letter, dated April 12, 1851: "One Myah Au (or Myat Oung) happening to stick out his horns a little sooner and a good deal farther than the other assistants, in the strife after regular pay, Mr. Abbott seized hold of him, and thrashed the whole company over his back so effectually that the poor fellow suddenly disappeared, and was not seen again by us for two years. A few weeks afterwards, however, we learned that he was not entirely annihilated; for Mr. Abbott received a letter from his church, stating that they had received him again in good faith, finding no fault with him. He ventured to appear cautiously at our last association, bringing a request from his church that he might be received into favor again, and the request was granted." Here again, Mr. Abbott did not mistake his man. The same Myah Au was finally set aside from the ministry in 1871, for forging an order for money in the missionary's hands belonging to his daughter, who had earned it by years of service in an English family, and had no thought of giving it into her father's control.

[2] For the views of the elder Vinton on this subject, see Missionary Magazine, October, 1846, p. 304. "We want no second-rate men...men that love to work, and that *will* work." For Professor Christlieb's strong expressions on the same subject, see his Protestant Foreign Missions, pp. 58, 138, and 238, English edition. }

But this is a digression. Mr. Abbott is now about to make a second attempt to enter Bassein in April, the hottest month of the year, by a more direct but harder route, up the Baumee River, through the pass to a place previously appointed within the bounds of pastor Bo's parish of Lehkoo. Previous to starting on the former fatiguing and dangerous expedition, the missionary had received a formal request from the Executive Committee that he would "abstain from all unnecessary exposure of his health." His reply of Nov. 2, 1848, is so characteristic that we quote from it.

"As it regards *'unnecessary* exposure of health,' I plead 'not guilty.' That my course of life has been attended with hazard and exposure of health in many instances, I admit. And that, in some cases, I have acted against the advice of physicians and friends is true. But I am yet to be convinced that I have not acted wisely. Not that I would justify 'unnecessary' exposure of life and health for a moment. The question to be decided is, when is *any* exposure of life and health justifiable? That missionary life involves exposures and perils from first to last, I need not inform the Executive Committee; nor that the course of some missionaries necessarily involves more exposure than that of others. This cannot be avoided, unless a man would be everlastingly *interpreting providences*, and do nothing else. But when are exposures which might be avoided, justifiable? Now, let a man take care how he interprets providence: for selfishness, timidity, and the love of ease are strong arguments; we are all liable to err on that side, and generally need no caution there.

"A case in point. At the close of 1844 I had an appointment to meet the Karen preachers near Ong Khyoung, in a small chapel, rudely built for the occasion on the sea-beach. My health had failed. Against the advice of the physician, with an alarming cough and an entire loss of voice, I started on that long journey to meet those beloved men, perhaps for the last time. My wife accompanied me with a sad heart, to see me decently buried in the jungle. I had some thoughts too. But I met those men, and preached to them day and night for twelve days; said the last word, and bid them adieu. Frequently during the time, especially late in the evenings, my dear wife would kindly come and whisper in my ear, 'My love, do you wish to live another day?' But I did my duty, and we both considered that I was only able to go through with those scenes by a special interposition of Divine Providence. I do not think it too much to say that the influence exerted at that meeting was made, by the grace of God, the efficient instrumentality of promoting the usefulness and steadfastness of those men during my absence. There was an exposure that might have been avoided very easily, but who shall say it was unnecessary exposure? I dare not."

He goes on to speak of the heavy labors before him, and of his determination to proceed, notwithstanding the precarious state of his health, and closes thus: —

"The committee may rest assured that I shall not expose my health unnecessarily. Their vote, so far as it indicates the interest they feel in my welfare, has awakened in my heart the most grateful sentiments."

From Sandoway he writes on the 15th of May of his second unsuccessful attempt to settle in Burman Bassein.

"From the tenor of my letter of last month you will expect to hear from me in Burma. I entered the country, as I proposed, by crossing over the hills from the head of Baumee River. But the governor of the district would not allow me to remain, and I was obliged to make my way back to Sandoway. He knew that the Karens were building me a house, and gave his consent to my residing in it. But, before my arrival, he changed his views; and his promise, which, I doubt not, was made sincerely, was of no avail. He wished me to remain, but under-officers had combined and succeeded in awaking his fears by threatening to impeach him before the king if he allowed me to remain. His anxieties were not a little increased by the results of my former attempt to enter by the Bassein River. When I left the river on my return, a small brig was lying in sight, which appeared to me to be a Madras vessel making her way up the coast. Word went up to Bassein that a man-of-war was off the mouth of the river, ready to enter, and avenge the insult offered to the 'English spy.' It had been represented to the governor of Bassein that I came in that character, as an agent of the English. That was the work of Catholic priests to prejudice the government against me, and prevent my entering the country. Consequently, the Bassein governor, being the highest officer in the province, called out all the other governors with their war-boats; and the fleet moved down the river to drive the foe into the sea, — when, on their arrival, there was not a ship to be seen. Then the other governors turned upon the Bassein gentleman, and handed him up to the king as an alarmist, a disturber of the public peace without cause. The result was, that the governor was taken to

Ava in irons. What has become of him we have not heard. This will indicate the commotion created by my first attempt to enter Bassein. The new governor has not yet arrived, and it is natural to suppose that the man into whose district I entered last was much in doubt as to what he should do with me. He dared not allow me to remain, and he was afraid to send me away. One good effect was produced by my last visit. The people now generally believe that I am what I profess to be,—simply a religious teacher. I have since heard that they say, 'That man would never come into our country as he does, and trust himself to our protection with none but Karens around him, were he not a true man.'

"My walk over the hills was very fatiguing, the more so as I was not accustomed to travelling by land. We were fourteen hours from the last village on this side to the first on the other. In that village was my house, or rather a large chapel, with bamboo work across one end for my sleeping-apartment. I arrived Saturday evening. That the Christians gave me a glad welcome is saying but little. Or that, in the course of that night, the thought that this was to be my home awakened a sense of desolation, perhaps I need not say.

"When I arose sabbath morning I could not take a step without excessive pain, arising from the long walk of the previous day. But that was soon forgotten. The pastors with their people began to assemble to see the teacher. At nine o'clock the chapel was crowded, ten pastors present, and a large number of people on the ground who could not get in. As near as I could judge, there were seven hundred [in the building]. I undertook to preach, but was unable to go through: the pain in my throat was too great. At noon the people who could not get in in the morning assembled: the house was again crowded, and they, too, must hear the teacher preach. I went through with the services and a sermon, with less pain than in the morning; and the people returned to their homes, except the villagers. I forgot the desolateness of my new home in the happy reflection that my position, although it might involve sacrifice and peril, was one I had long desired to occupy, as it affords facilities for *efficient labor*,—a position I would not exchange for any other, except a dwelling-place in heaven.

"Where should the father be,
But in the bosom of his family?"

God be thanked for such sabbaths in a heathen land!

"But my joyful anticipations were soon to be disappointed. At daylight the next morning Burman officers rushed into my sleeping-room, and ordered me, not very mildly, to start at once for the governor's court. I had seen Burman officials before, and had nothing to do but 'keep cool.' I finally succeeded in quieting their fury, and in getting them to leave my sleeping-room. After much ado they became more agreeable, and allowed me time to dress and take a cup of tea, as I did not know just whereunto the thing would grow, or when it would end. I got into a little canoe, and rowed down the creek to the bamboo palace of his Excellency,[1] where I arrived at nine o'clock.

{ Footnote: [1] This officer was the *pehnin* of Kyouk Khyoung-gyee. In Burman times this office is said to have been similar to that of a superintendent of police. Its powers were somewhat greater than those of a native assistant commissioner under the English government. }

It was the hour of the morning levee. The great man himself was seated on a mat at one end of a large hall, his silver boxes containing betel-nut, tobacco, lime, etc., spread around, and he reclining on a velvet cushion, 'as is the manner of Eastern princes.' The common people were at a great distance, bowing on their faces, while a few grave, elderly men were nearer, sitting in an upright position. I entered into conversation with the governor, told him distinctly who and what I was, and the object of my coming to the country. And he told me as distinctly that he dared not allow me to remain. I must return immediately, and wait a few months till the arrival of the new governor of Bassein, and till the matter could go before the king. He treated me very civilly, but was decided, and I was helpless. On taking my leave of him, I told him that I knew it was the custom of his country that those coming into the presence of a great man should take off their shoes, but trusted he would excuse me for not doing it: and as it was the custom of my country to take off the hat on such occasions, I would follow that; and I raised my hat, and gave him the best bow at my command, with which he appeared perfectly satisfied. I then made my way back to the village. I sent a request that he would allow me to pass through his district to Myoungmya, the district of the governor who invited me last year; but he would not grant it. Still, I left men around the court to hear and bring me word of what was said, for I knew my case would be freely discussed.

"These men returned at eight, P.M., with the word, that, unless the foreign teacher was missing the next morning, the head man of the village and the pastor of the church would be dragged to prison. *They* were made responsible for my immediate departure. I had determined to stay if possible, and see the end; but this was an aspect of things I did not like. What consternation prevailed throughout the village! How utterly unable are those who live in a land of liberty and law to estimate the results of despotism on the spirit of a people! Several of the women went into fits, so that we heard their screams in the chapel where we were sitting. Some wept, and some prayed. But the old men gathered around me and asked, 'Teacher, what shall we do?' Sure enough, here was a case to be decided, and not much time for a decision. But by nine o'clock we had asked counsel of God, and the matter was settled. Before eleven all my household furniture was tied again to poles to prevent slipping off; for the pieces were to be carried by two men each, through the jungles, over the precipices, rocks, logs, and ravines to Arakan. From eleven to twelve the people assembled for worship, and I endeavored to strengthen their confidence in the wisdom of Providence.

"At midnight we started on our dreary way back over the hills we had crossed two days before. The full moon was sailing through the clear heavens; and in its soft, melancholy light we travelled on cheerily, a few native pastors at my side, with whom I 'talked by the way' till near daylight, when the burden-carriers said if they could sleep one hour it would give them strength to climb the hills. As I knew the poor fellows needed rest, I ordered a halt; and they all dropped down on the ground by their burdens, and in a moment were in a sound sleep. I spread out my mat on the leaves, pulled a blanket over me, spread a handkerchief over my face, and gave myself up to the strange, wild thoughts the circumstances were adapted to awaken. The natives had told me that we were in a notorious haunt of wild elephants, tigers, and robbers. The men around me were all in a dead sleep. Through the opening foliage the moon's stray beams were playing with my eyes. Not a whisper was heard but the deep breathing of the sleepers. The events of the past few days, fraught with the interests of the kingdom of Christ and with the eternal destinies of men, passed in review. The fatiguing journey before us, with its perils, awakened anxiety; and the future was impenetrable. I, also, slept very quietly about forty minutes, and started up refreshed. The brilliant morning star met and gladdened my eye, beautiful emblem of the star of Hope, arising over these lands of pagan night. The men were soon upon their feet; and we marched on and still on, reaching the first village towards evening. It took us three days to procure boats, and get down to the mouth of the river; and three more to prepare a boat for Sandoway, where I arrived after six days at sea, having been absent twenty days.

"Since my return people have come from Burma, from whom I learn, that, early on the morning of my departure, officers came to the Karen village, and, seeing that I had gone, departed without molesting the disciples. Shortly after, a body of armed men came to the village, and simply wished to see the foreigner. They were supposed to be robbers; and, had I been there, blood might have been shed, perhaps my own. A report is in circulation there, that the king has actually issued the order that I be allowed to reside in the country. It is merely a report: should it prove true I should not be surprised. I cannot, however, make another journey to Burma till the close of the rains."

On the 6th of December, 1875, the writer had the pleasure of visiting the site of the historic meeting above described. Under the guidance of pastor Shway So, who was a participant in the meeting, I walked carefully over the little elevation, still called by the Burmans, in commemoration of the Christian multitudes there gathered in 1849,

"White-book Hill." My guide pointed out the exact site of the chapel erected for the occasion by Th'rah Bo, of Abbott's room, his cook-house, the Karen houses, etc. It is a slight rise of land only, within a stone's throw of the Moungbee, or, in Karen, the "Pineapple Creek," on the east bank, five or six miles north-west from Kyouk Khyoung-gyee, where Simons slept in 1835. There is not a soul living on the spot now. With my knife I carved Abbott's initials and the date of his visit on the trunk of a tree to mark the site.

The Karens say that the teacher was escorted both ways by a band of fifty or sixty men, who went over to Baumee to meet him and bring his luggage. One who carried him across the streams pickapack says that he had a bad cough and was spitting blood: though tall, he was, at that time, very spare and light. The party reached the village in the edge of the evening, Saturday. Though evidently much wearied by severe marching, he was overjoyed at his reception. Over a thousand Christians from villages far and near had assembled to meet him, and it was this going to and fro of the Karens that alarmed the Burman officers more than any thing else. He held a short service with them that night. The next day, Sunday, was a high day. Abbott preached with great power. One present says that the people listened with intense delight; that many were so moved that they could have suffered death for Christ's sake without shrinking. Mingled with his fervid teaching and exhortations were many expressions of joy that he had come at last to live and die among them. Although the separation was most painful on both sides, all the Karens who have conversed with me on the subject agree that it was best for them that he return as he did. His faithful attendant, Thahree, says that it was three or four months before the heavy furniture and boxes that were sent around by sea to Bassein came back to their owner in Sandoway.

The beginning of a distinct Pwo Karen department, in what is now known as the Bassein mission-field, is now to be made. Mr. Abbott, from the time of his first arrival in Sandoway, had done what he could for that people, and the Sgau preachers had co-operated with him zealously. A few hundreds had been converted and baptized. Pwo churches had been formed and pastors raised up for them, one of whom was already considered worthy of ordination. In consequence of the urgent representations of both Abbott and Beecher, Rev. H. L. Van Meter, another graduate of Hamilton, was sent out with his excellent wife, reaching Sandoway March 20, 1849. What they were enabled to accomplish will appear as the history proceeds.

CHAPTER VII.

"In Minahassa the great error that the Christians were never sufficiently trained to self-support is causing serious difficulties." — DR. CHRISTLIEB.

It is said that the *daimios* of Japan quietly yielded the larger part of their great power for the general good of the empire, and that thus, in a heathen nation, in our own time, one of the greatest revolutions in history was peaceably effected. In the Christian church, however, a reform is rarely, if ever, achieved without controversy, more or less bitter. Controversy is to be shunned as an evil; but neither Christ nor his apostles ever resorted to esoteric teaching, nor did they long suppress important truth to escape conflict with error. Christian frankness, with a full recognition of the merits of an opponent and his arguments, will enable a man like Abbott to present a difficult question calmly and convincingly to brethren more or less committed to opposite principles. This Mr. Abbott did with regard to the question of self-support in Burma. If, with equal wisdom and courage, the great question could have been widely discussed and rightly settled at home, how great would have been the gain! Instead of this, it was thought necessary to suppress the correspondence and the entire discussion as far as possible in America. The Christian public and the supporters of missions needed light, and still need it. May the great Father of lights prosper this honest effort to diffuse light among those who truly love it; and may he help us all to see eye to eye, and keep us in the peace of God!

A chief object of Mr. Abbott's visit to Maulmain had been to consult with his brethren there as to the system of supporting native preachers. We quote from his unpublished letter of Oct. 12, 1848: —

"The system of supporting native assistants—i.e., the plan by which each is to receive so much monthly pay—is coeval with the establishment of the Burmese mission, and is also the system of every other mission of which I have knowledge. This system, in my estimation, is fraught with the elements of destruction. From the

Burmese it was carried into the Karen department, and it has been practised among the Karens of Maulmain to this day. It is beginning to cause our brethren there intense solicitude. Mr. Mason at Tavoy, being farther removed from the influence of the Burmese department at Maulmain, has been able to discard it, and act independently. Here in Arakan, from the first, I have been determined to break it up, and introduce the system of self-sustaining churches...It is the *system* to which I object, and the spirit which that system is adapted to engender in the minds of all native preachers. Instead of having it as a fixed principle that all pastors are to be appointed and sustained by their own churches, that there is a mutual obligation and inter-dependence between pastor and people, and that every [preacher] is to have a church (except he receives a special appointment by the churches as an evangelist), this system relieves them of all sense of dependence upon their churches whatever, and they are simply the hired servants of the missionary.

"Now, in the Karen department *this system must be destroyed*. I was happy to find that Mason, Binney, and other Karen missionaries at Maulmain, are of one mind with Beecher and myself. *Churches are to sustain their own pastors:* pastors are to think, feel, and act accordingly. Evangelists are to be appointed and sustained *by the churches*. We will have a 'Union' here to act as the agent of the churches if necessary. And, if churches are poor (quite probable), and cannot support their pastors [wholly], we will write home to the Executive Committee, and they will make appropriations to help the poorer churches sustain their pastors and evangelists until they are able to do it [alone]. Such are the sentiments we are enforcing upon all our preachers, and such we believe to be the only system warranted by the word of God.

"But we meet at once with a difficulty not easily overcome. It is the system of patronage, spoken of above, which has shed its baleful influence over the entire mission. A large number of our preachers here, and a few at Maulmain and Tavoy, have risen above that influence, and we think will cheerfully rely on their churches for support, without feeling that they are undervalued by the mission because they receive no pay. But others here and at Maulmain seem to feel that unless they share in the mission patronage it is because they deserve nothing. They are constantly referring to the Burmese preachers who receive liberal and regular pay. They feel that they are not appreciated; that there is favoritism; that, while they are toiling in the jungles, obliged to trust to a handful of poor brethren for support, the Burman assistants in the city, a great company of them, with no churches and no responsibilities but to keep on good terms with the missionary, are enjoying liberal allowances and certain pay.

"We have been obliged to come out and declare that we do not approve of this system,...and that men are not to be valued according to the number of rupees they receive a month. For one, I am obliged from principle to continue to oppose the system of things at Maulmain, until a different system is adopted...Are the Executive Committee aware of the position of that church, with a missionary as pastor, some twelve or fourteen native preachers among its members on mission pay? Are they aware of the amount of money that church consumes each year? And what is the result? It numbered more than a hundred when I entered the mission thirteen years ago: it numbers about the same now. If the committee will take the trouble to compare the amount of money lavished on that church with the pittance expended on the forty churches [connected with Sandoway], they will see that my disapproval of the system is not so far wrong after all."

It is a tradition in Burma, that the great founder of the Burman mission was so deeply impressed with the falsity and the destructive nature of the Boodhist doctrine of merit, that, while he gave to good objects most liberally himself, he would rarely call upon the converts under his care for contributions for any object. He sought thus, it is said, to bring out in strongest contrast the Boodhist system with the Christian plan of salvation by free grace. Burman as well as Karen missionaries have since come to feel that this peculiarity in the early management of the mission resulted in a serious defect in the Burman work.[1] It is probably true, however, that the defect is due in a greater degree to the avarice which is natural to that interesting race, as well as to some others. Special pains and great patience are doubtless necessary to bring them up to the full measure of their duty in giving.

{ Footnote: [1] There is no doubt that Dr. Judson was well aware of the evils of so great a concentration of missionaries at Maulmain. Writing from that station to a private friend in the United States, Oct. 21, 1847, he says, "Brother Beecher is going round to Akyab to meet Brother Abbott, for the avowed purpose of opening his eyes to the beauties of Maulmain and the efficacy of 'concentration.' But this will be a failure, for Brother Abbott is almost the only missionary out who is not infected with the *Maulmania*. With him, indeed, it is *Maulmainphobia*, and I should not wonder if he succeeded in detaining the Beechers in Arakan. I sincerely hope he will, for they are really needed there much more than they are in this place." In justice to "the Beechers" we ought to add, that the writer of this letter was mistaken, probably, in supposing that they had any serious thought of leaving their appointed field for a station more attractive as a residence, but over supplied with missionaries. We have read Mr. Beecher's correspondence of that time carefully, and there is not a trace of wavering in purpose or desire. As soon as the arrival of his senior associate in Arakan was announced, he left Maulmain with his wife and household effects to join him. }

Another fallacy no less mischievous in tendency may here be noted. As ten or fifteen native preachers can be supported at the cost of one foreign missionary, it has seemed wise to many friends of missions to put as many of the native Christians as possible into the direct work of evangelization. By mapping out a town or district systematically, a few native brethren, when carefully superintended, will visit within a definite time every dwelling, and give to its inmates the oral offer of salvation, with tracts or Scripture portions. It has thus happened that many missions have employed a larger number of native preachers and other agents than the Christians of the country or district could possibly support; a larger number, too, than have given credible evidence of a divine call to distinctively religious work. In one of the Burman missions, e.g., nearly every male disciple, and several of the Christian wives and daughters, were for years under the pay of the mission as preachers, colportors,

Bible-women or school-teachers. To the poorer class of native Christians it is a decided rise in the social scale to escape from manual labor, to dress in a clean white jacket every day, and to be classed with writers and professional men. The rate of pay is not generally too high: the mistake is (with few exceptions) in employing them at all. By thus doing, the value of their testimony to the heathen around them is largely impaired; by taking so large a proportion of the membership from the supporting class in the church, and adding it to the class for whom support must be provided, it becomes impossible for the native church to maintain the establishment. Foreign money must do it; and the mission must be weighted, for an indefinite period, with all the baleful ills of the patronage system.

However plausible this plan may seem, especially in the beginning of a mission, when the converts are few and the missionary is eager to make as speedy and wide an impression as possible on the heathen masses, we look in vain to the New Testament for a precept or a precedent for this mode of evangelization. Great Britain and Germany were not thus converted to Christianity. Not thus were Christian churches and institutions planted and extended in North America. Individual missionaries there have been in every age sent forth by the home churches, and supported, to a greater or less extent, in heathen lands; but *in permanently successful missions, they have never subsidized their converts.* Not thus does the kingdom of God extend and establish itself in the earth. In successful missions the converts themselves quickly take up the burdens and responsibilities which the New Testament imposes upon them. There is a contagious life-principle in the gospel leaven, which causes it to work out in all directions, feeding upon and assimilating the inert masses with which it is brought in contact. If there is not life enough in an infant church to take root and grow in the fresh soil where it is planted, from resources right at hand; if there is not life and energy enough in it to become a tree, yielding shade and fruit for others, —the husbandman's labor is in vain: decay and death are inevitable. Unless the churches we plant in heathen lands speedily become a new base of supplies, and a new base of aggressive warfare, all the money in Christendom will not galvanize them into more than artificial life.

The urgent cry for pecuniary help which came from the Maulmain Karen mission in April, 1848 ("Missionary Magazine," 1848, pp. 451, 452), and the appeals for aid in the form of "Specific Donations" which are even now constantly made over the heads of the Executive Committee by Karen missionaries as well as others, are the direct result of this unscriptural system. To read the report of a mission composed of men like— —, and— —; to hear them talk seriously of resigning and abandoning their work to other denominations because they had received for their work, over and above their personal allowances and the generous help of English residents, only Rs. 4,446 (seven times as much as Abbott and Beecher had used in their more extensive and more difficult work), is a sufficient commentary on the enervating effects of the system they were under.

"The operations of the Karen mission have been so trammelled that the work has ceased to progress. It is no longer a matter of opinion. Many retrograde steps are already taken. Your mission as a whole is fast sinking; and the course now being pursued must inevitably ruin it, unless God in his sovereign pleasure does for it what we have no right to anticipate. We cannot consent to remain here to see it die."

No wonder Abbott felt impelled to visit them; no wonder his coming seemed, as one of them wrote, "almost as an angel strengthening us" (p. 117). A marked change is observable in a letter published soon after the lugubrious report and the visit. While there seems to have been no intermission in the payment of regular salaries to the pastors by the mission, Dr. Binney writes from Maulmain, Feb. 26, 1849:—

"These churches are, some of them, now able to support themselves, and ought to do so. Mr. Abbott has, I learn, commenced this work in Arakan. It ought to be done here; but, with my other work, I cannot commence what I know may demand much of my attention, at perhaps unexpected times. I have, therefore, endeavored to meet the case indirectly, leaving the work itself until more time and more favorable circumstances shall insure success. I have conversed freely with some of the assistants. They all think that something should be done. In conversation with the assistant in my school upon the subject [Rev. Pahpoo?], he thought the churches this year had better do what they could to aid our schools, and proposed himself to make an attempt. When I saw how he did it, I was most glad that it had been intrusted to him. Newville will give the schools this year over two hundred baskets of paddy, Kayin a hundred and ten baskets, Chetthingsville, a hundred baskets, and Ko Chetthing also a hundred baskets. This is in addition to their contributions for other objects, and is sufficient to show, that, with little or no aid, these churches can support their own pastors. They have given cheerfully."

Rev. J. H. Vinton at this time was in America. Fully convinced that the Karen work in his district was languishing for lack of money from abroad, instead of from an excess of foreign aid, he pleaded with the American churches for special help for the support of Karen preachers, and had obtained a special fund of five thousand dollars to be used for that object, over and above the ordinary appropriations of the society. A circular was addressed to each of the Karen missionaries by Secretary Peck, to know how much they needed, and how they would advise the money to be spent. We are able to give the replies of Abbott and Beecher only to this circular. It would be interesting to read the replies of others who then professed to have come to share in the new views, but they are not in our possession. The circular reached Sandoway Feb. 19, 1849; and Mr. Beecher replied under the same date.

"We hardly know what opinion to express respecting the manner of disposing of such a donation. Lest our opinion as a mission should conflict with that of a loved and worthy brother, or with that of any other station, we will express our views as individuals, to you as an individual, to be used as you may think best. I praise God for the increasing interest in the Karen mission,...but my joy would have been far greater if that five thousand dollars had been given for the establishment of a mission among the starving Kemees, who have so long been saying to us, 'Is there no man who cares for our souls?' If the entire sum must be appropriated to the one 'special purpose of aiding the preaching department of the Karen mission,' then my joy does not exceed my anxiety, —I may say, my sorrow."

After speaking of the dangerous and mischievous tendency of specific donations in general, he goes on to say, in the second place, —

"That amount above the ordinary appropriations is not now, and will not for many years be, needed for that particular object. To expend it all upon that object within three or four years would, I firmly believe, be attended with greater evils than would be experienced by calling home two-thirds of the Karen missionaries, leaving the native preachers to depend entirely upon their churches for support. As to Sandoway, we do not need any more this year than the estimate sent you some months since; and, whenever we may need more,...I prefer to trust to the willingness and efficiency of the Executive Committee to meet our wants, rather than to such special donations. If any of the money could be legitimately applied to schools, I would say, place Mrs. Binney's school, both as to buildings and teachers, above embarrassment...

"You may be surprised at some of these sentiments,...but, had you been with us in the Karen jungle this season, to see what we saw of the evil influence of *the hireling system* upon native preachers and churches, it would be sufficient to satisfy you of the correctness of our apprehensions respecting [specific] donations. Please excuse me from any responsibility as to the distribution of that five thousand dollars."

Mr. Abbott's reply to the circular is dated Feb. 26: —

..."We deem a reply demanded, and wish the following laid before the committee. By reference to my report for 1848, you will learn, that although our preachers have increased from thirty-six to forty-four during the year, although our schools have multiplied, and our operations enlarged, our expenditures decreased: so that of fifteen hundred rupees appropriated by you, we expended but six hundred rupees; and the statistics will show that the cause of truth has not suffered for want of money. Had we deemed it desirable, we should have expended all our appropriation. We hope and expect that this year our churches, preachers, and schools will be greatly multiplied;

but we do *not* expect that our expenditures will increase in proportion, for we believe that the system we have established will secure a support for the preachers, or nearly so, as was the case last year. As we do not expend all our appropriations, we require no extra donations.

"There is a representation from the Maulmain Karen mission in the Magazine received by last mail, to the effect, that, if Rs. 2,941 are not expended on their preachers,...many of them must be dismissed, and the most disastrous results will follow to the cause of Christ among that people. There must also have been a very strong representation of the case at home to secure that five thousand dollars to be expended in addition to the ordinary appropriations.

"Now, there is such a vast difference between the representations from these two stations, Maulmain and Sandoway,...that the question must arise, whence this discrepancy of views?...Does it arise from an inability on the part of the churches in Maulmain to support their pastors? I answer, No.[1] Those churches are able and willing to reduce the expenditure in this department one-half at least, so that the five thousand dollars might be appropriated to another purpose. Does it originate in the fact that jungle preachers in Maulmain cannot live as cheaply as in Bassein and Arakan, and, as a consequence, require more pay? I answer most unhesitatingly, No...How, then, can these most discordant representations be accounted for? Where shall we find the cause? *In the system established for the support of a native ministry in the Burman department of the Maulmain mission*...It has become to the native preachers the law of Christ's kingdom, the great principle that is to control their interests to all future time. It is vain to tell the Burman or Karen what our *theory* is on the subject; that it is but a temporary expedient to meet a present emergency, etc., so long as he has in the system itself a practical demonstration to the contrary, appealing not only to his selfishness, but to his sense of honor and justice...

{ Footnote: [1] It is to be remembered that Mr. Abbott had lived and travelled extensively in the Maulmain district, and knew whereof he affirmed. }

"A case that fell under my observation about twelve years ago in Maulmain is in point. One of the oldest Karen preachers, and one of the best, while receiving seven rupees per month, demanded of the missionary ten rupees, referring to the fact that the Burman preachers in the city were receiving fourteen and fifteen. He did not pretend that he could not live on his pay: that was not the question with him. If the Burman had fifteen, he ought to have ten. The missionary would not raise his pay; and the man left the mission service, and went to cutting down jungle to raise his own rice, when he could not realize from all his labor three rupees a month. Evidently it was not the love of money that drove him from the mission service, nor an insufficient support. It was a sense of injustice. He felt that there was gross partiality in the distribution of money, and that he was defrauded because he was a Karen. Like a true-spirited man, if he could not have what was right, he would have nothing...To show the Executive Committee that Mr. Binney agrees with me respecting the principle that should control us in this matter, I give an extract from a letter of his lately received. He says, —

"'Since you left, I have thought much of the course pursued by you with your assistants. It is the right course. Of this you have the best testimony, — their stability and progress during your absence. Do not alter it. When Vinton returns, I will do my best to pursue the same course here; and you know him well enough to know that he will be glad to find the thing possible. These men that work for pay are not the men upon whom the churches can rely. Explain to them the true state of the case. Show them how you consult, not their pleasure, or merely temporal good, but the good of their souls and of the cause, and then tell them what you have yourself done for them. Do not be afraid to say *I*, when your object is to do good. Paul has set us a good example on this point. You can tell them that the Maulmain teachers fully approve your course in this matter, and think it is one reason why God has so much blessed your people. We will try to follow on and support the cause by our example, as soon as we can get a little out of the fog.'"

Mr. Abbott continues:—

..."Will our system be permanent? But for the influence coming in upon us from Maulmain, it would...I am persuaded that the present state of things cannot continue. If the Maulmain brethren do not succeed in reducing the pay of their preachers, in many cases to nothing, and in all one-half, we shall have sad business here. Our preachers are not to be treated as slaves, and I shall not allow the beloved men under my charge to be degraded. An illustration:—on one side the river west of Rangoon is a preacher connected with Sandoway. He is pastor of a small church which cheerfully supports him. He receives not a *pice* from the mission. He is willing to labor, and suffer if need be, for the kingdom of heaven's sake, and would be satisfied with the support he receives, but for the fact that on the other side of the river, east of Rangoon, is a brother, pastor of a church better able and just as willing to support him, who receives eighty-four rupees a year from the mission. That is not an imaginary case, but a fact.

"To my mind there are but two alternatives,—they must expend *less* or we *more*. And as the extra five thousand dollars does not look like a falling-off in that quarter, the Executive Committee will not be surprised to receive an 'appeal' from Sandoway, demanding four thousand rupees a year to expend on our native preachers, to save the cause of Christ from ruin! We all know, and the committee should know, that it is absolutely essential that in the Karen department we act together. One principle only must reign throughout our entire mission. It is deemed advisable that I go to Maulmain for a few months, and I shall hope to visit Rangoon. I was acquainted with some of the preachers connected with Maulmain years ago. I have not forgotten them, and I trust they have not lost their regard for me. What can be effected, we know not: only this we know,—nothing good will be accomplished but by divine truth, under the blessing of Almighty God.

"Thinking you may like to know Mr. Ingalls's views on this subject, I send an extract from a letter received the day before yesterday. He says, 'The Burmans [in Akyab] have commenced a subscription for erecting a chapel, and some of them have put down fifty rupees. I shall soon commence one, without expense to the [Union]; and, with God's blessing, I will get the native preachers off their hands also. I most fully concur in all that you have written on this subject [the support of a native ministry], and will do all I can. But you must remember that I am still alone, and shall be, virtually, for some time to come...Such little men as you and I are, cannot, unless God shall sanction our views, contend with those whose years and standing are so different.'"

A copy of this letter was sent to Mr. Vinton by the same mail which took the original to Boston. Mason took some exceptions to Abbott's positions, which called forth a spicy, but friendly, rejoinder on the 1st of November, from which we make a few extracts: —

"Why not reform? What is the great difficulty in the way? One truth is clear, both from my reply and from your letter to me, that the difficulty does not lie in the Karen department itself. You find it in the weakness of — —'s faith. I find it in the influence of the Burmese department...You uphold the same system in Tavoy that they do in Maulmain. All your assistants rely on the mission treasury for support; and it is, of course, adequate and certain. Why should they complain? But your 'assistants in the jungle on four rupees a month never cry "injustice" when those in town receive ten.' Quite probable. If those assistants have imbibed the principles of their teacher, that the great truth, 'all men are created equal,' is 'an Americanism' and 'nonsense,' and if they feel the 'inferiority' which is attributed to them, they would make no complaint, of course, so long as they can get enough to eat. I might have had just such quiet times among the assistants and pastors west of Rangoon...If I had given them all regularly seven rupees, that is, if I had scattered thirty-four hundred rupees a year among them, I never should have heard it re-iterated in my ears, 'Why do you not give us as much as they do in Maulmain?' 'Can *you* not get as much money as they do in Maulmain?' 'We cannot live on less than they do in Maulmain,' etc. They would all have been as quiet as lambs, and I might have mistaken them for lambs.

"But supposing we all pursue this regular pay system: let us see whither it would bring us. To make a rough, but moderate, calculation, we have at—

Sandoway, say, 45 assistants, at "3,400" ", Burman say 20 assistants, at "3,300" Tavoy and Mergui, say, 40 assistants, at "2,400"

We have, then, a total of a hundred and forty-five men in the employ of the mission, at an expense of twelve thousand eight hundred rupees a year, a troop of mercenaries, all *natives*, bear in mind, over whom the rupee exerts a most bewitching, polluting, *hirelingizing* influence. Where shall we stop? We had better find out how far the Executive Committee will supply the rupees; for there we *must* stop, as the great power which has sustained the whole will have failed...

FACSIMILE OF MR. ABBOTT'S HANDWRITING, SANDOWAY,
NOV. 1, 1849

"Had you heard the discussions that I have had with our preachers on the subject of 'pay,' during these two years past, you would have gained a few ideas as to the working of the regular pay system of which you never dreamed. I suppose Karens here are about the same as Karens at Tavoy and Maulmain. My remarks do not apply to the majority of those here, I am happy to say, but to those who have been in the habit of receiving regular pay from the mission; so that I have the means of knowing what kind of a spirit that system is adapted to beget. I have endeavored to substitute the churches for the mission treasury; and it has cost me more anguish of spirit, and more hours of controversy and pleading, than all the other troubles arising from our forty pastors and five thousand converts, put together...I suspect that I have not much sympathy in this business; but, when my brethren shall attempt to bind their assistants to the cause of Christ, to poverty and self-denial, by the *truth*, by cords of *love* and not of gold, they will then learn that I am deserving of it...

"One thing is clear to my mind...Karen churches will feel no obligation to support their pastors, and will not do it cordially, so long as those pastors have access to the mission treasury. They will not labor and give their money to men who are supported by 'state patronage.' All that you and I can say or do will not alter the case, so long as they know we are giving their pastors money. True, some churches might give their pastors more than others, but that fact would not produce the evil you imagine. I need not stop to set you right,—I *know* it would not.

"You state, as one objection to my order of things, that there would be no provision for *itinerants*,—for men who have no churches. I will not attempt to annihilate that objection now, as it would compel me to take too wide a sweep, and to say things which I do not wish to be heard west of the Atlantic Ocean. *Pgah deene t'k'lu meh pgah t'goh tah naut'mee bah* [that sort of men are of no use at all].

"I am awaiting Brother Vinton's return with much anxiety. We shall hear from him what difficulties he has to meet in inducing his pastors to rely on the churches for support, and in inducing the churches to support their pastors. He will find the first much more difficult than the last, I can tell him...You say, if there is 'odium' attaching to the Maulmain system, it is 'common to every mission in India.' Certainly, and it is undoubtedly producing the same evils in every mission in India...What you say respecting Maulmain not being a proper place for the theological school under Mr. Binney is all too true. We have already seen the evils here to which you refer. That we are to *continue* to send young men to study [there] a few years, and then have them come back to us, filled with the idea that they are going to walk up to the mission treasury and coolly demand eighty-four rupees per annum, is not to be thought of for a moment. But what is to be done? That subject is going to cause us trouble. We have met the difficulty and must overcome it. But *how?*

"You give me credit for writing what I 'dispassionately believe.' Certainly: I give you credit for the same, and trust I shall be able to reciprocate the magnanimity and candor which you and Brother Stevens have exhibited. Should it be supposed that I have failed in this respect, I need not tell you it would cause me deep regret. The subject will agitate us more and more for a long time. It is one in which every member of our mission, Burman or Karen, is equally interested. My only object in writing the Executive Committee has been, that the whole subject may be brought distinctly before them; for, sooner or later, they will be called upon to act.

"Yours affectionately, "E. L. ABBOTT."

Nov. 17, 1849, he writes to Mr. Bright, the assistant secretary, —

"What shall I do? Go on writing, or demand four thousand rupees a year and spend it on 'assistants,' as others do, and then go on, and on, and still on; or shall I attempt to complete my *reform*, and try to induce others to do so? I am not willing to sit down quietly and see thousands on thousands expended for that object at other stations, when hundreds only are demanded here. We must have but one system for all our missions: they must come to hundreds, or we must go to thousands."

What was done with the fund of five thousand dollars, we have never heard. Doubtless a way to spend it was easily found; and doubtless a way will be found to expend the fund of thirty thousand dollars, or thereabouts, recently bequeathed to the A. B. M. Union for a like object. But if the position taken by Abbott and Beecher more than thirty years ago is correct, as we believe it to be, the spending of those funds in the manner designated by the Christian-hearted donors was, and will be, worse than waste.

The entrance into the way of self-support is always hard, and becomes more difficult with each year's overgrowth of weeds and briers. The movement will never come about of itself. Secretaries and executive committees have a duty to perform. In the "Missionary Magazine" for May, 1843, p. 112, the editor (secretary?) of that time says, —

"If other missions are more expensive, or less successful, it is not the fault of the missionaries; and if the Karen mission is cheaper or more successful than others, no credit is to be here attributed to the Karen missionaries above their brethren. *It is to be wholly attributed to peculiarly favorable providential circumstances.*"

From these remarks we dissent, of course, entirely, so far as they relate to economy in the management of the missions in question. Almost every thing, under God, depends upon the correctness of the missionary's views, and upon his ability to bring the native Christians to his way of thinking. Such an utterance from mission head-quarters, and the absence of an outspoken, consistent adherence to the policy of self-support, paralyze the arm of the man who believes in reform, unless he has the power and bravery of an Abbott. Insufficient discrimination, and excess in appropriations, and, above all, specific donations (not for the support of missionaries) from benevolent churches, Sunday schools, and individuals, increase the confusion, the waste, and the moral declension, which are to-day increasing in some of the fields of the A. B. M. Union.[1]

{ Footnote: [1] This remark, of course, is to be taken only as the author's opinion. He is not alone, however, in that opinion. A missionary correspondent writes from the field under date of April 24, 1882, as follows: "Our mission work needs to be enlarged, but not in the direction of more American money for so-called 'station-work.' Too much is expended in that manner now. In some quarters there is a tendency to pauperization. Each succeeding year too many missions want an increase of appropriations; and, strange to say, additional converts are made the ground for fresh appeals for more money."

Secretary Murdock uses the following language in his paper on "Apostolic Missions" (Magazine, July, 1883, p. 180): —

"There may be such a thing as nursing churches into chronic infancy and inertness, instead of exercising them into vigorous power and efficiency, by leaving them, under God, to their own resources...Possibly it would have been better for the cause of Christianity among the heathen, if this wise abstinence in pecuniary help to native churches and evangelists had been more closely imitated in our modern missions...It might have been better if [the missionary] had more carefully guarded the converts from the taint and the impediment of mercenary motives, by withholding pecuniary aid, except in cases of special need arising from providential distress or from considerations of public utility."

This subject will be discussed at greater length in the concluding chapter of this volume, to which the reader is respectfully referred. }

To the missionary brethren and sisters who still follow the old ways, and, in the language of a secretary of long experience, "estimate the possibilities of their success according to the amount of money they get from home, instead of trusting to the energies of the Spirit," only kind feeling and personal confidence are due. But can their plans, in so far as they are neglecting the resources around them, and relying on America for the support of their preachers and primary schools, be hopeful of permanent good? A native ministry which cannot so commend itself to fellow-countrymen and to resident English Christians as to secure a living is of little worth; and Christians who cannot be aroused to second the efforts of their missionaries and an enlightened government for the education of their own offspring are unworthy of the name. "American support for Americans, Karen support for Karens," with a modicum of foreign aid for advanced education, is as safe a rule for foreign missions in general as it has proved to be in the mission founded by E. L. Abbott.

CHAPTER VIII.

1850.

"The kingdom of heaven is compared, not to any great kernel or nut, but to a grain of mustard-seed, which is one of the least grains, but hath in it a property and spirit hastily to get up and spread."—LORD BACON.

Much for the time was doubtless accomplished by the discussions related in the last chapter, especially in the Karen missions; but the tendency to relapse is powerful in human nature, and reform must follow reform in endless succession. Thoughtful men may recognize the danger involved in church funds, and in the support of religion by the state, but how many churches in free America even were ever known to decline a legacy, the interest of which would be applied to meet their current expenses? It is remarkable that one of the younger members of the mission should have been permitted to become the leader in a reform of such vital importance and difficulty. The circumstances in which Mr. Abbott was providentially placed did much, doubtless, to make him the man he was; but rarely has any one done more than he to fashion the circumstances around him into conformity with the pattern which the Lord had showed him. Nor this alone in the matter of self-support.

The Burman pastor, Ko Thah-ay, had been ordained by Dr Judson and Wade in 1829, under peculiar circumstances. In the absence of the missionaries he had been persuaded by converts in Burma Proper to administer to them the ordinance of baptism. As he was a worthy and intelligent Christian, of mature character, it was thought best, after the fact, to give to him the rights which he had assumed irregularly. This seems, however, not to have been considered a precedent, either by the missionaries on the field, or the committee in Boston. At any rate, more than fourteen years had elapsed without the ordination of a second native in Burma.

In 1843 Mr. Abbott felt compelled by his own views of duty to ordain Myat Kyau and Tway Po, notwithstanding opposition on the field, and with the doubtful approval of the executive officers after the event (see chap. iv). The experiment succeeded so well, however, that other ordinations speedily followed. The fourth man, Kolapau, was ordained by the Tavoy missionaries at Matah, in 1846. Soon after, four young men were ordained by Messrs. Vinton and Binney, just after their graduation from the Seminary. Of this extreme step, the secretary who wrote so anxiously in 1843 now speaks as follows:—

"One of the most gratifying and auspicious incidents in the history of the Maulmain Karen mission the past year was the ordination in February, 1847, of four Karen preachers, graduates of the seminary— Prahhai, Kyapah, Aupau, and Tah-oo. 'Their examination was thorough, and well sustained for upwards of five hours. It was conducted in Karen, but interpreted sufficiently for others to know fully the merits of the case. Questions were freely proposed by the different members of the council, some of the most difficult ones being proposed by Karen assistants.'" ("Missionary Magazine," July, 1848, p. 260.)

We venture to call the ordination of these young men "an extreme step;" for, whatever may be true of Americans, a Karen, a Burman, or a Telugu fresh from school cannot be regarded as a "tried" man: and the event justifies this judgment. The annual report for 1851 (p. 270) speaks of Kyapah as "fallen;" Aupau, or Oung Bau, soon became deeply involved in secular business; while a third, Prahhai, was later under a cloud for years. Tah-oo, older than the other three, held out well, and did a good work. For the last twenty years, at least, the writer has not known such an experiment to be repeated by any missionary in Burma. The ninth man, the celebrated Sau Quala, was ordained April 28, 1847; the tenth, Ko Panlah of Maulmain, in February, 1848; and the eleventh, a Burman, Moung Pyoo, in Akyab in January, 1850. This year the missionaries at Sandoway were prepared to ordain four more, worthy and long tried men; but they were providentially hindered from doing so until near its close, as reported in the next chapter.

The Bassein churches are nearly ripe also for the formation of the first purely native missionary society of a general character in Burma. Mr. Abbott's published views on this all-important subject, and his well directed, vigorous action, stamp him again as emphatically the leader in the Karen Israel of that day.

We resume the narrative. Owing to the addition of the Van Meters to the Sandoway mission, Mr. Beecher built an additional dwelling-house the latter part of 1849, with "eleven glazed windows and two glazed doors, the remaining doors being panelled," at a cost not exceeding five hundred and fifty dollars. In Mr. Van Meter's first published letter from Sandoway, we find the following:—

"There are at least three hundred Pwo disciples already gathered in connection with this station, Shway Bo's congregation [church?] alone numbering one hundred. With such a beginning we surely cannot be discouraged as to the future, especially when we consider the limited means through which it has been effected.

"The present is a critical moment for this people. They have been so long asking for a teacher, and their cry has been so long disregarded, that they have begun to turn in another direction. A number of them have received a flattering reception from the Catholic priests at Bassein, who have been endeavoring of late to seduce the assistants and other Christians. Brother Abbott learned, only a short time since, of an attempt to seduce the Sgau assistants, by distributing money among them after he left for America. Quite a number of them received very unexpectedly a gift of five rupees each. But at present there is little apprehension as to their influence upon the disciples...There is nothing more trying to us just now than the fact that we cannot converse with these disciples, who, for the first time, have seen a teacher whom they could call their own...I hope that I may acquire sufficient knowledge to be able to converse with tolerable accuracy and freedom during my visit to the jungle next cold season. The Sgau school is in a very interesting state, there being upwards of seventy pupils. Both the ordained preachers and a number of the other assistants are receiving instruction from Brothers Abbott and Beecher in theological studies."

Dr. Binney reports this year, that ten of his twenty-seven pupils are from Mr. Abbott's distant field, and only two from Maulmain itself. Mr. Abbott left his station about the first of December, 1849, to meet the native preachers for a term of study in Ong Khyoung. Mr. Beecher, owing to the serious illness of his wife, did not follow until some weeks later. On the 11th of February he writes of Mr. Abbott's bad health and of his own labors: —

"On arriving at Ong Khyoung, Jan. 19, I found Brother Abbott, though convalescent, still suffering severely from a cough, and well-nigh worn out from the excessive labors of the season. Brother Van Meter was also there, having just returned from a visit to the Pwo villages farther down the coast. It was thought best, after a few hours consultation, that I should remain and aid Brother Abbott in instructing the native preachers, instead of proceeding to visit the churches as I had expected. The great majority of the churches in Burma have never been visited by a missionary, but, so far as we can learn, are quite as prosperous as those on the coast, which have enjoyed annual visits.

"The two weeks spent with Brother Abbott and the preachers were to me very pleasant and profitable. Such seasons as these afford the best opportunity for acquiring the language, so as to be able to use it with effect; for the discussions which naturally arise in a course of familiar lectures disclose Karen habits and modes of thought, without a knowledge of which it is impossible to interpret the language and doctrines of Scripture in a clear and forcible manner. The preachers have enjoyed a better opportunity for becoming acquainted with the doctrines of the gospel this season than ever before, and we have reason to believe that great good will result from Brother Abbott's well-directed and faithful labors with these chosen men."

After referring to the delay in the ordination of the well-approved, but self-distrustful candidates, he continues: —

"Immediately after this the preachers were dismissed, and I started for a short visit to the churches on the Baumee River. Nearly one hundred disciples from Burma were awaiting my arrival at Kyoukadin. They said, on taking my hand, that many of them had worshipped God six or eight years, but had never before seen a white teacher. The greater portion of them were females, who had travelled two or three days over the rugged Yoma Mountains, to see those who seem to be the objects of their highest earthly interest. They were disappointed in not meeting Brother Abbott, and had many inquiries to make respecting him. They often spoke of the interest they felt in us, of remembering us in every prayer, and especially of praying for the *mama*, after they heard of her illness: their desire to see her was 'greater than we can express.' Some of those who came from [Bassein] appear to be much more devoted than any I have seen elsewhere. Some of them have a singular form of Christian salutation. They take their teacher's hand, and, before speaking to him, spend a few moments in silent prayer, then warmly and repeatedly press his hand, and, when this is done, inquire after his health and answer his questions.

"This company, together with those from the vicinity, formed an attractive audience. It was easy and delightful to preach to them. There were seventeen candidates for baptism from Burma, and one from this side. After being formally received by their respective churches, we assembled on the river-bank, near by, to witness the profession of their faith...As each rose from the baptismal grave, praises were sung to Him who 'died for our sins,' and 'was raised again for our justification.' The commemoration of the Lord's death in the afternoon was also solemn and interesting. In the evening, bade the dear disciples farewell, each saying, as I gave the parting hand, 'Pray for us, O teacher!'"

On the 17th of February Mr. Abbott wrote a word as to his own health:—

"The doctor hardly knows what to do with my cough, fever, night-sweats, etc., but thinks they may be symptomatic of a sub-acute inflammation of lungs, etc. I have shut myself up, and am going to keep quiet a long time."

He writes again on the 18th:—

"I have had no fever for thirty-six hours, and trust I am improving. I suppose Sandoway is as good a place as I could be in for the improvement of health, excepting upon the sea; but I have no idea of taking a voyage at present."

It was not until the 12th of March that he rallied so as to send to the secretary an account of his work at Ong Khyoung this season. He writes with an apology for not rewriting and correcting his weighty communication:—

"You have learned, by a previous letter, that I spent the cold season with the preachers at Ong Khyoung. We have concluded not to attempt to get them together at Sandoway during the rains. I think this course carries out the spirit of the committee's instructions in regard to boarding-schools for preachers in a more satisfactory manner than a strict adherence to the letter would have done. The distance is so great, and the time of travelling falling within the hot and the rainy seasons, but few of them could be longer induced to come to Sandoway at all. I therefore made the arrangement with them that they all meet at Ong Khyoung in November, with the expectation of remaining three months. Every preacher connected with our mission was there, with one exception, and he was detained by illness.

"I deem it absolutely essential that I see all these men *together* once in the year. Even were I permitted to visit Burma, and go from church to church through the whole land, I should still deem it essential to have an annual association of pastors and churches, and to have them all together for several weeks, perhaps months. They require a more thorough knowledge of the Scriptures. They cannot go away to Maulmain and pursue a course of study that would require years. They have no libraries at their homes to aid them in the study of the Bible. They have no means in the jungle of acquiring knowledge, excepting what we give them; and, indeed, there is not a book adapted to aid them in understanding the New Testament. How can they 'understand' except some man should 'guide' them? What they hear one year, they forget before the next comes round, so that they require line upon line, and will for years to come. While at Ong Khyoung, I took them thoroughly through Hebrews and Romans, and also through some small primary works in theology.

"Again: all these men are laborers in the field,—with but few exceptions, pastors of churches. They not only have their own personal doubts and troubles, but, in many cases, difficulties with their churches in matters of doctrine and discipline. Pastors and churches may get into a quarrel here as well as in America. Divisions also have appeared between different pastors, and certain hard questions have agitated the whole community. They all come up to the missionary, each with his head filled with his own troubles or wrongs or difficulties, which he cannot surmount. All these matters must be settled, and these discordant elements brought into harmony, by the personal teachings of the missionary. All this requires time, patience, and power. I know not what others may do; but I cannot establish order and union, and control the whole, unless I have all the pastors in my presence.

"An important subject, and one that agitated us more than any other, related to the support of native preachers. In 1848 I sent circulars to all the churches, referring particularly to this subject, and requested them to send in statements to the association this year. Consequently the preachers brought each his epistle. I will translate one as a specimen of the whole. They differed only in immaterial points, and in the amount given to the pastors.

"'The year of Christ, 1849. The elders of the church at Great Rock, to Teacher Abbott: May the blessing of our Father God be upon you. Amen. We received your letter, and are very happy. The Lord Jesus Christ died for us, and we ought to do something to enlarge his kingdom. We gave our teacher, Shway Bo, during the year, twelve rupees, eight annas; sixty baskets of paddy; one hundred viss of dried fish (365 pounds); fifty viss of salt; a bundle of tobacco, etc. We are very poor, O teacher! (too true), and can do but little. Pray for us, that we may be blessed.'

165

"The letters indicate that the churches are beginning to perform this work in the right way. All were read to the association, and each pastor or teacher aided as his case might require. The churches did nobly last year; and, in my circular letter, I did not fail to tell them so. Eight pastors are supported entirely by their churches. They *voluntarily* renounced all aid from the mission,—noble-spirited men! The sacrifice they have thus made affords the most satisfactory evidence of the genuineness of their Christian spirit that I have ever seen exhibited in this mission. Besides these, there are thirty-seven, including five itinerants, aided by the mission. The whole amount expended during the year was about seven hundred rupees, an average of less than twenty rupees to each individual. The committee will not suspect that that money was expended on hirelings. These churches are *very poor*. Their taxes are heavy in this province; but in Burma Proper they are ground down to the dust, under the iron heel of despotism. We shall still require more or less aid from the committee,—that aid which has hitherto been so promptly bestowed.

"Evangelization also claimed a good deal of attention. It is a subject for these pastors and churches (as well as the missionary) to consider by what means the Karens now in darkness are to be evangelized. Whatever measures may be proposed by others, it is my firm belief that the Karen people are to be converted through the instrumentality of a Karen ministry,—of course under the instructions and guidance of the missionary. So it has been from the first, history being witness. At Maulmain and Tavoy, at Rangoon and Bassein, natives have done the work of preaching the gospel to their countrymen; the work of the missionary being to baptize converts, organize churches, and instruct and control the native ministry. Not half the converts have ever seen a missionary; and, if we cannot go into Burma, they never will.

"But how is such a ministry to be secured? Let us look at a few facts, and we shall be better able to answer the question. We have, in Bassein and Sandoway, forty-five native preachers; in Maulmain and Rangoon, I suppose forty; and in Tavoy and Mergui, twenty more,— upwards of a hundred already in the field. There are also a large

166

number in Mr. Binney's school; and a good many young men, who are now only school-teachers, will doubtless become preachers. Here we have an agency on which, it seems to me, we may rely. Consider also, that a large majority of these ministers—I do not like to hear them called 'assistants,' or 'native helpers:' they are ministers of the gospel, ambassadors of Christ, or nothing; at any rate, I like to feel that they are such, while preaching to them—these ministers are pastors of churches.

"Now, these churches should not only be self-supporting (if possible), but reproductive. They should be taught that the responsibility of raising up and sending forth evangelists to their fellow-countrymen rests upon them, and shown, that, what individuals cannot do, a combination may. I endeavored to make the pastors at Ong Khyoung understand that they, as a body, were deeply responsible in this matter; that they are to recognize and send out the heralds of mercy; and that they are responsible for their support. Evangelists of course are to feel that they are acknowledged by, and responsible to, that body, and not alone to the missionary. There is as yet no mechanical organization: the thing is in its infancy, the idea but just planted.

"Allowing, then, that we have the nucleus of an instrumentality by which the Karen nation is to be evangelized, the question arises, the most important of all, how is that instrumentality to be multiplied and rendered efficient? I am fully of the opinion, that it is *not* to be done by multiplying stations and large and expensive mission establishments; much less by a profuse expenditure of money on the natives. I think it is high time that the natives of this country, preachers as well as others, should begin to learn that mission money costs something,—that it is absolutely of some value, and that every missionary has not an exhaustless patronage, which he is at liberty to bestow at will upon men who may gather around his standard. The first successful preachers among the Karens—Ko Thahbyu and his co-adjutors in Maulmain, Rangoon, and Tavoy; and Shway Weing, Bleh Po and their associates in Bassein—were not men secured and held to their work by rupees. They went forth prompted by their own convictions and zeal, living as the fowls of heaven live, on the goodness of the Lord; and multitudes, through the divine blessing on their labors, became obedient to the faith. The men on whom I now rely for publishing the gospel abroad are not those who are tenacious for pay. 'Assistants' may be multiplied by money, but then you are not quite sure that you have added to the strength and efficiency of that agency which is to convert the people to God.

"The means by which an efficient ministry is to be secured are so simple that they need only to be stated,—the preaching of the missionary, attended by the power of the Holy Spirit sent down from on high. We have already all the human elements of final success; and may God Almighty speedily give us—missionaries, native preachers, churches, and all—the divine endowment! As a general principle, we cannot expect that a native ministry will be inspired with an enlightened zeal, except in proportion to their knowledge. If they are sanctified for the accomplishment of the great and glorious work proposed, they will be sanctified through the truth. That truth is to be preached to them by the missionary; and, admitting that the present stations are well sustained, and their operations efficiently conducted, under the influence of the spirit of God, not many years will have elapsed before every Karen will have heard of the great salvation.

"The present number of churches is forty. There are also a great number of Christian congregations which meet for worship regularly, and, in many cases, have a number of baptized Christians; but these are not included with the churches, as they have not regularly appointed teachers. The number baptized last year was two hundred and forty-four. Eight were excluded, and twenty died; which leaves a net gain of two hundred and sixteen for the year. There are many candidates for baptism, not only in the new regions, as stated last year, but connected with all the congregations in Burma. The conversions reported at the association indicate the continued triumphs of the truth; and, in many cases, they are of an unusually interesting character. Many of the old chiefs, patriarchs, or heads of families, call them what we may, who have hitherto resisted all the influences of the gospel, and clung to their old superstitions and sins, remaining either in a state of sullen resistance, or of deadly hostility, while their families and kindred have become Christians, have, within the year, bowed to the omnipotence of truth, and are waiting to be baptized. Many more would have been added to the churches, had there been ordained pastors to administer the ordinance.

"To supply this want, we had intended to ordain at least four of the preachers at Ong Khyoung. But Brother Beecher was detained at home till near the close of the session, and Brother Van Meter left when he arrived. It was desirable to have both present. Moreover, one of the candidates was taken alarmingly ill. Still the preachers, after a day of special prayer, selected two for ordination, having been taught that the entire responsibility rested upon them. These two did not object at first; but, as the time approached, they began to reveal their misgivings. Their earnestness in prayer and then mental struggles were intense; and they persisted in wishing to be allowed to wait another year, fearing to take upon themselves the responsibilities that ordination would impose. Action was finally postponed. I should like to live another year to see them ordained.

"The number of pupils in our village schools has not increased according to our wishes. The returns are not complete, but the whole number will be less than that of last year. Two difficulties have been met which we trust will not prove insurmountable. We lack a sufficient number of qualified teachers. To supply this need is one main object of our boarding-school, and should be of all boarding-schools in the Karen mission. No child should be brought into these schools to be taught what he can learn in his own village. Another difficulty arises from the poverty of the people. If they do all they can to support their pastors, they are not able in many cases to support schools. School-teachers must live as well as others. Still, I trust we shall be able somehow to supply this want. The Karens will learn to read in someway; but the influence of a good school upon the children of a village can only be appreciated by those who have witnessed its results through a series of years. We ought to have two thousand children taught in such schools three months each year, and we shall not feel satisfied till we can report that number.

"Hitherto, in our operations here, but little has been done systematically in sabbath schools. In fact, the native preachers did not see clearly how the thing was to be done. Fortunately, at Ong Khyoung there is a large church and congregation; and, the preachers being all present, I endeavored to enforce precept by example, and *show* them how it is to be done. We cannot expect that these schools will now be conducted on the plan of expounding Scripture. The Karens are not yet competent for that. Catechisms suited to their state of knowledge will be the only method for years to come. We have two of these adapted to the object, —Mrs. Wade's, which is historical; and mine, which is doctrinal. There are some other works, small, and good as far as they go. We hope the day will come when all Karen Christian congregations will learn their lessons from these and similar books during the week, and, on the sabbath, repeat their lessons to teachers competent to expound and enforce the great truths they contain. I rely on this kind of teaching as one of the most efficient instrumentalities for imparting Christian truth to the people."

In a postscript he says to the secretary: —

"I should like to give my reasons in full why I think that to multiply 'stations' will not probably augment the efficiency of the native ministry, or conduce materially to the extension of the gospel.[1] I am afraid that my thoughts about mission establishments in general will have to come out if I live...I do not care to listen to the advice of friends who are urging me to go home. I may perhaps go to Maulmain...I can only rely on the rich grace that abounds to sinners through Christ our Lord, and calmly await the decrees of Heaven."

{ Footnote: [1] So far as we can learn, Mr. Abbott was not permitted to set forth the reasons for these views; but the fact that these were his matured views should have due weight with all who are called to direct in mission affairs. }

During this travelling season, Mr. Van Meter visited five of the ten heathen Pwo villages on the coast of southern Arakan. In his account of the tour he gives a sketch of two valued Pwo assistants: —

"Thahbwah, our first Pwo teacher, has been preaching, since he left us, with much acceptance. He seems to be universally esteemed in the jungle for his amiable disposition, and his services have been sought for in more than one direction. He now leaves his own village, where there are but few Pwos, and enters upon a new field of much promise near Bassein. Thung Choke, the fourth assistant, the eldest of the four, and probably as intelligent and useful as either of his more favored associates, has been preaching and teaching for five years, at the same time assisting himself in part by manual labor, and in part by the practice of medicine, occasionally receiving a little help from his people. When asked by Brother Abbott if he now wished any aid from us, he replied, that, if it was desirable for him to give himself wholly to the work, he would require a little. The sum named, thirty rupees, was cheerfully given him. His whole library in Pwo consists of a copy of Matthew and a few tracts. I could give him only a soiled catechism picked up from the rubbish at Sandoway. He understands Sgau, however, and has the Sgau Testament. He has a congregation of over one hundred, not more than half of whom are professed believers. Tau Lau has ninety in his village: whether all baptized or not, I am unable to say."

On the 11th of May, at the request of the Executive Committee, the brethren in Sandoway organized themselves into a distinct mission by the choice of Mr. Abbott, chairman; Mr. Beecher, secretary; Mr. Van Meter, treasurer. We suppose that the only change in the working of the mission after this arrangement was in the matter of book-keeping. May 20 Mr. Beecher reports that Myat Kyau had baptized a hundred and sixty-five converts in Bassein during a recent tour. Tway Po, a month later, had baptized a hundred and forty-five in the same district, making three hundred and ten in all.

The boarding-school was dismissed at the close of September. Owing, in part, to the extensive prevalence of cholera in the Christian villages during the hot season, the average number of pupils for the term of five months had been only twenty. After the daily Bible lesson in the Gospels, Galatians, or Ephesians, arithmetic was the principal study. Mrs. Beecher's class of lads in English was sent over at the close of this term to join Mrs. Binney's school in

Maulmain. On the last Sunday the communion was celebrated; and a Burman disciple, Shway Eing, whose religious history is briefly sketched by Mr. Abbott in the next chapter, was received by baptism.

Nov. 20 Mr. Abbott, in replying to a letter from Secretary Bright, further unfolds his views on important questions of mission policy:—

"Our *theories* will not evangelize the Karens. Our machinery may, or may not, be the means by which it is to be done. We may theorize, and one say, 'Only give us lots of money to hire a host of preachers, and the Karens are evangelized:' or, 'Let us pursue this or that course, and the Karens are evangelized.' I think, however, there is common ground where we can all stand. That missionaries are going into every small village, or city even, of Burma or China, is not to be thought of for a moment...Heathen countries must be evangelized through a native ministry. That ministry must be educated *by foreign aid*. Give to them and their country the Bible and theology, education to teachers and ministers, books, etc., and a general guidance such as Paul gave to the churches he had planted. Of course missionaries are to plant churches in great cities, as Paul did. But these ministers, when educated, must not become the hired men of the missionary. After we have given to the country or people an educated ministry, teachers, the Bible, and a literature, *the rest must be self-sustaining*. Karens must sustain Karens, is a sentiment I have re-iterated to our native preachers here. Churches must sustain themselves, *must begin, must learn, and believe and feel that that is the law of Christ's kingdom*. This missionaries must teach if we would have the native ministry and people believe it and begin to act upon the principle.

"As to securing a native ministry, we are getting on admirably,— thanks be to God for ever and ever!...We have men enough to preach the gospel to every Karen hamlet in a very few years.[1] We want— *we want now*—the Holy Spirit, power from on high to effect the evangelization of the Karens, more than we want men or money or theories. So I believe, and so I teach."

{ Footnote: [1] I believe that this has been done over and over again in all the Sgau villages that remain heathen in the Bassein district.— ED. }

Mr. Abbott's tender regard for his friends appears in this, as in so many of his letters. This time it is, "How are they at Haverhill? and why does not Train write me?" In the next it is, "Kind regards to the executive officers at the Rooms, not forgetting Brother Shaw."

Again in December he writes,—

"Common schools form one of the most important departments of labor and usefulness to which our minds can be directed. What would the United States be, with all her other institutions of religion and learning, were it not for 'common schools'? And what will the Karen people be without them? I am not sure but we shall deem it a duty to ask for an appropriation for them. We shall not hesitate to do so, if we think money can be expended in that way without doing more hurt than good."

Again, we quote for the benefit of sickly persons, who desire to go out as missionaries:—

"If——is really 'a consumptive case,' he will find this a bad place for him. He might live longer here than in a cold climate, and *he might not*. This is a bad climate for feeble lungs. Such cases ought never to come on a mission.——was one,—well to-day, and a cough to-morrow; no heart or strength to engage in that hard labor which anticipates its results for years to come; away on a trip for health, and better; a brief time of study; then a cough again, discouragement, and all given up. It requires good health and all one's energy to prepare for labor in the mission field."

It is unnecessary to say, probably, that the disease which was now so soon to end Mr. Abbott's valuable life and labors was not brought with him to Burma. It was, without doubt, the direct result of years of exposure, overwork, anxiety, and grief.

CHAPTER IX.

1851.

"We who are to be the spiritual conquerors of the world should send, not our mediocre men, but *our very best,* —those who, not only in faith and self-denial, in courage and meekness, but also in linguistic attainments, in capacity for organization, in many-sided, practical resource, far surpass the clergy at home." —DR. CHRISTLIEB.

The annual associations of the native churches in Burma have a retrospective as well as a prospective character. The results of the previous year's labor are reported and tabulated, while plans are formed, and funds provided for the work of the year to come. As the Burmese lunar month is followed in the appointments from year to year, to secure as much of the moonlight and nocturnal coolness as possible, both for the meetings and the long journey to and fro, the time varies, generally falling within the limits of the new year, but sometimes, as on this occasion, at the close of the old. As this is the last general meeting which the beloved Abbott will ever hold with his beloved Karens on earth, the good man's report of the meeting, and the thoughts suggested to him by the proceedings, will be read with peculiar interest, notwithstanding the length.

"*Sandoway, January, 1851.* I have just returned from the annual meeting, held at Ong Khyoung from the 12th to the 16th of December. Most of the preachers were present, and a good number of the elders, but not so many of the latter as we hope to see in future years. Written reports were read from nearly all the churches: the exceptions were Pantanau and the churches east of that place. The letters in general indicate a degree of stability and prosperity highly satisfactory. The statistics for the year 1850 are as follows: Forty-four churches, forty-eight native preachers, five hundred and twenty-nine baptized, fourteen excluded, and a hundred and fifty-one deceased. These forty-four churches include the eight in Arakan, but are exclusive of many little clusters of Christians in various places not organized as churches. They all have worship regularly on the sabbath, have succeeded to some extent in establishing sabbath schools: all aid more or less in supporting their own preachers. The majority have convenient places of worship; and they are, as a whole, maintaining the institutions of the gospel and the order of the Lord's house according to the divine pattern."

Again the missionary gives expression to one of his fondest hopes: —

"The Karen churches, especially in Burma, are fulfilling a high mission. The proud, pharisaical Boodhist, the polluted idolater, the wicked of all grades, are reading the blameless, virtuous lives of the Christian Karens, and are becoming convinced that a religion that can produce such fruits is divine. An impression is thus being made which promises glorious things for Burma. Not a few Burmans are already attracted to the truth by that blessed influence. God confounds the wisdom of this world and things that are mighty by those that are weak and simple. May we not hope that the Karen churches will become the consecrated instrumentality for the conversion of Burma to God?

"The churches succeed in supporting their pastors beyond my expectation. Their letters read at the association show that they are beginning in the right way. That work, however, will demand the exercise of a powerful guiding influence; more especially, as there are conflicting views, and, what is worse, conflicting practice, among those who 'episcopize' the whole. It becomes us all to take care how we lay the foundation, and with what we build; for posterity will judge our work. In one view of the case I am not without apprehensions, but in the light of the promises all is clear. Our preachers are multiplying: we now have forty-eight, including the six ordained pastors. There is also a large class studying at Maulmain. Upon these men depend our hopes of the final triumph of the gospel, and the perpetuity of Christian institutions in the land. There are varieties of character, and degrees of influence and efficiency among them; but, taking them all in all, we have an excellent company connected with this mission. And we record, with devout gratitude to God, that none of them, during the past year, have given us occasion to weep over their downfall.

"Most of those baptized were connected with churches in Burma, and were baptized by the native pastors. The few in this province and around Sandoway were baptized by Brother Beecher. One of the pastors from Rangoon baptized a good many near Pantanau, I suppose near one hundred, which will make the whole number baptized during the year over six hundred, all of whom are connected with established Christian congregations. Including the deaths in the Pantanau churches, and those who, though not baptized, died in the Christian faith, we may safely say that four hundred have died during the year, the greater number of cholera. Whole villages are broken up by that fearful disease, and scattered like leaves before the storm.

"One of the chief obstacles to the social improvement of the Karens is their disposition to rove from place to place; to build light, frail huts, here this year, and away to another spot the next. The chief cause of this propensity is the prevalence of violent contagious or epidemic diseases. Some of our best and largest villages, not only in Arakan and Burma, but in Maulmain and Tavoy, have been broken up from this cause. It is an evil which the present generation, I fear, will not be able to remedy. But what a consoling reflection, that instead of meeting death with dread, and the awful forebodings which the approach of eternity awakens in every heathen mind, so many of the Karen people now walk through the dark valley fearlessly, singing, —

'Welcome the tomb!
Since Jesus has lain there, I dread not its gloom!'

"Among the deceased was Wah Dee, the pastor at Great Plains. He had gone into Burma, was attacked there with cholera, and was soon with the dead. He emigrated to Arakan in 1841, and settled with the people of his village at Buffalo. In 1842 I baptized at that place seventy-five within one hour, I recollect. Wah Dee was of the number. He moved with his village to Great Plains, and was the faithful and beloved pastor of that church till his death. He was emphatically a good man; not great or learned, but a man who made full proof of his ministry, and is blessed in his death. He ruled his own house and the church of God well, and his name is fragrant and hallowed. His family will not be forgotten or neglected.

"The day-schools have not come up as we could wish: not more than two hundred have been connected with regular schools this year. The cholera broke up many; in some of the largest villages, indeed, there was no school at all. We lack teachers. More have been demanded than we could supply from our station-school. To provide for that demand will claim all our time during the rainy season. Common schools, among this uneducated Christian community, next in importance to a native ministry, call for our vigilant and constant care.

"During the meeting three brethren were ordained to the work of the ministry,—the same who were before us a year ago. They came accompanied by the elders of their churches, who testified to their character and standing, and also to the wish of the people that they might be ordained. They were examined and accepted Dec. 14. They passed the examination very satisfactorily, and were unanimously approved. I needed no new tests to satisfy my own mind; for I have watched their course from the beginning, and was ready to ordain them a year ago.

"On the 15th they were recognized as ministers of Christ, by the laying on of hands, and by prayer. Brethren Beecher, Van Meter, Tway Po, and Myat Kyau participated in the imposition of hands; and Myat Kyau offered the consecrating prayer. The services throughout were adapted to make a deep and lasting impression, and were listened to by a large congregation with breathless attention. It added not a little to the interest, that Brother Van Meter gave the hand of fellowship with an appropriate address in Pwo. It was new to the people to hear that language from a missionary. Nearly all understood, and all listened with delight. It was the *installation* of the Pwo department.

"Another interesting feature of the exercises was the address of Tway Po,—the more interesting to me, perhaps, from the reminiscences which it awakened. The congregation were evidently deeply affected. In the midst stood the three men who had been recognized as ambassadors of Christ. Before them, a few feet distant, stood Tway Po facing them, leaning gently with his right arm against one of the large pillars that support the roof of the chapel. The personal appearance of Tway Po is prepossessing, his manners dignified and ministerial. He is mild in his address,—mild but effective, quietly forcible,—of few words, but those well chosen, and adapted to touch the heart. He opened his mouth, and gave to his ordained brethren a few words of admonition to fulfil with fidelity the ministry they had received of the Lord Jesus. There they stood, Karen charging his brother Karens to magnify their office as the messengers of heaven to a wicked world, and enforcing the admonition by words of wisdom and truth. As I looked and listened, I experienced one of those rare moments, when the recollections of past years, their mingled emotions, hopes and fears, come rushing in upon the mind in a torrent, and gushing tears relieve the agitated heart.

"These men before me have passed over from demon darkness into the kingdom of God's dear Son. What a translation! The ignorant, degraded, devil-worshipping Karen is now the sanctified minister of righteousness, standing in the great congregation of God's people, Karens like himself, pouring forth from an enlightened heart those truths which were to be the guide of his brother ministers in discharging the solemn responsibilities which their ordination had imposed,—truths which he had so recently learned and made the guide of his own life. What a transformation of character! It was a joyful sight,—joyful not only as an historical fact, indicative of the triumph of the gospel and the sanction of God, but by its bright and inspiring promise of the future. Would that all the friends of missions could have been there to witness the scene. But it would have been necessary, perhaps, that they should first share in my experiences, in order to sympathize fully with my sensibilities. We commended the beloved men to God and to the word of his grace, and sent them forth on their career in the name of the Lord. We shall watch their course with unabating anxiety, and with prayers to the great Head of the church, that he may keep his own to the end. Glory be to his holy name forever!

REV. MAU YAY OF KYOOTOO

"The names of the three men ordained are Mau Yay, Myat Keh, and Po Kway.[1] The first is pastor of the church at Kyootoo, where I sat on my mat at midnight, in the open air, many years ago, and preached the gospel of Christ. The 'young chief' of those days is a member of that church. It is large and prosperous, has built a beautiful place of worship, supports its pastor, and makes liberal contributions for benevolent purposes. Mau Yay has been acting pastor of the church since its formation ten years ago, and has maintained a reputation without spot. The other two are younger, but their reputation is as fair as his. They have been for several years acting pastors of large churches, which support them entirely, maintain among themselves the institutions of the gospel and schools, and contribute largely for other objects. Thus they start on their career with bright prospects, but God alone seeth the end. My yearnings over them, who can declare!

{ Footnote: [1] The latter died near the close of 1880. He was the father of sixteen children, by one mother, including Rev. Myassah Po Kway, whom many friends in Hamilton, N.Y., and Plainfield, N.J., will remember. Myat Keh was the pastor and uncle of Moung Tway, well known in Cambridge and Newton, Mass. The two first named still live, full of years and honor. Three abler or more devoted servants of Christ, it would be hard to find in any Eastern land. Their career speaks well for the capacity of their race, and for the training and discernment of their first teacher, Mr. Abbott, as also for the later influence of Mr. Beecher. Neither of the three ever had the benefit of study at Maulmain or Rangoon. }

"The fourth candidate, a Pwo, was detained on the way by the illness of a travelling companion. The Pwos in Burma must have one of their own people ordained. Shway Bo was approved as a candidate a year ago, and he will probably be ordained later in the season at Buffalo.

"During the association, a society was organized which, in other lands, would be called a 'Home Mission Society.' Hitherto, this work has been conducted here as in other missions, —by native preachers in the employ of the missionary. That system has its evils, which none can know but those who have endeavored, after the preachers and churches are brought under its influence, to break up the system, to substitute for the mission treasury the native churches themselves, and cast all the preachers on those churches for support. Preachers have been employed by us here, as in other places, who are now, or should be, employed by a missionary society conducted and sustained by the Karens themselves. At this point we have finally arrived, with a fair prospect of success. That *pastors* are to be sustained by their own churches, if possible, need not be repeated. The object we propose in organizing such a society is not to beget a missionary spirit, or to awaken missionary zeal, or to create that disposition in the churches which prompts to effort for the conversion of the world. That is not the work of a missionary society, but of the pastor; and, if not effected by him, the most that a society can do will be to produce fitful efforts, a convulsive, momentary zeal, which dies as soon as the cause that produced it is withdrawn. We organize a voluntary association to give expression to the faith and zeal, the prayers and benevolence, of the churches; to open a channel through which streams may flow out to bless and fertilize surrounding deserts. When a combination of churches can effect this object more efficiently than individual churches, then it is the duty of churches to combine.

"Were there but one Christian on earth, it might be said to him, 'Thou art the light of the world,' and it would be his duty to enlighten the world in the best way he could. Were there but one church on earth, consisting of twelve men, it would be said to that church,—to the twelve individuals,—'Ye are the light of the world,' and it would be their duty to enlighten the world. Could they do it better as individuals, each acting on his own responsibility, then it would be their duty to act as individuals. What one man might not be able to effect, the twelve combined might; then it is their duty to unite, and act as a society. Individual and united action are both alike duty. Were there but twelve churches on earth, numbering one thousand members, it would be said to the twelve churches, and to the thousand members alike, 'Ye are the light of the world,' and it would be their duty to enlighten the world. What one church might not be able to accomplish, the twelve acting in union might. Then it is their duty to act in union. The command binds each individual of the thousand, as an individual, as a member of the church, and each church as a member of the whole.

"What particular direction the action of the whole, acting as a society, may take, rests with the one thousand individuals to decide. All must act individually if that is the best way; by individual churches if that be better; or the thousand must act as one man if that be best. And let individuals beware how they decide, lest their action stop short with individual or church action, because they can find no New Testament model for a 'Missionary Union.' Should they refuse to combine, what they might effect, acting in concert, is not done. The world is not enlightened; and the saying, 'Ye are the light of the world,' so far as relates to those twelve churches and that one thousand individuals, *is not true.*

"It is a simple truth, that every individual is responsible for all that he might effect, as an individual, as a member of an individual church, and as a member of the great Body,—the Church Universal, acting in concert and union. Each individual church also is bound as a member of the whole.

"But what is an individual church? Supposing there are fifty members, men and women, in a particular church: what is that church but fifty individuals, who live in one place, and write their names in one book, and, in many matters, act in concert as one body? Those fifty individuals can never lose their personal identity by being absorbed in what they call a church,—can never lose in the church their individual responsibility to God, or their obligations to a dying world. If they can, take away those fifty individuals, and where is the church?

"Each individual is bound to do what he can to enlighten the world as an individual, or as a member of the church; which may act, in turn, either as a church, or in concert with every other Christian and every other church, in any way and in all ways that may effect the object proposed. Individual and united action, whether that united action be said to be by churches or individuals, are both alike *duty*, from which no one individual, however feeble or poor, may for a moment hope to be exempted. Would to God that the three hundred thousand individual Baptist Christians of the Northern states would all ponder well their individual and united obligations to Christ and a world sinking to hell, and, all acting in concert through that glorious 'American Baptist Missionary *Union*,' send out men chosen of God, who should go into all the world, and preach the gospel to every creature!

"The above train of thought was suggested in view of the fact, that we had superinduced upon the Karen churches, organized after the pattern of the New Testament, a 'society' composed of individuals from all these churches, whose object it is to enlighten the world. We not only believe that every individual shall give an account of himself, but we believe also that 'Union is strength,'—that, if the united action of all the people of God may accomplish a great and good object, which individual action cannot accomplish, then united action is a duty binding upon every child of God. Hence our Karen Home Mission Society. It is, of course, but an infant, yet of fair proportions and cheering promise.

"Three missionaries are appointed, and are to be supported for the year 1851, wholly by the native Christians. The society is under the direction of the Karens themselves,—its secretary, treasurer, and committees, all Karens. Of course the missionary will keep in sight to advise, impel, or restrain, as need may be. The American Baptist Missionary Union is the parent and patron of the society, and may be a contributor. We trust it may yet rejoice over the triumphs achieved by its own offspring. It is our expectation that the support of all the preachers who require aid, the supply of poor churches, and the sending of missionaries to regions beyond,—indeed, all the operations of the 'home department'—will be conducted by this society. The Karens, and, indeed, all converts from heathenism in our missions, contribute liberally to objects of special interest,—more liberally than Christians, as a whole, in America. It is not so easy, however, for these converts to feel it a duty to support their own pastors and the interests of their own churches,—a duty to be performed year after year, with none of the peculiar satisfaction which attends the offering of their substance to the Lord on special occasions and directly to the missionary. Their liberality should be enlightened, lest it be vitiated by the old superstition, that offerings must be made to the gods, that is, to the pagodas and priests, no matter to what purpose the offerings might finally be devoted, whether they go to the fire, to dogs, or to scoundrels; only *make offerings and secure merit*. To enlighten the people at this point, and direct their contributions into legitimate channels, demands, in my estimation, the earnest and prompt attention of the missionary. All the preachers manifested an interest in the formation of the society. Many of them had the contributions of their churches in hand, and were inquiring of us what to do with them. Now they have an object to which their offerings may be legitimately devoted. More than that, a new door of hope is thus opened to their countrymen, who still sit in darkness and the shadow of death. A resolve was made unanimously to pursue the great work of home missions until 'every Karen family shall have seen the light of God.'

"There is a division in one of the largest churches, which once numbered two hundred and seventy-six members. It will probably destroy the church. Indeed, their large and beautiful chapel is deserted and going to decay, the two parties going each a different way. They will be gathered again, we hope, in other churches.

"There have been but few cases of apostasy or discipline. In this respect, we have reason for rejoicing and gratitude. The principal source of anxiety, in my own mind, is, a defect of energy, of efficiency, of enterprise, in our preachers. Perhaps, bringing with us the sentiments and the spirit characteristic of America, we expect too much of them. Perhaps we do not make sufficient allowance for the fact that they have just emerged from the lowest depths of social degradation, of ignorance, indolence, and filth. As to the moral and religious character and influence, not only of the preachers, but of the Karen Christians as a whole, they are certainly exhibiting to the world a powerful testimony in favor of truth and righteousness. There is also improvement; so that, on the whole, we have abundant reason to magnify the riches of God's grace, and take courage.

"I could have wished to remain longer at Ong Khyoung with the preachers. I would desire no happier life than to live and die among those beloved men. They have shared in my sympathies and toils, as they have been my companions for years. Their filthy and indolent habits *did* try my patience, but their marked improvement has awakened my joy. For their well-being I have experienced a depth of watchful solicitude which no mortal can ever appreciate. They have won my confidence and love. To them the strength of my best days has been devoted. The Lord bless them, and make them faithful, beloved pastors, and successful heralds of salvation."

It was not thought prudent for Mr. Abbott to remain in the jungle beyond the few days necessary for the meetings. He says,—

"To be unable to pursue my labors longer among the preachers and churches at this time causes regret. It is the less, however, as Mr. and Mrs. Beecher are there...Whether my intended trip to Maulmain and a few months sojourn there will afford me any permanent relief is perhaps doubtful. As I hope to be near the Press, and able to write a little, perhaps my time will not be entirely lost."

Writing from Dr. Stevens's house in Maulmain, Feb. 20, he says,—

"I have been here a few days, and am intending to spend the rainy season with Brother Mason at Tavoy...No bleeding from the throat since the violent hemorrhage three weeks since. Hope a season on this coast may be useful...We are discussing important subjects here, and the future brightens. I have strong hope that a reform will be effected in some departments. We are all on the most cordial terms,—perfect friendliness and confidence. Thanks to God for that!"

To return to Sandoway: Mr. Beecher writes, March 14, as follows:—

"After the meetings and ordination at Ong Khyoung, I remained there nearly four weeks, instructing a class of thirty preachers. They were occupied chiefly in the study of Galatians. An exposition was also given them of the more difficult portions of James and the First Epistle of Peter. Ten school-teachers and boys were instructed in arithmetic by an assistant. A few evenings were occupied with lectures on astronomy, in which all seemed interested, the people of the village also attending in good numbers.

"While with the preachers, the letters of the churches read at the association were carefully reviewed, and the cases of discipline mentioned were examined. A table of statistics was also made out from them, by which it appears that thirty churches have contributed to the support of their pastors, on an average, twelve rupees and seventy baskets of paddy each, besides other articles. Moreover, they have contributed about fifty rupees towards the support of two or more itinerants among the heathen. In order to increase this fund, and to complete the arrangements for this new enterprise, the preachers have appointed a meeting to be held in Burma the first of this mouth.

"Only twenty-six of the Sgau preachers have been aided this year by the mission; and they have received, on an average, only twelve rupees each. This, with what they receive from their churches, and what they can do for themselves, without diminishing their usefulness as pastors, will render them as comfortable as the majority of their people, and that is all that is desirable. Among other good results of their depending on the churches for support, is that of stimulating both pastors and people to build up large and permanent villages. Pastors, too, are more anxious to gain the favor and confidence of the people, and the people are more interested in their pastors. The pastors and churches have yet many things to learn before they will fully understand their mutual duties; and errors, the result of ignorance, already appear, which, without careful correction, will work mischief. But we are encouraged by their readiness to listen to instruction, and yield to the wishes of the missionaries, to hope that the system of ministerial support which has been established among them will, in due time, be attended with all the advantages here that attend it in America.

"While with the assistants, the disorderly conduct of one of their number, Too Oo,[1] 1 was brought to my notice. His case was carefully examined before all the assistants. He was charged with abusive treatment of his wife. He frankly confessed that he had frequently beaten her when angry, and acknowledged that he was easily irritated, and his temper ungoverned. He had often been entreated and rebuked by his brethren, with all longsuffering and forbearance; had as often promised repentance and reformation, but had returned and done the same things. The assistants heard with patience all that he had to say but when the question was put, whether they would fellowship him as a preacher, not a word was said or a hand raised in his favor. This act of discipline, though done in my presence, was none the less their act; and though it was deeply painful to us all, to have one who has been for years laboring as a preacher thus silenced, still the determination to preserve a high standard of moral purity in the ministry, which the assistants have manifested on this and other occasions, is bright with promise for the future character of the churches. The preachers were dismissed, Jan. 8, and the rest of the time at my disposal was spent in visiting the churches on this coast.

{ Footnote: [1] The same who afterwards became a pervert to Roman Catholicism. See p. 104. }

"Were it consistent with faithfulness to present only the bright side in our missionary reports, I would gladly speak only of the churches at Thehrau and Great Plains. But, in the primitive church, those who made the mission reports were not silent respecting the errors of the converts. The church at Ong Khyoung has suffered from the change of pastors in 1847. Tway Po, who had gathered the church, left at that time to build up a new interest at Thehrau. His successor, Myat Kyau, is a better preacher than pastor. The church is not united or cordial in supporting him. Their love for each other, for their teacher, and for Christ has grown cold, while their love of money and the world has increased. A few, however, are faithful, and we hope that another contemplated change of pastors will tend to produce a favorable change in the people.

"The church at Khyoungthah is a feeble band. Their pastor, Shway Meh, lacks energy, and needs additional instruction to prepare him for efficient work. But he appears anxious to improve, and we hope he will be able to study with us during the coming rains. The church appear willing to aid him according to their ability.

"Bogalo, pastor at Sinmah, is dissatisfied with the fruit of his labors there, and goes to build up a new interest near Buffalo. The church seem to regret his leaving them, and would aid in supporting him as far as they can; but he will not remain. The church at Buffalo have built a neat and durable chapel, and are gradually increasing in numbers and strength, though they are still few and feeble. They find it difficult to obtain sufficient food and clothing for their own families, but promise to contribute five rupees towards the support of their pastor.

"Weeks before we arrived at Great Plains, we had heard with deep sorrow of the death of Wah Dee, the beloved pastor, while on a preaching tour in Burma. His elder brother had been from the first the head man of the village and the main pillar of the church, which had been gathered and called from Burma, chiefly through his influence. He had given freely, and labored hard to erect an elegant and substantial chapel. We had heard the old man relate the history of the church, and wept with him as he recounted his toils, his trials, and bereavements. One hundred families had followed him from Burma nine years since. Some were disheartened and returned; some had gone to other villages; his wife had been taken from him; and now Wah Dee, his pride, his chief joy and hope, had been suddenly removed. Stroke after stroke had fallen upon the head of the worthy patriarch; and he showed how near he was to being heart-broken at the last blow by his often assuring us with tears and sobs, 'My heart is not yet destroyed.' We found, on arriving, that the old man was still as untiring in his labors as though he believed the life of the church and the prosperity of the village depended upon his efforts. In season and out of season he was the counsellor of the young, the friend of the poor, the comforter of the afflicted, a bright example of that faith which works by love.

"But the village! They had told us nothing about this. Many came to the river to greet us, and, during our long walk to the village, talked to us of their lamented pastor, of their fears on account of robbers, and their troubles with the Burman tax-gatherer; and we thought of little except the words of comfort and encouragement we should speak to them. We had a faint recollection of the scattered and shabby houses which composed the village three years before. We had heard of changes, but were expecting to see little beyond an ordinary Karen village. But never were we so agreeably surprised as when we stood in front of the late pastor's dwelling and looked at the new village. The carefully built houses standing in rows; the ground under and around them free from rubbish, as if often swept; the well-cultivated plots of vegetables; the street, wide and straight, and neatly bordered with fruit-trees and flowers,—altogether formed a pleasing picture.

"We were fast forgetting the sad thoughts that had filled our minds, and were expressing our pleasure at the neatness and prosperity of the village, praising also the industry and good taste of the villagers, when one and another, the old head man among the foremost, came near, and said, 'It was all done by Wah Dee,' 'It was all planned and directed by Wah Dee,' 'Wah Dee, though dead, has become a sweet-smelling savor.' Nor did the village lose any of its charms during a stay of three weeks. We found the people intelligent, industrious, and anxious for instruction. At first our mornings and evenings were wholly occupied with visiting twelve or fifteen sick persons, all but two of whom, by the blessing of God, soon recovered.

"The death of one of these served to exhibit in a painful degree the ignorance and superstition that still darken the minds of some Christians, even in our more intelligent villages. A bereaved father came to us just as we were leaving, and with a sorrowful face entreated us to pray for his daughter, who had died a few days before. We were the more shocked, because that subject had often been remarked upon during our stay, and once when he was present. How hard and slow the process of thorough conversion from heathenism! The majority of the church showed at the covenant-meeting a degree of intelligence and spirituality that much exceeded our expectations. Their afflictions seem to have been sanctified to their growth in grace.

"Soon after our arrival, a school of thirty-five interesting children was gathered, and taught by one of our Sandoway pupils. The attendance was good while we staid; but it was expected that when we left the older pupils would be needed to aid their parents. It was decided, in accordance with the wishes of the church, that the son of the deceased pastor, a promising young man [Shway Au], should take the place left by his father, as soon as he should be prepared by age and study. His uncle, in the mean time, will continue to conduct worship, and watch over the church, as he has done since Wah Dee's death. We bade the people farewell, wishing that it were practicable to make their village our home.

"A day and a night's sail towards home brought us to Thehrau, where the Christians have literally caused 'the wilderness and the solitary place' to be 'glad for them.' Four years ago the place was a dense wilderness; but the rice-field has appeared instead of the jungle; the habitations of men are now seen where were then only the haunts of wild beasts. Christians now walk in company to the house of God, where, a few years since, roamed the wild elephant; and the voice of prayer and praise is heard where the moaning of the forest was only broken by the yell of the tiger and the barking of the deer. This people have shown much spirit and enterprise in building up their village, and are making pleasing advances in civilization as well as in Christianity.

"Their pastor, Tway Po, to whom the praise is chiefly due, has so often been mentioned that you must begin to feel acquainted with him. He has everywhere the same dignified yet winning manner, but needs to be seen in his own village and in his own family to be perfectly known and appreciated. No native preacher has a stronger or better influence abroad, and none is more beloved and respected at home. Even the worshippers of nats and idols, who will not believe the doctrine he preaches, look to him for counsel in trouble. We had often been amused to see how much more at home he appeared than the other assistants, when sitting in our chairs. When we saw him in his own house, we understood the reason. His whole house was well built; but his room, which is used also as a conference-room, approached the civilized standard more nearly than any thing we had before seen among natives. The floor, rafters, steps, and door-frames were of sawn plank. The room was furnished with two tables, two or three chairs, and a couch with turned legs. Upon the tables were a small variety of books, in Karen and Burmese, also papers and pamphlets, all arranged with care. But what gave a charm to the whole was that the furniture was of his own manufacture. As we passed by or entered this room from day to day, and saw Tway Po—*Rev.* Tway Po, we should say, for no minister was ever more worthy of the title than he—sitting by his table, reading and studying, or conversing with those who sought his advice, we often wished that our brethren who feel such an interest in this people could see him, looking so much like an American pastor in his study. Let the prayers of Christians ascend to the great Head of the church, that he will raise up from among this people many Tway Pos."

The Van Meters spent two months in the jungle this year. Mr. Van Meter reports the membership of the Pwo churches as increasing somewhat.

"One of the little bands [Shway Bo's] has been scattered and peeled by the iniquitous misgovernment of the land. The congregation has been reduced from one hundred to thirty. Still they are not lost. As regards the support of Pwo assistants, all are necessarily dependent on us for more or less aid. The few Pwo churches are still feeble, and not far enough advanced in the knowledge of their obligation to fulfil this work, had they even the ability...Two of the churches have supplied their preachers with nearly one hundred baskets of rice, together with fish, tobacco, and a little money. All the assistants are in the habit of working a part of the time for their own support."

After the interesting meetings at Ong Khyoung, Mr. Van Meter went two days farther down the coast, to Buffalo, where he had a class of ten Pwo students and assistants for five weeks. The Sgau Christians built them a good house, he says, and they worked hard, mostly on the Book of Acts, and Old Testament history. He tells of a curious incident that occurred at Sinmah. One of the assistants took him aside, and gravely informed him that the villagers intended to become Christians to a man, provided Mr. Van Meter would induce the government to deliver them from an oppressive tax-gatherer.

The principal event of the season was the ordination of the first Pwo Karen pastor, Shway Bo, at Buffalo. He still lives, a useful man, respected by his own people and the missionaries. He is the father of Moung Edwin, who is known somewhat widely in the United States. Mr. Van Meter says of the candidate at that time, "He is young, but no novice, and exhibits a [good] degree of knowledge, tact, independence, and maturity of character...He has enjoyed the advantage of a systematic course of study at Maulmain." At the ordination Mr. Beecher preached the sermon, Mr. Van Meter gave the charge, Tway Po offered the ordaining prayer, and addressed the congregation, and Myat Kyau gave the hand of fellowship. Mr. Beecher writes again, June 10, of the first meeting of a native missionary society on Burman soil, of the opening of school, and other matters:—

"Since I last wrote, young men and boys have come from various parts of Burma, and from this coast, to attend our school. They brought letters from many of the pastors, and verbal reports from others, from which we learn that the churches are steadfast, and many of them growing in numbers and in grace. Mau Yay, since his ordination last December, has baptized ninety-seven in Bassein.

"The convention for completing the organization of the Home Mission Society was held near Bassein, in accordance with the appointment made at the association. A good number of the preachers were present: more would have attended, did not the jealousy of the Burmese render large assemblies of Karens unadvisable. Contributions were sent in from nearly all the churches, amounting to over a hundred rupees. This was divided between a Pwo and a Sgau preacher, who are to labor exclusively among the heathen of their respective tribes. About fifty rupees had been previously raised, which is to be appropriated to the support of another missionary already appointed, but detained from his work by sickness in his family.

"These churches have, from the first, been accustomed to make annual contributions to the mission; but this is the first time that the funds have been devoted particularly to this object, or that the responsibility of expending the funds has been thrown upon themselves. This first effort is comparatively small, but it promises to grow and wax great. (The fact[1] that this convention of native preachers [in the absence of a missionary] have decided to give, and two of their number have accepted as their entire support, fifty rupees a year, is worthy of consideration. They are here expending their own money, or money from their own churches. They will not be likely to give their missionaries more than is necessary, nor will the missionaries be likely to accept less than they actually need for support; so that we could not find better qualified judges of the amount necessary for the support of native preachers than these men on this occasion...But to convince the brethren of other stations that five rupees a month even is sufficient—*Hic labor, hoc opus est!*)

{ Footnote: [1] The sentences enclosed in parentheses are restored from Mr. Beecher's original letter. They were omitted in the Missionary Magazine. }

"Since we returned from the jungle, nearly eighty families of Christians have emigrated from Burma to this coast, being driven out by the exactions which the king is making to carry on war with the Shans. This will increase our jungle-work next year, and will make it more impracticable than heretofore to attempt a school for preachers in the cold season. We have a boarding-school of twenty-four pupils."

Mr. Abbott arrived in Tavoy, March 27. He spent several weeks at Monmogan, by the sea, with some advantage to his health. From that place he sent an interesting account of Mrs. Abbott's labors for the Burmans of Sandoway. It belongs to this narrative of the doings of the Bassein Karen mission; and perhaps no better place can be found for it than just here, at the point where the still sorrowing husband wrote it, as a just tribute to the memory of that devoted wife, and no less devoted missionary, Ann P. (Gardner) Abbott.

"When I arrived at Sandoway in 1840, I could not use Burmese with any fluency, and did not attempt to preach to the Burmans at all, though we were surrounded by a Burman population, with no one to preach to them. I had enough to do for the Karens, and could not think of preparing myself to preach in Burmese.

"Mrs. Abbott had studied Burmese intensely: she had mastered it, and spoke it with remarkable fluency and correctness. Our house stood out of town by the wayside. In front there was a large veranda, that passers-by were accustomed to enter, either to seek rest and shelter from a burning sun or from the rain in its season, or attracted by curiosity to see the foreigners and their children. That veranda was Mrs. Abbott's chapel. There she used to take her seat, with a bundle of tracts and the Scriptures, which she would read and explain to all that would listen. Occasionally a large group would sit in silence for hours, held there by the influence which Mrs. Abbott exerted over them by her presence and the perfect manner in which she spoke their language. Her command of Burmese was a passport to their hearts; and well did the meek preacher know how to avail herself of it to secure an introduction for that gospel which bringeth life and immortality to light.

"Another means of usefulness was in ministering to the sick and afflicted. The *mama's* fame for goodness and skill spread to all the villages round about; and the lame, the halt, and the blind were brought in to receive medical aid. Did a child tread upon a coal and burn its foot, it was sure to be brought by its mother to the *mama* for help. Many children of the land are afflicted with sores, arising, no doubt, from their habits of life. Such cases were attended to at once, their sores or wounds washed and bandaged, and directions given how to take care of them. And, when all was done, the poor creatures would sit down on the mat at her feet, and listen to the reading of a tract, or to words of wisdom and truth. Thus Mrs. Abbott, like other women in our missions, exerted an influence over heathen women as nearly divine as any thing we can conceive of in this fallen world.

"For five years she thus pursued her way, amidst domestic cares and sorrows, in weakness and affliction, ever ready to divide her solicitude between her own feeble infants and the heathen women who might gather around her door. With a fidelity and meekness seldom surpassed, and never ostentatiously displayed, she discharged the daily obligations of life; and with a faith that never wavered she bore the burdens which her missionary life imposed. All the labor in the Burmese department she performed: all its responsibility devolved on her, and well did she sustain it. Although subjected to trials peculiar to herself and to her position, known only to ourselves, she labored for the welfare of the heathen with a constancy untiring, ever exhibiting a Christian magnanimity as she walked on in the pathway of life. She fulfilled her mission of suffering, of toil, and of holy influence, till she sunk suddenly, but gently, into the grave.

"She died in the evening. During the night the news had reached a few villages near, and in the morning it spread; so that, early in the day, groups of women from the town and the surrounding country came flocking in to get a last glimpse of the *mama* before she was hid away in the tomb. Some undoubtedly came from curiosity. A foreign lady had died: it was a strange thing in the land. Many came with a spirit of mourning. Mrs. Abbott was a woman capable of making an impression upon *minds*, of exerting an influence that should be long felt. Such an influence she had affectionately exercised over those women. Many of them deeply lamented her death. They would stand around her lifeless form, and express their grief and affection. They would speak of the sacrifice she made in coming to their country, and of her goodness and kindness to them. Then they would bewail her death, a *mother's* death, and, turning to her motherless babes, would give vent to their tears. To this day they remember her, and her praise is still on their lips.

"The native officers of the place came, and proposed to make a large gilded coffin, and to carry her to the grave with pomp and parade. Not that they intended any religious ceremony, or any compliance on our part with their ideas of things: it was simply the prompting of respect and good will. But it was not congenial to my spirit to have so much noise and display. We buried her at evening. The people had all gone to their homes, except the few native Christians and two English gentlemen. We laid her in the new-made grave, and she slept with her infants already there. How sweet the slumbers of the grave! There she rests from her labors, and her works do follow her: yea, the people rise up and call her memory blessed. A plain monument is erected over the spot; and a marble slab simply tells the stranger that it is 'the grave of Mrs. Abbott.'

"The first convert from the Burmans was Ko Bike, a man advanced in life, and, for a Burman, a grave, moral character. He had visited our veranda, and had heard from Mrs. Abbott truths which made him wise unto salvation. After a time he asked for baptism, and in 1843 was baptized by Brother Stilson. Since that time, he has uniformly maintained an exemplary Christian life. He was cast out and abused by all his acquaintance and neighbors, and, worse than all, by his own wife and family. He suffered provocation from his wife, adapted, *I* should think, to arouse the spirit of a man. But through it all Ko Bike maintained his integrity. I have seen the good old man weep like an infant when speaking of this: all else he could bear with composure. And he finally triumphed. All his family are either Christians, or friendly to the truth. When I returned from America, I found Ko Bike the same, and he has maintained a good profession till the present time.[1] He talks to the people a good deal, and distributes tracts, and, although not a great preacher, his piety and personal worth give him a good influence over the people.

{ Footnote: [1] It was not this man, but a Karen of the same name, living in Maulmain, I believe, who regarded himself as "ordained to make up deficiencies." This Ko Bike afterwards removed to the compound of the Burman mission in Bassein, where he died, trusting in Christ, in extreme old age, about the year 1869. }

"The next convert was a priest. He, too, was first attracted by curiosity,—a white *woman* could speak his own language well. It was a great condescension in a Boodhist priest to go at all into a house where there was a woman; a greater, to sit down in her presence, especially for *him* to sit on a mat upon the floor, and the *woman* in a chair above him; greater still, to listen to a woman's reading or instructions. But the priest *did* sit down at the feet of the woman, and listen to her words long and attentively. He came occasionally for months, and Mrs. Abbott cherished a hope that he was earnestly seeking the way of life. At length he disappeared. For a long time we heard nothing of him, till at last word came from his monastery that he was dead. It appeared that his fellow-priests had become alarmed at his frequent visits to our veranda, and had persecuted him; and that, while he was ill, they had tried to force him into the observance of heathen ceremonies. We heard, also, that to the last he refused to comply. A mystery hangs over his last days, as we could learn nothing except what came through the priests. From all we could gather, we indulged a hope that he died a Christian.

"Ko Bike's son also embraced the gospel in those days. His case was not perfectly satisfactory, but so much so as to justify his baptism...The wife of Ko Bike had begun to bend before I left for America; so much so, that she would come to the house and see Mrs. Abbott. She had not *sehed* (to abuse with words, which means a good deal among Burmans) her husband for some time. She would allow him to pray in the house in peace. Had not for a long time dragged him about the floor by the hair of his head, and had not even run away from him recently. When I returned from America, she was still more like a Christian, and has since, on the whole, exhibited a good temper, although she occasionally lets the people about her know that she still has a spirit of her own. She does not, however, exhibit the violence of former days, and in no case the vileness. She is a changed woman, and regular in her religious course; has been asking for baptism, and, I presume, will be baptized during the season. Ko Bike's children and grandchildren are being trained up under Christian influence, and from his good example his neighbors are learning the way of life. He has achieved a noble victory, and is mightier than he that taketh a city.

"There are two other Burman members in the little church, —an old man named Shway Eing, and his daughter, who came over from Burma. This daughter was left motherless when an infant, and her father gave her to a Karen Christian woman to nurse. Of course the infant was nurtured in the 'admonition of the Lord,' and, when quite young, was baptized by a Karen pastor. Ko Bike's son heard of this girl, —a Burmese and a baptized Christian. He went over and sought her hand, married her, and brought her to Sandoway with her old father. He had renounced Boodhism thirteen years before, under the influence of 'the young chief' of those days, who had just escaped from prison at Rangoon. The old man remained a nominal Christian till he came to Sandoway, not fully settled as to the doctrines of the gospel. He revealed to me all his doubts, which I endeavored to remove; and during the whole season, whenever I said any thing [in the chapel], it was in Burmese, for the benefit of that old man, and Ko Bike and the other Burmans. Shway Eing apprehended the truths of the gospel with remarkable clearness, and began to declare them to his countrymen, though at first rather timidly. Still he was not very urgent for baptism, and I allowed him to take his own course. He was finally baptized by Brother Beecher. He preaches well, and promises to be an efficient laborer. His influence over the heathen is excellent, and under his teachings quite a number are considered good inquirers.

"Thus you will see we have a small Burman church at Sandoway, a nucleus around which, we trust, will yet be gathered a great company of believers. The gospel is preached there, truth is communicated to the people, and we now need nothing so much as the Spirit from on high. Our brethren and sisters there are studying Burmese, that they may be able to labor for the people around them. They all must be there from March to November of each year, and, if they have health and will, can do much for the Burmans without impeding their Karen work."

There is some confusion and conflict of plans about this time in the Karen department. Mr. Abbott, still eager to get into Burma Proper, to be nearer his converts, was proposing in March to go soon to his old station, Rangoon, hoping even that he might be able ultimately to reach Bassein from that point. Mr. Vinton did not favor the plan. In August the Maulmain Karen mission, in view of Dr. Binney's return to America, and of Mr. Vinton's desire to remove to Rangoon, proposed formally that Mr. Beecher come to Maulmain and take charge of the theological school, until some one should be sent out from home for that work, *or that the school be temporarily transferred to Sandoway*. This vote, however, was rescinded a month or two later, and Mr. Beecher, who had already reached Akyab on his way to Maulmain, returned to his station. But the stirring events of the next year were to increase the confusion, and suspend temporarily all plans for the upbuilding of Christ's kingdom in Burma Proper.

Self-Support

"I will overturn, overturn, overturn it: and it shall be no more, until he come whose right it is; and I will give it him." —EZEK. xxi. 27.

CHAPTER X.

1852.

"The nation and kingdom that will not serve thee shall perish: yea, those nations shall be utterly wasted."— ISAIAH.

In the Magazine for March of this year, we find a glowing account of the Bassein Christians from the pen of Dr. Kincaid. He had sent Burman assistants with letters and books to visit the disciples in that region. Some of the Christians returned with the messengers, and they had a united Karen and Burman service in the mission-house at Rangoon, of which the warm-hearted doctor writes, "The sweetness and harmony of Karen voices in singing, especially in their own language, exceed any thing I ever heard. It is like what one imagines the music of heaven to be."

The assistants reported one church with which they spent the Lord's Day, they preaching twice in Burmese, and the pastor once in Karen. "The church numbered nearly four hundred. Their chapel is forty cubits square, well built, and surrounded by a neatly-kept plot of ground. Near it stands a schoolhouse, twenty-six by twenty-eight cubits. A large number of the members came together when the messengers arrived; and when they saw the books and letters, and were assured of being remembered, they were affected to tears, and some wept aloud for joy. I received a letter from the pastor of this church [Mau Yay of Kyootoo?—ED.], and will give you an extract:—

"'May the grace and fellowship of the Father, Son, and Holy Ghost, be with you! with my love, and the love of all the sons and daughters of God in this church. I am one of the least of all the disciples, and know but little of God's word. Divine grace has made me a teacher of the gospel, and by the sacred imposition of hands I am made a pastor. Daily I study the Bible, and pray for a larger measure of the Holy Spirit, so as to teach and guide this flock of little ones. I have but little knowledge, and can teach only what I know. I, the pastor, and all the church, rejoiced greatly when we heard that you had come into this Burman kingdom, and we cease not to pray for you. Our Father who is in heaven will hear our prayers. We all desire greatly to see you, and to hear more fully the deep things of God, that we may grow and be established in every virtue.'

"Among the letters received is one from a Burman who has been taught the way of life, and baptized by a Karen pastor. The letter is imbued with Christian sentiment, and breathes the spirit of one redeemed unto God; and yet the writer has never seen a missionary...The word of God is making a deep impression on many Burmans in the neighborhood of Karen churches. The two Burman assistants I sent out were much gratified to find so many of their countrymen favorably affected by what they saw and heard among the Karens. This is most encouraging. As the Karen churches become mature in Christian knowledge, a mighty moral influence will go forth, lifting the cloud of darkness from the worshippers of Gaudama. Already an army of ten thousand stand up on the side of God, clothed in the Christian armor. Their strong, simple faith gives to their whole character a dignity and grandeur which compel the heathen to take knowledge of them, that they are divinely taught.[1] About forty of them have come, within twenty days past, for books and advice, several of them coming over a hundred and fifty miles, through districts infested with robbers, and amidst almost incessant storms. I feel ashamed and am rebuked when I look on this people, braving danger, and suffering privations and hardships, to procure portions of God's word...

{ Footnote: [1] If the hopes expressed by Dr. Kincaid, and shared equally by many Burman and Karen missionaries, have failed of fulfilment, as we are constrained to admit that they have for the most part, we suggest, as the only adequate explanation, the twofold fact that American Baptists have not extended the aid which was essential to a thorough Christian education of this people, and, on the other hand, this help failing them, the Karens themselves have settled down into half-helpless contentment with ignorance, or the barest modicum of knowledge, too often, it may be, preferring a shadow to the scarcely proffered substance. How long before the grave defects in our system shall be remedied? }

"One other fact among many. Two young Karens from Pantanau were sent here by their pastor to bring letters, and get a few books. Ten New Testaments, a 'Pilgrim's Progress,' seven tracts, and two hymn-books were wanted. They remained two days, and then set out on their long journey back. The books were carefully rolled up, and put in the bottom of a basket, and then the basket was filled with rice and dried fish. This done, they gave the parting hand, and in a tremulous voice said to each of us, 'Pray for us, that we may not fall into the hands of officers with these books.' Two Christian boys, sixteen or seventeen years old, trusting in God, make a journey of a hundred and thirty miles to get this handful of books. Here is faith that will remove mountains."

Dr. Dawson also (same volume, p. 98) gives Burman testimony to the excellent deportment of the Karen Christians. Rev. Dr. Stevens says (*Ibid.*, p. 20) that Burman priests "from the region of Bassein have borne honorable testimony to the Christian character of Karens in that province." He gives an interesting incident related by one of the Bassein priests, which well illustrates Karen and Burman character. "Before he became a priest, a Karen chanced to come along one day, while he was reading aloud Mr. Comstock's 'Way to Heaven.' After listening attentively for a while, he begged him to go to his village, saying that the Karens there would like much to hear that book...On reaching the man's house, the whole village came together, and he read to them. They listened with deep attention till he came to a passage where Jesus Christ is spoken of as dying on the cross for sinners. Here, he said, *they began to weep*, and the tears trickled down their cheeks. They were not satisfied with a single hearing. They urged him to repeat his visits, which he did, going from place to place among them, reading that book, and receiving a number of presents for his pains. Here, thought I, is Brother Comstock speaking, though dead, and preaching to Karens by means of an idolatrous Burman. The priest showed no marks of a salutary impression made on his own heart by the reading of the tract, although he was evidently familiar with its contents. Nor does it appear that he was actuated by any other motive than that of 'making a gain' of them. But, 'whether in pretence or in truth, Christ is preached; and therein we do rejoice, yea, and will rejoice.'"

Six months before the second war began, Dr. Kincaid writes again:—

"I feel ashamed when I look on this people, so full of faith and steadfastness, so certain that the day of deliverance is at hand, and that the empire of darkness will be overturned. The seal of God is on them...While the Burmans are groping their way amidst the darkness of pantheism, and are toiling under the weight of a superstition more degrading than popery, the Karens are inquiring for God's book; and the God of the Bible is their refuge."

The time has now come when the faith of these simple-hearted disciples is to receive a rich reward; but they must first pass through a period of sharpest trial. Some hundreds, under the lead of Englishmen, must take up arms in defence of their homes, and to gain that sweet liberty which they have never known. Some must die a soldier's death, and others win a martyr's crown. The cruel and haughty governor of Rangoon has again threatened to shoot every Karen found with a Christian book in his possession (E. L. Abbott, Nov. 23, 1851). He has treated hundreds of British subjects with the grossest injustice and cruelty. Many have been stripped of their property. A few have died under Burman torture. British ships have been illegally detained, and their captains treated with outrage. At last a deputation of four British officers from the commodore has been insulted at mid-day, before throngs of barbarians, at the governor's residence. The measure of Burmese cruelty, oppression, and insolence, is again full to overflowing. After years of forbearance, the English Trading Company under Lord Dalhousie will again strike, and strike so hard as to roll the tyrant's frontier up stream, full three hundred miles from the sea. Thus God works out the deliverance of his people.

Meanwhile, Messrs. Beecher and Van Meter at Sandoway were doing what they could, at such a time, to carry on the regular work of the mission. The Beechers, in attempting to reach Thehrau,—the place appointed for the association this year, — were driven out to sea in an open canoe with no keel. Their lives were in peril for some hours, and the main object of their voyage was defeated. Mr. Van Meter started a little earlier, and arrived at his destination just as the storm reached its height. The meeting, though marred by the absence of the Sgau missionaries, was of great interest. After a week's continuance, it was suddenly broken up by the announcement of open war. We give extracts from Mr. Van Meter's interesting account: —

"The weather was not settled, although I did not leave until Dec. 4. A storm had been threatening for some days; and I encountered rough weather each day of the passage, increasing in violence towards the last. The sea was so heavy, and the sky so threatening, that the boatmen hesitated very much to make the last day's run. Upon urging them, however, they started; and we made a very good run to the mouth of the Thehrau. Before I could leave my boat, the storm commenced, with heavy rain, and lasted for several days. All this time we were anxiously awaiting Brother and Sister Beecher. On the eighth day we gave them up, concluding that they had either met with some misfortune, or, in consequence of war rumors, had returned to Sandoway. Some of the Karens who came over last from Burma had brought alarming reports; but, as there was still some doubt, we remained together, hoping that the Beechers would yet come.

"During the first few days we had preaching, generally twice a day, by some of the assistants, and conference on various subjects. At length we had to take up the business of the churches, reading letters, collecting statistics, etc. Sabbath came, the seventh day we had been together; and the question arose, Shall we partake of 'the great feast,' or postpone it a few days longer? It was finally deemed best, all things considered, to partake of it at that time. We did so in the evening, and a most interesting season we had. The services were chiefly conducted by the ordained brethren, one of the Sgaus breaking the bread, and the Pwo pastor pouring the wine, with remarks from each, in their respective dialects...

"There was not so large a number present as at our previous meeting, nor is the increase among the churches as great as last year. Still there are encouraging signs. One of the pleasing features of last year, the presence of duly accredited delegates from the churches, was repeated. The character and intelligence of those present speak well for the churches which sent them...The interest in home missions is on the increase. The number of missionaries is to be doubled this year. The meeting on Saturday evening was of much interest. Thahbwah, the Pwo missionary, gave a detailed account of his first tour, the villages visited, his reception, and the general aspect of the field. He evidently magnified his office, and seemed elated by his success. He had preached in many places, and seen many tokens for good. The most encouraging result of his labors was the conversion of a small village of six or seven houses. They have asked for a teacher, and promise to build him a house, and help him otherwise, as they are able. A young licentiate received permission to go and labor among them.

"At the close of Thahbwah's remarks, I endeavored to impress upon all the importance of their carrying forward this work with diligence, and the solemn responsibility resting upon them in view of their position in this dark part of the world. They were evidently a chosen people. Years and years of labor had been bestowed upon the Burmese, but they opposed and resisted. God then turned to the poor, despised Karens, and had brought them into his kingdom by thousands. He had rejected the Burmans, should we say? No: he had set them aside for a season, and chosen the Karens. God had committed this work into their hands, and who could set limits to what he might accomplish by them among the tribes and nations in this and adjacent lands? If they would do the work, God would be with them: otherwise he would commit it to others.

"The interest excited was deep and solemn. This was evident from the fact, that, although the hour was late,—we had listened to a sermon from one of the assistants before Thahbwah gave his report,—there was no restlessness, nor did one of the large congregation go out. During the closing prayer, also, there was a silence, which seemed to indicate that all hearts were deeply engaged.

"Another encouraging feature was the character of the preaching to which we listened day after day. The speakers seemed to have more freedom and confidence, and there were more variety and compass in the discussion of their subjects than I had before witnessed. It was with no ordinary interest that I listened to the opening and closing sermons. The former, by Mau Yay, was a very fair introductory sermon, and was filled with reflections suitable to the occasion. He is an earnest and effective speaker, and took the lead in almost all our discussions. The passage chosen by him was in the second chapter of Colossians. A happy allusion was suggested by the fifth verse; viz., the similarity in situation and interests of the *absent* teachers to those of Paul, as there expressed. The concluding sermon was preached by Tway Po, sabbath morning. His dignified, authoritative, and yet affectionate manner reminded me of some of our good old pastors at home, and, for the time, made me almost forget that I was in the Arakan jungles. The fixed attention and interest manifested on both these occasions were highly creditable.

"Monday evening the subject of common schools was under discussion. Some English friends in Akyab had made a contribution to aid such schools, and Mr. Van Meter urged the pastors and elders to make more earnest efforts to give a primary education to all the children. They discussed the matter for some time, and admitted fully the importance of the subject; but I waited in vain to hear some practical suggestion. At length I proposed a resolution, that they would each and all make special efforts to establish and support schools in the villages during the coming year. The number of scholars reported was only one hundred and thirty-three; but less than two-thirds of the churches were represented.

"We had just commenced discussing the need of regular postal communication between their villages and Sandoway, at least, every other month (their papers, letters, etc., now often lie six months at the mission-house without an opportunity of sending), when a note was received from Mr. Fytche, informing us of warlike movements in Burma. I told the Karens at once: they were terrified, and made immediate preparations for leaving. The note came about ten, P.M. I divided what money I had with me, in small sums, among the more needy; and before daybreak almost every man had disappeared. On the previous day they had selected as many books as they could carry; but they durst not take one with them, nor any thing else that might excite suspicion as to whence they had come. This was certainly prudent, nor would I detain them under such circumstances. It was near midnight when we took each other by the hand. It was a solemn parting. Should we ever meet again? What awaited them on their arrival? Would they ever reach their homes at all?

"A larger number of Pwos than usual were present. A class of ten young men came over with the assistants. They were prepared either to remain and study with me in the jungle, or to go to Sandoway in my boat, if advisable. They dread the long journey on foot and its exposures, many of them suffering severely from sickness whenever it is attempted. Among the company were the wife and child of Shway Bo, whom we ordained last year, —the first instance, I think, of a Pwo woman coming from Burma on such an occasion...

"Sickness caused the absence of the two [Pwo] assistants. One of them has been partially insane for some time past, an infliction, some think, from a *poongyee* [Burman priest] whom he had visited for the purpose of discussing the comparative merits of Christianity and Boodhism. That the *poongyees* possess some mysterious power to inflict serious injury, and even death, upon persons at a distance, is still firmly believed by many Karens; and doubtless this belief exerts a very unfavorable influence over them. It seems impossible to convince them of its absurdity. When pressed, they reply by referring to the fact that such things are recognized in the Scriptures, especially in connection with the miracles of Christ upon those possessed of devils."

Mr. Beecher gives an account of his visit to the Ong Khyoung church, which he found in a more flourishing state under the joint labors of the young pastor, Tohlo, and "the efficient and intelligent" schoolmaster, Shway Bwin. After baptizing six candidates, and administering the Lord's Supper, he makes his perilous but unsuccessful attempt to reach Thehrau. Voyaging on that rocky coast, as our missionaries of that time constantly did, in small, smooth-bottomed native canoes, seems to us reckless and dangerous in the extreme. We quote from the latter part of Mr. Beecher's letter:—

"We had a gentle, favorable breeze till about ten, A.M., when the east wind rose so strong as to drive us from our course, and, still worse, prevented us from returning to the land. To run against such a wind in such a sea was impossible. The boat pitched and rolled so, that the men could not stand without holding on. The wind continued to rise, driving us farther and farther out to sea. About two, P.M., the boatmen, fearing, that, before the wind would change, we should be driven so far from land as to suffer for want of provisions, if not from the violence of the waves, cut away our boat-cover. This left Mrs. Beecher and myself exposed to the burning sun. Those were long and anxious hours; but, thanks to our heavenly Father! we were spared from much suffering, other than the intense anxiety. As the sun was setting, the wind died away to a gentle breeze, so that the boat became manageable, and we turned towards land; but, as the wind was still unfavorable, we were till the third day, at evening, in getting to Gwa, the nearest land we could make. While waiting there for our boatmen to rest, and to have the boat repaired, Brother Van Meter came in, and at the same time a steamer direct from Bassein, bringing such reports of movements at Rangoon, that it was deemed prudent for us to return to Sandoway.

"My disappointment at not being able to reach the association was the saddest of my life. That meeting, which has ever been so full of interest and importance, had been this season more than ever the subject of thought and prayer; and then, when within a day's sail, to be driven off by adverse winds, was a severe trial. But we have the consolation of knowing that all these things are ordered by infinite wisdom and goodness.

"Only thirty churches were reported, as follows,—baptized, 178; died, 27; excluded, 4; net increase, 147. Contributions: for support of pastors, Rs. 178-13; taxes paid for pastors, Rs. 22-8; for home missions, Rs. 88; for the poor, Rs. 17-4; sundries, Rs. 7; total, Rs. 329-9, besides rice and other provisions supplied to pastors...The churches on this coast, with one or two exceptions, are prosperous. In Burma the Karens are suffering severely from the exactions of their rulers; but we trust the day of their deliverance is at hand."

As Sandoway was more exposed to an attack from the Burmese than either Kyouk Pyoo or Akyab, the missionaries remained there in some suspense, daily expecting intelligence that might compel them to remove to one of those stations. Near the end of January, however, the Burmans professed so strong a desire for an amicable settlement, that it was believed there would be no war. Mr. Beecher was still anxious to visit the churches on the coast. He hoped, also, that some of the Bassein pastors might come over, and give him an opportunity of learning the condition of their churches, and of affording them some aid and advice in this time of trial. They had already sent once to Sandoway to inquire respecting the intentions of the English, as they had heard contradictory reports, and knew not what to do or expect. The Burmans had charged them with being the cause of the ships-of-war going to Rangoon, and of the troubles which followed, and had told them that they should suffer for being so friendly to the English. All their arms had been seized, and oppressive demands had been made upon them to supply the king's army with provisions; but none of the Bassein Karens had been called to go in person as soldiers. Accordingly. Mr. Beecher, assured by the English officials that there would be no war, left his home and family (Jan. 29), and went directly to the most southern church at Great Plains. We reprint a part of his letter:—

"I was highly gratified to find the people healthy and contented, and was greeted by them with many expressions of joy. The village of the old patriarch had been enlarged by additions from Burma, the fruit-trees had thriven, the flowers had not been neglected, and the appearance of neatness and comfort observed last year still pervaded the village. The old man, with a new wife and renewed youth, was active and useful. Shway Au, the young pastor, with a discretion above his years, and a degree of energy seldom exhibited by Karens, had discharged the responsible duties of his office with such zeal and faithfulness, that he may be said to have fully observed the precept, 'Let no man despise thy youth.' I need not say that a people with such an elder and such a pastor are prosperous...A new village has been formed this year by a number of families from Great Plains. Sah Gay, the pastor, is of a retiring disposition, but has firmness of purpose and good common sense. He has the cordial support of his people. Provoked to good works by the [parent] village, the colonists have made praiseworthy improvements, and promise to make still more. The people of both villages assemble together in their commodious chapel sabbath mornings, but meet separately in the afternoon. Neither ask any aid in supporting their pastor this year, and they have jointly contributed over ten rupees for the Home Mission Society.

"Early Sunday morning we repaired to the seaside for a baptism. A neat little basin among the rocks, with a smooth, sandy bottom, afforded a convenient and attractive baptistery. The solemnity of the service was deepened by the sound of many waters rolling upon the long beach, and breaking upon the rocks around. Here twenty-two were buried with Christ in baptism. In the evening a goodly number partook of the broken bread and the wine in remembrance of Christ. Having made arrangements for a school, which commenced the day after I left, with thirty pupils, I bade the people farewell for another year.

"On arriving at Buffalo, Feb. 10, I immediately sent for Tway Po. He, and nearly all his people, had left their village, and were stopping at the mouth of the river, a few hours distant from their homes. Some weeks before, the rendezvous of a band of robbers was discovered in the thick jungle near their village; and, though the robbers had been thwarted in some way, still Tway Po and his people were so much alarmed by their narrow escape, that they durst not remain there longer. It was known, besides, that robbers in Burma, instigated, no doubt, by Burman officers, had declared intentions of violence to Tway Po. 'It is not his money, or the property of his people, that we wish,' say they, 'but his life; for he has been chief in leading so many Karens away from Burma, and in getting favors for them from the English.' It was his life, doubtless, that they were seeking; but God took care of him and his people. We hope that the day of their deliverance from robbers is near. The church at Buffalo has received additions during the year from Burma. They have enlarged and improved their village, and wish to make still further improvements. They appear united and cordial in the support of their pastor [Kroodee], and have given him more than they promised when I was with them last year.

"The day had been nearly spent in inquiries, etc., when, at the hour of evening worship, a letter arrived from Mrs. Beecher, containing news of the battle at Rangoon, of the certainty of further hostilities, and the necessity of her going to Kyouk Pyoo in case of danger at Sandoway. I was then only a day and a half south-west of Bassein, and at least eight days from Sandoway. Reports reached us that a man-of-war, lying at the mouth of Bassein River, had sent men ashore for water, two of whom were shot by the Burmese, and that the ship, in turn, was battering down the Burman stockades. My position, to say the least, was not pleasant; and though I longed to remain and labor a few days, prudence dictated a speedy return. Accordingly, after a season of prayer, the evening was spent in distributing medicine, and imparting such counsel as the occasion seemed to require. Tway Po had arrived. Bogalo, the pastor of Sinmah, was present. Myat Kyau had failed in an attempt to enter Burma, and was stopping a few days at Buffalo. Regretting to leave my work unfinished, the hope that I was leaving it to enter shortly a wider field in Bassein rendered the prospect before me comparatively bright.

"On my way home I saw a few members of the church at Sinmah. The pastor has pursued a course which has alienated and divided his people. His chief fault is in his novel and somewhat arbitrary mode of discipline.

"I was much gratified with the appearance of the church at Khyoungthah during my stay of a few hours. Twelve or fourteen families from Burma have been added during the year, and, though they have suffered from sickness and poverty, they seemed hopeful, and were intending to improve their village. They are united in their pastor, and contribute according to their ability for his support.

"I reached home in good health after a journey of a day and a half by boat, and five days' and a half most fatiguing travel by land. I should be ungrateful not to mention the kindness shown me by the Burmese through whose villages I passed. On arriving at a village, I went to the house of the *thoogyee*, or head man, by whom I was always welcomed; and the best which his house or village afforded was immediately set before me. The men who followed me, too, were well supplied with food, and, though money was always offered in return, it was very seldom received. It is worthy of remark, also, that as soon as the people, Burmans or Karens, learned the news of the battle, and the probability that the entire province of Pegu would come under British rule, they all, without exception, manifested delight. The people of Arakan, having experienced the blessings of the mild and just government of the English, are warmly attached to it. And, what is still more remarkable, all natives who come from Bassein and Rangoon are unanimous in representing that the mass of the people there are anxious to throw off the oppressive yoke of the king, and would hail with delight the advance of British troops into their country. May the Karens soon experience the blessings of freedom, and their missionaries be permitted to live and labor among them, for their social and spiritual improvement, unmolested!"

The Van Meters went to Akyab the last of January, and from thence, in March, to Maulmain. The Beechers staid on at Sandoway until near the end of March, when that station was menaced by a body of two thousand marauders from Burma; and they retired to Kyouk Pyoo, where they spent the rainy season with the deeply afflicted Mrs. Campbell.

No one watched the progress of events more keenly than Mr. Abbott. The capture of Martaban (April 5) and of Rangoon (April 14), followed shortly by the successful storming of Bassein itself, filled his heart with gratitude and joy. Though sadly broken in health and spirits, his mind is much occupied with thoughts about his dear, scattered Karens, and with plans for the future. On the 12th of May he writes from Maulmain as follows:—

"It will be no news to you that Rangoon is a British possession. Bassein will be taken soon, and the lower provinces of Burma will probably be annexed to the dominions of the East India Company. I have made several attempts to reach Bassein, and hope to succeed next time. That place will become the centre of our missionary operations, hitherto conducted from Sandoway. The war will throw every thing into confusion. Villages and churches will be broken up and scattered, pastors killed, and every thing in desolation. The work of years is to be done over again,—villages are to be gathered, churches to be re-organized, a station to be built up, provision made to meet the increased demand for trained preachers and school-teachers; and the Home Mission Society, on which so much depends, is to be resuscitated. With increased facilities for labor, the demand for labor increases.

"I do not see how Sandoway can be abandoned at present. The mission property, the Burmese church, the Karen interests in the vicinity, the station as a centre of missionary operations, should not, it seems to me, be all abandoned at once. If Brother Beecher remain there a year or two only, I should hope that a native pastor from Akyab might be found to occupy the post, so that that interesting field may not be left desolate.

"Then what are we to do at Bassein? I had hoped to see that mission in a state that would justify my leaving it, for a while, at least. Five years have passed since my return; but never was my presence more imperatively demanded than now. Three years more, at least. *We must have help now.* I therefore propose to the Executive Committee to appoint Brother Thomas of Tavoy as my colleague, to come and join me at once...Think of all those churches and pastors, that great field, hitherto so flourishing, now so desolate! Moreover, my poor health will not justify high hopes. Brother Van Meter will go with me, but what can we do?"...

Those who have any acquaintance with the history of missions, from the days of Paul and Barnabas until now, will perceive without surprise that there was at this time a difficulty between those excellent brethren, Abbott and Beecher, which seemed to prevent their laboring harmoniously at the same station. Details are uncalled for. As we have already said, they were unlike in disposition. Both were intensely human, liable, like the best of human kind, to err, and, doubtless, both did err. Each, by the grace of God, did a splendid work, in which they both now rejoice, as they also rejoice each in the other's perfections before the Lamb of God. Him they both loved and served on earth with an intensity of purpose that few of the present generation have approached; and him they both are serving and loving in heaven, world without end.

The Executive Committee were not unwilling to comply with Mr. Abbott's earnest request; but, before Mr. Thomas could become a missionary in Bassein, he must needs do ten years and more of hard, successful work in Henthada. Messrs. Abbott and Van Meter left Maulmain for Bassein in the steamer *Tenasserim*, July 10, arriving on the 12th. The Boodhist *kyoung*, or monastery, which they secured for their temporary abode, was situated on the north side of Aylesbury Street, between Merchant Street and the Strand Road, quite near the present compound of the Roman-Catholic mission. We quote from Mr. Van Meter's interesting journal: —

"*July 11, 1852, Sabbath.*—Reached Diamond Island at six, P.M. Weather very pleasant since leaving Amherst. We had a fine run, from mouth to mouth, in thirty-two hours, the distance some two hundred miles. Anchored at the mouth of the river. A beautiful harbor.

"*12th.*—Anchored off Bassein at one, P.M.; distance, seventy miles. The appearance of the country on either bank is very pleasant and inviting, more so than any river I have yet seen in India. Was disappointed in the appearance of Bassein; scarcely any elevation in or near the site of the town. Ruins of houses, stockades and fortifications, are visible in every direction. The town is hidden from view by a massive brick wall, extending for nearly a mile along the east side of the river. Some houses are left on either side of this fortification; but every thing is swept clean in front of it. Going on shore, we found the place little more inviting within than without. Many beautiful trees had been destroyed by the Burmese; and the English, as a prudential measure, were cutting down the remainder. Hardly a house was left standing, save those occupied by troops and their officers. These were principally old *kyoungs*. The fortification, as stated, is of massive brick-work in front and to a considerable distance on both sides, but is extended by stockades. The whole area thus enclosed is about one square mile. Before, and at some distance from, each of the gateways, is a mass of masonry ten or fifteen feet thick. The entrances are passages of solid brick-work about ten feet wide, fifteen feet high, and thirty feet long. There are many brick walks in the town, some extending a good distance outside, but much out of repair. They are lined on either side with pagodas, idol-temples, *kyoungs*, etc. A large pagoda, said to be a hundred feet high, stands on an elevated platform connected with the front wall, facing nearly the centre of the town. It has been gilded recently, and is quite imposing at a distance.

"As soon as we had come to anchor, Brother Abbott sent off the few Karens that had come with us [including Dahbu, Shahshu, Poo Goung, Yohpo, and Thahree, then students, but since excellent ordained ministers, every one.—ED.], to learn if there were any others in or near the city. They soon came back accompanied by several, whom they found stopping here. The meeting was an unexpected and happy one. Shway Weing, 'the young chief of former days, is now in great favor with most of the officers, and has been appointed head man of all the Karens and Shans in this district. He has a great deal to do, also, in supplying provisions for the officers and men. He is the same uncompromising Christian as ever. Immediately on our arrival, he sent off men in various directions to tell that the teachers had come to Bassein.

"Our first object was to find a good place for residence. We found a substantial *kyoung*, almost new, standing in a beautiful grove, a short distance from the south gate of the town. I must not forget to mention the very considerate conduct of Gen. Godwin. Just before reaching town, he came and inquired very kindly about the health of Mr. Abbott, remarked the severity of his cough, inquired as to our intentions, and if there were any thing he could do for us. He said, further, that he would speak to the officer in command to aid us in securing a place of residence. I should mention, also, that yesterday one of the staff-officers expressed a deep interest in our work, and inquired how he could aid us, observing that he had a handsome allowance, and had no object in laying up money.

"*13th.*—Called on Major Roberts, the officer in command, and were very kindly received. He at once granted our request for the *kyoung* above mentioned, or any other building not yet occupied, that might suit our purpose, and kindly proffered further aid. A pious officer of the Fifty-first European also gave us a warm reception, and pressed us to tell him of any way he could serve us. He took a deep interest in the Karen Christians from the first, and had ordered books from Maulmain, some of which he had received and distributed before we came. He is expecting another box shortly. Some pious European soldiers were also much rejoiced to learn that we had come.

"*14th.*—The *Sesostris* left early for Rangoon, with the general and staff on board. I spent most of the day on shore, superintending the demolition of a large *kyoung*, to get materials to finish the one assigned us, the roof of which had been stripped off only a few days before our arrival. I felt almost guilty in thus destroying the property of others; but it is the order of the day. The Karens have begun to come in already, both preachers and people. Had a respectable congregation this evening. Brother Abbott spoke to them briefly, but with difficulty, as he is suffering again with a bad throat.

"*15th.*—Still busy in bringing materials from the demolished *kyoung*. All the *kyoungs* here are of timber, and they are neither few nor small. There is another large one standing in our enclosure, which, though quite old, will answer very well for a schoolroom and Karen boarding-house. A large amount of timber has been put into stockades; and buildings of all kinds have suffered a common destruction for the sake of the common defence. Brother Abbott was not able to go on shore this evening. I had the pleasure of addressing

216

a congregation of at least sixty, among whom were the ordained preachers Myat Keh, Po Kway, and Shway Bo.

"*16th.*—People continue to come in from villages one, two, and three days distant. Many of them are Pwos, who never before saw a Christian teacher. The Pwo assistants are but few, and live some distance above Bassein. I have been astonished to find that almost every Pwo who has yet come in is as ignorant of God and true religion as the most benighted tribes of Africa. When questioned, their reply is, 'We know nothing of God or religion, but the worship of pagodas and idols and *poongyees;*' and yet very few that I have seen are idolaters. When asked why they, knowing that the Sgaus worshipped the true God, and had a holy book, had not worshipped the same God, they reply, 'How could we without a teacher? We have never seen one who could speak our language. But now, since the teacher has come, we will all become Christians.'

"I visited the 'mud fort' this evening, where so many of the Burmese were killed in the late assault by the English. It must cover an area of some four or five acres, and has a large tank near the centre, intended to destroy the effect of shells from the ships! The whole was built in two months; from a thousand to fifteen hundred men being employed on it. The front was protected by a novel kind of *chevaux de frise*, made of bamboos firmly twisted and bound together at the base, but bristling with points as thick as quills on a porcupine's back. The English, however, took the liberty of selecting their own road, and all this labor was worse than useless; for the place became a snare, and the common grave of many who aided in building it.

"Addressed the people again this evening, their numbers still increasing. The Karens who took me to the steamer after dark were more than once on the point of turning back, 'afraid the foreigners would shoot them.' It is very unpleasant to live on shipboard at such a time, instead of with the people. And yet, unless we could get within the stockade, this is much the best place for a quiet night's rest. There is no knowing how near a band of Burmese soldiers or robbers may be. But, if our house were in order, we would go into it at once.

"*17th.*—Brother Abbott still unable to go on shore...Shway Bo had to return to-day, as word had come that Burman troops were approaching his village. Those living above here are very anxious to have the steamer go up, and drive away the Burmese. They are said to be two thousand strong, distant only one day's march. Several companies have come in to-day, one numbering fifteen persons, three of them preachers.

"*18th, Sabbath.*—Met for the first time in the new house. It is but partly covered. The covered room, which is some fifteen by thirty feet, is much too small: there were about seventy crowded into it, and at least twenty outside. No women or young children present. Some eight or ten were preachers. Had an interesting season; spoke from Ps. ciii. A large number of Pwos present,—substantial, honest-looking men. All seem ready to enter the kingdom at once, but want a guide. Oh that the Lord of the harvest would raise up and send forth laborers into his harvest, apparently so ready for the reaper! I am anxious to have a class of young men in training as soon as possible. Two or three assistants have come in from Arakan. They say that the people are all moving eastward. We tell them to wait a while, and on no account to come yet. I begin now to feel that there is work for me here.

"*20th.*—Have been on shore all day, and taken meals in native style,—without knife, fork, or spoon. Mau Yay came in to-day with a number of new Pwos. The latter were anxious to know whether they must worship the priests or not. They seemed much surprised when told that priests were like other men, and that none but God should be worshipped. For two weeks we have been living on board a war-steamer, with every thing in readiness for action. Now we have a little more of this than ever, as this has become the guard-ship since the departure of the *Sesostris*. The thirty-two-pounders fired at nine, P.M., make a disagreeable noise to one not accustomed to such sounds. We would not have chosen such a situation; but we have uniformly met with the kindest and most respectful treatment from all the officers.

"*23d.*—For two days have been wholly occupied on the house. There is a good deal yet to be done, and not a carpenter to be had. Some twenty Karens are on hand, all very willing to help, in their way. They are useful in heavy, rough jobs, but poor helpers in other kinds of work. They have already broken my saw, two chisels, hatchet-handle, etc. Nevertheless it would be very hard to do without them, especially as they work for nothing, and find themselves. Brother Abbott came on shore yesterday morning much improved. Had worship last evening in the larger room (thirty feet by fifty), which we take for a chapel. The part which we shall occupy is about half that size, and was formerly used by the *poongyees* as a dormitory and a place for keeping idols, sacred books, etc.

"After the service last evening there was a meeting of the preachers. Twelve were present. The four ordained men, Tway Po, Mau Yay, Myat Keh, and Po Kway, had been appointed a committee to inquire as to the losses of all the assistants, and their present needs. The case of each was taken up separately, and duly recorded. The result was, that some two hundred rupees were asked for to be divided among fifteen assistants. This sum, it must be remembered, is all that they have received for about two years; Mr. Beecher having been unable to reach the last annual meeting. Arrangements were made to-day for the school. No Sgaus are to come who cannot read. An exception will be made in favor of Pwos. We do not wish a large number, but tell them to select from each village three or four promising boys that are most anxious to learn, and send them in by the next full moon.

"*26th.*—By working hard and late on Saturday, succeeded in enclosing the chapel and a tolerably comfortable room for each of us. Several of the assistants and others came last evening, after worship, to ask if there was more work to be done; if not, they must return tomorrow. I must now let work alone for a while, and give all my time to the people, who still come in small companies, two or three daily. Mr. Abbott came off on Saturday, and brought all his things, his health much improved. He was able to preach Saturday evening, and twice yesterday, and does not seem the worse for it. Had a delightful sabbath. The day was very pleasant, and this increased the cheering effect of the services. The congregation consisted chiefly of Christian Sgaus, who have been gathering here for several days. Immediately after each service, I got the Pwos around me, and read and talked with them about the great God and the dying Saviour. Must always begin with the first elements of Christianity in talking with these people. The progress is slow at first, as many words and phrases have to be explained; and the difficulty is increased by the fact that the book dialect differs from that spoken in this section.

"*29th.*—There is a great Pwo population east and north of Bassein, and there are not a few below also...The most interesting company came in yesterday. They are all Christians, and came with Thahbwah. He says that in that village, Kyootah, there are fifty-two worshippers not yet baptized. One of the old men who came with him wept for joy. Here is precious fruit. Oh that it may increase a thousand-fold! They have a good school in the village. The other Pwo assistants, two of them, at least, are so far north that they dare not move. They are subject to constant oppression and exactions by the Burmese."

Mr. Abbott, writing July 24, gives an interesting view of the state of the churches in Bassein:—

"Nearly all the preachers have reported themselves. Five have died this year, including Myat Kyau, the first ordained Karen pastor. All these, with one exception, died of cholera, and they were all valuable men. I have not time to give further particulars. A great many disciples died of the same disease; but I have not learned the whole number. Many of the Karens have suffered extreme oppression. Nearly all their chapels have been demolished by the Burmese, so that there are but five or six left standing in Burma. Still the people were wonderfully delivered from the most extreme sufferings they apprehended in case of war. Many of them were confined, to be executed as soon as the English should approach the country. But the war steamers came up, and took Bassein before the Burmans had time to execute their threats upon the Karens; and, after the town was taken, they all betook themselves to flight, and the Karens escaped. They consider their deliverance a wonderful interposition of Providence. Some districts, however, are still overrun by bands of robbers. In them the people are oppressed to the last point of endurance.

"There are seven or eight hundred European and native troops in Bassein, and a company of artillery,—enough to protect the place against any Burmese force. They are not likely to be attacked, as the Burmese army is dispersed. Still the English forces will not go out into the surrounding country to protect the people during the rains."

On the 26th of August Mr. Van Meter again writes:—

"The two principal Pwo churches which are above Bassein have been unable to communicate with us, as the old [Burman] governor of Bassein is still occupying that region with some soldiers. We hope to hear from them soon, as the steamer moved up unexpectedly five days ago, and no doubt has made thorough work this time. The Christians in those parts have been in much danger, merely because they are Christians; for, as you know, all the blame of this war is laid on the Karen disciples. Their preachers have been fined very heavily, some having to pay upwards of two hundred rupees, and there were strong fears that it would come to worse. Already the Burmans had forbidden them to worship, commanded them to destroy their chapels, to drink arrack, and do things that would destroy their Christian character. None had yet yielded to any but the first of these arbitrary requisitions; but it was feared they would be compelled, unless deliverance soon came.

"Our school began at the 'death of the moon,' two weeks since. We had difficulty in getting a place for cooking and eating, as it is almost impossible to procure building materials. So we took possession of a third *kyoung*, a short distance away. Abundance of rice, with a few other articles, has been furnished by the Karens. What had to be bought was bought by the assistants in adjoining villages, at the best advantage. The people in this region seem to be coming to recognize more and more the justice of the principle that *Karens are to help Karens*, while the American churches take care of the 'teachers.' There are upwards of eighty students here at present, most of them young men. A number of the younger preachers are here also. Many of the young men have been studying for two or more years, and are therefore, in a measure, prepared to appreciate the daily lectures of Brother Abbott on the Scriptures. Other classes are conducted by the more advanced students under his direction. We have not yet heard how soon Brother Beecher will be able to join us.

"I have a little nucleus of six Pwo pupils, all of whom have learned to read within the year. I feel almost unwilling to detain any of the few who have been with us at Sandoway, or any of the Pwo assistants, as the time seems so favorable for labor among the Pwos. There are large districts near by, occupied almost exculsively by them, which no Pwo preacher has ever visited. A few days since, Shway Bo, accompanied by one of our former scholars, started for Shway Loung, one of the largest Pwo districts, containing a thousand houses. He is a competent man, and we hope that a flourishing church will spring up there as the fruit of his labors. They have taken books, and will commence a school at once, if scholars can be had. The other assistants are at present engaged in their respective fields, but are intending to go out into new fields as soon as arrangements can be made to supply their places. Even since our arrival here, I have learned of two or three young men coming forward as assistants, of whom I had not heard before. And thus we hope the Lord will furnish laborers for the great Pwo field, as he has for the work among the Sgaus.

"The country, on every side excepting the west, has been overrun for some weeks past by robber-bands,—men who but lately were in the Burman army, but are now scattered in companies of two or three hundred each. Constant reports of their depredations were reaching us; but it was not until lately that they began burning and sacking villages. The Burman head man over Bassein is devoid of principle, like all his kin, and is strongly suspected by the English officers, of playing a double game. Some of them are watching him very closely. 'Only give us some proof,' they say, 'and we will soon bring him to account.' He sent out his men, but accomplished nothing, and the robbers were only getting bolder, and coming nearer and nearer to Bassein. The same man made a great ado when told that Shway Weing would have exclusive control of the Karens. Indeed, Capt. I— —, a great friend of the Karens, tells me that he made such an uproar, that the major had to put him down summarily. At first he would not hear to it at all. How could he govern the country, and have a Karen govern at the same time over the same country! After leaving the presence of the officers, they say, he was so enraged that he struck Shway Weing, as they were going along together. But he will not attempt that again; for, as Capt. I——says, if they did not lay down the law, and the consequences he would meet if he ever dared to repeat the act, it was because the interpreter was afraid to tell him what they said. They even threatened him with the bastinado, if he ever interfered with Shway Weing, who, they told him, was entirely independent of him.

"Shway Weing is now absent, has actually gone to fight the Burmans. He left here last Saturday,—offered to go of his own accord,—took some fifty men, two or three old muskets, and a few *dahs* [large knives]. He went with the sanction of the officer in command, who could not, however, furnish him with arms. Brother Abbott tried to dissuade him from going, unless arms and ammunition were furnished him, and says he would not be surprised if he should be killed, for he is no coward. Still, as Brother Abbott said at the time, 'he knows what he is about. He has not been the son of a chief all his life, without getting some ideas of chieftainship.' His intention probably is to 'set a thief to catch a thief.' This he can do by collecting three or four hundred Pwo robbers, who are not scarce in these regions. Inspired with the idea of fighting against the Burmans with the sanction of the English, fighting, too, for their own country, they would be a formidable enemy for any equal number of Burmans. Shway Weing is a noble specimen of the Karen, very amiable, and much esteemed by all who know him. He looks young, but is not far from fifty. He often speaks of the time when he alone, of all the Karens in this region, worshipped the true God. I forgot to mention that he is head man over the Talaings also, and they are much attached to his rule. Burmans even have complained that they could not have him [for their ruler].

"*30th.*—We have received news from Shway Weing. He has raised some four hundred men and a hundred and fifty muskets. Those who had not fire-arms were armed with spears and swords, just drawn from their hiding-places. He did not intend to move, however, till he had increased his force to seven hundred or eight hundred men. We have recently heard that armed boats, and a considerable native force, have been sent from Rangoon to Pantanau in pursuit of the Burmese. Shortly after our arrival here, a company of Pwos came, who said that they were Christians, and were very glad to see us; they had given up all hope of seeing a teacher, since theirs had been taken away to Ava. One of them very communicative, repeated a portion of their creed (Roman Catholic), and sung a hymn in good style, the subject of which was praise to the great Creator. All the sentiments were quite evangelical, until near the close, when Mary came in for a share of divine honors. The man was a little suspicious, however, and soon inquired if we were the same as their teacher. He said they had no Bible, but had other books. Just before leaving, he inquired where 'that teacher Abbott' was. He seemed to be taken quite aback when Brother Abbott told him he was the man. He has not been here since. A few boys have been in, who said that their parents were disciples, but did not worship, now that their teacher was gone; that they could read, but not our books.

"Brother Abbott has been very poorly. Says he knows he is growing weaker every day, and was never so weak before. He has lost flesh very fast of late. His cough distresses him constantly, and, with frequent other complaints, it must be literally true, as he himself says, that he hardly has a moment of freedom from pain."

For more than two months Mr. Abbott was permitted to continue his instructions to the faithful band of Karen ministers, young and old, who loved and revered him as few men have been loved by their children according to the flesh. For their use, he had just carried through the press two sizable and well-prepared volumes of Notes on the Book of Acts and on the Epistle to the Hebrews. At last his strength is all gone. The willing spirit can no longer force the worn-out body to do its bidding. He himself sees that he must leave Bassein and the dear Karens forever. On the 27th of September Mr. Van Meter wrote to the secretary:—

"You will not be unprepared to learn that Brother Abbott has at length decided to quit the field. Since my last, he has been failing more and more, reviving, perhaps, for two or three days, but only to fall lower the next time. This decision cost him a long and dreadful struggle. Night after night did he toss on his bed, scarcely closing his eyes at all in sleep. He said it seemed as if he would be 'recreant to God and man' to leave this field, so inviting, just when he was so well prepared for this peculiar work. Ah! when will these bereaved children ever see another father such as he?"

When the decision was finally reached, he called the preachers around him to receive his last words,—words never before committed to paper, but still heard upon the lips of children's children in the land of his imperishable labors: "The kingdom of Christ is here in Bassein. You must care for it, and labor for it faithfully. Do not rely too much on the white teachers. Rely on God. If his kingdom prospers, it will prosper through your efforts. If it is destroyed, it will be at your hands." To his faithful Thahree and other young men he said, "The American Christians have spent much money on you. Be diligent and zealous in the Lord's service. Do not look for government employ." To all of them he said, *"Pgah ler a'mah ah tau tah t'thay bah nay, mau a'thu t'mah sgah lau tah t'gay"* (He that cannot make an increase, let him not diminish). By which he is understood to have meant, if you cannot increase in wisdom, in the love of God, in contributions, in numbers, etc., at least, let every man and every church *hold its own*. Let there be no falling off in any good word or work.

One of the native Christians who was present says,—

"We pitied the teacher very much. There was nothing left of him but skin and bones. He could not walk. As he left us, he said, 'If I do not die, I will come again; but I am very sick. As the Lord wills.'"

Nov. 6, writing from Maulmain on his way to America, Mr. Abbott says,—

"When the Karen preachers and students heard the first lisp of my design, the scenes through which I passed till I left, I am not able to describe. All the ordained pastors, and many of the preachers, were with me to the last. I was able, from time to time, to tell them all my plans for rebuilding their chapels, and gathering their scattered flocks. Our intercourse for the last few days was sad. Many bitter tears were shed; and the pastors clung to me as though they would not give me up."

Mr. Van Meter, writing at the time, says,—

"Such is the depth of feeling among the Karens, that they can hardly approach him without weeping. Several times, within a few days, I have seen one and another come to him; and, before a word could be uttered, the tear starts, the bosom heaves, and they turn away, and weep like children about to lose a fond and revered parent...Myat Keh gave a long exhortation to the Karens, Sunday evening, on the necessity of faith in prayer, and, by way of application, urged them all to try its efficacy in the case of their teacher. He himself spent the whole night in prayer."

Perhaps the only parallel to these scenes is Paul's parting with the elders at Miletus. Yet the Karens are far from being a demonstrative people. It has been said even, that they are not susceptible of gratitude. As with other races, something depends on the man who serves them and on the value of the service rendered.

GRADUATES OF THE BASSEIN KAREN GIRLS' SCHOOL, 1872

CHAPTER XI.

1853.

"Keep open among the heathen the doors that are open, and open those that are shut." —*Moravian Motto.*

"Human kindness is a key that unlocks every door, however firmly it may seem to be closed against us."—REV. W. LAWES, *New Guinea.*

"*Kindness*, but not gifts. Galleon-loads of silver and gay clothing will not purchase love for the missionary, or recommend the Saviour of sinners to any people."— *Anonymous.*

In October a flotilla of seven or eight steamers, and a detachment of three thousand men, proceeded up the swollen Irrawaddy. Prome and Henthada were occupied, with little or no opposition. Soon after, Pegu, the former capital of the Talaing kingdom, was taken, after a stubborn fight of a few hours. On the 20th of December, 1852, the whole of the ancient kingdom of Pegu was formally annexed to British India by proclamation of the Governor-General. Salutes were fired, and the administration of the new province was committed to the able hands of Capt. Phayre, the kind friend of the Sandoway missionaries. To Capt. Fytche, who succeeded Phayre in Sandoway, the charge of the turbulent Bassein district was soon intrusted. Meanwhile the barbarous predatory warfare, in which alone the Burmans are adepts, continued to rage over the entire country, outside of the garrisoned towns, and beyond the range of armed steamers. The Karens in their retired villages, and on account of their well-known attachment to the English, were exposed to the full force of the enemy's fury and hatred. Murder, tortures, robbery, and incendiarism were constant occurrences. Mr. Van Meter's journal, which follows, gives a vivid picture of what the Christians had to pass through in the transition from Burmese to English rule. Had the Karens been properly armed by the English, and allowed to fight under leaders of their own, doubtless they would have proved even a better match for the Burmans than they were.

"*Sept. 22.*—Sad news came in to-day of the destruction of two Karen villages...

"*23d.*—Heard to-day of the destruction of Kan Gyee's village. He is a younger brother of Shway Weing, and third in authority over the Karens in this region...

"*Oct. 2.*—Reports constantly arrive of the continued depredations of the Burmese in Karen villages. Two or three companies are in daily from the north or from the east. The people are flying, or if they dare to remain at home, and receive the Burmese, are subjected to the most relentless extortions. The Burmans have again appointed their own governors over all this part of the country. The steamer went up the river again on Monday, but did not accomplish much. Her shells were poor, and burst at a short distance from the ship. Have just learned of a spirited and successful resistance made by the Karens at Kyootah. The Burmese had decided to attack the village on Sunday, supposing the Karens would then be at worship, and off their guard. A few, however, with only four muskets, were on the watch for them at a point where the stream becomes quite narrow. The Burmese came in twenty boats, large and small. The Karens attacked them just at the right time. Thirteen of the Burmans were killed on the spot, and the others took to flight, leaving twelve of their boats behind. Kan Gyee came in yesterday, and gave an account of an attack by the Karens on Tantazin, known to contain those who had plundered and burned their villages. Two Burmans were killed, and six muskets taken. They could not take prisoners, as they would be pursued by a large Burman force, which was near by.

"*14th.*—Two Sgau Karens were 'cut to death' by the Burmans yesterday, at Paybeng. A man in to-day says the Burmans have carried off two children of his. Shway Weing's son is lying here very low of cholera. There have been a number of fatal cases here within a few days. War and pestilence—what occasion for gratitude, that thus far the complement of the fearful trio, *famine*, has not made its appearance!

"*16th.*—Shway Weing reports that the Karens resisted an attack of the Burmese two days ago in Theegwin. Sixteen of the enemy were killed.

"*17th, Sabbath.*—Some ten or fifteen women and a number of children, accompanied by two or three men, came in to-day from Paybeng, flying from the Burmans. The wife and child of one of the men died on the way, of cholera: others were left sick at the village, and some on the way, with a few faithful ones to watch over them. Three came in from Kindat. The people there are in constant fear. They say that the Burmans above now talk of compelling the Karens in that quarter to go and fight the Karens who are making such a spirited resistance below; *but they are to have no arms!* This idea, to drive Karens before them when making an attack, so as to protect themselves from the shots of the enemy, is quite original.

"*20th.*—Capt. Burbank of the *Pluto* is very anxious to render aid to the Karens. He will go down immediately, and drive off the Burmans, if the major will consent. He gave Shway Weing eighteen hundred charges of powder; and Capt. Irby supplied him with five hundred balls. Powder is very scarce. It is rather anomalous for a missionary to have the request for gunpowder, coupled with that for medicine, many times every day. Shway Weing's son is out of danger.

"*22d.*—Some Karens from above have just brought down the head of a Burmese chief, who was on his way, with four hundred and fifty men, to attack Kyouk Khyoung-gyee, two hours above us. Thirty Karens and eight Burmans, with about twenty muskets, lay in ambush, and attacked his party in front and rear, as they were passing between a hill and the river. More than ten of the enemy were killed, and several wounded: the remainder escaped.

"*25th.*—Kan Gyee is just in from Kyootoo with five prisoners. A party of fifty or sixty came to plunder and destroy what was left at this village. The Karens attacked them, taking five prisoners and one musket.

"*28th.*—Heard this morning, that three young men were killed a day or two since in Labogala. They were taken while driving buffaloes. Two were also taken, under similar circumstances, in Theegwin, four days ago, and tortured to death, by making incisions all over their bodies, and rubbing salt into them.

"*30th.*—The Karens say that their buffaloes are killed by the Burmans, who sell the meat, and buy powder of their friends in and about the town, and then go back to fight them. 'But what object can they have in fighting with you?' I have asked again and again. 'What do they expect to gain by it?' From all that I can learn, there seem to be three classes of Burmans,—those who fight because they are compelled to, those who do it for plunder, and those who do it from hearty good-will. The latter lay all the blame of the war on the Karens, because they have adopted the religion of the English. Kyootah has had to submit at last. The village is destroyed. The Karens say, 'If we kill ten, they send fifteen; if one hundred cannot conquer us, they send two hundred; if that will not do, they send three hundred; and so on, until they completely overpower us.'

"*Nov. 1.*—Called at the mess of the Ninth Native Infantry, and mentioned the great need of the Karens for powder. A spirited contribution was immediately set on foot. I thought it best to take up with a suggestion of one of the officers, to send off a servant of his to try and buy some, as the Burmese [traders] are now refusing to sell to the Karens.

"*3d.*—The Karens in Labogala repulsed an attack of the Burmese, and killed three. As usual, none were injured on the side of the Karens,—a fact which they often mention with much feeling, ascribing it to God's goodness. Capt. Grant, a great friend of Shway Weing, gave him a very pretty brass-mounted sword yesterday, with this note: 'I have presented a sword to Moung Shway Weing-gyee, as he is a sterling, honest man, and head of the Karens in this district.'

"*6th.* —A great fight just reported, and the Karens victorious. The Burmans had built a stockade at Magyeegon in the Pandau district, and garrisoned it with two hundred men. The assaulting party consisted of two hundred Karens on land, and eighty Burmans in boats. The fight lasted, from a little after noon, until near sunset, when the garrison made their escape as they best could. Three officers, having secreted themselves in the jangle, were captured and killed. Several others were killed, and a number of muskets taken; but none on the Karen side were injured.

"*9th.* —The Karens took eight Burman prisoners at Zanwa-khyoung. They were found under very suspicious circumstances. Four of them were brought in to-day. We hear that two steamers came down to Shway Loung; and, upon inquiry as to the authors of the disturbances there, all the blame was laid on the Karens. Two Karens who tried to reach the steamers were taken by the Burmans, and killed. Have just heard, that, of a number of Karen women kept prisoners at Kyoung-gon, three have already died through the violence offered them by their brutal captors.

"A large number of Karens came in to-day to help build me a house. I have decided to build a good-sized house inside the stockade. Have had quite enough of the jungle, in which our *kyoung* stands. I have not been well for a number of weeks, and the officers all advise the change. The European troops that have just come to relieve those who have been here since the town was taken have been getting large quantities of gold and silver images from the old pagodas, which had been dug over and over again for that purpose. Several hundred have been taken out by them already. I had heard, but had never before seen or imagined, how much Boodhism costs its stupid devotees, from whom you can hardly get the least pittance for a neatly printed volume in their own language, on the most interesting of subjects.

"*12th.* —I was a good deal annoyed yesterday to hear that the Karens who brought in the four Burman prisoners were *themselves in the stocks, and the prisoners set free.* I called on the major, and represented the case rather strongly. He charged Shway Weing with falsehood.

He said the prisoners had been placed in Shway Weing's hands; that no one else had any control over them; that he had not ordered the Karens to be put in the stocks, etc. The matter was much complicated by the appearance of Nga So, second in authority to Shway Weing, who was introduced by the interpreter as having a complaint to make against Shway Weing. Early this morning I called them both, with other Karens, and examined into the whole affair...Shway Weing says, that, if I were not here, he could not stand it, but would leave the place at once. [Nga So still lives, and draws a pension from the English Government; but he has never professed Christianity. — ED.]

"*16th.* — Pah Yeh, one of the assistants, came in to-day from Pandau, very urgent to have the steamer, or some boats, go up immediately. The Burmans have come down upon one of the villages, and carried off the preacher Thah Gay, his son (Shway Nyo, who has been studying for some time), and a number of the villagers. Pah Yeh thinks they will go on, and do the same in other villages. The people are in great distress, the Burmans all around them, and they cannot escape. Three men came in to-day with a long letter from Nahkee, assistant at Khateeyah, two hours this side of Pantanau. The Burmese there also are oppressing the Karens worse than ever, and have forbidden them to worship God, on pain of death. They have been compelled twice to go to the *kyoungs*, and offer obeisance, if not worship, to the priests, and were fined almost to their last *pice*. A small schooner had been seen there, and two gunboats. One of the latter was fired into, and a man killed. If these things are so, a strong force will soon be sent thither from Rangoon.

"*18th.* — A few weeks since, nearly the whole village of Peeneh-kweng, below us, on the west side of the river, was swept off by small-pox. Twenty-eight died within a few days, the preacher (Kyah Gaing) among the rest. Many of the dead were left unburied in their houses. Bad news from the north and the east, — the Burmese coming down in force upon Nga So and his little band of two hundred men. Word comes, that, unless they have help from the steamer, they will be overwhelmed.

"*20th.*—More definite news respecting the movements of the Burmese. They are coming in three directions,—from Kyounggon, five hundred; from Myau Mya (?), two hundred; and from Kyouk Khyoung-galay, from six hundred to a thousand. One Karen village, Kyongebyin, is already in the hands of the enemy. The Burmans surprised them by night, and secured twenty prisoners. The steamer went up the river this morning. Meekoo (a student severely attacked by cholera) is out of danger, but very weak. All the Karens who were helping on the house have returned. It is a time of distressing anxiety.

"*22d.*—Most encouraging tidings from the seat of war. The Karens have retaken Kyongebyin by storm. There was a total rout of the Burmese. Over twenty were killed on the spot, and the Karens are in hot pursuit. The only spring at this place was in the jungle, a considerable distance from the village. The Burmese had made several attempts to get water; but the Karens were watching, and fired on them whenever they came near. Water they must have; and so a captain, with sixty men, was sent for a supply. The Karens attacked, routed them, and killed their leader, and immediately made a general attack on the village. Shortly after this, two of the *Rattler's* boats went up the Dagah to aid this force, and, in conjunction with two hundred Karens, attacked a large body of Burmese at Thabau-ngoo. The Burmese fled, leaving almost every thing. Capt. Mellish wrote a glowing account of the affair, speaking in the highest terms of the bravery of the Karens. We have just heard that the Karens in Labogala intercepted a party of fifteen men, conveying powder to the Burman force in that quarter, a few days since. Eleven of them were shot in the boats, and the other four killed with the sword. So much for the late unjust proceedings here in relation to prisoners. Forty pounds of powder were taken...Formerly Nga So and his party had but forty muskets: they now have over two hundred. Sah Shway in Labogala had but twenty-eight: he now has one hundred. Shway Weing tells me that all together some five hundred muskets have been taken from the enemy by the different parties of Karens.

"*27th.*—The Karens frequently express their gratitude for the presence of a teacher. One said this evening, 'Teacher, if you had not been here, we could not have staid in the country.' A few days since, a man who had just come in from Me-gyoung-t'-yah exclaimed, 'O teacher! we come in and see you here, and it makes us very happy.' And I, for my part, all alone as I have been for the last two months, ask not to be anywhere else on earth but in the midst of these dear disciples. Among such a people missionary labor is a pleasure.

"*Dec. 6.*—Have been out, with several of the assistants and Shway Weing, for the purpose of selecting a good site for a Karen village near Bassein. Nearly every eligible place is already occupied by the Burmese. We have fixed upon a place [Singoung?] about four miles below, just a good distance from the city. All seem to approve of the choice, and there will probably be a large Karen village there before many months. There is no prospect yet of quiet. A large number of refugees came in three days ago, most of them from Kyootah, one of the first villages destroyed by the Burmans. They brought a number of buffaloes, several canoes, a large ox-cart, and a full proportion of little ones. They are all living in our *kyoung*, outside the stockade. I see them generally morning and evening, and give medicine and advice to the sick. Three men came in yesterday from Shankweng, a long way up the river: they fled from their village three days since. They came to inquire whether it would be wrong for them to acknowledge the rule of the Burmese, and thereby to save their property, especially their paddy, which is now ready for the sickle. I told them to return at once, to make their most respectful obeisance to the *mingyee*, and be quiet until the English take the country.

"*7th.*—A schooner is just in from Rangoon. It is seven weeks since I heard a word from any part of the world, excepting a short note from Sandoway. The days of my loneliness are ended. Brother Beecher has come. The captain of the *Rattler* has very kindly brought down three hundred baskets of paddy from a Karen village, respecting which I had written him. The great object now is to cut and save all the paddy we can."

Mr. Beecher, leaving his family at Kyouk Pyoo, had started for Bassein, *viâ* Rangoon, on the 27th of September. Writing from Rangoon (Oct. 25), he says, —

"I am happy to be re-assured by Brother Vinton that his views respecting the principle of native preachers being supported by their own churches are the same as those entertained by the Bassein mission, and to hear also, that he has already put his views into practice among the churches in Rangoon and in Maulmain, as far as he has been able."

It is but just to say here that this statement is quite correct so far as the Rangoon Karen churches are concerned. Beginning on this principle, with the deterrent example of his old field, and the stimulating example of Bassein to sustain him, Mr. Vinton succeeded in establishing that mission on the basis of self-support, where it has stood ever since, second only to Bassein in that respect. It was not so easy, however, to undo the mischief already wrought in Maulmain, as we shall see further on. Mr. Beecher writes again from Bassein, on the 28th of December: —

"You will rejoice, with us and the suffering Karens, to hear that Pegu has been proclaimed British territory. The Commissioner of Pegu, Capt. Phayre, kindly sent the mission a copy of the proclamation, accompanied by a letter, in which he speaks of the Karens as follows: —

"'I am particularly anxious that your Karen people should receive protection, and be put under people of their own race. I hear but one account of the Karens from every officer of the force, namely, that on all occasions their information has been the best, and their assistance the most hearty. We must not forget such good will as has thus been shown us.'

"This is truly glad tidings, and a day of deliverance to this long-oppressed people. Blessed be the Lord, who 'bringeth the counsel of the heathen to nought,' whose eye 'is upon them that fear him, upon them that hope in his mercy; to deliver their soul from death, and to keep them alive in famine.' Were it not for this timely proclamation, to be followed up, we hope, with vigorous measures for the suppression of the large robber-bands which are now laying waste the country on every side, this people must soon have famine added to the other horrors of war. But the hand of Providence, which has been so remarkably displayed in the preservation of his people during the whole war, is now again extended for their deliverance. I find, on careful inquiry, that the Karens—in about fifteen engagements fought for the defence of their homes, their wives and children—have killed one hundred and sixty-five of the enemy, while only three of their own number have been killed, and three wounded; and this, although they were disarmed by the Burmans at the opening of the war. They are still fighting in self-defence; and reports of [skirmishes], with various success, come in almost daily.

"Karens, distressed with fears that their villages will be pillaged and their crops burned by robber-bands, come in daily for counsel and aid, and to beg that we will intercede with the military and naval commanders in their behalf. On returning to my house, after an effort to aid them, a few days since, I saw at a distance a small company, who appeared like Burmans, approaching the stockade. Two men were mounted on large ponies, and near them were two others, bearing aloft, upon staves ten or twelve feet long, large red umbrellas. 'None but Burmese captains have such umbrellas as these,' said an astonished Karen by my side. They enter the stockade, come around, and stop in front of my house. One advances towards me. 'Is it you, Po Kway? And what are these?'

"'It is thus, teacher. Three or four hundred Burmans had stockaded themselves near a Karen village. Eight days ago a detachment made an attack on the village very early in the morning, and took several women prisoners. The Karens rushed to the rescue as soon as they could rally fifty-six fighting men. They came upon the Burmans while eating their rice, fired upon them, shouting, and brandishing their swords and spears. The Burmans fled in confusion, but not till six of their number were shot down. The women were all rescued; and the men, in returning, took these umbrellas, several muskets, swords, and spears, which the Burmans threw away in their flight. The ponies also were taken there. One of them lacked a bridle; but the Karen who captured him made the fetters he had wrenched from his own feet serve for bits. Ropes completed the bridle; and the late prisoner in irons now rides his enemy's steed. Teacher, we have brought the umbrellas for you and the officers to look at, and do with as you like, and the ponies for your use, if you wish them.' One of the umbrellas I must keep to commemorate the valor of the Karens; and one of the ponies shall henceforth serve their teacher.

"Such are the scenes of war in one part of the district; but in another, how different! Not two days' walk from the scene just described, Thah Gay and Tau Lau, with many of their flock, are in the hands of merciless robbers. From day to day the fiends wreak their vengeance on these defenceless disciples of Christ. They are pierced with swords and spears, savagely beaten, suspended by their necks from trees, and let down just before life is extinct, to recover strength for a repetition of the cruel torture. Day after day, and week after week, for two dreadful months, do these men thus die daily. Word was brought yesterday that they were released from these sufferings by death, and that they were strong in faith to the last. The news was a mournful relief to our painful anxiety. May this state of anarchy, terror, and woe, soon be succeeded by the blessings of peace under a firm and just government!

"*Jan. 8.*—Annexation was proclaimed in Bassein on the morning of the 3d. It was read in three languages to the attentive multitude. Twenty-one guns from the stockade, and as many from the steamer, thundered forth the decree of a mighty nation. What various emotions are awakened in the awestruck crowd! The soldier is elated with thoughts of glory. The haughty Burman hears in those peals the doom of his kingdom and his religion, and trembles. But the long-oppressed Karen hears a voice proclaiming liberty to the captive, freedom to worship God. And, louder than trumpet-blast or cannon's roar, the messenger of God hears the voice of his ascended Lord speaking to the Christians of his native land, 'Behold, how plenteous the harvest, how few the laborers, how wide and effectual the door, how few to enter in! Awake, put on thy strength, O Zion! Awake, and come up to the help of the Lord against the mighty!'

"The imposing ceremony is over; but the enemy is not yet subdued. Scarcely has the voice ceased which proclaims Pegu to be British soil, and its inhabitants subjects of British rule and protection, when news arrives of another conflict between the Karens and the banditti. Two Karens have been wounded, and four Burmans killed. The lives of the Karens were spared; but five thousand baskets of rice, their staff of life, which they had striven long and hard to defend, were devoured by the flames. In this hour of distress they come, beseeching us to intercede with the Commissioner for protection. Their foes are threatening still further devastations. Their case is presented, is regarded with favor. Inquiries are made, plans formed, and at the appointed hour the steamer starts on its errand of mercy. The mind is relieved of a burden of anxiety. Patience, too, whether its work has been perfect or not, has had work enough in obtaining definite information from natives of indescribable stupidity; and the whole frame, in constant excitement for days and nights, needs relaxation. The steamer has been gone only a few hours, when Tau Lau, only a week since reported to have died under torture, makes his appearance, and tells his tale of sufferings, from which he barely escaped with life, wounded and naked.

"Shway No, [Nyo?] who has been missing two months, and was known to have fallen into the hands of robbers, comes as Tau Lau's companion. He was redeemed for thirty rupees, and has since lived secreted. They bring word that Thah Gay, too, is still alive, but that the tortures he is suffering are worse, if possible, than those of which he was reported to have died. He is alive; but an awful death is awaiting him, together with thirty-nine others. They are crowded into one prison, and allowed, from day to day, barely food enough to prevent starvation. Beneath their prison-floor are piled the fagots which are to burn them alive. More than seven hundred rupees have been extorted from their friends by false promises of release. Perhaps the hope of obtaining more money delays their doom; but the language of the tormentors to their victims more probably expresses their real intention, 'We shall despatch you as soon as we can catch a few more of you.' Thah Gay is loaded with three pairs of fetters, and split bamboos are so applied as to pinch his flesh, from his toes to his shoulders.

"Sad and anxious faces again approach the missionary, and he is implored to aid in delivering Thah Gay and his flock from such sufferings and impending death. Oh for the arm of a Samson! But help can come alone from Him whose arm is not shortened; and the prayer that has been going up in their behalf for weeks is now offered with renewed fervor. But faith without works is dead; and, after a night of prayer, Tway Po and Myat Keh ask our opinion of this plan: 'We have resolved to go in different directions, and, calling together a company of our brethren, make an attempt to rescue Thah Gay.'—'Go. And may the Almighty go with you, and grant you success!' Muskets and ammunition are sought, arrangements are made, and they come again to my room. Fervent prayer is offered; and they go forth, asking us earnestly to continue to pray for them.

"The new order of things imposes heavy duties upon the missionary. Crowds throng his house from day to day, plying him, with a thousand questions as to the intentions of the English, their form of government, etc. One company of thirty or forty no sooner depart satisfied than another company arrives, equally ignorant, equally curious, and equally persevering in trying the strength and patience of the missionary. The Karens, by their hearty and efficient aid during the war, have merited the special favor and protection of the English, and are to be under petty magistrates of their own race. Our opinion is sought as to who are best qualified for these offices. Thus the temporal as well as the spiritual welfare of thousands is affected by our words and acts. Who is sufficient for these things?

"Do Christians in America rightly estimate the importance of their mission-fields and the magnitude of mission-interests? Will men of influence, of experience and wisdom, who turn a deaf ear to the claims of the foreign field, be found guiltless at the last day? If a new college wants a man of learning and practical wisdom for professor or president, he is soon forthcoming, when, perhaps, the whole institution might be blotted from existence, and its proposed work be done elsewhere, without endangering half the interests that are imperilled at some mission-station for want of that same man to guide its momentous affairs.

"Feb. 5.—The expedition sent to disperse the bands that were laying waste the country to the south and east so effectually routed the banditti, that the people in that region, under the temporary jurisdiction of Shway Weing, are now returning to their devastated homes in peace. The Karens who thought to release Thah Gay found their number too small to make the attempt with any hope of success, and gave up the plan. Tway Po returned to Arakan, to bring his family and congregation from the unhealthy and unfruitful jungles by the sea to the fertile and salubrious plains of Bassein. Other pastors and elders from Arakan seek advice as to the wisdom of following his example.

"The steamer *Zenobia,* from Maulmain, reached this place on the 20th ult., bringing my family with the Van Meters—all in usual health. The steamer's boats and crew, since her arrival, have been actively engaged in dispersing the Burmese forces. The first expedition, to the vicinity of Pantanau, where the Karens have suffered severely, was in every way successful. Ninety Europeans, with their Karen allies, gained a brilliant victory over three thousand Burmans; that number being swelled by camp-followers to nearly ten thousand. Forty were found dead on the field, and two hundred and fifty were taken prisoners. We hope that this will prove to be the finishing stroke to the war in this district.

"Encouraged by news of the near approach of a European force, a large body of Karens made a rapid march upon the Burmans, who have held Thah Gay and his villagers. They were in time to save all but Thah Gay. Two days before the attack of the Karens, the Burmans fastened him to a cross, and disembowelled him; when, life not being extinct, they shot him twice, and cut his throat.[1] Thus has perished a good, faithful, and promising pastor. Nahkee, who long lived secreted, has at last escaped from his enemies, and is now with us. We hope that the country will soon become settled, and that we shall be able to prosecute our labors without interruption."

{ Footnote: [1] For a sketch of this martyr's death, see Missionary Magazine, October, 1856, pp. 388, 389, also Karen Morning Star, May, 1853, pp. 139-142. This man is often called Klau-meh. His zeal and success as an evangelist were remarkable; and to save his life he would not deny his Lord, even under excruciating and long-continued tortures. }

On his passage to Maulmain for the ladies and children of the mission, Mr. Van Meter, in his little cutter of twenty tons, was blown off to sea when almost in sight of Amherst; so that the voyage, which should have occupied but six days, was lengthened to sixteen. Writing (Jan. 27), after their arrival in Bassein, he says, —

"Capt. A. Fytche, our old friend at Sandoway, has been here some weeks as deputy commissioner. He is away now with an expedition, clearing out two or three places above this which the Burmans have long made their headquarters, and which no European force has ever succeeded in reaching. A large force of Karens co-operate with the Europeans. A bamboo house has been put up on the Catholic compound since my departure, and we hear that they have quite a large attendance of European soldiers. We do not hear of their doing much in native work.

"Since the arrival of the *mamas,* our *kyoung* has been full nearly all the time, principally of Burman women and children, who have their curiosity greatly excited by the presence of two American women with their children. Mrs. Van Meter has sat two hours or more each day, reading and talking to them in their own language. Even now many of them listen with interest to what is said, although the greater part, of course, come from mere curiosity. Doubtless willing ears will be found to listen for the truth's sake as she acquires greater facility in the language. As to the Karen field, we could hardly ask for any thing more encouraging. Had a large company last Sunday, including many Karen women."

From Mr. Beecher's pen we have the following account of the first annual association held within the limits of Bassein: —

"The meeting was opened Feb. 22, and closed on the evening of the 25th. Many circumstances combined to render it a season of joyful and melancholy interest. The fact that we met, not, as formerly, on the inclement coast of Arakan, at a distance from the homes of the Karens and from our own, but in the midst of our people and at our own doors, in our own field rescued from the despot and persecutor, and that we were thus enabled, at its centre, to devise measures for the edification of the churches, and the preaching of the gospel among the heathen at greater advantage than ever before, was fitted to awaken in us all lively gratitude and joy.

"But a view of the desolations which disease and war have wrought among the preachers and their flocks mingled sadness with our joy. Seven of the pastors whom we have been accustomed to meet on these occasions have gone to their rest. Six fell by disease: the seventh, Thah Gay, was the victim of Burmese cruelty, and died, to use his own words, 'the death of Christ.' While such a marked providence has been displayed towards the Christians, that very few have died on the battle-field, we have been called to mourn the loss by sickness of 141 members of our communion, and 119 members of Christian families, who had not yet received baptism.

"The recent death of Thah Gay, with all the aggravating circumstances fresh in our minds, the presence of his family, bearing the marks of long and bitter suffering, and their tale of woe, told with tears and sobs, excited our deepest sympathy and sorrow. Two or three of the preachers are still in the hands of a cruel Burman chief, about whom we have great reason to be anxious. A few preachers were absent through fear of cholera and small-pox, which are beginning their annual ravages around us; but it was highly gratifying to meet thirty-nine of our brethren in the ministry on this important occasion. The work of ruin wrought by the war has been great. Twenty-five churches have been scattered, their chapels and villages destroyed, and in many cases all the personal property of the people wrested from them. Great numbers are thus reduced to beggary. In two or three townships, providentially, the Karens have been able to raise and preserve their usual amount of rice, which, if distributed with the Christian benevolence which we expect, will do much to relieve the destitute. Still there are many who will suffer, we fear, after all that we can do for them, from insufficient food, clothing, and shelter. The preachers, on this account, will require much more aid from the mission this year than they have received for several years past. The appropriation, six hundred rupees, when distributed among those whose claims are the most urgent, will do but little towards meeting their most pressing wants.

"Perhaps half of the churches that have been scattered are returning to their former places of abode, and will gather around their former pastors. Some of the members will remain where they fled for refuge, a part uniting with other churches, and others forming new ones under other pastors. Years must elapse before the churches will be as well organized and efficient in supporting the preaching of the gospel as they were before the war. We are grateful that we have at this juncture a class of ten young men well prepared by their studies at Sandoway and Maulmain for ministerial work. Four of these are appointed over churches left destitute by the death of pastors. One was appointed over a new church, which welcomes him with the promise of support. His labors commenced with the reception of ten members, who were baptized by the ordained brother who accompanied, and introduced him to his field. Four others, each with an associate, have gone forth as missionaries to the unconverted. Two, who have enjoyed fewer advantages in education, but have proved themselves efficient laborers, were also appointed to labor among the heathen, making six in all, who, with their associates, will do missionary work, and be supported mainly by the funds of the Karen Home Mission Society. It will be impracticable for them to do much during the rains, and probably those who do not succeed in so far discipling villages that their constant presence and teaching will be required will then pursue their studies with us.

"There are many thousand unconverted Karens near Bassein, who afford a promising field for missionary effort, besides yet greater numbers still further away, of whom we know comparatively little. One object of those sent forth will be to explore those fields. Besides the efforts of those who devote themselves exclusively to mission-work, it will continue to be our earnest endeavor to impress on every pastor his duty to labor constantly for the conversion of the heathen in his own vicinity. The vast field seems ready for the harvest. The Lord has raised up in all fifty-five native laborers to enter in and reap. Let prayer be offered unceasingly, that these laborers and their teachers may be full of the Holy Ghost and of faith, that much people may be added to the Lord.

"The unsettled state of the people during the war, the loss of nearly all their books, the interruption of religious services, has been attended naturally by many departures from holiness and rectitude. Twenty cases of discipline were reported at this meeting, about half of which were for violations of the seventh commandment. The unsatisfactory manner in which many of these cases were treated shows that we have before us a most important work, — to bring these converts from heathenism, pastors as well as people, up to the Christian standard of discipline.

"We are glad, however, that the dark picture of this year is relieved by some bright spots. Amid the confusion, the gloom, and declension that have attended the war, the life-giving influences of the gospel have been felt. During the year twenty-eight families, numbering in all about a hundred souls, have professed to abandon the worship of *nats,* and to believe on Christ. These have not yet been instructed sufficiently to receive baptism...The pastors feel the importance of establishing common schools, and will exert themselves to do this as fast as they recover from the effects of the war. The association being in session upon the Thursday set apart in our native land for special prayer for colleges, the subject of education was brought up, and this custom explained, after which an hour was spent in prayer with the Karens for the same objects.

"Our statistics for 1852 are: churches, 50; baptized, 43; excluded, 10; died, 141; whole number of communicants, about 5,000; preachers laboring as missionaries, 6; appointed at the association, 10; died, 7; whole number of preachers, 55; pupils taught in common schools, 184; in boarding schools, 80."

Mr. Van Meter adds some particulars respecting the Pwo work: —

"Of the four older assistants, three were present, the fourth being kept away by sore eyes. This was the third time he had been prevented from attending by a similar cause. When help was again asked for him, I mentioned that this was the third year that he had failed to come, and, more than this, that he had sent neither delegate nor letter. They immediately began to plead for him, that it was not owing to indifference, that he had a large heart, and was very zealous in the work of God. I was glad to hear this; but, to conform to our rules, one of them promised to see him on his return, and to send back a written account of his labors and the state of his church. I will then send him the amount awarded by the committee for the present year. The assistants have wrought in their former fields, as far, at least, as the unsettled state of the country would allow. They have all performed more or less missionary work.

"Thahbwah has been laboring in a new field, nearly east of Bassein, with much encouragement. He wishes to remain there a while longer, until the work is so far advanced, that another with less experience can carry it forward, when he will leave for another part of his inviting field. Shway Bo started last August for Labogala, but was prevented from reaching that place. He then set out for Shway Loung, but had hardly entered on his work, when the first battle was fought in that region, since which, all has been in confusion. He has baptized twenty-two of those for whom Thahbwah had been laboring.

"Besides these, there are three others recognized as assistants in part. One of these, Leh Soung, I saw first in November last. He has been for some months acting pastor at Paybeng. He is a young man of much promise, although he has never been in our schools; has a good knowledge of Sgau and of Burmese. He has not yet asked for help from the mission. Another, Shway Leng, has been engaged most of the year in preaching, and teaching a school of twenty or thirty scholars at Kyootah. The third, Pyah Thay, brother to Thaing Kyo, has just gone as a missionary to Pandau and vicinity. Ten rupees were given him, and will insure him against want for at least two months...Tau Lau goes to Pandau also, the district in which he resided before the war, and where most of the Pwo Christians have been gathered. The two largest Pwo churches were formerly there...Another missionary to the Pwos is a young man who has been studying in Maulmain. He is a Sgau, but has a good use of Pwo and Burmese. He has a heart for the work, and is to go to Keh Boung, a long way to the north-east of Bassein, beyond the other assistants.

"One alone, of all the Pwo Christian villages, escaped the destroyer. Their paddy, buffaloes, books, and other property, shared the same fate, except what was carried off by the enemy. It was not at all uncommon, in former years, for paddy to sell at five rupees a hundred baskets. Now it is not to be had for less than thirty, and, in some places, forty rupees. Its exportation, we hear, is prohibited. Still it must continue very scarce until the next harvest, and even longer, unless the country is quiet at sowing-time, and the crop equals the ordinary yield. We have fears for the people. It will be very difficult for many to support their families. Not a few will have to depend largely upon charity. We have just prepared an address, soliciting aid for the destitute. We hope that it will meet with a ready response from the officers, as many of them have expressed sympathy for the suffering Karens."

In April of this year the fighting was supposed to be over; but the rejoicing of the Christians over the return of peace was somewhat premature. Nine Karen missionaries were actively engaged in preaching among the heathen during the dry season. Four Karens were appointed *goung-gyouks*, or magistrates of districts corresponding to our counties,—an office of rather low order, but of considerable responsibility. Their names were Shway Weing (our old friend, "the young chief"), Nga So, Shway Myat, and Kangyee. Several others were appointed *thoogyees*, or tax-gatherers. Thus was the door at once thrown open for the long-oppressed Karens to rise in the scale of influence and civilization. A friend may be permitted to doubt, however, whether they were fully prepared at that time to enter the door. At all events, the subsequent course of three out of the four magistrates was singularly unfortunate. Mr. Beecher writes, April 21:—

"The war, I said, is past. Yes: the storm has swept by, and in the calm that follows we are learning the sad extent of the destitution, wretchedness, and ruin which it has wrought. Almost daily small parties come in from the despoiled villages to implore our aid in obtaining rice, to ask our intercession with the government that they may be exempted from taxes this year, and to make numberless inquiries on points civil, social, moral, and ecclesiastical, to say nothing of those surgical and medicinal. We have thus constant opportunities for learning the state of the churches, and for inciting them to efforts for the education of their children, and for preaching to the heathen. These parties are often composed of heathen Karens, giving us good congregations in our own houses. They listen attentively, and take tracts and books home with them, that they may there learn of the religion we preach. Many of them say that they will worship God as soon as they can learn the way.

"The interest among the Burmans continues unabated. Twice have parties come to my room, saying, 'Teacher, we would listen to the doctrines of Christ.' On one occasion, being pressed with duties to the Karens, I directed a Karen preacher to explain the gospel to them, when, as too often, instead of preaching Christ, he began descanting on the folly of idolatry. One of the Burmans immediately checked him by saying, 'We know all about our own gods, and modes of worship. What we wish, is to learn about your God and the doctrines you believe,' and again desired that the teacher himself would preach to them. I need not add that the desire was gratified to the best of my ability. It would thus appear that there are those among this people who would take the kingdom by violence; but how much is due to mere curiosity, time alone can disclose. A Burmese missionary should soon occupy this promising field.

"I learned last evening of the conversion of four or five families at a village about thirty miles east of us. Four or five persons have been waiting there several years for an opportunity to be baptized. These, with the recent converts, form a company of twenty-five or thirty candidates. An ordained pastor will at once go there, and I hope soon to report the organization of a church. The man who has been instrumental in the conversion of these and many others has never been recognized as a preacher, and has studied only enough to learn to read; but what he could learn of the gospel he has been faithful in making known to others while laboring as a farmer for the support of his family. Mau Yay has just returned from a tour to the west and south, in which he baptized forty persons, and collected thirteen rupees for home missions."

April 22 he adds this sad intelligence: —

"A mysterious providence has this morning thrown our whole mission into mourning. Our dearly beloved brother, Tway Po, died about nine, A.M., of cholera. He had commenced building a large village [Kaunee], about four miles north of the town, with very cheering prospects, but has thus been cut off in the midst of his usefulness. It is also our painful duty to record the death, by cholera, of another preacher, Kyau Too. May these afflictions be sanctified to our spiritual good and the advancement of Christianity among this people!"

To these losses by death was added, before the close of the year, that of Nahyah, the valued pastor of the church at Kyootah.

In September was held the first regular meeting of the Bassein Karen Ministerial Conference, — an institution which has proved to be of great value, and which has continued its meetings every three or four months, substantially unchanged, to the present time. As it was a beginning of so much importance, we transcribe Mr. Beecher's account of the first meeting: —

"The meeting opened on the morning of Sept. 3, and closed on the 6th. It was a season of deep interest to ourselves, and we have never seen the Karens enter more heartily upon any enterprise than they did upon the objects of this gathering. Forty preachers were present, a good number of delegates, and, on one occasion, a congregation of about five hundred. The first half-day of the conference was spent in devotional exercises; the remainder of the day and evening, in listening to oral reports from the preachers, of their labors for the six months since the Association. The object in requiring these reports was to learn definitely from each his views of their responsibilities and duties as pastors, and preachers of the gospel, the manner in which they spend their time, and the standard of discipline which they endeavor to maintain in their churches. The facts which were brought out gave us excellent opportunities for correcting what was erroneous, for encouraging and promoting what was right, and suggesting what was deficient. While it appeared that some of the pastors have very inadequate views of their calling, we were much gratified by the evidence given that others have a just sense of the sacred responsibilities of those to whom are committed the care of immortal souls. So in discipline some had been negligent, while the larger number had tried to follow the Bible standard in maintaining the purity of their flocks. All seemed highly pleased with the plan for the pastors thus to meet in conference, and after full discussion voted unanimously to meet hereafter every three months.

"The meeting of the Home Mission Society [which followed] was largely occupied with encouraging reports from the missionaries. Two young candidates for the ministry, Kweebeh and Thahpah, on arriving in Laymyetnah district, about three days north of Bassein, found that the children in some of the villages were anxious to learn to read Karen. Their parents, though somewhat averse to it, gave their consent. One of the young men taught the children, while the other preached in the neighboring villages. The children were taught first the story of Jesus, and their duty to believe on and worship him. They did soon believe, and wished their parents to accept the new religion; but they were told to wait till next year, as they (their parents) were not ready yet. The children then told the teacher, 'Come to us next year, and teach us again; and, if our parents still wish to worship *nats*, they may do so, but *we* will worship God.' Soon after they left that vicinity, a Karen family which they had visited professed conversion.

"The society was re-organized by the election of Karen officers. More than two hundred and thirty rupees were collected at the meeting, wholly the contribution of the churches in a year when the scarcity of rice almost amounts to a famine. Four missionaries were appointed for the next six months, and others will be appointed as soon as the season favors jungle-travelling."

Mr. Van Meter adds, that, after careful deliberation, it was voted to have meetings for prayer and Scripture-reading in the village chapels every Wednesday and Saturday evening, also that the old custom of meeting in the chapels for worship every evening be recommended to those living within a convenient distance.

At the December meeting, Rev. J. H. Vinton of Rangoon was present, and added much to the interest and profit of the occasion. Myat Keh reported by letter the baptism of seventy-two persons since the previous quarterly meeting. Mau Yay had baptized sixty, and Po Kway forty, of whom twenty were recent converts from heathenism. Eleven missionaries were appointed,—two to the Shway Doung field, near Prome; two to the Henthada district; and the others, Mau Yay among the number, to labor nearer home. Thus early was the work of foreign missions definitely entered upon by these churches, which seem almost to have reached maturity at one bound, without passing through the cradle at all. But another year of war and warlike rumors must elapse before the Bassein Christians can fairly settle down to the work of the second period of their history,—the period of reconstruction and consolidation.

We close the chapter with our last extract from Mr. Abbott's pen—a tribute to the memory of his dearly loved Tway Po, whom he was so soon to follow to the better land:—

"I baptized him in 1842, 1 think, at a village in Arakan. He began preaching at Ong Khyoung, and I ordained him the second year following. He was with me a good deal at Sandoway, and constantly with me when in the Karen jungles. He was the companion of my missionary labors, in travel, in sickness and sorrow, by night and by day. He was my counsellor in all matters relating to the organization and discipline of the Karen churches. He apprehended the great truths of the gospel, the mysteries of redemption by faith in the blood of atonement, with a clearness and strength seldom surpassed even in Christian lands. His unimpeachable character as a man of prayer and of entire devotion to the cause of Christ, his aptness to teach, his goodness, his sound judgment, his wisdom in counsel, his capacity to govern, his reputation,—'well reported of by them that were without,'—his meekness and humility, which covered him as a garment of loveliness,—all recommended him as a candidate for the ministry.

"Tway Po increased in wisdom and knowledge, and in his usefulness as a pastor. He had my entire confidence, and soon won the confidence and love, not only of his own church, but of all the churches and preachers among the Karen people. When I left Burma in 1845, I relied upon him to take my place. During my absence he and Myat Kyau baptized many hundreds, formed churches, and set over them preachers and teachers, as much to my satisfaction as if I had been on the ground. Myat Kyau was a man to be respected and esteemed; Tway Po, a man to be also loved. Both were men of unyielding integrity and unwavering fidelity, and each in his own way was useful to the cause of Christ. Translated from the darkness of heathenism into the kingdom of God's dear Son, the first ordained among the Karens, they both fulfilled the ministry they had received of the Lord Jesus with fidelity and honor, and have their reward."

CHAPTER XII.

1854.

"Let me plead for the foreign missionary idea as the necessary completion of the Christian life. It is the apex to which all of the lines of the pyramid lead up. The Christian life without it is a mangled and imperfect thing."—REV. DR. PHILLIPS BROOKS.

In the early part of the year, nearly all the northern and eastern townships of Bassein were again in a state of insurrection. Among the more notable of the rebel chiefs, so called, of this and the previous year, we find the names of Nga Tee-lwot, Nga Thein, Nga Thabon, the Talaing chief Myat-toon, Nga Thah-oo, and Hlabau. By his energy and success in putting an end to the raids of these emissaries from the court of Ava, Major, since General, Fytche, the deputy commissioner, distinguished himself, and secured rapid promotion. For his official reports of the military operations in Bassein for 1853 and 1854, in which it appears that the Karens bore an active and creditable part, reference may be made to his work, "Burma, Past and Present," vol. ii. appendix B, pp. 221-238.

The family of Nga So still cherish the following certificate, among others, given to their father by Major Fytche and other officers. Similar testimonials were doubtless given to the other Karen captains, which we have not happened to see.

BASSEIN, Dec. 4, 1860.

Ko Tso, *Myo-oke* of Theegwin, was one of the earliest and most zealous adherents of the British Government in this district. On my arrival at Bassein, and publishing the proclamation of annexation, he joined me with a body of some twelve hundred Karens, and assisted greatly in driving the Burmese troops out of the district, and in dispersing the marauding bands. He is the only Karen *myo-oke*, remaining out of four which I appointed on the settlement of the district. Ko Tso may always be depended on as a most faithful servant of the government in any emergency, and he possesses great influence amongst the people of his own race. I have had good reason also to be satisfied with [the discharge of] his court duties as *myo-oke*.

(Signed)
A. FYTCHE, *Colonel,*
Deputy Commissioner, Bassein.

About this time we first hear of the priests of a new Hindoo (?) deity called "Maulay." His worship included offerings of money to the priests, with much feasting, dancing, etc. This deity was expected soon to make his advent, with all the ancestors of his disciples in his train, with all manner of worldly and sensual delights for the faithful. These priests and their devotees occasioned much excitement, and their proceedings began to assume more or less of a rebellious character.

To add to the confusion and uncertainty, the government was now seriously contemplating the removal of the district headquarters from Bassein to a place three tides down the river, on the west bank, called Negrais, or Dalhousie. The removal was actually determined upon. Some *lacs*[1] of rupees were expended in preparing a site for the new town, landing-places, etc., when suddenly a furious storm, accompanied by a great tidal wave, so wrecked the place, that the project was abandoned. The removal of the mission establishment would have followed the success of this measure as a matter of course; and, as it was, some delay in erecting necessary buildings in Bassein, and no little uncertainty, resulted.

{ Footnote: [1] A lac is one hundred thousand. }

Mr. Beecher's account of the interesting meeting of the association at Kohsoo was not published, possibly, because of the strong ground which he took, as always, on the necessity of more extended facilities for education at Bassein than the Executive Committee at that time were prepared to grant. We give the more important paragraphs: —

"The year has been one in which many of our brethren have had to struggle with the reverses, temptations, and sufferings attendant upon war and famine. We are thankful that the great body of believers have remained steadfast during this fight of afflictions, though we are pained to learn that a few have turned again to the weak and beggarly elements of heathenism. The meeting was held, Feb. 13-15 inclusive, at the large and flourishing village of Kohsoo [pastor Myat Keh's], situated about six miles north-east of Bassein. The preparations made by the villagers, and the hospitable spirit manifested towards the delegates and visitors, breathed a hearty welcome to the anniversary; and the season seemed to be one of sweet social and religious intercourse to all present...Fifty churches were represented by delegates and letters. Forty-five pastors were present, and eight preachers of the Home Mission Society. All of these, and a large number of delegates, seemed ready to strive together with one heart and mind for the promotion of the great objects of the mission, entering heartily into our plans for the evangelization of the heathen, the edification of the churches, and the education of their children and the ministry. In this harmony, as well as in the greater directness and efficiency of the past six months' labors, we would acknowledge the blessing of God upon the quarterly ministerial conference.

"The statistics taken show that three pastors and 248 church-members have died, and that forty have been excluded. The number of deaths is unusually large; cholera and small-pox having raged with great violence during the year. But what filled our hearts with greater sorrow was an event unprecedented in our history, which we should shrink from recording, did not fidelity require it.

"Among the forty excluded persons were sixteen who had turned back from the straight and narrow way to dishonest heathen practices. In the reverses of the war, they had suffered from their Burman enemies extortion upon extortion, and cruelty upon cruelty, until in the extremity of their wretchedness, to satisfy the cravings of hunger, they plunged into a life of plunder and robbery, and are not disposed to forsake it, though the circumstances which first led to it have passed away...

"A few bright features. It has been noticed with anxiety in previous years, that, while we could report good numbers of baptisms, but few, and in some years not any, of the baptized, were recent converts from heathenism; the additions being either from the families of church-members, or from converts who had long been waiting for an opportunity to be baptized. But, by the blessing of God upon the labors of the year just closed, we are permitted to rejoice over 200 converts, who within the year have renounced heathenism, and enrolled themselves among the believers in Jesus. The greater part wait to be instructed in the way of the Lord more perfectly. The whole number baptized in the twelve month is 519. The number reported as being now connected with the churches of this mission is about 4,300; but there are many other Christians, scattered by the war to distant and unexplored regions, whose names would probably increase the number to about 5,000. This, it will be perceived, is the number that was reported in 1850. The churches, therefore, while losing so many by death, have still, in respect to numbers, maintained their ground.

"In order to put this people upon a permanent course of progress,... greater efforts must be put forth, and better results attained, in respect to *education*. We have been greatly hindered in our efforts for common schools, by the unsettled and poverty-stricken state of many of the villages; but we are thankful to report 330 pupils in common schools, and about 150 in the boarding-school. The whole number of pupils again is only about equal to that reported in 1849. In regard to education, therefore, we have this year only reached a point which had been before attained, from which we have been receding for three or four years. But, under the more favorable influences which are now rising around us, better results will be shown in the year to come. We feel that this is a subject of vital importance to the stability and purity of the churches, and we shall not relax our efforts until we see something like an adequate degree of progress. Some of our brethren at home have been talking about 'colleges' for the Karens. They have far outstripped us in this matter, for we should be glad to see schools worthy even of the name of academies springing up in our missions.

"Accordingly we ventured to propose at the association that such a school should this year be attempted, and that two or three others, somewhat above the ordinary common school, should also be established at points distant from the first and highest. We must wait patiently to learn the result; for new ideas, however carefully planted, do not, in the minds of Karens, come to maturity during one meeting. For them to support their children at school in their own village, or to send them to the missionary to be supported from foreign sources, are ideas which they can understand and appreciate; but to send their children to another Karen village to be taught by a Karen teacher, at the expense of their parents, is an idea which must be explained and urged again and again, before they will be half as ready to pay five rupees for tuition as they are to pay the same for tobacco. Nevertheless, when the thing has once taken root, and given promise of fruit, it will not be unappreciated or neglected. Whether we see any thing like an academy this year or not, we expect to see common schools of a higher order, and in larger numbers, than we should have seen otherwise, and we hope for the day when academies worthy of the name, taught and supported by Karens, shall enlighten and adorn these provinces. But we meet with serious difficulties at the very outset, from the want of suitable text-books, and teachers qualified to carry out the plan to success. How these books and teachers are to be supplied, to meet the ever-increasing wants of a rising people, is a question worthy of more attention than it is receiving. If the time has not yet come for establishing colleges among the Karens, it is not because thoroughly educated Karens are not needed to strengthen these churches, and guide this people in their upward course, but because the preliminary steps were not taken years ago, or, if taken, were not encouraged and followed up.

"There is another reason for more vigorous efforts in this direction...The Roman Catholics have met with better success in Bassein than elsewhere in Burma. Their converts here, according to their own statement, number between four and five hundred souls, including children probably. But what is of more serious moment to us is the fact that about seventy of their converts were once among our own church-members. This falling-away was previous to 1849; since then, excepting a few who were first excluded from our churches, none have been turned away from their faith in Jesus to the worship of the Holy Virgin. The check which was given at that time to Romish efforts among the converts of our mission must be attributed to the more enlightened views of the Bible and the history of the church, which were then given to the preachers and teachers in our schools and at our general meetings...

"We need not, brethren, attempt here to show how much we need your prayers, your counsels, and your abundant aid, in order that the great tree which has already grown from the mustard-seed may, through the increase of enlightened faith and holy love, strike deeper and wider its roots while extending its branches. Let it not, through the large number of uninstructed and unstable converts, stand in danger of being ere long shattered and prostrated by the violence of some wind of false doctrine.

"The available funds of the Home Mission Society for the year have been three hundred and sixty-two rupees, besides one hundred and twenty-five rupees more contributed at the meeting. Under the patronage of the society, the gospel has been preached, during the year, in more than seventy heathen villages, in some a second time for weeks in succession, and with great encouragement. Eight preachers were re-appointed to labor during the coming season.

"We are encouraged to hope that the churches will this year take a still higher stand in regard to the support of their pastors. The committee to whom the subject of aiding the feebler churches was referred reported only eighteen as needing aid from the mission; and none of these were regarded as needing above fifteen rupees for the whole year, and the majority are to receive less. The whole amount now thought to be needed for this purpose is two hundred and eight rupees,—a little more than one-half of the amount contributed by the Karens to the Home Mission treasury in this year of scarcity. Bassein, therefore, is now virtually able and ready to support the preaching of the gospel within its own borders."...

In March and April, Mr. Beecher made a tour of eighteen days among the churches and heathen villages in the northern part of his district. During this tour he formed the church at M'gay-l'hah. At Shankweng he baptized twenty-two persons, and at Shway-nyoung-bin, nineteen. Myat Keh, after a long tour among the churches and some of the heathen Pwos south of the town, reported the baptism of fifty and the hopeful conversion of twenty-eight Pwos. Shway Bo baptized seventeen about the same time; and Mau Yay, fourteen, — all after the meeting of the association. Mr. Beecher gives an interesting account of the quarterly ministerial meeting held in Mohgoo, about twenty miles west from the town, May 13-15 inclusive, from which we quote: —

"It was gratifying to find a neat, commodious, and substantial chapel just rebuilt. The floor was of *sawn boards*, as yet quite a novelty in Karen villages, though we hear of several churches following this example. The people here have suffered little from the war, and find themselves able to support Moung Bo, their pastor, entirely, and to expend, for Karens, a liberal sum on their house of worship. The pleasant contrast between this house and the places where we have preached, and called upon the name of the Lord, in heathen villages, often led us to repeat, 'How amiable are thy tabernacles!' The attendance at this meeting was a renewed proof of the deep interest which this people feel in the work which we are striving to promote. We had feared that they would be so busily engaged in building their houses, and preparing for the rains close at hand, that few would be present; but we were happily disappointed in meeting thirty-one pastors, five or six of the itinerant missionaries, and a congregation of more than five hundred on Sunday, besides many who returned home on hearing that small-pox had broken out in the village. Letters of regret were received from several pastors who could not attend.

"Saturday, the first day, was occupied with the reports of the pastors, and the examination of Tway Gyau for ordination. Our time was too limited to allow all the pastors present to speak; but those who were called upon spoke of the exercises of their minds, and their views of their calling, with greater freedom and intelligence than ever before. At our first conference, nine months since, it was with difficulty that some of them comprehended what we meant by asking them to relate their Christian and ministerial experience. The contrast at this meeting was a gratifying proof of their growth in grace and the knowledge of Christ.

"The Christian experience and call to the ministry of Tway Gyau, as brought out in his examination, were very satisfactory; but his blameless Christian life for fifteen years, and his success as a pastor for twelve, were the best proofs of his fitness for ordination. His church were unanimous in asking for his ordination, and all of the ministers and elders present approved. He is truly a *good* man, blessed, in a less degree, however, with the same excellent traits of mind and character as his lamented brother Tway Po. I spent a sabbath with him a few weeks since; and his house, furnished with tables and chairs of his own manufacture, and books bearing marks of faithful use, reminded me strongly of what I had seen at the house of the beloved and studious pastor of Thehrau. Brethren Mau Yay, Po Kway, and Shway Bo (Myat Keh was detained by illness) performed very appropriately the parts assigned to them. The silence and attention of the congregation throughout the exercises were marked. The same may be said respecting the dedication of the house in which we held our meetings, which occurred sabbath morning, — the same day with the ordination. We regretted the necessity of crowding so much into one day, but could not avoid it without protracting the meeting to an extent which the heat, the near approach of the rains, and the anxiety of the people to return, would not warrant. This dedication is the first that has occurred in Bassein, but will not, we hope, be the last.

"One new church has been formed during the quarter: about a hundred and fifty have professed conversion, and a hundred and seventy-six have been baptized. Another indication of the progress of Christianity and its constant attendant, civilization, is seen in the fact that the churches of this mission have now in course of erection about twenty chapels and as many schoolhouses. The treasurer of the Home Mission Society received a hundred and sixty-three rupees during the quarter. Upon making known to the society the request of Brother Kincaid for Karen preachers to labor in Prome, two young men of excellent character were immediately appointed, and were soon on their way."

Mr. Van Meter, in his tours, which were prolonged through the entire hot season, visited seven villages of heathen Pwos south-west of the town; also, on the east, Paybeng, where the ordinance of baptism was administered for the first time to twenty-three candidates, and two substantial men were set apart as deacons; P'nahtheng and vicinity, where he again set apart deacons, and baptized fourteen persons, — one a man reputed to be a hundred and eight years old; and eleven villages in the Shway Loung district. The people of one of these villages were loyal, but had fallen under suspicion. A Burmese head man had been killed somewhat mysteriously. This their enemies had seized upon, and made a case of murder. A number of their principal men were indicted.

Mr. Van Meter writes: —

"I had myself become bail for six, who, not suspecting such a charge, had come to town in company with the head man of their district. The commissioner finally dismissed the whole affair without a formal trial; but for the time being they were in great trouble, and could think of little else...

"Many declared their willingness, and even earnest desire, to become worshippers at once; but how could they without a teacher? We were completely thronged, at a village in the south part of the district, for two days. A company of young men met us before we reached the place; and so anxious were they to have us go to 'the big house' (most houses here are small), that they cut a passage for our boat a long way up a narrow creek. They then brought presents of their choicest kinds of rice. A number expressed an earnest desire to learn to read, and a willingness to aid in supporting a teacher. We talked, prayed, and sang with them again and again. Our time was too limited to reach the village, which had been reported to us as containing many worshippers; but we met the young man who had been acting as teacher there. We learned from him that most of the people had fled, or been carried off by small-pox. The head man, of whom we had great hopes, was among the first victims. There were but thirteen households left of the former twenty-seven.

"We returned, with the promise and prospect that schools should be established in two places. Two young men who spent part of last rains with us were the only persons able to read in Pwo. They were accepted as teachers, and a support promised them...During the whole of this trip the Karens took us from village to village, and brought us home. This is a saving to the mission, and aids in cultivating a disposition towards us which it is very essential they should have, if we are to do them any good, or they are to be of any use in the cause of Christ." [1]

{ Footnote: [1] The peculiar opinion here expressed was strongly held by Mr. Van Meter, and acted upon more or less throughout his course; but it is doubtful whether such a policy would contribute to the success of most missionaries. }

At the second quarterly meeting in August, "Brother Dahbu" preached the opening sermon, which, no doubt, was a good one. The meetings were excellent, as usual. Seventy-nine baptisms were reported for the quarter, and forty-four village schools, with eight hundred pupils in attendance, all, with four or five exceptions, supported by the Karens themselves. But the great step forward, after long preparation and deferred hope, was taken at the meeting in October. We leave Mr. Beecher, tho man who did so much to bring about the grand result, to tell the story.

"*Bassein, Oct. 29, 1854.*—The first three days of this week have been occupied with the third quarterly meeting of the Ministerial Conference and of the Home Mission Society. We have seldom, if ever, attended meetings of deeper interest, or greater importance. They were held at Naupeheh, about twelve miles in a westerly direction from Bassein. About forty preachers were present, including four or five of our missionaries. The increasing interest which the Karens take in these meetings was manifest in the congregation of about eight hundred that gathered on the sabbath preceding the meetings. The rising sun of each day saw preachers and people assembling for prayer and praise; and the voice of supplication and singing is in no place more pleasant or cheering than in the Karen jungles."

At the request of the church in Naupeheh, their pastor, Tohlo (father of Moung Yahbah, who is known to friends in Hamilton, N.Y.), was examined with a view to ordination. The examination was very satisfactory, and on Wednesday he was ordained; the first prayer being offered by Tway Gyau, the sermon by Po Kway, the ordaining prayer by Myat Keh, the hand of fellowship by Shway Bo, and the charge by Mau Yay. The sessions of the Home Mission Society began Monday, P.M., with an instructive sermon by Po Kway, appointed at the previous meeting, which was followed by reports of the missionaries. We continue the quotation from Mr. Beecher's letter.

"The measure which we had anticipated with deeper interest and anxiety than any other—the accomplishment of which marks a new era in the history of this mission, if not in the history of the Union— was effected Tuesday morning. Since the time when the preachers consented to rely mainly upon their churches for support, we have constantly cherished the hope that the day was not far distant when these churches would undertake *the entire support of native preaching*, both among churches and the heathen. That day has dawned. It was Tuesday, Oct. 24. Believing that the funds of the Home Mission Society would warrant such a measure, a committee was appointed on the previous Saturday to take the subject into consideration. Ample time was thus given for entering upon the measure deliberately, and with a full understanding of its nature. Myat Keh was the chairman of the committee, and presented a resolution, of which the following is a translation:—

"'We, Brethren Myat Keh, Shway Bau, Oo Sah, and Tootanoo, are agreed, that for preachers, pastors, and ordained ministers, we should expend no more of the money of our American brethren. So far as there is occasion to help support them, we will do it ourselves. But for books and schools we greatly need help, and we request that our dear brethren in America will continue to aid us in these things.

(Signed)
'MYAT KEH. OO SAH. SHWAY BAU. TOOTANOO.'

"A free expression of the views of all present was encouraged. Some of the pastors were not without misgivings as to the ability of the churches to support both pastors and native missionaries without aid from America. But after they learned that the funds of their own society were sufficient to meet all the outlay for these objects for the past nine months of the current year, and leave a balance of nearly three hundred rupees in their treasury, and especially when they were told of the large deficiency in the treasury of the Union, and of the embarrassment which many American pastors meet, whose churches contribute, as well as themselves, to the support of Karen missions, their misgivings gave way to a conviction of duty and to a readiness to undertake to carry out the resolution; and it was passed by a unanimous and hearty vote."

The vote, no doubt, was apparently "unanimous and hearty;" still, as on a similar memorable occasion in 1849 (see Chap. VI.), there was probably a minority who gave up the last hold on American support with reluctance; and it is almost certain, in the author's judgment, that the action never would have been taken by the native brethren alone, nor without the pressure of Mr. Beecher's strong personal influence, exerted right in the line with all the teachings of their revered teacher, Abbott. Such a leading, controlling influence must be exerted by the missionaries, combined with the constraint of a gradual reduction, and finally an absolute withholding, of appropriations and donations from America, before self-support can be expected to prevail throughout our foreign missions. But the action was nobly taken, and it is historic. The Karen pastors even now refer not infrequently to this meeting at Naupeheh and to the resolution which they adopted with fear and trembling. Old Shway Bau especially loves to rehearse the trial of his faith and the consequent blessing which came to him, somewhat in this wise: —

"When it was announced at the meeting in Naupeheh, that no more funds were available for our support from America, my heart sunk within me.[1] What should we do? Brother Myat Keh and Brother Po Kway, however, said that it was no matter; the Lord would provide. Still I was very anxious, and went home much cast down. Pretty soon one of the church-members was looking around in my house, and saw that the salt jar was nearly empty. The next day he came and filled it. Not long after, one of the sisters observed that the mats were getting old and ragged, and said that the teacher must certainly have some new mats; and the mats came. And so it was. There was no lack. Paddy, fish, clothes, and every thing that we really needed, was supplied as abundantly as before. And how was it about the preaching? Before, we were not fully dependent on the churches. In a measure, we were sent and paid by the missionary. We felt our importance, and perhaps we put on airs. But, after this, we could not help loving our people, and working for their souls."

{ Footnote: [1] Shway Bau, it will be remembered, was a member of the very committee which valiantly brought in the resolution to dispense with further assistance from America. This is his confession, made before the Bassein Association in 1870. }

Mr. Beecher was hopeful and enthusiastic over the stand that had been made, and not without reason, as the far-reaching results continue to prove. But some one in Boston either did not share his faith to the full, or deemed the expression of it impolitic; for the following paragraph, now restored in parentheses, was suppressed:—

("We have therefore the pleasure of informing the Executive Committee, that the appropriation of six hundred rupees for the preachers of this mission this year will none of it be required, and that we confidently hope that there will never again be occasion for making appropriations in aid of native preaching in Bassein...The measure is important, not for the amount of money that will be immediately saved; but the principle developed is big, and bright with promise. The child is still many years from maturity when he begins to walk alone; but the future man, resolute in purpose, strong in action, is there seen. Time and training only are necessary to develop all his wonder-working powers.")

FACSIMILE OF MR. BEECHER'S HANDWRITING, BASSEIN, OCT. 29, 1854

The services closed on Wednesday with the commemoration of the Lord's Supper by about five hundred communicants. One hundred and four baptisms were reported since the previous quarterly meeting, and about fifty professed conversions from heathenism. Twelve preachers were appointed to labor as missionaries for the remainder of the year. We continue our quotations from Mr. Beecher's letter.

"We now learn that the number of schools is forty-three, and of pupils eight hundred and thirty-four. Some of these schools have been of a higher character, that is, more thorough and extended in some studies (especially arithmetic, land-measuring with the cross-staff, and Burmese), than at any previous time. The school of the highest order [at Kohsoo] has exceeded our expectations. For four months it numbered forty-five, and in the fifth month, fifty pupils; while a school of the ordinary class of fifty pupils more was taught in the same village. We have called it an 'academy,' not so much because it resembles academies at home, any more than the Karen theological seminary resembles Newton Institution, but because it is as much superior to ordinary village schools here as academies at home are superior to ordinary common schools, and because the principle of its support is as different. The Karens have shown their appreciation of superior teaching by sending from home to this and other good schools, at their own expense for board, and, in many cases, for tuition, eighty-seven pupils,—a thing never done before by Karens, at least in Bassein. In this extension and elevation of our village schools, as well as in the support of native preaching by native Christians, we rejoice in the realization of hopes long cherished, and sought by earnest prayer and labor.

"At the same time, we are sorry to say that what has been accomplished in the way of schools this season has been done under great disadvantages, and the prospect before us is darkened by recent arrangements. We find ourselves embarrassed and hindered, from the want of an adequate number and variety of text-books and of properly qualified teachers...We see converts and pupils multiplying around us, but no adequate provision for the instruction of pastors and school-teachers. The boarding-schools for instructing the pastors of fifty churches, and the pupils of five thousand communicants, are limited by the Deputation to fifty pupils for both Pwo and Sgau departments![1] The best qualified teachers of the forty-three schools of this season have told me that they could proceed with their present classes but little farther, without more study with me, and that they were greatly embarrassed for want of books. The average time which the Bassein pastors have attended our boarding-schools, as appears from statistics carefully taken in February, 1852, is *less than eight months*. Every variety of books now in Karen could, all of them, be carried by a man of ordinary strength from Rangoon to Bassein, and would gladly be carried by one of only half the zeal of 'the young chief,'—when he exposed his life in 1838, for the sake of bringing to Bassein a few Christian books,— were it necessary to do so, in order to obtain them...

{ Footnote: [1] Instead of fifty pupils, the Sgau and Pwo boarding-schools in Bassein had over four hundred in attendance in July, 1883. }

"Not a month has passed since the return of the Deputation; but Karens have already asked me earnestly, if there was no place for their children to study English in Maulmain. And, when told there is none, they have asked, 'Can we not send them to Rangoon, to Akyab, or Bengal?' And, when asked why they were so anxious to have their children study English, they have replied, 'In order that a few may become thoroughly educated teachers and ministers, and sufficiently learned to aid us in our efforts to rise from the degradation which has so long oppressed us.'

"The leading and more intelligent Karens are constantly devising and suggesting plans for the elevation of their race. I will here mention one of many instances that have occurred during the past year. At the recent conference, Tohlo came to me and said, 'Teacher, I have thought of a plan which I wish to suggest: whether it will hit your heart or not, I do not know.' — 'Let me hear it.' — 'It is this. Thahree's church do not like their present location. They will come to Kyouk Khyoung-gyee and unite with other churches; so that he will not be needed as a pastor. Let him aid you in teaching; so that you can call a large number of young men to study with you in town.' — 'But why should not these young men go to the academy, or to other good schools?' — 'These are all very good, teacher; but young men who study only in the village schools do not amount to much. They have not the influence or the character of those who study with the missionaries in town.' The fact is one which had escaped my observation; but on looking around I find that there is hardly one efficient pastor or school-teacher who has not been made efficient, mainly by his training in the boarding-schools. I will only add, that the hearts of this people are deeply moved and anxious on the subject of education. There is manifested a hungering and thirsting for knowledge, and, first and strongest, for a knowledge of God's word, which can no more be satisfied with what may be obtained through existing arrangements than the famishing soul of poverty could be satisfied with the crumbs which fall from economy's table.

"The Bassein Karens are in constant communication with the Karens of Maulmain. Since commencing this letter, I have mailed a dozen letters from Karens here to those in Maulmain. Five or six of Mr.

Binney's best scholars are among our most efficient preachers and school-teachers. The other preachers acknowledge their superior qualifications; and these young men and other Karens know well without information from missionaries, what have been, and what now are, the advantages of going to the theological seminary. I shall continue to encourage candidates for the ministry to go to Maulmain; and, when they are satisfied that they will enjoy better advantages there than at Bassein, they will probably go.

"It is far from pleasant to reflect upon the doings of the Deputation; but, as a watchman on the walls of our Karen Zion, is it not my duty to inform the Executive Committee and the churches, in whose hands God has placed so largely the educational as well as the religious destinies of this people, of their views, and their aspirations after that knowledge without which they know, as well as we, that they cannot rise in the scale of Christianity or civilization?

"In less than nineteen years from the time the Karens of Bassein first heard the gospel, they are ready to undertake the entire support of native preaching in fifty churches and among the heathen around them; and, except for books and three or four teachers, they are supporting the primary education of more than eight hundred pupils. At this rate of progress, what will be their numbers, their abilities, and their educational wants, nineteen years hence?

"In connection with these facts, consider, also, the rapidity of conversions and the growth of churches in Rangoon, Shway-gyeen, and Toungoo; and let the Baptists of America, in the fear of that God who has committed such momentous interests to their hands, inquire what are their duties to the present and future Baptists of Burma. What do American Baptists wish or expect this people, so remarkable thus far in their religious history, to become? What ought to be their religious and literary character? Do they wish it to be like their own? If so, then why should not a literary and theological institution be at once established, which shall rapidly become like their own in the variety and extent of the studies pursued? We cannot close our remarks on this subject more suitably than by quoting from the report on the Karen missions, read by the Rev. Dr.

Ide before the Union at Albany. 'Has not the time come for placing the educational branch of the Karen missions on a broader and more stable foundation? Has not the time come for a more systematic endeavor to consolidate these scattered tribes, to give them nationality, [?] and, by means of intellectual and spiritual culture, elevate them in the scale of social order?'"

In his extended comments on this letter, the Corresponding Secretary has no word of appreciative praise or of thanksgiving for the unparalleled step taken by the Bassein Karens. Because they have assumed the entire support of their pastors and itinerants, he seems to feel that they must be able to support all the schools they need. We quote a few sentences, which fairly indicate his bearing towards a movement which transcended in importance, probably, any other that he was ever called to consider.

"They ask help to support their schools; but which is easier, so far as concerns the readiness of a people,—to educate the young, or to support the ministry? As to plans and views held by Karen Christians in regard to schools, or theological training, or the study of English, our readers will be at little loss to attach to them their due importance, if they consider how limited must be the intelligence to which Karens can have yet attained on such topics, and how little they are accustomed to form opinions irrespectively of their missionary teachers."

From personal knowledge, the author can testify with certainty, that it was the Karens themselves, and not Mr. Beecher, who were demanding facilities for English education. It is barely possible, also, that the Karen instinct, in this regard, had more of wisdom in it than the elaborate judgments of the pious and learned brethren of the Deputation.

In closing the record of this year, we must not omit to mention that the father of the Bassein mission, Rev. E. L. Abbott, passed away on the 3d of December, in Fulton, N.Y., aged forty-five. Obituaries may be found in the "Missionary Magazine" for March, 1855, and March, 1874.

Mrs. Martha (Foote) Beecher also, who had embarked on the *Collingwood* at Rangoon, in January, with Rev. Mr. and Mrs. Benjamin and Miss M. Vinton, to return with her infant to America, died unexpectedly on the 3d of March, and was buried at sea. She was a good and useful woman, of many amiable traits; and her loss was a heavy one to the mission, as well as to her husband.

CHAPTER XIII.

1855, 1856.

"Missionaries of Christ have other relations besides those sustained to the Board, and other responsibilities and duties besides those for which the Board holds them accountable to itself. It is from another and higher source they derive their authority to organize churches, and ordain preachers and pastors." — *Memorial Volume A. B. C. F. M.*

Corresponding to the political turmoil and uncertainty depicted in the last two chapters, was the excitement in mission circles, growing out of the action of the Deputation from the society's headquarters in Boston. Better men than the Rev. Drs. Peck and Granger could hardly have been found in America; better intentions than they brought to their work could not have been desired: and yet the troubles and heart-burnings which followed their visit to Burma are only now passing into the dim border-land of forgetfulness.

A rigid New-Testament ideal of missions, and a slightly exaggerated authority on the one hand, a magnifying of "Baptist principles," and perhaps an extreme sense of personal independence on the other, furnished a background for the dissensions between the Deputation and a minority of the Karen missionaries. The contention was sharp and long. Good men on either side did not refrain from impugning the motives, if they did not impeach the characters, of their opponents. It is safe to say, probably, that both were partly right and partly wrong. Certainly donors have a right to say how their gifts shall be expended. If secretaries and committees are responsible to the bodies appointing them, then men sent on the Lord's missions, even, are in a degree responsible to the human agents who send them; and, if they cannot conscientiously carry out the policy of their supporters, they should resign, and seek support elsewhere, as Beecher and his associates did.

The issue would have been more doubtful, had it not been for a third party,—English Christians residing in the East, and especially the Christian Karens, whose existence and determining power would seem to have been, for the time, almost forgotten by the Deputation. Had not the Karens clung loyally to their missionaries, refusing to receive any new men whatever, the executive officers and the denomination would have been more resigned to the loss of the uncompromising men with whom they had to deal. As it was, it cost the society the loss of the larger, and by far the stronger, half of the mission churches.

And what was the gain? A deserved rebuke was given to that show of equality by which the same importance is attached to the needs and claims of a circle of ten churches as to one of fifty, and to the injustice which would lay down the same Procrustean limitations to the schools of long-neglected, uprising Bassein, with its five thousand adult Christians, and to Tavoy with its thousand Christians then surfeited with instruction and pecuniary aid. The station-schools now range in number of pupils from fifty to two hundred and fifty, without fear of interference, so long as a due proportion of their support comes from local sources. The virtual prohibition of English teaching is so far removed, that in every mission-school in Burma to-day, English is freely taught, and, in most of them, to an undesirable majority of the pupils; but the error is left to correct itself, as it surely will in time. More than all else, the watchword, "partners, not employees," began to be heard; and the sympathies of the denomination at large were so clearly with the missionaries, that a former secretary has written, "Coercion, as often as tried, has failed." [1]

{ Footnote: [1] The principle that the station and work of missionaries shall be assigned by the Executive Committee may have received needed emphasis by the action of the Deputation, the Committee, and the Board at this time.

There is also the correlative principle, embodied in the Regulations since 1859, that changes of fields of labor "shall be matters of negotiation and agreement between the committee and the missionaries." But we are unable to see wherein Mr. Beecher had violated either of these principles in spirit. His written instructions from the Board, in 1846, contain these words: "The designation of Mr. Beecher is to the Arakan Karens and to those who connect with Arakan...The Karen aspirants to the ministry, who come over the Yoma Mountains that they may learn the way of the Lord more perfectly, must not be left to ignorance and vain imaginings. So, too, of the multiplied Christian villages and churches in the province of Bassein, the present hive of the Arakan Karens. These are all proper parts of one diocese. The central point of influence over it remains to be ascertained...Mr. Beecher will ultimately, however, and at no distant day, remove [from Maulmain] to Arakan, or to Bassein, if accessible, or wherever he shall find the most fitting place for doing his assigned work."—*Quoted from BEECHER's Defence*, December, 1854, pp. 20, 21. }

It is easy to be wise after the event. To us, now, there seems to have been but one thing to do when Abbott's health failed, and he was compelled to leave the field with no reasonable prospect of a return; and that was for Beecher to enter into the place and the work which were clearly his by providential appointment. He had indeed been sent by the Board to Sandoway, but Sandoway was nothing but a back door to Bassein. For six years he had been laboring, by direction of the Board, for the Bassein Karens, and for them alone. When the front door was opened wide, when the few churches remaining on the coast were leaving *en masse* for their old homes in Kyouk Khyoung-gyee and Theegwin, why should not their teacher follow, and follow promptly? He could do nothing more in Sandoway. The place and the work in Bassein were his, and he knew it. Missionary brethren in whom he confided urged him to go; the Karens claimed and called him, and he went. But instead of confirming his judicious action, and praising him for his zeal, it was thought fit by the officers of that day to try him for insubordination.

It was a grand mistake.[1] A careful perusal of the Karen minutes of the Bassein meetings, annual and quarterly, that followed the departure and death of the senior missionary, proves conclusively that the Karen pastors and elders desired and would have for their leader the man whom they knew and loved next to Abbott, and no other. The repeated unsuccessful attempts to put other men into Beecher's place prove the same. That mistake of twenty-five years ago will not be repeated; but how long will it be before the obvious right of those seventy-seven self-supporting churches to express a preference in the election or the withdrawal of their American leaders is accorded?

{ Footnote: [1] We have the best authority for saying that Secretary Peck himself became convinced finally, that the policy which bore his name was a mistaken one. A letter expressing this was written by him to a friend who still lives to adorn one of the highest positions in the Baptist denomination of America. }

Rev. J. L. Douglass and wife, the first Protestant missionaries to the Burmans of Bassein, arrived Nov. 23, 1854. As he always manifested a deep interest in the Karens, and did no little to help them, especially at times when they were without a missionary of their own, his name will often occur in the course of the following fifteen years. He also had studied several years at Hamilton, N.Y.

The annual meeting of the association was held on the 1st and 2d of February, at Kwengyah, the most northern Christian village in Bassein, seventy miles above the town. Mr. Beecher was the only missionary present. Statistics presented at the meeting gave a total of six hundred and forty-four converts baptized during the year, twenty-two excluded, and one hundred and sixty died. A good degree of union and brotherly love prevailed among the churches and preachers. Three new churches had been formed within the year, making the whole number fifty-three, each of which was supplied with a pastor. There were also ten evangelists laboring either as missionaries or as school-teachers among the heathen. The number of pupils in forty-three village schools was nine hundred and thirteen. Naupeheh and P'nahtheng were beginning schools of a higher class, similar to the one opened a year before at Kohsoo. Mr. Beecher relates some incidents of his tour to the meetings and beyond.

"I left Bassein Dec. 28, and spent about ten days in visiting Christian villages north of the town, on and near the Bassein River. At four villages I found converts waiting to make a public profession of their faith in Christ, and had the pleasure of baptizing eighty in all. About twenty of these are recent converts from heathenism: the others have been waiting several years for an opportunity to receive the ordinance...North of Kwengyah there are numerous heathen Karen villages, some of which have given us much reason to hope that they would turn from their soul-destroying nat-worship to serve the living God. I visited five or six of them last year, and have just returned from a tour of about three weeks among them. A circle of six or eight small villages near the borders of Henthada had promised the preachers, that, if I would make, them a visit, they would build a small chapel. Three weeks before my arrival, they had begun the work. We were not a little disappointed, therefore, on reaching their place, to find the people so far from meeting us in a chapel, that they were reluctant to listen to us when we went to their houses. And although they entertained us with all hospitality, yet, when pressed to embrace the gospel, they told us plainly that they could not do so at this time. Thus, after exhorting them faithfully to repent 'while it is called to-day,' we were compelled to leave them in their blindness. I have since learned, that this sudden change in them was chiefly occasioned by rumors that disaffected Burmans were plotting a rebellion against the English, and threatening, in case of success, to massacre all white foreigners, and all who were found believing and practising the doctrines of the white books. We have abundant reason to believe that the gospel which has been preached to this people has made an impression on their minds, and we hope to hear before long, that many in this region have turned to the Lord. While making this tour, I was much gratified and aided by the labors of the Karen missionaries, whom I frequently met, and some of whom constantly travelled with me."

The aid asked for the schools of both departments of the Bassein mission this year was six hundred rupees for the normal school in town, and three hundred rupees for village schools. How much, if any, was granted by the society, we are unable to state.

Mr. Beecher, heart-sore with his heavy domestic bereavement, and smarting under what he felt to be the unjust censure of the Executive Committee, left Bassein, with the formal approval of the Bassein mission, on the 19th of February, for Calcutta, whence he sailed, in the American ship *Wisconsin*, for New York, arriving at that port Sept. 28. Meanwhile, the work among the Sgau Karens of Bassein was left mainly in the hands of the native preachers until Mr. Beecher's return.

The quarterly meeting for May was held at Kaunee, a little way above the town. The chapel, enlarged on three sides for the occasion, was quite insufficient to accommodate the multitude. Mr. Van Meter writes that thirty-six preachers and over twelve hundred disciples were present. Three additional Karen missionaries were sent to aid Mr. Whitaker and Sau Quala in Toungoo, making six Bassein men in that most promising field. Among them was one who still lives, spoken of by Mr. Whitaker as "the faithful Kyoukkeh." These, with two in Henthada and two in Prome, made ten foreign missionaries from Bassein, besides the laborers in the great home-field. The baptisms and contributions were up to the usual average. Yoh Po, in charge of the academy at Kohsoo, had one hundred and thirty pupils in attendance. Poo Goung at Naupeheh also had made a fine start. Besides the work done in these "academies," in the town school, and in the usual number of village schools, twenty-one young men had gone to Maulmain to study the Bible with Dr. Wade, and ten or twelve to Rangoon to study English in Mr. Vinton's school, making a total of more than one thousand Bassein youth under instruction.

The meeting at the end of July was held in town, and was described as a good one. Eight missionaries were appointed to the home-field, and eighteen pastors were aided from the home mission treasury to the extent of from five to ten rupees each. At this meeting Mr. Douglass had the pleasure of baptizing a Burman convert, of whom he writes:—

"He had frequently heard the gospel from a Karen preacher who lives near his village, and who said he had every evidence that the man was a Christian. At the close of the morning service on Sunday, the Burman and a Pwo Karen related their religious experience, and were unanimously received for baptism. We went to the water, where, in addition to the Karens, about one thousand Burmans assembled. One of the Karen ministers, who speaks Burman as readily as his own language, gave a short discourse on the authority and nature of baptism; and after singing and prayer I administered the impressive ordinance. The crowd around me, and the solemnity manifested by all present, brought vividly to my mind similar scenes enjoyed in my native land. These are all I have baptized...yet I do expect to see a Burman church in Bassein."

The next quarterly meeting, held at Mee-thwaydike, continued four days, and was enriched by the presence and counsels of Rev. Mr. Thomas of Henthada. About one hundred "new worshippers" were reported, forty-six of whom were Pwos. Four missionaries were sent to labor, under Mr. Thomas's direction, in Henthada district. Other statistics as usual. Several cases were brought to the notice of the conference, in which native doctors had attributed sicknesses to witchcraft. A circular letter of warning and wise counsel was accordingly prepared by Tohlo, and sent to the churches. Of the time spent at this meeting, and in visiting a few of the Bassein churches, Mr. Thomas writes, "A more intensely interesting and important week, I never passed."

The year 1856 opens with the annual association at P'nahtheng (pastor Po Kway's village), Jan. 21-23 inclusive. The usual large number of preachers and people were in attendance. Our reporter is Rev. Mr. Van Meter.

"The interest was heightened by the presence of Brother Brayton from Rangoon. Brother Crawley from Henthada came in just at the close. Though his late arrival was much to his and our regret, the disappointment was in a measure forgotten in the pleasure of a short visit with him in our homes at Bassein.

"Features of peculiar interest attach to this meeting. First, there was a larger number of Pwos present than on any similar occasion. This was owing to the fact that the place of meeting is further east than the places at which we have met formerly, also to a real increase of interest on their part. Our three largest Pwo churches are in this vicinity, and were well represented. Another peculiar feature was the ruling of a native moderator throughout the session. The man chosen was Mau Yay, the eldest of the ordained men, who has acted in this capacity heretofore for the Home Mission Society. He succeeded very well, considering that much of the service was new to him. Another was the formal appointment of a committee of laymen and preachers to take charge of and disburse the funds of the association, also to have the power of appointing missionaries, in fact, the Executive Committee of the Bassein Home Mission and Preachers' Aid Society.

"They entered upon their duties with any thing but an empty treasury, for the money-box required the strength of a man to lift it. You must not estimate the contents too highly, however, as our representative of value is the hard metal, and the box held not a little of the baser sort. The contributions for the year were Rs. 708-11-6. Of this amount, nearly one-half, Rs. 312-13, was given during the last quarter, most of it at the meeting. More than Rs. 400 were left in the treasury after paying off all claims for the past year. There have been paid during the year—to missionaries, Rs. 228; to preachers, Rs. 93; and, in consideration of the large balance on hand, an additional sum of Rs. 160 was appropriated at this meeting to aid twenty of the more needy preachers.

"Moreover, the association has now virtually assumed the support of the two academies. I had not been able to pay the principals of either in full for last year, but I had aided them as our small funds would allow. Seventy rupees remained due to one of them, which the pastors paid, thus discharging our debt. While we are far from undervaluing rupees, especially at this time, we regard the money-value of their aid as insignificant in comparison with the cheerful cordiality with which they assume these responsibilities; and more, because it is a further development of the principle of self-support, which must lie at the foundation of all healthy growth. I have but little doubt as to their ability to support all they have now undertaken, and that involves, in fact, the relinquishment of their last hold on the mission-funds, except for the school at Bassein, and books. The school, also, we hope, will be sustained by them principally this year. I have advised them to tax themselves for this object to the amount of one basket of rice per house; and most of them have consented very cordially, the more so, because the same thing has already been done by the churches of Rangoon for the support of the school at that place.

"The baptisms for the year were four hundred and five, including four Burmans. The number of Pwos baptized last quarter was twenty-nine, perhaps more. New worshippers for the year exceed a hundred and thirty, and of this number seventy-three are Pwos. New interests have started, and are progressing in several places. The new Pwo church at Tee Chai, formally recognized on the first day of the year, shows genuine vitality in its growth and fruits, and is a glorious memorial of the power of divine grace. I baptized thirty-three at the time of organizing the church, and over twenty have since been added by baptism.

"Some of the old churches are more or less unsettled and scattered, from the extensive changes taking place in the location of their villages. Their great object now is to get eligible situations, on the banks of large streams, for the greater facility of trade and travel, the necessity no longer existing for them to hide in the jungles. This has, of course, been a serious hinderance, especially when, from difference of opinion or from other causes, the villages have been divided; a part only going to the new locality, the remainder perhaps unable, or not wishing, to make the change immediately. Some other difficulties have marred the peace of individual churches, but nothing very serious. By far the most unpleasant event of this kind took place in the Kaunee church, deprived, by the death of Tway Po (nearly three years since), of one of the most faithful of pastors. A 'lying spirit' entered into one formerly a member of the church. He pretended to frequent interviews with Tway Po, their deceased pastor, at his grave, and finally succeeded in leading the widow entirely astray. They were both excluded. Both, however, we are happy to say, seem sincerely penitent, and are asking to be received again into the church."...

A serious calamity was in store for the missionaries in Bassein. The old *kyoung* that had sheltered them for four years was in an unhealthy situation. They had secured a very eligible compound "of some five acres," on the ridge overlooking the river, where the circuit bungalow now stands. Messrs. Van Meter and Douglass had erected each a dwelling-house of moderate cost. Mr. Van Meter had removed, with his family and furniture, to the new house only a few days before a fearful conflagration broke out in the town (Sunday, P.M., March 16); and "within fifteen minutes from the outbreak, our house was a mass of blazing ruins. ...Not a book, a spoon, nor even my watch, was saved. All my manuscripts with my library are lost. I saved nothing but the clothes on me at the time, and Mrs. Van Meter and the children but a handful more." The Douglass house and all the mission-property in Bassein, except a part of the material prepared for Mr. Beecher's house, were likewise consumed. To this succeeded a heavier loss to the poor Van Meters. On the 6th of May their eldest daughter, Anna, aged seven, was removed by death. She was the first of the mission-circle to be buried in Bassein.

In this time of hardship and loss the Karens most cheerfully rallied to the assistance of their American friends; although, to most of them, they were not their own teachers. They had themselves come out of the furnace of affliction too recently, and they had too much of the spirit of Christ, to forget their duty. Within a short time they contributed over a thousand rupees in cash, besides some useful articles, to repair, in part, the loss of the two families.

Of the quarterly meeting in April we have no account, the missionaries being prevented from attending by the fire. The next was held (July 17-20) at Kyootah, a village already mentioned as devastated by the Burmans during the war. The support of the academies was continued. Two hundred and forty rupees were given to aid the needier pastors for that quarter, besides the regular pay of the itinerants. To crown all, by a most cheerful and unanimous vote, a hundred and twenty-five rupees were given to the A. B. M. Union towards the liquidation of their debt. We add Mr. Van Meter's account of the ordination services, and his summing up of the benevolence of the Bassein churches for the year 1855. How would he have rejoiced to know, that, in twenty-five years more, the five thousand rupees would become twelve times five thousand! Of the candidates ordained, Th'rah Nahpay had been subjected to cruel tortures for his faith, from the effects of which he never fully recovered up to the time of his lamented death in 1880.[1] The other, Th'rab Oo Sah, will be remembered as the companion of Myat Kyau in his first great baptizing tour in Burma Proper (Chap. V.).

{ Footnote: [1] For many years the suffering old man never came to town empty handed; and he rarely returned without the gift of at least one bottle of good Dr. Jayne's Liniment, to mitigate his pains. }

"Neither of the men ordained is from the *schools*; but they are tried men, and known of all their brethren. The younger of the two, Nahpay, is a preacher and pastor of much promise, and has been talked of as a candidate for some time. I gained my principal knowledge of his attainments and worth while he was studying with us last year. The elder one, Oo Sah, was the first missionary sent out from the Bassein churches on the organization of the Home Mission Society, in 1850.

"Before fully deciding to ordain Oo Sah, two or three others were mentioned as suitable candidates; but we found them quite reluctant to assume the responsibilities of the office. One, Shway Bau, as to whose qualifications his brethren were fully agreed, gave, as his reason for declining, the fact that his church, and especially the deacons, had not yet so learned their duties as to leave him free to do the work of an ordained man. 'The honor of the pastor is identical with the character of his church,' said he; and, while having so much to do in 'serving tables,' he felt that he ought not to undertake the higher duties. This he said with strong feeling, which was appreciated by his brethren in the ministry. And this, let me say, is where these pastors experience their greatest trials, and where they most need prayer and sympathy. One of the candidates was examined by the native pastors alone. They also took all the exercises of the ordination, except the address to the congregation; and each one performed his part well.

"I have the pleasure of sending you at length a statement of what the Bassein churches did in 1855 for the support of the gospel among themselves and for extending its blessings to others. The amount contributed shows how their liberality has abounded, and what an increase we may expect from them in the future, should no untoward influence, no 'root of bitterness' or division, spring up among them.

Could we get full reports from all the churches, the amount would much exceed the figures now given. We report in round numbers, where the returns were not complete.

For Home Mission Society	Rs.	721
For aid of pastors	"	700
For school-teachers	"	600
For chapels	"	1,000
Aggregate	Rs.	3,021

Besides these, smaller sums have been contributed in aid of poor members, etc., and, for the support of their pastors, 3,500 baskets of paddy, which has been selling for Rs. 50 per hundred during a large part of the season. Let this be put down at a fair valuation, say Rs. 1,500, and we have a total of Rs. 4,521. The churches, moreover, have paid for books, principally hymn-books and Bibles, from Oct. 18, 1855, to July 31, 1856, Rs. 430. For the earlier months of 1855 the record is lost, but it may be safely put at Rs. 50. This will make a grand total, for all these objects, of Rs. 5,001.

"In this connection, we wish to make particular mention of the prompt and generous offerings sent us by nearly every church upon hearing of our serious loss by the fire of March last. Most of them made up and sent in at once what they had to give: others did not send in till after some weeks. The total thus given is above a thousand rupees. Unfortunately, the first hundred and eighty rupees of this sum were stolen soon after they came into our hands, and have not been recovered.

"Upon reading the above, you will surely say that the Bassein Karens have done nobly. But it may be asked, in return, 'Are they not overdoing? May it not be asking too much of them within so short a time? and may it not be a spasmodic effort, that will be followed by a corresponding decrease of contributions for some time to come?' Of this we have yet to see the first signs. On the contrary, they seem only prepared to do the more. For instance, they have given for our buildings, in materials, labor, and cash, upwards of one hundred rupees, and for our school in Bassein the additional sum of two hundred and thirty-six rupees, besides furnishing all the rice and fish that we need. The two hundred and thirty-six rupees were given by young men who were employed last season as government surveyors. Is there not encouragement here for the friends of missions? Is there not occasion for devout thanksgiving to God, who can bring good out of evil, that, in this time of trial, his work has been so little hindered; that, indeed, this very embarrassment has been made, as we believe, occasion of blessing to these churches, in leading them to know and feel the obligation and the pleasure of giving and doing for Christ and his cause? In view of these results, we can even rejoice, and thank God for the losses and afflictions that have so recently come upon us in quick succession; believing that they are not the effects of a blind chance, but the wonderful working of Him who doeth all things well, in the great love that he hath for this portion of his Zion.

"While on this subject, let me notice, to the praise of His grace, a few items as to the liberality of individual churches. Within a few days after the fire the pastor and deacons of the Kohsoo church came in, and laid down before us sixty rupees. We declined taking so much; but they insisted, saying that it was sent by many persons, as a most hearty freewill offering on their part, in this our time of need. This church is giving a full support to their pastor, Myat Keh, sustains a good school, etc. Tohlo, the pastor at Naupeheh, said that he was away from home; but, immediately upon learning of the fire, he hastened home, and was engaged the whole night before coming in, in collecting for us. He brought nearly forty rupees. Other churches did almost as well. And that this liberality towards us has not hindered other contributions is evident, we think, from the amount paid to the Home Mission Society for the past six months. The Kohsoo church alone contributed above fifty rupees [to that society] at our last meeting. True, these are among our ablest churches; but there are instances of equal liberality, in proportion to their ability, among the smaller ones."

Again: on the 27th of September Mr. and Mrs. Van Meter report their "hands full of most interesting and encouraging work." Although three or four Burmese carpenters were still employed on their dwelling, they had been able to carry on a school of from twenty-five to forty scholars the past two months; the Karens defraying the entire expense of the session, including the cost of the temporary buildings erected for them. They were to have a short vacation; after which it was proposed to have another session of at least four months, to afford the village teachers and others an opportunity for further improvement. The instruction was to be given by one of the best Karen teachers, under the supervision of the missionaries. Mrs. Van Meter writes:—

"One day this week the Commissioner of Pegu, Major A. P. Phayre, spent nearly the whole day in our school, at his own suggestion, and appeared highly gratified. He wished us to send a subscription-paper requesting aid from the residents of Bassein, which he headed with a donation of one hundred rupees and a very flattering notice of what we are doing. We have in this way received about two hundred and thirty rupees. Yesterday he sent us an order exempting from taxes all young men who are engaged either as scholars themselves or in teaching others for half the year. This will be a great encouragement, as well as aid, to the Karens...The Commissioner spoke to the Karens strongly against meddling with English unless they were prepared to give their lives to it, commencing with eight or ten years of study...You will rejoice with us, that the Karens are so able and willing to help themselves, and also that God has blessed them with rulers who care for their interests. My heart was touched last evening by a young Karen who lives here in town, and whose earnings are twenty rupees a month (with a family to support), handing me twenty rupees entirely unsolicited."

The October meeting was held at Lehkoo, ten or twelve miles north of the city. We extract from Mr. Douglass's account of the services the following:—

"Saturday morning at sunrise I went into a neat chapel that will seat eight hundred persons, built a few months since by this church. Within five minutes after I entered, about four hundred and fifty members came in to hold their morning prayer-meeting. They commenced by singing an excellent translation of the hymn,—

'Rock of ages cleft for me,
Let me hide myself in thee.'

"As the rising sun appeared, dispelling the darkness, and shedding light and comfort around, I thought how beautifully it illustrates the moral change which the Sun of righteousness has brought to many of this people. Twenty years ago the name of Jesus was unknown in all this district: now the dense jungle around us is made to echo with the song of praise, and hundreds unite in their petitions at the throne of grace. At half-past nine, A.M., a plain, impressive sermon was preached from the parable of the wise and foolish builders (Matt, vii. 24-27). The remainder of the day was spent in hearing accounts of the condition of the different churches, and what has been accomplished since the last meeting. In the evening a sermon was preached before the Home Mission Society by one of the ordained brethren. It was founded on Rom. viii. 14, and was an able and clear presentation of truth, enforced by Scripture illustrations, showing how Paul and others were led by the Spirit in preaching the gospel in places where Christ was not known. On the sabbath sermons were preached by three young men, who, for strength of mind and literary attainments, stand pre-eminent. They received their theological training from Dr. Binney in Maulmain, and are a good illustration of what grace and education can do for many of this people."

Fifteen home missionaries were appointed; and the meeting closed Monday, P.M., with the administration of the Lord's Supper to more than eight hundred disciples.

In the report of the Prome mission for this year we find our old friend Maukoh (pp. 26, 29, 39) and another Karen preacher from Bassein exploring that district on both sides of the river, for the purpose of ascertaining the whereabouts of their people, and preaching to them. In the journal of that most excellent missionary, Mr. Whitaker, under date of Jan. 2, 1857, we get a glimpse of what our Bassein men are doing in Toungoo. He says, —

"Lootoo and Klehpo, two of our most efficient preachers, were kept at home by severe illness. Kyoukkeh has just returned from a tour to the east, in which he penetrated to the eastern limit of the Pakus. At Mu-khe, the most easterly district, he found the people engaged in mining. The chief of a large village, on hearing of his approach, said, 'Let him come up here, and we will make two or three holes through him with our spears: if he does not die, we will believe him, and worship his God.' Hearing this, Kyoukkeh, true to his nature, set out at once for the village. Having arrived, he said, 'I heard you were going to pierce me with your spears. I am here now: if you wish to pierce, pierce. I trust in God, and have come to preach his word.' In his emphatic language, 'They were dumb, and listened attentively to my words.' He staid with them several days. They made fair promises; but he thinks them still undecided, and fears, that, on his return, they took to their heathenish customs again. Two teachers have since been sent into that district. Kyoukkeh has now gone with several others to preach in the region west of Toungoo."

Thus closes the record of two years more of mingled trial and blessing in this vineyard of the Lord's own planting.

CHAPTER XIV.

1857.

"Out of utter defeat, it is God's prerogative to bring victory; and even from fratricidal conflict He can bring a higher harmony and good, that had else been unattainable." — *Anonymous.*

In the report of the Maulmain Karen mission for 1856 we find a sad picture of the effects produced on native Christians by overmuch temporal help from their missionaries.

"The churches feel but lightly, as yet, the importance of sustaining the institutions of the gospel, schools, etc., among themselves. In this respect the churches of this district present a marked contrast to those of Tavoy, Bassein, the infant mission of Toungoo, and perhaps other fields. But one church has supported its pastor during the past year. They seem to have become rooted in the belief that the missionary must do every thing for them, and this not only in religious matters, but, what is still more trying, in temporal things also. It is painful to see how ready they are, in every case of real or fancied want or trouble, to come to us. When we have no means of helping them, and our judgment tells us that we ought not to help them if we could, it is almost impossible to shake them off. They will not believe but that 'the teacher' has unlimited resources at his command...Most of the pastors have been helped so long, that they have lost their early missionary spirit." —*Missionary Magazine*, 1856, pp. 256, 257.

To gain satisfactory results, native Christians of Asia, as well as Christians in the new States and Territories in America, must be trained *from the first* to right views and correct practice in regard to bearing their own burdens. The above quotation is necessary to enable the reader to understand the position in which Rev. Dr. Wade and Rev. C. Hibbard found themselves, with a theological seminary on their hands, and the oldest circle of churches in Burma still clamoring for the daily bread of their pastors; while, through the dissensions that had been raised, the mission treasury in Boston was empty, and burdened with debt. Something must be done; and good Dr. Wade, in all his fifty years of wise, devoted service, never proposed a wiser or more practicable plan than the one we now record. If we mistake not, the correspondence throws no little light upon the "education question" in Burma to-day.

The Maulmain Karen mission wrote to the Executive Committee in November, 1856, on receiving the schedule of appropriations for that year: —

"Under these circumstances [the inadequacy of the appropriations for schools], which a previous letter of yours had led us to anticipate, we have felt utterly at a loss what to do. It seems impracticable to keep up a theological seminary in this expensive place, with the appropriations you make to it. It has been strongly suggested to our minds, as Rangoon is not open to us, that the school had better be removed to Bassein. The Bassein native brethren *urge* it, promise help in feeding and clothing the pupils; and the prospect is, that a large school would cost the Union less there than a small one here."

Meanwhile the mission had addressed a circular to their brethren at Bassein and other stations on the expediency of the measure, in view of this and other considerations; to which, in due time, answers were given.

In the following month Dr. Wade wrote again: —

"With the appropriations you have named for this year we cannot continue the school at the rate of expense unavoidable in Maulmain, where most of the pupils have to come from a distance, where the prices of provisions of all kinds are extraordinarily high, and where the native churches can not or will not aid with a single basket of paddy, or stick of fuel, without receiving city prices. I therefore beg the sanction of the Executive Committee, if my health allows me to continue in charge of the school, *to remove it at once, before it is positively broken up, to a place among the churches where the churches want it and will do something for its support* [Italicized by the editor], and where the expense of the school will be less than here...We have therefore proposed Bassein as the most eligible place, and particularly because the churches and pastors there, so far as we can learn, are exceedingly anxious that I remove the school thither, and pledge their aid in its support, so far as concerns the board of the pupils. The expense of new buildings for the school will be, in the minds of the committee, I suppose, the strongest objection to a removal; but a theological school of fifty pupils there will in my opinion cost less in two years, with this expense included, than here, and, I am inclined to think, less in a single year. Here a school of fifty pupils cannot cost less than twenty-three hundred rupees. Last year a less number (not including the wages of Pahpoo and Shwayhai) cost above two thousand rupees; and the price of provisions, fuel, etc., is constantly increasing in Maulmain." —*Missionary Magazine*, 1857, pp. 386, 436-438.

The views of the several missions on the question raised by Dr. Wade's circular, so far as they have transpired, are as follows. The Bassein mission, of course, earnestly favored the plan. The Maulmain Karen mission advocated the change, as we have seen. The Henthada mission, while they thought it "desirable and best for the cause to remove the seminary to Bassein," were of the opinion, nevertheless, "that the arrangement should be only temporary," and that the school ought eventually to be located at Henthada. The grounds for this opinion were stated to be, the greater centrality of that town, its superior healthfulness, and the fact that it would be far more favorable to the morals of Karen pupils than any large seaport could be. For these three reasons, two of which sound strangely to one who knows Bassein, and for a fourth, which long since vanished away (viz., that Henthada "must always be furnished with doctors, as it is and must be the headquarters of a thousand sepoys," while the unfortunate residents of Bassein will have to seek medical aid "in Dalhousie, or at some place still more distant"), it was finally decided by the Executive Committee, Dr. Wade at length concurring, to remove the seminary to Henthada, and that with no promise whatever of aid from the churches of that station.

If, instead of opposing both these plans, Dr. Binney had seconded the original plan of Dr. Wade, and gone with the seminary to its natural home in the great heart of the Bassein churches, —all hungry for just such help as Dr. Binney and the seminary would have given them by their bare presence and the pursuit of their own special work, —his own usefulness, and that of the institution he loved so well, would have been trebled. But, not knowing Bassein, he saw not his golden opportunity, and for him it passed by forever.

The report of the annual meeting held at Yaygyau in January of this year gives evidence of solid progress, and renewed occasion for thanksgiving. There was a falling-off in the number of baptisms; but it was the result, perhaps, of greater care in instruction, and more strictness in the reception of candidates. Among an ignorant people there is always a strong tendency to depend more on the outward rite than on faith in Christ, and evidence of the new birth. At a meeting of Pwos, held a few days before the association, Mr. Van Meter writes:—

"We received but six from among more than twice that number of applicants. Many were disappointed: but we told them, after a careful examination, that we dared not at this time receive more; and that, so deplorable was their want of knowledge of the first principles of the gospel, they ought, for the credit of the Christian name, to be better prepared to 'give a reason for the hope that is in them.' Formerly this could hardly be expected; but now books and schools are multiplied, and there is not the excuse for ignorance that there once was.

"One new church (Adalouk) is reported, numbering eighteen members, with a congregation of forty or fifty. It is composed of both Pwos and Sgaus, and has for its pastor Kwee Beh, one of our active and worthy young men. He studied several years in our mission-school, and has since been engaged as a teacher and missionary. We could wish the churches had been more earnest in carrying the gospel to their heathen neighbors; but, while the funds and disposition have not seemed to be wanting, the men to do this work have been far too few. We hope the day is not distant when many of the members, as well as all the pastors, will feel a deep individual responsibility in this matter, and when it will not be regarded as entirely the work of the paid missionary.

"Most of the churches formerly in Arakan have selected places on this side of the mountains, but [a few churches and] a number of families remain behind. One of the churches has been severely tried through the apostasy of its pastor [Sah Gay, spoken of in the next paragraph]. All traces of the tendency towards spiritualism have disappeared. The decided measures taken with the first offenders seem to have had the desired effect. It was not found necessary to cut off others, and even those cut off have since begged to be restored.

"There has been no increase in the number of preachers during the year, if we except those who have just returned from Dr. Wade's school at Maulmain. Several of these are now out as missionaries, and some of them may be included among the preachers in our next report; but most of them, we hope, will return to their studies. Our whole number of pastors and preachers, fifty-nine, is less by four than last year. One, an excellent and faithful pastor, has died. Two have gone to labor in other fields, — one to Henthada, the other to Rangoon. One [unordained] has been deposed, Sah Gay by name. He had not attended any of our general meetings, and, as might be expected, had become alienated from his brethren, fell into sin, and finally made shipwreck of his faith. This is a most afflictive event; but it gives occasion for gratitude that such things have been rare indeed in the history of this mission.

"While the contributions to the Home Mission Society have largely increased, the direct result of missionary labor is small. Most of our young men being engaged either in teaching or studying, but few are left for missionary work, except the pastors. About twenty of these in all have been out during the year. They visited a large number of villages, were well received, and in some places urged to return. The number who joyfully and heartily receive the Word is small; yet seed has been sown, from which fruit may be gathered hereafter. Ten missionaries were appointed at the annual meeting, but the late insurrection has been a serious hinderance to them. Six of them were brought in as prisoners only a few weeks since, under suspicion that they were emissaries of the rebels. The Burman official even went so far in one village as to order all who had listened to or received them to be severely beaten. No violence was offered to the preachers, and they were released almost as soon as they reached Bassein. We are happy to add, that Major Fytche administered a severe rebuke in open court to the head man who had seized them, and beaten the people. The Karens will know now that the government has no sympathy with any such abuse of authority, and that their rulers have not the least objection to their becoming Christians. Yet there are still many whose common excuse is, that they dare not become Christians for fear of the Burmans; and the most absurd reports and falsehoods are so far credited that many dare not allow a 'white-book man' to enter their houses.

"In two places decided impressions seem to have been made, — one in the extreme north of the district, among the Sgaus; and the other east, among the Pwos. Two old men from the former place were present at the annual meeting, and seemed deeply interested in the proceedings. They both declared, for themselves and their village, their full adoption of Christian customs and a determination to abide in them.

"The schools have been well sustained, though the number of scholars is less than in 1855...The serious hinderances occasioned in all our operations by the fire, and sickness in our family, and especially by the loss of all our school-books, will be apparent on a moment's consideration. Even in our town school, as many as two or three had to use the same book in more than one class. Thirty-nine pupils were in attendance, of whom twelve were pastors of churches. Our chief dependence must be, for the present, on what can be done in the rainy season."

The academies continue to prosper. Kohsoo reported ninety-three pupils; Naupeheh, sixty-five, with two young preachers in attendance; while P'nahtheng, the youngest, had eighty in her school, all the expense of teachers, and aid to youth from other villages, being borne by the church in P'nahtheng alone. The other two schools drew fifty rupees each from the Home Mission Society, and six rupees a month extra for the principal. The returns for the year are given by Mr. Van Meter:—

"Baptisms, 270; new worshippers, 45; communicants, 5,250; churches, 51; preachers (ordained, 8), 59; schools, 38; pupils, 882.

CONTRIBUTIONS.

For the Home Mission Society	Rs.	849-15-10
For support of pastors (cash)	"	1,292-15-6
For support of pastors (paddy, 4,126 baskets)	"	1,650-0-0
For schools, teachers' wages, pupils' board, etc."		910-0-0
For new chapels	"	1,222-15-0
For the poor, cash and paddy	"	192-9-0
For miscellaneous objects	"	1,714-11-9
Total	Rs.	7,833-3-1

The first quarterly meeting held at the remote village of Podau in March was smaller than usual, but the interest manifested was fair. Mr. Van Meter writes:—

"The whole number of baptisms for the quarter is a hundred and twenty, of which forty-seven are Pwos. Twenty of these I baptized a few weeks since at Tee Hai, the new and growing church in Shway Loung district. Forty were baptized at Podau during the meeting, many of them from Laymyetna, in the extreme north of Bassein, of whom mention was made in our last annual report. The missionary has continued to labor among them, and these are the first-fruits. The delegation appointed to visit the churches in Arakan report those who still remain as steadfast in the faith, and mindful of their obligations to support gospel institutions. Shway Nyo, one of the two pastors who had been remiss in attending the quarterly meetings, and reporting their churches, was heard from by letter at this time. The other, Sah Gay, deposed at the annual meeting in January for immorality, we were pained to learn, gave no signs of penitence.

"Some of the pastors complained of a disposition, on the part of a few of their people, to absent themselves from worship without good reason. The presence of Burmans in and near their villages, and the practice of their heathen customs, is a source of serious annoyance to others. This is partly owing to the fact, that now many of the Karens are living in much more eligible situations than formerly, on the banks of large streams, and near main thoroughfares, and hence are more liable to disturbance than when hid away in secluded places. Still we tell them they must avoid commingling with the heathen as far as possible, by letting it be known that they have selected such and such places for themselves, where they wish to dwell in peace and quiet as Christians, and by warning off at once all others.

"There is continued improvement in their houses and chapels. They are not only larger, but in many instances have an air of comfort and finish which a few years since was wanting. The substitution of sawn timber for bamboo and rough jungle wood is doubtless the chief cause of this improvement.

"The most cheering feature of this meeting was found in the reports of the ten or twelve missionaries who have been out during the quarter. The year 1856 seemed remarkably barren, but the fruit of seed then sown is now beginning to appear. With but one exception, all reported cases of hopeful conversion. One says, 'At Nehyagon, far north of Bassein, three houses worship.' A young man was left there to teach them to read. At another place are some twenty worshippers: a teacher was left there also. Two had learned to read, and five or six were asking baptism. Shway Bau went over nearly the same ground, and found appearances far more encouraging than at any former time. Some seven families seem in earnest in seeking the kingdom of heaven. A third, Shway Min, labored in Theegwin. Two houses, about ten persons, are worshippers. Thahbwah reports, among other encouraging cases, fifteen houses at Bo-bay-eng[1] ready and anxious to receive a teacher. Shway Meh, who went as far as the Henthada district, reports as the result of labors at Kyeikpee five houses of new worshippers."

{ Footnote: [1] For many years favorable reports were brought back by native missionaries visiting this place. The people were pleasant, and ready to receive evangelists with hospitality when they came: they would even promise to accept the gospel at a more convenient season in the future. Jan. 27, 1880, the author baptized a man and his wife at this place, so far as he is aware, the first and only fruit gathered from the annual visits and somewhat desultory efforts of over twenty years. }

The second meeting of the year, held July 3-5, in Taukoo, one of the western villages, is briefly reported by Mr. Van Meter.

"This meeting, we believe, will be long remembered by all who attended it as one distinguished by the special outpouring of the Spirit. I witnessed at this time, what I have so often longed to see among the Karens, a melting of hearts before God and one another, manifested by simple but earnest expressions of deep and ardent feeling, confession of sin, and praise to God's rich grace. It was good to be there. So many wished to give utterance to their feelings, that the [covenant] meeting, which was held till quite late on Saturday night, was continued through the greater part of the sabbath, the interest increasing to the end."

This was the last meeting attended by Mr. Van Meter prior to his return to the United States. He sailed with his family, *viâ* England, at the close of the year. Rev. Mr. Beecher and Mrs. Helen L. Beecher arrived in Bassein, for his second term of service, on the 17th of September. They were hospitably received by Mr. and Mrs. Douglass, and he at once set about the important work of obtaining a suitable site for the Sgau Karen mission compound and the erection of the necessary buildings.

Although various attempts were made to keep up the connection between the Sgau churches and the A. B. M. Union, all of them failed, and the field naturally passed under the patronage and control of the Free Mission Society. In this change of relations, which at the time cost so much bitter feeling and regret, we can now clearly see the hand of Providence. To Mr. Beecher's strong views on the subject of self-support was now added the pressure of necessity. The younger society, with its smaller constituency, could not do for its missions all that the older organization had been accustomed to do; and thus the Karen stripling continued to use and develop his own legs, to his own unspeakable advantage.

The quarterly meeting at Kyun Khyoung, Oct. 2, was attended by Mr. Beecher alone of the missionaries. Mr. Van Meter sent an unfortunate letter on behalf of his society, the sole effect of which was to strengthen Mr. Beecher's position in the eyes of the Karens, if indeed it needed any strengthening.

Rev. Mr. Thomas having been directed to assume charge of the Sgau churches of Bassein in addition to his former field, retaining Henthada as his residence, made an important tour in the Bassein district in the months of December and January. His views and methods of labor differed materially from Mr. Beecher's. He was in favor of subdividing the churches and of multiplying the number of paid preachers, and to do this he would draw largely upon the Christians of America for pecuniary help. That he was a rare missionary "goes without saying;" and the estimate which his journal gives of the condition of the Bassein churches at that time is very valuable, though perhaps slightly colored by his views of mission policy, and not quite accurate in every case. During this tour of two mouths and a half he baptized one hundred and eighteen converts, and administered the Lord's Supper thirty-four times. We deem ourselves happy to find a picture of the Bassein Christian villages, and of a missionary's every-day work among the people, so graphic as this from Mr. Thomas:—

"Dec. 10.—This morning retraced our steps to Padin-gyau, whence, after breakfast and a short season of devotion, we took our course by the foot of the hills to the south. Here, again, all was not poetry. We soon entered a swamp, where the mud and water were from a foot to four feet deep. It was not until we had struggled on for a mile, that I found we were in the midst of a slough not less than three miles in length. But there was now no alternative: we must go forward. Ere long, the coolies, worn out with fatigue, were falling into the water with my luggage. At first I was very careful lest I might wet my feet, to prevent which I put myself into an almost horizontal position upon my horse. But I found this operation so painful, that I was obliged to let my feet dangle in the mud and water. So, after a struggle of an hour and a half, we emerged on the south side of the slough, the most pitiful appearing objects imaginable.

"We soon forgot our past trials in view of events to come and in contemplating the beauties of nature which were scattered around us in profusion. We passed through one populous region of Burmese and a few Karens, when we reached a lowly hamlet of five or six houses, quite in among the smaller hills. Here we found three baptized converts and a few candidates for admission into the church.

"*11th.*—I baptized four Karens this morning, who, with the three who went a long way to be baptized by one of the Bassein pastors last year, form a very interesting company of believers. There is reason to think that two or three more families will soon join themselves to the people of God here. After administering the memorials of Christ's dying love to these weak lambs of the flock, we set out for Kwengyah, the most northern church of the Bassein mission. We walked till after sunset, when we reached a large region of heathen Karens, many of whom once threw away their foolish, degrading customs, only, however, to embrace them again after a short time. After preaching and talking, we had but a few hours to sleep, before we were again on the road, which we followed until afternoon, when we reached a part of the Kwengyah church. I was received with the greatest apparent love and joy, no way of showing which being unemployed. At evening we came on to the main body of the church, where we were made to feel how different the disciples are from the heathen, among whom we have been mostly during the last ten days.

"*14th.*—I bade adieu to Kwengyah, having spent two days with the one hundred Christians there. I found no cases of discipline. The members seem to be men and women of much maturity of Christian character. They are entirely estranged from their former degrading customs. They support their pastor, and take a commendable interest in education. The missionary spirit they manifest is very pleasing. Two or three members of the church are sent out to preach to the heathen. The church remember these evangelists in their prayers. The pastor of the church [Sau Ng'Too] is a good and able minister, with a few unpleasant peculiarities. Yet he tries to magnify his office, and might with safety be ordained. But even here one would be glad to see an improvement in their houses and in the clothing of their children. Yesterday I baptized ten converts, and administered the Lord's Supper, which had not been observed here before for two years. If this sacred means of grace is neglected thus in many places, the ordained men need to be spoken to on the subject. On the whole, our friends in America may confidently trust in the Christian stability of the Kwengyah church.

"Evening.—I have been with the church at M'gayl'hah about half a day, but sufficiently long to learn that they are in a very bad state. The pastor was educated at Maulmain. He is a good man: he has efficiency, but a very inefficient way of showing it. He is heartily discouraged. The members, he says, do not exert themselves to send their children to school, nor to attend meeting themselves. Some of them have not been seen in the chapel for a whole year. Some attend meeting in the morning, but spend the remainder of the day in visiting the heathen; while some have been guilty of more serious offences. I am told, moreover, that the better members of the church, even, do not seem disposed to take any action in regard to the unruly. Were we to see a person insensible to his condition while some of his limbs were actually decaying, we should regard him as in a dangerous state. Such are my feelings as to this church. I have sent for a neighboring pastor to be with me to-morrow to aid me in trying to 'strengthen the things that remain.' I find that here, also, there has been a strange neglect of that ordinance which is so essential to growth in grace even in America. The Lord's Supper has been administered here but once for at least four years.

"15th.—During the meetings to-day the state of the church appears no better. One has been excluded, four refused admission to the communion: indeed, more than half of the church have absented

themselves. It is painful to see how much of a piece every thing is here in M'gayl'hah. Two young women presented themselves as candidates for baptism, but they were not aware that they were sinners. They could not tell who Christ is, nor whence he came, how he died, or whether or not he arose from the dead; and yet they were children of members of this church. I need not add that they were not baptized.[1]

{ Footnote: [1] It is but just to say that this church, with the same pastor, Too Po, has stood, for the last twelve years at least, among the best in the district for intelligence and piety. }

"Since writing the above, I have come down the river only an hour's sail; yet all is changed. I am among the members of one of the larger churches in Podau. The village [Nyomau] is on a rise of land. The houses, all fronting the river, with front yards swept, and surrounded with ornamental trees, present an unusually pleasant appearance. The deacons [see Shway Bau's own testimony concerning them, p. 258] who have just called upon me were neatly and becomingly dressed, and are men of serious and venerable bearing, and appear quite worthy, either here or in any part of the world, of the office which they fill. After worship this evening, the pastor, Shway Bau, a very capable man, called on me with his family, who with others sung sweetly the songs of Zion, and conversed until a late hour. It is impossible to repeat the conversation: however, I feel confident that the gospel has made a deep and saving impression in Podau.

"16th.—I have just left Podau in my little boat. The meetings to-day have been full of interest. Nine young persons, of the most interesting character, have been baptized.

"Evening.—We arrived a little after dark in Hseat-thah, where there is a small church. The scene has changed again. Appearances are less pleasing than in Podau. But discipline does not seem to be called for. This church may be described as 'faint,' and very faintly 'pursuing.' Here were ten candidates, five of whom were rejected because they knew nothing of Christ.

"*18th.*—I have been in Yohplau [Shankweng] about twenty-four hours. None of the members of this church seem to have offended openly, yet there is a want of something. The pastor [Pah Yeh] is a man of good abilities, but does not throw his whole soul into the work. He exhibits a sad lack of spirituality, and so do the whole church. The members are not all worldly: there are some living Christians here who seem to have been quickened by the administration of the ordinances. To save such churches as this from utter worldliness, American Christians need more spirituality, which must be transferred to these churches, by the blessing of God, through their missionaries. Oh for vital godliness!

"*19th.*—I came on this evening at a late hour to Thrai-oo. Here is the headquarters of a large church, say two hundred members; but they are now scattered in three different places, some near the sea, over a hundred miles distant. Those present seemed to be benefited by the ordinances of God's house. Here I met the daughter of that apostolic man, Myat Kyau, the first Karen ever ordained. She is a woman of uncommon abilities, but is out of health, and is married to a very worthless man. A son of Myat Kyau was so promising, that he was sent to Calcutta, at the expense of an English officer, to complete his education and to study medicine. This had the effect to ruin him. He is now, I think, in government employ as an apothecary, has married a heathen Arakanese woman, and, that he may be a perfect gentleman, he drinks brandy, etc., to excess. These are the relics of a man who baptized more converts than any one in Burma, except, perhaps, Quala.

"*20th.*—Sabbath evening. I have spent this day in [Meethwaydike], where I spent a week with the missionaries and Karen pastors some two years ago. There has been a very large congregation all day. Not a few have come from the nearer churches to listen to the Word, and to commemorate the Saviour's love. During the past two years this church has increased in numbers, but I fear it has decreased in piety. Several of the members have of late visited heathen feasts, but they profess penitence. Here is one of the ordained pastors, [Oo Sah]. He appears to be an honest man, but of abilities too limited to perform properly the duties of a minister: however, he will not knowingly go astray.

"*21st.*—I have spent this day with a small church. Here, as in many other places in this part of Burma, paddy has been almost ruined by an excess of water: hence the members are about to try their fortunes in another place. It takes but little to put a whole Karen village thus upon the wing. They will go to a new region, and build new houses, when some disease may break out, and scatter them again. The people seemed to be blessed by the word and ordinances of Christ.

"*22d.*—Here in Yaygyau is one of the larger churches, and an ordained pastor of very decent abilities, [Nahpay]. Here, as in most other places, there is a sad want of spirituality. I have seen many members of this church in Henthada, and have been shocked at their disregard of the sabbath: hence my sermon was specially pointed on that subject.

"*23d.*—The past night and day have been spent in Kyau-t'loo. Here is a small church, which has just expelled from their number two members, for the sin of adultery. Yet the church is not destroyed: no, most of the members seem to be filled with faith and love. This day has been one of the pleasantest of days to me. The members are poor, but 'rich in faith.' I was taken by surprise this morning, when the elders of the church not only received me with gladness, but even, while shaking hands, poured out their souls in praise and prayer to God for his goodness in guiding me to them: hence it sometimes took ten minutes to shake hands with one. Have baptized five here.

"*24th.*—Have spent the past twenty-four hours at Lehkoo, with a large church of about a hundred and fifty members. Here, as well as in Kyau-t'loo, the members are not a little dissatisfied with the limited power of the church. They are told that the church as such can simply expel an adulterer from all church-privileges; that churches have no power to fine and flog unruly members, however great their offences. Furthermore, to flog a man, unless it be done by the magistrate, would be an offence against the government. We urged them to consider that to have the hand of fellowship withdrawn by Christ's constituted agents, the members of a church, ought to be feared far more than the loss of a few rupees, or the infliction of stripes. We spent a great part of last night on this subject.

"*25th.*—We are now half a day's row north-west from Bassein town. Received a most cordial welcome from the church in [Kaukau Pgah]. Arose early, and went two or three miles to preach to a small village of heathen Karens, who listened well. Preached in the morning. At noon examined candidates for baptism. Six were baptized. Broke bread to a house full of members. Preached again at evening to a large number of Christians, several of whom will probably be baptized to-morrow. The Christians in this region appear extremely well [see pp. 5, 239]. Their pastor, Dahbu, is a very superior man,— one of the best, educated in Maulmain. I have been surprised to learn to-day that the widow of Ko Thahbyu, the first Karen convert and 'apostle,' is still living. I have spent considerable time with her, and have been much pleased with her cleanly appearance and her apparent heavenly-mindedness. Not long after Ko Thahbyu died, she came to this vicinity; and she says, 'I think I shall remain here until God calls me.' I learned nothing new of special interest from this aged saint.[1] But as I sat conversing with her about her tours in the Mergui, Tavoy, Maulmain, Rangoon, and Arakan provinces, I was affected even to tears; for there rushed into my mind the scenes of my past labors, the whole history of the Karen mission, and all the wonders God has wrought among this people...I dare not baptize in the name of Christ persons who know nothing about him. I fear many of the preachers neglect too much *the* gospel,—'Christ and him crucified.'

{ Footnote: [1] She still lives, 1882. }

"*27th.*—Sabbath evening. I have spent this holy day in the midst of the Christians of [Naupeheh], one of the western Bassein churches. The pastor, Tohlo, has long been ordained. I regard him as one of the most able, refined, and reliable ordained men in all Burma. He spent a great deal of time with the lamented Abbott.[2] He was with him as a student, an assistant in school, and as an associate. He was perfectly acquainted with that servant of Christ; and he saw no failings in him which prevent him from loving Mr. Abbott as a father, and revering him as a true minister of the gospel. Here is the seat of one of the three Bassein academies. I have taken special pains to ascertain the real merits of these schools; and, although far from perfection, I am convinced that they are doing a good work. The large chapel has been literally crowded all day, and I have preached the gospel, with the most precious liberty, from 1 Cor. i. 30. The state of things here is very encouraging; and one feels, while in the company of such a pastor and such Christians, that Christianity will not soon die out in Bassein.

{ Footnote: [2] It was Rev. J. L. Douglass, I think, who remarked, that for a Karen young man to follow Mr. Abbott as a horse-keeper for a year or two was equivalent to a liberal education. }

"But I have been made sad in the midst of my joys by the intelligence that Brother Van Meter and family are embarking on the English ship *Fort George*, to proceed, *viâ* England, to the United States. This induces me to leave all for a few days, and go to the town. In the absence of Brother Douglass[1] it will be necessary for me to look after mission property.

{ Footnote: [1] Attending his sick wife to Singapore, on her way to America and the better land. }

"*28th.*—Reached the city about three, P.M. Found a number of large ships lying at anchor, besides a steamer, and, as usual, a large number of Chinese and Burmese boats. On landing, I was attracted by the houses of Brethren Van Meter and Douglass. They are modest structures, but very pleasantly situated. So here I am in the society of missionaries. It sounds so odd to hear the English language spoken!

"*Jan. 2, 1858.*—I have spent the past two days at Shanywah, six or eight miles below Bassein. Here is a small church, rather, the chapel of a church, whose members live in three small villages. There seems to be but little life either in pastor or people.[2] I have done all in my power to quicken them. This has been a lonely place in which to pass

New Year's—some two hundred miles from my family. Yet God is near.

{ Footnote: [2] This church again, under the able ministrations of Rev. Pohtoo, has become one of the very best churches in the Bassein association. }

"*4th.*—Arrived at Kaunee last evening. I spent the sabbath with a larger church, which is in a more encouraging state than the one at Shanywah. Yet I find, as in almost every other place in Bassein, a want of spirituality. The fact is, we need a revival of religion, oh, how much!

"*5th.*—Returned to town this morning to see Brother Van Meter off, also to make arrangements to preserve mission-books, which, if left as they now are, will be ruined by rats and white ants in a month or two.

"*9th.*—I am again in my little canoe, with my face set towards the Karen jungles south-west of Bassein. But we make no progress; for the tide has left us stuck fast in the muddy channel of [Tahkeing *Yaygyau*]. It is sunset before the water lifts us out of the mud, and there is a good half day's journey before us; so that we shall not reach Thehbyu before midnight.

"*11th.*—Spent the sabbath yesterday with the large church at [Mohgoo], with apparent profit to the people. In this region the Karens are better off than in many other places, and seem grounded in the faith. I have walked to-day three miles, and administered the ordinances to a very well appearing church of a hundred members [Taukoo], and returned again. These disciples, at least many of them, are evidently some of the 'holy seed' to whom pertain the promises. Isa. vi. 13.

"*12th.*—This day has been spent in trying to unite a church rent asunder by dissension. The pastor has left the village, where are the chapel and the homes of the main body of the church. He will be followed by most of the members. We tried to urge the pastor and his party to return with us, and see if all could not be reconciled. They declined. They had been told that they must return. One or two ordained men had told the pastor that he must return, or leave the ministry. He and his party think this a stretch of ecclesiastical power. Many of the church are determined to call the pastor to another place, and he is as determined to obey that call. Hence, in the absence of serious offences, it remains for us to induce them to live apart in peace. You will at once see how much this body resembles too many churches in America. Schisms are not confined to Burma: indeed, they seem to be fewer here than they are at home.

"*13th.*—I came on an hour or two, and reached another large church [Layloo], whose members seem more nearly like the heathen, as far as refinement goes, than almost any other Christians in Bassein. The pastor, an old man, and almost entirely without education, told me just now that he understood nothing in the Karen almanac which I gave him yesterday. It is painful to see men of so little ability in such places. But time will enable us, with strenuous effort, to remedy this evil. As we pushed off from the shore to-day, many voices called out, 'Do come again; come often!'

"*14th.*—Had a pleasant time for twenty-four hours at the village of Tway Gyau, another ordained pastor. He is evidently a good man, but of few words and of moderate abilities. The disciples here also are about to remove to a new place. It is easy to find a place to establish any number of new villages, for this country is nearly destitute of inhabitants. I have felt pressed in spirit to preach from Hab. iii. 2: 'O Lord, revive thy work.' Let all join in this petition.

"*17th.*—I have been visiting several places where there are a few Christians, a few heathen, and also two small churches. At one of the latter places, Ng'Kwat, I found the people divided as to where to pitch their frail houses. After preaching this afternoon from Heb. x. 25, I baptized five, and administered the Lord's Supper. I have also visited and given medicine to many who are afflicted with that scourge of the land, intermittent fever. I find here, and at several other places, young men, who, if they were moved by the Holy

Spirit, might preach the gospel. But we hear of very few coming forward, and confessing, 'Woe is me if I preach not the gospel.'

"*18th.*—Here in Karah Kyee [now Hsenleik] there was a large church: but it has decreased about one-half; for since the pastor died, two years since, the church have not secured another. To-day, with great unanimity, a man from the theological school has been chosen.

"*21st.*—Again in Bassein, having completed the circuit west of the city. I am about to leave for a long tour among the eastern churches. I expect to continue it by land until I reach my home in Henthada.

"*Evening.*—Here I am in Kohsoo, one of the most refined Christian villages in Bassein. The pastor, Myat Keh, is one of the most popular of our ordained men,—a man of great power in exhortation. Here is the first academy established in the district. It is cheering to see the improved houses, and the general appearance of the village. Good chairs are no strange thing here; while in the house of Yoh Po, the teacher of the academy, I see, from where I sit writing, a very neatly dressed Karen woman[1] sitting at work in an American rocking-chair.

{ Footnote: [1] This intelligent Christian woman is a daughter of the pioneer evangelist, Mau Koh. The rocking-chair referred to is still in existence, and has given rest to many a weary missionary. }

"*24th.*—Spent yesterday in a Pwo Karen village. I have not been to a Pwo church before, during this tour. I find here in Kyun Khyoung a small one. The members are feeling sad and disheartened by the departure of their teacher, Van Meter. How many times I have been asked by Pwo converts, 'Is teacher Van Meter to return? If not, will another man be sent to the Pwos?' I have generally answered thus: 'If he does not return quickly, another man will be sent to you.' I have given this answer in view of the importance of this field.

"The Pwo Karens in Bassein are probably more numerous than the Sgaus. I have been surprised to find so few heathen Sgaus south of the most northern church connected with Bassein. There is one populous region of heathen Sgaus just east of the town. It is wide, but its inhabitants are few when compared with those of Henthada. On the other hand, there are some Pwos in almost every part of Bassein; while in the south and along the seacoast there are few Sgaus, but a great many Pwos. So, again, to the east from the ocean, along by Pantanau, to Donabew and even to Henthada, the inhabitants are nearly all Pwos.

"These Pwos are not hardened above all others. Brother Van Meter baptized a number just before he left. There are also six little churches already, which need the watch-care and aid of a Pwo missionary. Besides, the present is a peculiar time. The Pwos have been drawn into difficulty in connection with the 'Maulay' sect. Some of them have been shot by government agents, and the rest fear lest they may be suspected of belonging to that strange sect: hence, to avoid suspicion, they are professing Roman Catholicism in large numbers. They have their children sprinkled, and conform outwardly to the rules of worship. But it is said that their lives are unchanged. I feel an inexpressible weight upon my soul while I write, because at this juncture we have no missionary among the Pwos of Bassein. Hence this digression.

"25th.—I have spent this sabbath in Th'mah-t'k'yah ['A Hundred Alligators']. An interesting feature in this church is, that among its members are three Burmans. I have already found six Burman Christians in the Bassein (Karen) churches. One of these is at present pastor of a small Karen church. I have also seen one Shan convert. To-day I have been entreated to baptize a Bengalee. He certainly understands enough to be a Christian. But he is a Bengalee, and has no wife. Though he has been in Burma a long time, and in this village more than a year, yet one fears some sinister motive.

"27th.—Spent yesterday with a new church, where I baptized four. After calling at P'nahtheng, arrived to-day at [Kyootah], the place where the association meets. The third academy is at P'nahtheng. It is not so firmly established as the one at Kohsoo.

"*30th.*—Since the last date I have been engaged day and night in the meetings of the association, the Home Mission Society, and the Ministerial Conference. These meetings were all mingled together in the most indiscriminate manner. I tried hard to have them attend to [the business of] one body at a time, but was unable to break over their old customs. This irregularity was the cause of fearfully long sessions, wearying out most of those present long before the meetings closed: hence, while hundreds more were present in the village, the meetings (some of them) were thinly attended. Mau Yay was chosen moderator. If he is the best Karen for that office, there is not one fit for it. However, the meetings were all harmonious, and some of them devotional. It is regarded by the Karens as a good meeting. The statistics indicate a fair state of religion among the churches. The contributions compare well with those of former years. Two hundred and fifty-five have been baptized, and some new worshippers are reported.

"*31st.*—This forenoon was occupied with the ordination of Toothah, the pastor of the church with which we meet. In the afternoon I took the lead in the communion-services, and was determined to have one service only endurably long. But after we had sung, and were ready to leave the house, Mau Yay arose, and begged to say a few words. The privilege was granted, of course, and the good brother spoke at least half an hour. But his speech was on a very important subject, and, though long, was of great interest.

"*Feb. 3.*—I left Kyootah early Monday morning for Henthada. Our course, for there was no kind of a road, lay to the east and northeast. Two whole days we travelled without meeting a single Christian. Indeed, we found but very few people of any kind, and nearly all of them were Burmans and Pwo Karens. We invariably stopped among the latter tribe, who freely provided us with food, and a sleeping-place in their houses. They also listened attentively to the gospel, but seemed not at all inclined to submit to it. Late last evening, when every one of us was ill from excessive weariness, we reached Eng-gyee, the most southern church of the Henthada mission. It would have been agreeable to my feelings to spend most of the day in sleep, but there has been too much to do. We have had four services, besides examining, and going two miles to baptize, two converts."

As this meeting at Kyootah was felt by all parties to be a critical occasion, Mr. Vinton of the Free Mission Society came over from Rangoon to sustain his associate, Mr. Beecher. His lamented decease occurred very soon after his return. Outwardly the meeting was harmonious, the three American brethren being about equally prominent. The one decisive thrust which seems to have determined Mr. Thomas to go directly back to his own field after the meeting, and to have nothing more to do with Bassein, was delivered by a Karen, none other than the leonine veteran, Mau Yay of Kyootoo, who still lives to preside, in his own fashion, at the meetings of the Home Mission Society. We quote Mr. Thomas's vivid description of the scene:—

"Mau Yay is the oldest of the ordained Karen pastors. He is unusually large, and rather uncouth in his personal appearance. He has but little education, even for a Karen pastor. He is not eloquent, in the common acceptation of the term; yet there is power in his speech, for there is soul and common sense in all that he says. He appears to be quite ignorant of the fear of man. Hence it is that on all occasions Mau Yay is put forward as the mouth-piece of his brethren.

"Fancy, then, this man of the jungles, with turban but ill arranged, with two or three coats on (one over the other), with a soiled silk handkerchief flung around his neck, containing a little change tied up in one end, and his keys attached to the other. The immense congregation is assured that he has something of importance to say: hence all listen attentively while he passes in review the history of the creation, of the fall of man, and of the redemption by Christ. The kingdom of God must be extended; Satan's head must be crushed.

"Now, all this is very good in its place; but why does Mau Yay rehearse these great truths here and now, seemed to be the inquiry of all present. Indeed, it was not until he had nearly exhausted our patience, that he brought out his great thoughts; viz., that Karens, in order to act well their part in the world's redemption, must be educated. He naturally passed from this to the means of obtaining an education. With great boldness and force he urged that they, the churches of Bassein, ought to call a teacher, not exactly a missionary, from America. They were able, he said, to pay the passage of a family, and to support that family alter their arrival. He continued, 'Let the missionaries now in the field give themselves to the work of the ministry, and go to the regions beyond; but let us have a family who will remain among us, and instruct our youth in English, in Greek and Hebrew; then may we ourselves hope to understand the word of God.' He urged his brethren to act at once, and to act unitedly. Said he, 'Let the five thousand Christians of Bassein but contribute four annas (twelve cents) each, and the passage-money for our teacher and family is paid.'

"The proposition was unhesitatingly accepted, and all present agreed to make the effort at once. I spontaneously arose, and said, 'Brethren, go on. Your fathers and brethren in America who have long labored for your good will rejoice to hear that you can get on without their special aid; that they no longer need to watch over their mission in Bassein, as a mother over her helpless babe, but that they may dismiss you as a well-grown man, able to provide for himself.'

"These were my sentiments on that sabbath evening, Jan. 31, 1858; these were my sentiments daring my return home; they are my sentiments now that I am again in this town, the centre of the Henthada mission. Brethren of the Missionary Union, with many prayers and tears you have sown the seed of the kingdom in the districts of Bassein and Rangoon. That seed has taken root; it has sprung up; it is now bearing fruit. You have done your work in the Karen departments of those fields. Now, therefore, commend those churches to the God of missions, and let them choose and support their own theological and literary instructors. Indeed, let them be just as free in these matters as are the churches of New Hampshire and Vermont, but let me remain in the Henthada and Tharrawaddi districts, and spend all my time and strength henceforth in trying to win these numerous heathen to Christ, and to make these churches equal and even superior to the churches of Bassein. Help, brethren, by your earnest prayers, by your silver and your gold, and, depend upon it, in less than another quarter of a century your special aid may also be dispensed with in both these wide provinces.

"Yours in the gospel of Christ,
"B. C. THOMAS."

This faithful missionary did his best to rescue the heathen of Henthada and Tharrawaddi, and to breathe his own earnest spirit and warm religious life into the churches of his planting. He did his best, doubtless, to use wisely the silver and the gold which came to him from the home-land, according to his expressed desire. But the snare that was in the lucre was scarcely escaped, perhaps, by his people; nor is the need of special aid less keenly felt to-day, perhaps, although the quarter of a century of which he wrote was complete last February. If there were, or if there be, in the Bassein Sgau churches any less spiritual life than in other circles of Karen churches, which the author strongly doubts, it may be the fault of their overworked missionaries: it certainly is *not* the fault of the system of self-help to which they have been so rigorously trained. It may also be said, that the greater degree of benevolence developed, and their pre-eminent zeal for education and foreign missions, will go far to atone for any slight deficiency that some may seem to detect in the direction aforesaid.

In closing the chapter, we must not fail to give the following translation of the historic letter which was prepared by the Bassein pastors at Kyootah, and sent to the Executive Committee of the A. B. M. Union at Boston:—

"We, the ordained preachers of the churches of Bassein, have received your letter, in which you say that you had compassion upon us while we were yet in darkness, and sent teacher Abbott to instruct us in the word of God; and again, that, though teacher Abbott is dead, love is not dead, and that you will have more regard for us in the future than in the past. You also say that teacher

311

Thomas is of like mind and spirit with teacher Abbott, and direct us to receive him as our teacher.

"In reply, we are happy to inform you that we have not forgotten the great blessing we have experienced through your sending to us teachers Abbott and Beecher, and, more, that we never shall forget it, or cease to pray that God will abundantly bless you for what you have done for us.

"When teacher Abbott left us, he said to us that Mr. Beecher was to become our teacher in his place; and, when Mr. Beecher left us for America, we hoped to receive the additional favor of your sending him back to us. As you, however, did not send him, another missionary society kindly received him, and sent him back to us. We have therefore received favors from both these societies, neither of which we can ever forget.

"You say that you send teacher Thomas to become our teacher, and direct us to receive him. As to this, we know not what to think. Teacher Thomas wrote and inquired if we would receive him; and we replied, 'Come and visit us, and stir us up in the faith and fellowship of the gospel: coming in this way, we will cordially receive you.' But we also told him that our own teacher, Beecher, having returned, we had received him as our teacher, as at the first. What you say to us, therefore, respecting teacher Thomas, greatly embarrasses us, for the following reasons:—

"Teacher Thomas has work of his own, and he cannot do both that and the work here; and, should he become our teacher, that work must go to pieces. Moreover, it will have the appearance of an attempt to interfere with the work of our teacher, and will greatly perplex the minds of many of the disciples. For ourselves, we cannot but regard the two teachers as brethren; and what one does, the other should consider as done; and what the other does, his brother should consider as done. Moreover, we have learned through teacher Kincaid that you have decided to invite back teachers Beecher, Vinton, and others, in order that all may be one again, as formerly. We do therefore greatly rejoice; for, should the Executive

Committee earnestly invite them to return, it might be the means of uniting the two societies in America, and, if not, they would no longer throw obstacles in each other's way. What one did, the other would consider as done, and there would be no interference with each other's work.

"We think, therefore, that we should receive teacher Thomas only as a visiting brother, as we have received teachers Brayton and Vinton. Beyond this, we do not think that we ought to receive him.[1]

(Signed)
"MAU YAY. NAHPAY. SHWAY BO.
MYAT KEH. OO SAH. TOOTHAH.
PO KWAY. TWAY GYAU. TOHLO."

{ Footnote: [1] There may have been a little ploughing with the Karen heifer; but the letter was substantially their own, and its positions were fully indorsed by the great body of the Bassein disciples. The one concession which would have been most highly prized by the Karens, and which would have done more than any thing else to elevate them, and keep them friendly, if not loyal to the Union, was to have transferred the Seminary to Bassein, as urged by Dr. Wade. Beecher would have co-operated cordially with Dr. Binney, but the latter was fated to go and labor for years in a locality where it was obvious to himself afterwards that he had but a scant welcome. }

CHAPTER XV.

1858—1862.

"Christianity has been in all its history the patron of sound learning. It has gone teaching all nations. The light of knowledge has followed it around the world, as the light of day the sun. It can hold men only by going before them; and *the narrowest policy of missions ever conceived is that Christianity can employ preaching, but not the school.* When a people become Christian, they next call for education, and they will fall to those who furnish it for them. Without education, religion itself runs out."—PRESIDENT SAMSON TALBOT.

In returning to Burma, Mr. Beecher clearly apprehended the great want of the Christian communities in Bassein to be increased facilities for Christian education. Up to that time they had enjoyed but twenty-six years of labor from foreign missionaries, including Abbott's period of service, Van Meter's, and his own. Twenty years of that labor had been done at arm's-length; the missionaries being shut up between the mountains and the sea, in remote Arakan, where but a few scores of the people could see them for a small part of the year. Six years only of white man's time had been given them in Bassein itself. Other stations had received more thousands of dollars in aid of schools and preachers than theirs had received hundreds. While the villages of Maulmain and Tavoy had received long visits from their numerous missionaries, more than half of their chapels had never been entered by an American "teacher." They had indeed escaped the evils of petting and superfluous aid; but the substantial benefits of Christian light and training—full rations of the very bread of life, and full draughts of the water of life—were beyond their reach. True, many of them could read; but what had they read? They had learned to worship, to pray, and to sing; but how well? Very partially, indeed, had the love of God and the light of life supplanted the slavish fear of Satan's hosts and the darkness of death.

Improved facilities for *Christian* education is what Mr. Beecher sought, and his successors still seek, for that people. We emphasize the adjective; for no extension or improvement of facilities for secular education offered by an enlightened, but, in religious matters, necessarily neutral government, can lessen our obligation to aid in providing for the children of our converts the religious atmosphere and training of positively Christian and Baptist schools of an advancing grade. To give over the brightest and most aspiring of our Christian youth to the moulding influence of irreligious, neutro-religious, or Boodhistic masters and text-books for eight or ten years at the most plastic period of life, in the hope that we can subsequently, at Sunday services and (for a few of them) in distinctively theological schools, renew the lost impress of early lessons, may be tried, if you will, in America; but in Burma the experiment will be a failure, and the outcome worse than vanity and vexation of spirit. To leave, moreover, as we are still doing among the Karens and Telugus, a larger majority of the children of converts to grow up in ignorance and superstition than does any other missionary society of which the author has knowledge, is to incur sooner or later a fearful penalty. To the duty and direful necessity thus laid upon us, the missionaries, and even the half-enlightened Christian parents of Bassein, have been from the first more keenly alive than the best of their friends in the far-off land of schools and churches.

Mr. Beecher, therefore, in communicating to the Executive Committee the conditions[1] under which he would be willing to return to his field under their auspices, frankly wrote:—

"In regard to the first condition, I would say the great object to which I intend to direct all my energies, and employ all the means placed at my disposal, is, not merely to Christianize the Karens, but to bring the converts forward as rapidly as possible to that high state of intellectual and religious culture which shall enable them to go forward in their growth and in the support of religious and literary institutions, independent of foreign aid.

{ Footnote: [1] "1. That I shall return to Bassein, and perform the same work that I undertook at my first appointment; and in this work of preaching the gospel, superintending native churches, raising up a native ministry, and educating the Christian population, I shall be left unrestricted, except by the aggregate of the annual appropriations of the Executive Committee.

"2. No permanent change shall be made in the place or kind of my labor, except by mutual consent.

"3. The Executive Committee shall not dismiss or recall me unless I shall have had an impartial hearing by my associates, and have been pronounced by them unworthy of my standing.

"4. Any statement communicated by any one on the mission-field to the Executive Committee or executive officers, injurious to my Christian or missionary character, shall be immediately made known to me, or the paper containing such statement be returned uncopied to the author." }

"In order to prosecute the work successfully, I deem it necessary that I should not be required to follow out *in detail* any routine of measures which the Executive Committee shall prescribe; but while I shall not feel at liberty to exceed the appropriations, nor to divert them from the object for which they are designated, yet with regard to the number of pupils who shall be instructed in the normal and other mission schools, and the course of instruction to be pursued, I shall expect a large liberty, only promising that the funds of the Union shall not be used to support pupils studying English, unless by specific permission of the Executive Committee."

Considering the fact that a powerful attempt had been made to keep him out of his appointed field of labor, and that an official letter had passed him on his homeward voyage, recalling him from the field, on the strength of unfriendly representations which he had had no opportunity to meet, his conditions seem to us not unreasonable; but they were rejected. Coming out as he did, unfettered, under the auspices of the Free Mission Society, he addressed himself manfully to the important work which he had planned, in the face of many obstacles. With the narrowest resources, he had a poor but united and enthusiastic people at his back. With the blessing of God on their help, he may yet accomplish great things.

The position which Mr. Beecher occupied at this time was a proud one, and his victory was assured. Chosen by the Karen Christians for what he was, and not for what he might bring; with no bag of American money for monthly or quarterly distribution among the preachers; with no funds even for the support of teachers or needy children in his schools; his whole power and influence due to the weight of his personal character, to the truth which he may draw from the word of God, to the teaching and the examples which he may cite to them from the Christian civilization of his own land, and, above all, to the gracious help of the Holy Ghost, who had called him to this very work,—he proceeded to lay the foundations of Christian institutions, and to mould and develop the people, whom he loved, for God, depending solely upon the pecuniary help of the poor, and such local aid as might offer. It is painful to see how few missionaries of the present day are content to occupy just such a position.

The first work of the missionary was to secure a suitable piece of ground for the mission establishment and a large boarding-school. As the government had at last given up the plan of removing the district headquarters to the mouth of the river, land was more difficult of acquisition. For the Karens, however, a location somewhat removed from the heart of the town would be preferable. The credit of selecting the present beautiful and sightly Sgau Karen compound clearly belongs to Mrs. H. L. Beecher. Others thought that "White Book Hill" (Sahbyugon), as it is now called, was too far from the town, or too far from the river. There was no road to it. There would be danger from tigers, robbers, etc. Besides, it was an old Burman burying-ground, and many Karens feared that they would be pestered by ghosts. But one fine morning the ponies were mounted, and the hill was reached by a circuitous route through the potter's village. Mrs. Beecher favors us with some interesting reminiscences:—

"The whole place was covered with scrubby jungle, and was uninhabited and neglected. A Karen boy climbed a tree, and declared that he could see the river. Altogether our visit satisfied us that it would be the best place for a large school, and so clearing and building were begun immediately. The beginning, like that of many good works, was under great difficulties. It was the time of the commercial panic in America, and it was very difficult to get money for the work, or for any thing else. I remember that one Saturday night we had no money to buy the necessary food for Sunday even, when a friendly Chinaman came, and lent us quite a sum of money, without interest or security. Indeed, we had many proofs of the Lord's care over us. We had hardly moved into our new house, and it was by no means finished, when a terrible cyclone swept over the city, and tore down nearly all the houses both of the natives and the Europeans. Our thatch all stood straight up, and we had to hold our umbrellas over our heads. I remember well, how, during that anxious night, Mr. Beecher called me to kneel with him, and I cannot forget the fervent and trusting petition that he presented, that our house and those mission-buildings might be spared. And they were spared, somewhat injured, but not one destroyed. The next year a similar tornado came; but we were better prepared, and suffered even less. We had several earthquakes, too, the first year or two; and lightning struck one of the Karen houses, but the fire was soon put out. I have often wondered, in thinking over those days, how we were cared for, and all our wants supplied.

"The dry season of 1858 was a period of great interest. As soon as the first building, the old schoolhouse, was put up, we moved into it. It had no glass windows, and was rough enough; but we were very happy there. It was so quiet and sweet all around us, so many birds sang (more sweetly than I supposed tropical birds could sing), and the jungle, which came almost to our door, abounded in the most beautiful flowers, and every thing was so fresh and hopeful. Every week, Friday or Saturday, we visited some Karen village, and spent the sabbath with the people. In that way, although Mr. Beecher had to spend nearly all his time week-days in looking after the building, still, much important work was done, and preparation for the rainy-season school was made.

KAREN MISSION-HOUSE, BASSEIN, BUILT BY MR. BEECHER IN
1858

"That rains, nearly all the pastors came in to school. It was the first
time they had ever had the whole Bible to study from. I wish I could
give you an idea of the intense interest they exhibited as the types
and shadows of the Old Testament were explained to them. Many of
them said that they had never in all their lives learned so much as
they had in that one season. Some of them brought their wives.
There were also several young women. And Po Kway brought his
whole family, excepting Myassah, who was studying in Rangoon. Po
Kway was one of the most interested students. I recollect how
amused I was to see him make quite a nice suit of clothes for his little
girl, Mah Loothah. His wife, when she first came, was quite
homesick; and of course I felt somewhat anxious in beginning to
teach so large a class of women when I had been so short a time in
the country. My first essay was at a Saturday morning prayer-
meeting. I read to them about Timothy, his mother and
grandmother, and talked a little upon it. I saw no particular response
in their eyes, such as I had been accustomed to see from my dear
girls in Rockford [Ill.]; but in the evening, Th'rah Kway came, and
said to me, that, since his wife had heard my talk about Timothy, she
was no longer homesick. I believe that I was never more comforted
in my life. That was indeed a busy rains. Besides finishing the

buildings, and making roads, and a bridge across the creek, the school must be carried on with very imperfect machinery...

"The Karens, especially Th'rah Kway, soon spoke of an English school; but we kept putting it off, from time to time, as well as we could. Two great difficulties were in the way,—one, the state of public sentiment at home; the other, the want of a teacher. However, as the Karens were so determined, we at length began, with Santhah only to help. Sahnay came afterwards, and so things went on. It was simply impossible for Mr. Beecher or me to do any thing in that school except to keep a general oversight. I also taught the girls to sew, etc...No one knows better than you what the work was that pressed on my dear husband's time and strength, and finally pressed the very life out of him."

Mr. Beecher, writing to a private friend in February of this year, says,—

"The Karens propose to pay the cost of the buildings I am now erecting, which will be, when completed on our present plan, some two thousand dollars, they holding the property as their own."

The Karens were full of enthusiasm, no doubt; but, by the time their school-buildings were erected and paid for, they were quite willing to have the Free Mission Society meet the expense of the mission dwelling-house, and retain control of the entire property. In consideration, doubtless, of the loyal services of the Karens in the late war, the government generously gave to the Free Mission Society ten acres of land on the crown of this hill, and made it free from all taxes, "so long as it shall be used for *bonâ fide* mission-purposes." Sixteen acres have since been added by purchase from native grant-holders; so that the mission now owns twenty-six acres, including the entire hill, the whole forming a mission compound unsurpassed, in Burma at least, for beauty, extent, and healthfulness.

On this fair hill Mr. Beecher proceeded to establish in 1858 the "Bassein Sgau-Karen Normal and Industrial Institute." At the importunate and long-continued solicitation of the Karens, the

English department was added in 1860. His grand object, as clearly set forth in a prospectus published in 1861, from which we quote below, was to increase the numbers and efficiency of the native agency, and through them to elevate the entire people in the scale of Christian civilization.

"The gospel has awakened such new life and enterprise in this people, that they desire to advance in civilization and social refinement, as well as in Christianity. To do this successfully, they require a much better educated class of preachers, of school-teachers, and other lay-helpers, than those who are their present mental and spiritual guides. All praise is due to the zeal and faithfulness of these laborers as *pioneers*; but the great majority of them were so sadly illiterate when converted, and have since (almost unavoidably) made such meagre attainments, that they are incapable of raising their people, in the social scale, much above their heathen neighbors. The object of our plan, therefore, is to raise up an agency well qualified to promote education, civilization, and social reform, in connection always with progress in the Christian life, or rather as the fruits of that life.

"The Karens have been so long an oppressed people, that all enterprise has been crushed out of them. They have been made to regard themselves as inferior in mental and physical abilities to the race that ruled them, if not to all other races. It is not strange, then, that they have little heart, even if they had any encouragement, to learn any thing from their more skilful but haughty and contemptuous neighbors. Being destitute of a literature and science, as well as of mechanical skill, they are impressed with the belief that they can make little or no progress without foreign aid, and without a wider range of thought and enterprise than can be found through their vernacular. Not that the masses can be taught in any other than their own language, but that a portion of the agency which enlightens and guides the masses requires that mental discipline and that knowledge which can be acquired to better advantage by studying the English language than by any other means within their reach. And if the standard of moral excellence, social refinement, and ennobling industry, which has been attained in England and

America, is to be the model for moulding these converts, then must the same means be used among Karens that have proved effectual among Anglo-Saxons.

"Impatient of longer delay, the Karens have come forward this season, and with great exertion have raised funds for erecting a small schoolhouse and dormitories, barely sufficient to accommodate the one hundred pupils who have been admitted from a much larger number of applicants. Besides these, we have eighty in the vernacular department.

"In order that these pupils may be fitted for the work now needed among their people, it is evident that they must be taught the natural sciences, physiology, and hygiene. All observing Europeans remark their unproductive and wasteful methods of cultivating and cleaning their great staple, rice; and no one who has noticed how much laziness, disorder, and looseness are attendant upon their sprawling postures in their unfurnished houses, can have failed to reflect upon the healthful moral influence of chairs and tables in daily use. In connection, then, with studies that will enlighten, strengthen, and elevate them, they need to be taught practically some branches of mechanical industry.

"These considerations seemed to indicate that it was highly important to establish somewhere among the Christian Karens *a Normal and Industrial Institute*. Believing that Bassein is a most favorable place for such an institution, we propose, with the divine blessing, to give the schools now in our charge this character, as far as the means intrusted to us will permit. These schools are in fact already assuming this character. All the pupils in both departments are now required to perform some kind of manual labor three hours a day. Ten of the vernacular pupils are at work with carpenter, joiner, and wheelwright tools. From fifteen to twenty are required to clean the rice used by the school; and they are doing it this season with mills, fitted up mainly by the pupils, which are regarded by all as a decided improvement upon the mills in common use. Six lads have become quite skilful in making low seats, or *morahs*, of rattans and bamboos. Sixteen women and girls are instructed in needlework.

A large number of the smaller boys are at work clearing and grading the mission premises, which were covered with dense jungle. This work will soon be finished, when there will be some seventy-five lads who would gladly work at useful trades, if they could be supplied with the necessary tools and workshops."

None over thirteen years of age were admitted to the English department, unless they had previously received instruction in that language; and all entered under a pledge to remain ten years, if approved after due trial. The English classes continued in session nine months in the year; and, from the outset, the expenses of board, lodging, and native teachers, were mainly borne by contributions in money and paddy from the Karen churches. Although an appeal for outside help, either in money or school-material, was issued with the prospectus, but little aid was received. The work, however, went on, gathering volume and steadiness year by year, as we shall see hereafter.

The first building erected on the premises was the old schoolhouse, fifty-two by thirty-four feet, which stood about ten feet west of the present girls' school, between it and the mission-house; next came a line of dormitories, running north and south, a few steps east of the schoolhouse, each thirty-four by seventeen feet, in which were used for posts the iron-wood slabs obtained in squaring the posts of the mission-house, also built in 1858. The small English schoolhouse, which stood a few rods north of the mission-house, was erected in 1860 or 1861, and was more substantial than either of the earlier school-buildings. All of these accommodations for the school probably cost the Karens, with Mr. Beecher's careful management, not less than three thousand or four thousand rupees. Of course, all were roofed with thatch, and made of cheap jungle-wood; so that the best of them, with annual repairing, lasted barely fifteen years, when, with the increased resources of the Karens, they gave place to a more substantial class of structures.

But a burning desire for education, and enlarged plans for promoting education, were not permitted to interfere with the religious work of this people. In April, 1858, another quarterly meeting of the Conference and Home Mission Society was reported by Mr. Douglass. Mohgoo was the place of meeting. A memorial service of deep interest was held, in view of the recent death of Rev. Mr. Vinton. Lootoo, one of the faithful missionaries to Toungoo, was present, with seven young converts who had returned with him to study in the Bassein schools. His account of the work in which he and his companions had been engaged, with the lamented Whitaker, excited much interest. Mr. Douglass's story of the way in which the first debt in the Bassein Karen mission was managed is worthy of insertion: —

"After one of the young men from Toungoo had given some account of his own people, and the work among them, the committee of the Home Mission Society gave their report. They stated that six men were ready to go as missionaries; that the three young men who had been to Toungoo had returned in debt; that paying them and the other missionaries had exhausted all the funds, and left the treasury with a deficit of ninety rupees.

"As this is the first time the Home Mission Society has been in debt since its formation, the announcement created at first a little despondency; but instead of passing a resolution to retrench, to appoint no more missionaries, and to recall some already appointed, they voted unanimously, after a little conference, to appoint the whole six. The question was then asked, Could not a contribution and subscription be taken on the spot? This idea met the approval of all; and in a few minutes three hundred and forty-seven rupees were raised, a large portion of which was paid at once, and the remainder promised within three months, thus cancelling the debt, and more than providing for the six missionaries for three months to come. All then united in the closing season of thanksgiving and prayer."

At the October meeting held in the town of Bassein, the foreign missionary spirit of this people was again manifested. Most missionaries had long believed that the main body of the Karen people would be found in Upper Burma. The Karen Christians had come to feel a strong desire to send missionaries thither to their own unknown kindred. Mr. Douglass narrates the circumstances: —

"Soon after the meeting commenced, a spirit of fervent prayer was manifested. Never have I attended a meeting among the Karens where the Spirit's power was more visible. Resolves of a bold character were made with reference to educational and missionary operations. Early in the meeting there was a call for volunteers to go to the Karens north of Ava. Some expressed a wish to go, but no appointment was made until sabbath evening; and the inquiry continued as to who would lead the way as a pioneer into that vast region between Ava and Assam. At the close of the services sabbath morning, in a conference of the pastors, I ventured to ask if Rev. Po Kway was not the man. He was taken a little by surprise. But the question was no sooner asked than all saw, and soon heard, that his mind was full of the subject, and that he only wanted the concurrence of his brethren fully to believe it his duty to leave his church, his wife and children, and go. This concurrence was promptly given; and that evening, Po Kway and two younger men were appointed for the work.

"An address followed, showing that to sustain these men and the others under appointment, and to carry out the resolutions passed during the meeting, fervent prayer must continue to be offered, and all they possessed be consecrated to God. A contribution was taken for missions, amounting to over one hundred rupees. Po Kway and the young men will go three or four hundred miles north of Ava, and spend about six months preaching and exploring, that they may learn the number of the Karens there, the dialect spoken, and the willingness of the people to receive the gospel. He will then locate the young men at suitable places, and return here to report. Po Kway's intellectual power, education, eloquence, and devoted, consistent piety, cause him to stand pre-eminent among the ordained pastors in this district. He is about to commence a work which we hope will not be less glorious in result than that which Quala began in Toungoo five years ago."

To tell the story of this mission in a few words, the party went, in company with Rev. Messrs. Kincaid and Douglass, as far as Ava and Mandalay. Leaving the capital in January, in a Burman boat, two of them went north to Bhamo, the present seat of the Kakhyen mission, whence they soon returned home. As we now know, there are nowhere, north of the frontier, Karens who speak the dialects used in Lower Burma; so that the expedition only served to settle the question of there being no Karen field in that direction, and to prove the zeal and devotion of those who composed and sustained it. The information obtained concerning the Kakhyens was correct, and of some value.

In November we find Mr. Douglass organizing the Pwo Karen church at Thahyahgôn, now one of the largest churches among that people. As the village has recently been set off to the new district, of which Maoobin is the chief town, there is some talk that the church may join another association. Most of the original members were converted under the ministry of Thahbwah, with whose name and work we are already familiar. The little Sgau church at Kwengyah (south) also originated about this time, through the labors of Ko Thahno, one of Mr. Douglass's Burman assistants, — the only instance, in Bassein at least, of a Karen church founded by a Burman preacher.

At the annual meeting in Kohsoo, in February, 1859, the deputy commissioner, or governor, Major Brown, was present, and made a brief speech on the importance to the Karens of educating their children. Several other English officers and merchants were present, and expressed themselves as much pleased with the singing and the general appearance of the Karen Christians. Th'rah Po Kway gave a report of his mission to Upper Burma; Shway Bau spoke of his labors among the Kyens in the Prome district; while Thahbwah and others gave an account of their labors in the home field. The subject of building permanent villages, and of breaking up, as far as possible, the Karen habit of roving from place to place without sufficient reason, was made prominent. Strong resolutions on this subject and on education were discussed and adopted. The aggregate of contributions was greater than in any previous year. At the closing session, Sunday, P.M. (the meetings began on Thursday), twelve hundred disciples partook of the Lord's Supper with thankfulness and joy.

In November, 1859, the hand of fellowship was withdrawn from Thahbwah, for ten years a Pwo evangelist, for immorality. The church at Thahyahgôn, which he had been instrumental in founding, and which comprised several of his near relatives, excluded him promptly and unanimously, and chose a young Sgau preacher in his place. When such straight-forward discipline, regardless of the ties of kindred and clan, becomes the rule among Karen churches, it will be a happy day for them, and their glory will be less frequently dimmed than it is at present.

Dr. Kincaid reports this year four Karen preachers laboring in the Prome field, sent thither and supported by the Bassein Home Mission Society. This service was continued year by year, both among the Karens and the Kyens of the Prome field, until 1863, when Dr. Kincaid writes as follows: —

"I have frequently mentioned the young Karen preachers from Bassein. They were supported for a year [three years?] by the Bassein churches. I have now assumed their support. Up to this time, twenty have been baptized as the result of their labors. And this is not the only result. The seed of the kingdom has been widely scattered, and I know there are many who can no longer make offerings to the evil spirits. The gospel in its power has reached them. Twenty or thirty have been taught to read the word of God in their own language. One year ago they were degraded heathen, and did not know a letter of the alphabet. These preachers are both firstclass young men,[1] and have been remarkably well instructed in the Scriptures. To Mr. Beecher and the Bassein churches I am under great obligations for such faithful and well-trained fellow-laborers, — men who are not eye-servants, and do not need prompting to go into the field, and work, — men who do not see 'a lion in the way.' One of them has been very ill with fever for three months. He is still feeble, and I have provided him with means to ride from village to village, and go on with his work."

{ Footnote: [1] Myat Koung and Shway Nee are referred to. }

327

Mr. Thomas also reports two brethren laboring in his field, under the support of the Bassein churches, in 1859, and five the year following. The contributions of the Karens in Bassein are reported by Mr. Douglass as steadily increasing. Owing to the alarming state of Mrs. Douglass's health, her husband was obliged to return to the United States in the summer of 1860. The Pwos continuing to ask earnestly for a missionary of their own, Mr. and Mrs. Van Meter were sent back to them, arriving in Rangoon Sept. 29, 1860. Their ship, the *R. B. Forbes*, which carried several other missionary passengers, became a bethel during the voyage; all but two of the crew and officers, from the captain down to the cabin-boy, professing a hope in Christ. Bereaved of their little son soon after their arrival in their own home, Mr. and Mrs. Van Meter seek comfort and joy in the avenues of usefulness which open to them on every side.

Six Chinamen had been baptized in Bassein, of whom Dr. Stevens writes, "They owe their knowledge of Christ mainly to the Karens, among whom they are accustomed to trade." In the absence of Mr. Douglass, Mr. Van Meter looked after the interests of the little Burman church and the Chinese converts, as well as he could. As Mr. Beecher was no longer connected with the parent society, he also reported, from time to time, the progress of the Sgau work. This service, so little appreciated at the time, was the more valuable from the fact that the Free Mission Society seems to have taken little pains to preserve in permanent form the current history of its missions. Mr. Beecher's original letters to the secretary of that society are believed by Rev. Dr. Brown to be no longer in existence; and we have been unable to find anywhere a file of the society's organ, the "American Baptist."

The meeting of the Bassein Association at Kaukau Pgah, in February, 1861, was an occasion of more than ordinary interest. Dr. Binney, from the seminary in Rangoon, was present, and gave valued assistance. The impression left upon his mind by this his only visit to Bassein can be inferred from the following paragraphs written to the secretary:—

"I was very much pleased with what I saw and heard. The meeting of the association opened punctually at the time appointed, and every thing moved on as though they were used to it. During the three days' session, the letters from the churches were read, and the queries, theological and casuistical, noted. The discussion of those queries went through the whole session, and added great interest to the meeting. The churches, ministers, and schools are in a very encouraging state: to me it appeared especially so, as their efforts rely largely upon Karen support. It was truly cheering to see eight hundred or nine hundred Christian Karens collected together for such purposes, and to witness the intelligence and energy with which they attended to the business. Sabbath forenoon there were not less than a thousand Christians present, nearly all from abroad, and among the best members of the churches. I was gratified to meet many of my own and some of Dr. Wade's old pupils, and to see that they are among 'not the least valuable men here.' I was not ashamed of any who took a public part, as most of them did. I am quite willing the tree should be judged by the fruit. Mr. Beecher speaks well of them. But the places assigned them, and the manner in which they performed their duties, was most conclusive to me. The senior pastors, whom Mr. Abbott ordained, are strong, reliable men. They reminded me of some of our fathers in the Baptist ministry at home, who learned the value of an education from the want of it, and resolved that their sons in the ministry should not suffer as they had done. They were the men who provided institutions, and urged young men to go to them in our own land; and the same class are nobly doing a similar work in Bassein. They see the advantages of education, and how it would add even to their own usefulness. They took part in all the discussions respecting education, and manifested a warm sympathy in all our remarks in behalf of village schools, Mr. Beecher's school, and my own."

The ordination of Dahbu, the pastor of the church, on Sunday, gave great pleasure to all. He had studied under Dr. Binney in Maulmain; and the doctor writes of the examination, conducted by himself, that it was one of the best that he ever attended. At the ordination-service, Dr. Binney gave the charge to the candidate, and Mr. Beecher addressed the church. We continue our quotation: —

"As soon as Mr. Beecher closed his address, an elder of the church arose, some distance from us, and in a short speech responded to the address. This part was not in our programme, and it took us all by surprise; but it was beautifully and touchingly done. In a few remarks, simple and to the point, he, for himself and for the church, accepted, as from the Lord, the precious gift of a pastor, with all its accompanying duties and responsibilities, and pledged himself and the church to an effort rightly to sustain the relation; so that God might be pleased, and that pastor and church might be happy and useful, and, in closing, asked the prayers of all, that God would help them to be faithful. It had a very good effect upon the large assembly. The whole proceedings and my visit have greatly encouraged me in my own work. It is not in vain: it is worth living for, and, if need be, dying for."

For more than twenty years now, that church, as well as their admirable pastor, have nobly redeemed the pledges made that day.

Mr. Van Meter was present, and took a part in the association at Kaukau Pgah; but the Pwo churches were not well represented. They had a separate meeting, immediately after, in a Pwo village, looking forward, no doubt, to the formation of a separate Pwo Karen association. The connection of the Sgau churches with a distinct American society, and the not unnatural feeling that they and their work were somewhat overshadowed by the larger Sgau body, made a separation seem advisable to them; and it took place two years after, with kind feelings on both sides. If there had not been, somewhat later, a little too much eagerness to draw away, from the older organization, churches in which there were a small minority only of Pwo members, fewer regrets would have followed the change. At the supplementary meeting of the Pwos, Thahbwah, the fallen Pwo preacher, was fully restored to his place in the ministry and to his salary from America.

During the year 1861 thirty-five native evangelists were commissioned by the churches of this district; some for a short period, others for the entire year. Of these, twenty-two were Sgaus, eleven Pwos, and two Burmese. Two of the Sgau preachers were expected to go a long way towards Ava, in search of large Karen communities reported in that direction. At the association in M'gayl'hah, in February, 1862, it appeared that eight new churches had been formed during the year, three of which were among the Pwos. Two hundred and eighty baptisms were reported, and seventy-seven "new worshippers;" the number of pupils attending the schools was three hundred more than the year before; while the contributions for the English school in town had increased threefold. At the same time, in order to secure three thousand rupees and fifteen hundred baskets of paddy annually for the support of the town school in both its departments, the Sgau churches voted to assess themselves thenceforth yearly one rupee and a half-basket of paddy per member for this object. The contributions for all purposes this year reached Rs. 10,637, of which Rs. 1,219 came from the Pwos. Two unordained preachers, Shwaythee and Pohdee, were set aside for immorality. We should not omit to mention that Mr. Van Meter acknowledges one hundred baskets of paddy and some money, given to him this year by the Sgaus for the Pwo school.

During the year 1862 there was more than ordinary encouragement in the work for the heathen of Bassein. Mr. Van Meter's journals speak of several new villages that seemed to be turning to the Lord. He draws a pleasing picture of a scene which transpired in November: —

"Immediately after Yoh Po's sermon, we proceeded to the examination of Shway Wing, a Chinaman, for baptism. Mau Yay, also a Sgau preacher, aided in this; but so imperfect is the candidate's knowledge of Burmese, that Ko Han, another Chinaman, had to interpret for him. A strange sight this, but one of deep significance, may we not say?—a Karen examining a Chinese, through the Burman language, as a candidate for membership in a Burman church, and that through one of his own people as interpreter, in the presence of an American missionary, who must in some degree bear the responsibility of the decision. He seemed unwilling to admit that he was still under the influence of sin, and an actual transgressor; but he finally admitted the fact, if he before denied it. Our chief dependence, of course, is on the knowledge of his life and conduct for the past two years, while going in and out among us as a believer in Jesus. There was entire unanimity in his reception."

As this year of our Lord (1862) closes, we hear grateful tidings from Bassein laborers in distant fields. One who had wrought among the northern Bghais of Toungoo for two or three years, "with much success," was ordained by Dr. Mason and his assistants. Toowah, then fresh from his studies in the seminary, now one of the veterans in the Henthada field, sends the following comforting message to his aged mother in Bassein:—

"Six young persons are learning to read with me. The parents have already become disciples. Others seem about ready to follow. I hope many more will become Christians here soon. I hear that my mother is anxious about me, because I am in Myanoung [a region infested with robbers]. Do write her a letter, and tell her not to be anxious about me, for I am safe. Burman officials greatly hinder the work. It is truly distressing to me to hear them curse and revile the disciples.—TOOWAH."

Sahpo, small of stature, but brave and true, writes thus to his beloved teacher Thomas:—

"Dear teacher, since I parted with you in Henthada, I have been on a preaching-tour, quite to Enmah [near Prome]. Some, mostly the young, listened attentively; but the older people are less desirous of hearing the gospel. I saw a great many villages in Enmah; and as I went from village to village, almost alone, O teacher! I felt my own weakness. Then I remembered Joshua going about the walls of Jericho, and took courage. Do remember these Karens in your prayers. I am sure that ere long God will enlighten the hearts of these multitudes. And why not? God can command the stones, and they become the children of Abraham."

On the 18th of May Mr. Beecher wrote in his private journal:—

"Had the great pleasure of welcoming back to his native land, to our family, and to a share in our labors, Brother Sahnay, after an absence of seven years and two months."

Long before this, the pupils had made such progress in the use of tools in the industrial department of the Institute, that he had written:—

"Instead of the old, stupid excuse for indolence and inefficiency, that 'Karens cannot do these things,' they reply, to propositions for new branches of industry, that they are able to do whatever their missionary will teach them."

The first public examination of the English school was held on Thursday, Nov. 6, 1862. Several of the English residents were present, and expressed themselves well pleased with the progress of the pupils.

CHAPTER XVI.

1863-1866.

> "'There are heathen enough here in America. Let us convert them before we go to China.' That plea we all know; and I think it sounds more cheap and more shameful every year." —REV. DR. PHILLIPS BROOKS.

A multiplicity of cares and heavy burdens were rapidly telling upon Mr. Beecher's constitution. To his other trials and anxieties were added open opposition, for a time, from one who owed all his education, and opportunities for extensive travel, to himself and to the American Christians whom he represented. Whatever may have been the need twenty years ago, now, certainly, there is little occasion for the natives of Burma to subject themselves to the risks, and Christians in America to the heavy expense, of ocean-passages, and years of sojourn in a foreign land, to acquire an education. Facilities better adapted to their wants are now to be had at their own doors in Burma; and our missions should be saved the distraction and trouble which have been too often caused by superficially educated but self-confident young men returning from their somewhat dazzling experiences in the new world to their native wilds in the newer old world. Happy will it be if the great body of native pastors and Christians to-day, and onward into the future, shall have the good sense and loyalty to put down the spirit of pretension and discord as it was summarily put down by the God-fearing, missionary-loving Karens of Beecher's day.

Early in 1863 four more tried men were ordained to the full ministry of the Word; viz., Thahdway, the able and popular pastor of the church in Kyun Khyoung, one of Dr. Wade's pupils; Thahree, so long Mr. Abbott's faithful personal attendant; Kroodee, also one of Abbott's men, not great in intellect, but the model pastor, who said, as he lay a-dying in 1872, with a beautiful smile breaking over his face, "The angels of heaven have received me;" and Tsa Laing, an approved Pwo pastor. This accession brought up the number of

Karens hitherto ordained in Bassein to sixteen, of whom fourteen were living; twelve of them, the apostolic number, being Sgaus.

In February, as already foreshadowed, two associations were held in different villages, the Pwos finally separating themselves from the Sgaus. Mr. Van Meter reports a serious division in the Thahyahgôn church, caused by two or three quarrelsome and boisterous men. He relates, that soon after one of their outbreaks, two of these men happening to be in one house, a stroke of lightning deprived one of both wife and child, and marked the other, probably for life. The result was a new chapel, an enlargement of the village, great union in the church, and such a warm and hospitable welcome to the Pwo association as is rarely seen even among the Karens. The cast-iron theory of natural events had not then penetrated the Karen jungles.

On the 6th of January thirty-six baptized believers united in forming the Institute Church, — the first Karen church established in the town of Bassein. As their action, and the covenant to which they subscribed, had been duly approved by a council from the neighboring churches, the new church was received into fellowship at the following meeting of the Sgau association.

A mission to the Karens of Zimmay in Northern Siam (now again revived, in 1881 and 1882, under more hopeful auspices) was then in progress. Sahdone and three companions, all recent pupils of Dr. Binney, left Bassein for that distant region, after appropriate farewell services in the school chapel, on the 30th of January. They went *viâ* Maulmain, with a company of traders, but found the difficulties and dangers of the way so great, that they stopped short of their destination, and returned. The mission to the Karens and Kyens of Prome was still prospering, but the missionaries were suffering a good deal from fever. Thirty-one Karens altogether had professed their faith in Christ since the four brethren then engaged in that work first entered upon it. Single churches were at this time contributing as much as four or five hundred rupees a year for various objects; and Mr. Van Meter states that one (Sgau) village brought in no less than five hundred baskets[1] of paddy for the use of the town school. Grants-in-aid were also offered to the jungle schools by government this year, for the first time, — five hundred rupees a year for three years to the Pwos, and fifteen hundred rupees to the Sgaus.

{ Footnote: [1] Rather more than that number of bushels. }

The rainy-season term of the English school opened May 5, with forty pupils present the first day. On the 11th, however, owing to an outbreak of cholera and small-pox in the town, and the death of a pupil from the latter disease, Mr. Beecher felt obliged to dismiss the school for three weeks. How often has this seemed to be necessary in later years! Aug. 9 Mr. Beecher writes in his journal: —

"Received a letter from Dr. Binney, notifying me that I should probably be invited to a council in Toungoo to see what can be done to arrest the progress of Mrs. Mason's heresies among the Karens. Replied to Dr. Binney, that, if invited, I should consider it a most disagreeable duty to attend. Would that God in his wisdom and mercy, however, would order some more effectual means of saving those feeble churches from ruin!"

Mr. Beecher was absent on this painful business during most of September and October.

During this year one of the Bassein evangelists in the Prome district, Moung Coompany, was earnestly engaged in reducing the Kyen language to writing. He succeeded in making a spelling-book and a small hymn-book in that language, which were printed by Rev. Mr. Bennett. High hopes were entertained of his continued usefulness among that people, all of which were blasted, first by his downfall in dishonest debt and adultery, and, later, by his becoming a rank heresiarch, and doing all the harm he could in two or three misguided churches of his native district. The love of the Chinese church-members seemed to be waxing cold, when, fortunately, about the close of the year, Mr. Douglass reached his old field in Bassein again. Mo Nyo, a third Pwo pastor, was ordained about the same time.

Dec. 24, Mr. Beecher writes in his journal:—

"Had a visit from Poo Goung. Was much gratified to hear that fourteen or fifteen young men wish to study the Scriptures and arithmetic with him, as soon as the hurry of harvest is over.[1] God is thus beginning to grant an answer to my prayers, that he would create a hungering and thirsting for a knowledge of his Word in the hearts of the Karens."

{ Footnote: [1] These studies had hitherto been pursued only in the rains. }

In January, 1864, the association was held at P'nahtheng with much *éclat*. At the urgent invitation of the church in P'nahtheng, the Burmese association just held in Bassein was adjourned to join with the Karens in their annual gathering. Dr. Stevens, Messrs. Crawley and Douglass, Mrs. Ingalls, and perhaps other Burman missionaries, were present with several of their assistants and disciples, and added much to the joy and profit of the occasion. Dr. Stevens writes thus:—

"The Karens urged their plea by the statement that they had long prayed that God would visit the Burmans as he had the Karens, and incline them to his service. They now saw their prayers answered, not only in the conversion of the Burmans, but in bringing a Burmese association to hold its session in their midst. They felt, therefore, that they could not be deprived of the privilege, nor could we decline such an invitation. The session was truly interesting, uniting the Karen and Burman disciples in closer bonds, and producing a deep impression in the minds of all, missionaries and converts, that the kingdom of Christ is taking firm root in this land."

Mrs. Ingalls also writes:—

"It was a glorious sight to see that representation from the Karen churches of Bassein, headed by fifty pastors. Some of them had passed through bitter trials, but these have made their faith strong in the power of the eternal God. I had met many of these men when I first came to Burma with my dear husband; and it was sweet to renew our acquaintance, and together mingle our tears, and talk of the Lord's goodness. They very much enjoyed this meeting with the Burman brethren. One day I saw two men with arms clasped about each other's neck, and I paused to know the reason. One was a Karen preacher [Myat Koung, probably.—ED.], and the other a Burman preacher. They held each other a moment, and then, half releasing themselves, the Karen exclaimed, 'We were enemies once, but now we are brothers!' And then, with overflowing hearts of joy, they bowed upon the grass, and mingled their prayers of love and gratitude."

Let it be noted, that, at this great meeting, the first on the list of resolutions adopted was this: "*Resolved*, That Bassein ought to beg until it gets an American teacher to come and help in the teaching of the Bible." In other words, Mr. Beecher, the native pastors and Christians generally, had come to feel the urgent necessity of having a Bible-school for the Karens in Bassein itself. That an urgent call went home to the Free Mission Society there is no reason to doubt. But the call, though often renewed to the mother society as well as to the daughter, remains unanswered to this day. The contributions of the Sgau churches for this year, including Rs. 144 given for the entertainment of the Burmese association in Bassein, foot up to Rs. 11,174. The number of Sgau communicants was 5,431, or, including the Pwo and Burman Christians, 6,064 members of Baptist churches in the Bassein district.

The meeting of the Pwo association, also, was a pleasant occasion; and the reports of the itinerants among the heathen showed that much aggressive work had been done, not without a prospect of rich results. So great had been the strait for money in the mission, owing to the war in America, that the Pwo mission house and compound (now owned by Mohr Bros. & Co.) had been sold during Mr. Van Meter's absence, and the proceeds used to keep in operation the missions of the Union in Henthada and Bassein. He had now secured for eight hundred rupees a new home for the Pwo mission, opposite the Burmese mission compound; and this fact gave satisfaction and hope to the Pwo Christians, who cheerfully made a contribution for the erection of temporary buildings for the use of their children in the town school. The deputy commissioner, Major Stevenson, attended this meeting on two of the days. Mr. Van Meter says of his visit, —

"His object is to become acquainted with the people, and to have them become acquainted with him, and know that he is their sincere friend, personally and officially. As an earnest Christian man, he gives his support to every measure that tends to elevate the people; and he believes firmly that the prevalence of Christian truth will do this most effectually. When in the city, it is his custom to have religious services in the court-house, sabbath afternoon. At this time he invited all to tell freely of any grievance, present any petitions, or make any inquiries they wished. In order to attend the better to such business, he had brought with him two court-writers, who made on the spot a memorandum of all matters of importance. Six of the preachers, who had not yet received their tax-exemption papers, gave in their names, and will not need to go to court in the city. He addressed the association on the subject of schools, especially village schools, stating the deep interest felt in this matter by government, and the conditions on which aid would be given."

During this year, several new adherents are reported at Myat-laykhyoung, where the Romanists are said to be making strenuous efforts to get a foothold.[1] The Zoungyahgyun church receives eighteen new members from the heathen, and doubles its congregation, largely through the labors of Myat Thah, a native of Paybeng, and long a member of that church, but now for many years the ordained assistant of Rev. Mr. Brayton in Rangoon. Mr. Van Meter's "heroic" method with a niggardly Sgau Christian in this village would hardly be adopted by pastors in the United States who are afflicted with covetous members in their churches. He writes: —

"One of the wealthiest men in the place, who ought to be the leading man in the church, is so wretchedly mean in giving for the support of the gospel, that his example is most pernicious. I have lately instructed the pastor to say to him and his family, that they must give up to a certain amount (say, ten baskets of paddy), or nothing at all would be received from them. This, perhaps, may shame them into doing their duty. It will at least show the others that we can do without the gifts of some men, and they be no better off, and the church no worse off."

{ Footnote: [1] It was about this time that a Roman-Catholic missionary, depending on the co-operation of a deputy commissioner of the same faith, went to work systematically to compel some of his Karen disciples to unite in forming a large village in the south-eastern part of the district. Things went on pretty smoothly, until one man—not daring to refuse, yet determined not to obey—hanged himself. This brought the business to light, and very soon put an end to it. }

At the two associations held in March, 1865, exactly four hundred baptisms were reported—a larger number than in any year of the preceding ten. Three hundred and sixteen of these were Sgaus, two were Shans, the remainder Pwos and Burmese. Upwards of one hundred "new worshippers" are reported among the Karens, of whom seventy are Pwos. Two new churches were received. The schools numbered one thousand and six Karen pupils, and the outlook was full of encouragement to the friends of missions. Among the subjects for earnest prayer presented by Mr. Beecher at the Sgau association were these, "that God would stir up the disciples' hearts to hunger and thirst for the Holy Word," and "that God would bless the work of the society in America, in sending an additional teacher to Bassein." A resolution was passed also, which may sound strangely to Americans. It was to the effect that any applicant for baptism who cannot read, and who has no understanding, is to be refused. The resolution is justifiable on the ground that learning to read the phonetic Karen is so easy, and the facilities for so doing so widely diffused, that a persistent neglect to acquire the ability to read would indicate an utter lack of appreciation of the worth of God's word and the dignity of the Christian calling.

This year Myat Koung, the evangelist in Prome, was ordained under Dr. Kincaid's direction. Tahpooloo, also a Bassein man, was ordained pastor of one of the Maulmain churches. A little later, Sahpo, of whom we have already spoken, was ordained in one of the remoter villages of Henthada; and, about the same time, Shwayleh was set apart to the work of the ministry by the laying-on of hands in Toungoo. This Shwayleh was connected with the work in Toungoo almost from its beginning; and, according to Dr. Cross, he was one of the very few who were not shaken in mind, or entangled in the new customs and the new religion invented by Mrs. Mason. The year after his ordination, he made a speech at the association, of which we have a report by Dr. Cross. His statements are so true, and so worthy of consideration, that we reproduce them. He said, —

"You see the Bassein Karens everywhere, in all parts of the mission-field. Your own pastor and his wife are from Bassein, and you may see many others as the leading men among you. Why is this difference? I answer, It is because the first disciples in Bassein were made to know by trials and cruel opposition the value of books, and how much it costs to possess and read them. I was obliged, when a lad, to hide my books in the ground, or in a hollow tree, and steal opportunities to read them by night, for fear of the Burmans. They killed one of my uncles, by tearing out his bowels, for having and reading books. It was these trials, and the faithfulness with which they held on to their Bibles, that made the Bassein disciples what they now are, in comparison with others. No others have paid so much attention to the Bible and to schools, and no others have made so great advancement, or sent so many preachers to other places, as they." —*Missionary Magazine*, 1867, p. 413.

A fortnight before this speech, two more Bassein preachers, Lootoo and Klehpo,[1] were ordained by Dr. Cross, making six Bassein men in all ordained in foreign parts within a twelve-month. It is necessary to speak of these things to show the far-reaching results of Abbott's and Beecher's labors, and also to show how highly Bassein Karens have been appreciated in fields remote from their native district.

{ Footnote: [1] For Rev. A. Bunker's estimate of Klehpo, and his efficiency in stirring up the Toungoo Christians to self-help, see Missionary Magazine, September, 1875, p. 404. }

In October, 1865, at Rangoon, was formed a society from which great things were expected, and from which great things ought yet to be realized,—the Burma Baptist Missionary Convention. Beecher, Douglass and Van Meter, with several of their native assistants and brethren, participated in the first session of this body; the former taking an active part in the drafting of the constitution.[1] In the resolutions which were adopted on education, we find an appreciative notice of Mr. Beecher's schools in Bassein. Directly after his return, in early November, the quarterly meeting of the Sgau pastors was held; an unusually large number being present. There was an animated discussion on the subject of the new convention; but a decision to unite with that body was not reached, although it was earnestly advocated by the three Bassein missionaries. Three new Karen missionaries were appointed to Prome, and two to Toungoo to assist Rev. Mr. Bixby in work for the Geckos.

{ Footnote: [1] The author was associated with him in this work, and he remembers distinctly that Article V—"This Convention shall assume no ecclesiastical or disciplinary powers"—was proposed by Mr. Beecher, and adopted without dissent. To the close of his life he held this principle of the Free Mission Society to be of vital importance. }

As too often happens in our "hand-to-mouth" way of conducting foreign missions, help came when it was too late to relieve and save the patient, suffering burden-bearer. Rev. William M. Scott and wife, from the vicinity of Philadelphia, sailed from Boston, July 28, under appointment by the Free Mission Society, to aid Mr. Beecher in educational work. Touching at Galle, they reached Rangoon Dec. 13, and Bassein near the close of 1865. Dr. Scott was a regular graduate in medicine, and had had some experience in school and medical work among the freedmen. He was a good man, of very fair abilities, and if he could have had a fair chance (which could only come by using his eyes and ears for a year or two, with the senior missionary in principal charge), he would have succeeded well. Instead of addressing himself to the uninterrupted study of the language, the state of Mr. Beecher's health required him to take charge of the

English school almost immediately, and that step was only preliminary to heavier burdens.

At the association in Thahbubau, March 1-4, 1866, Mr. Beecher presided, apparently with his accustomed energy. The Scotts were there, young and buoyant. Mr. and Mrs. Carpenter from Rangoon were present also, by invitation, and, without suspecting it, received their first introduction to the scene of their future labors. To their eyes every thing was hopeful: there were no signs of the coming change. Preparations for the erection of a house for the Scotts were actively progressing. The Karens had brought in over thirteen hundred rupees for that object. The scholars were clearing a site for the house, and the posts and lumber were contracted for. Mr. Beecher was complaining a little of a sore mouth, but neither he nor his friends regarded it as an alarming symptom. The stroke came at last, as tropical storms sometimes come, almost without warning. He had not taken to his bed, or given over his accustomed duties for a day. Even after the arrival of Mr. Scott, he kept about his work from morning till night, and too often, in his restless dreams, from night till morning. In less than a month after the meeting at Thahbubau, the startling news came that Brother Beecher was far gone in consumption of the lungs,[1] and that he was positively ordered to leave the country without delay.

{ Footnote: [1] Physicians in England decided that his lungs were unaffected, and that he died of chronic disease of the liver. }

They had but one week in which to pass over the work into other hands and to make hurried preparations for the homeward voyage. The wife and mother, almost an invalid, rose to the emergency. Her sick husband and four little girls—the eldest under eight, and the youngest in very poor health—must be got ready, or at least made comfortable, for the long passage around the Cape. Kind friends gave their assistance. Boganau, a lad in the English school, was ready to go and help take care of "the teacher," though there was not time to seek the consent of his parents. A ship must be chosen, and the choice rested with Mrs. Beecher. There were three in the river, loading for England, two of them comparatively new and fast. The third, the *William Chandler*, was a lumbering old craft, but stanch, and nearly as comfortable for a family as the others. She had a close netting around the poop, which would make it "so safe for the children." This, with the fact that she was to sail a day or two before the others, decided the question. They would go in the *Chandler*, although the port-officer said afterwards that he, or any seafaring man, would have chosen either of the others in preference. The event proved that a kind Providence directed the choice. The *Chandler* was left far astern by her fleeter companions. The *Mystery*, in which the children wanted to go, because she had numerous pets on board, sailed into a storm, and was lost south of the Cape; while the other, a fine new iron ship, was never heard from again. We can take but a few sentences from Mrs. Beecher's very interesting account of the voyage, and her husband's last days in England:—

"When I found how hopeless my dear husband's case was, I dreaded exceedingly to go to sea; but our kind friend, Mrs. Wells, suggested that there was a possibility of recovery; and kind Capt. Wells, while taking us to the ship in his comfortable boat, gave me this advice, 'Live in the day, and don't be anxious about the morrow.' Although my heart had been like lead, I really think that we took his advice. It seemed as though we thought but little, and did not even pray much, during those sad first days of the voyage, but left ourselves quietly in the hands of our loving Father, and he cared for us.

"Our state-rooms were very comfortable, but Mr. Beecher was unable to come down. He remained on deck, where there was a rattan couch, the inclination of which suited him exactly; and they put up an awning over him, which protected him from the sun and the dews of the night. For about six weeks the thermometer did not go below 82°, day or night. My dear husband sometimes appeared to be dying. There was no doctor, and no woman but myself on board; but the Lord sustained us. Mr. Beecher began gradually to improve; and by the time we had crossed the line, and had reached the delicious trade-winds, he seemed to me to be almost well again. How pleasant every thing was then!...But all too soon we reached the region of change and storms again. As we approached the 'Cape of Storms,' the barometer began to fall alarmingly, and the wind and sea were so high, that we had finally to heave to. I shall never forget that night."

They had pleasant weather from the Cape to St. Helena, and from thence to Falmouth. Mrs. Beecher, however, was alarmed by the re-appearance of bad symptoms in the patient, especially by the swelling of his feet. On the 6th of August, eight days from St. Helena, they crossed the equator again; and Mr. Beecher writes in his journal the last words, it is believed, that he ever wrote on earth: "How highly are we favored by the Father of mercies!" They reached Falmouth Sept. 12, and Plymouth on the 14th, all, as it was supposed, in greatly improved health. Although much encouraged by hopes of the invalid's ultimate recovery, it was thought best to remain there quietly for some time before attempting the Atlantic voyage. Mr. Beecher was very weak, but as peaceful and happy as a child.[1] He took omnibus-rides daily, and enjoyed calls from the pious and learned Dr. Tregelles and a few other friends. On Saturday, Oct. 20, he took his usual ride, and on Sunday would not permit his wife to remain at home from chapel to be with him. Monday morning, at four o'clock, after a slight exertion, he fainted as was supposed; but he never revived. His trusting spirit had passed home to God. His remains were interred in the burying-ground of the George-street Baptist Chapel. Through all this time of sickness and sorrow the kindness of their English friends, many of whom were old friends of Mrs. Beecher's father, Rev. Dr. C. H. Roe, was unbounded; while the devotion of young Boganau was like that of a son. It was not until the 11th of June following, that the bereaved family reached their friends in New York.

{ Footnote: [1] A resolution received at this time from the Executive Committee in Boston, cordially and unanimously inviting Mr. Beecher to return to the service of the Missionary Union, gave him much pleasure, and he even indulged the hope of going out again to Burma under their auspices. }

The record of Mr. Beecher's labors in the mission-field we have already given in an imperfect manner. While he never overlooked other departments of the work, it is evident that his attention was largely drawn, from the outset of his career in Burma, to the educational necessities of his people. Nurtured for many generations in ignorance and superstition, surrounded still by the grossest superstitions, accepting Christianity, but still inwardly prone to superstition, as the sparks to fly upward, he saw no hope for the growth of the Karen converts in love to God, no hope for their growth in holiness and all Christlike graces, but through giving them far better opportunities for a Christian education than they had ever enjoyed. That he was right, and that those who opposed him in this respect were wrong, is certain. He did not exaggerate the deplorable need, nor was he mistaken in the remedy which he sought to apply. He was not permitted to see the walls rise far above the surface; but the foundations which he so wisely laid, still remain, and will remain, we trust, for ages to come, the firm basis of a massive structure, which shall ever grow in breadth, height, and solidity, fulfilling for all time the educational needs of that people.

Born of stanch antislavery, Baptist stock, it was impossible for Mr. Beecher to "lord it over God's heritage." He himself testified repeatedly, and to the truth of that testimony those who have succeeded him can bear witness, that there are no churches in the world more independent, none, as he said, more "provokingly independent" sometimes, than the Karen Baptist churches of Bassein. He rejoiced in that independence. Only when he saw them going astray from righteousness and from the New-Testament pattern, did he interpose, not personal authority, but the authority of God's word, which liveth and abideth forever.

A friend who was most intimate with him for many years writes thus of Mr. Beecher: —

"The strongest impression left on my mind as to his character is the direct and childlike nature of his faith. His business was to do his Father's work; his Father's, to supply the means. And his prayers were most remarkable for their directness and trust. He was not surprised at the answers to them, which were constant, and often striking. He expected that they would be answered; and, like a child with a father, he brought the little as well as the great things, and, asking in faith, received the answers continually.

"The next thing that is impressed upon my memory is his extreme attachment to his work. It was the delight of his life. He might weary in it, but he never wearied of it. He desired no change, no recreation. Few could work on so steadily as he. The Karens often spoke of his industry. From early dawn to the hour of retiring at night, with the exception of meal-time and a short ride or walk daily, he was continually at work at one thing or another, and I well remember on our voyage home, when I was speaking of the pleasure of meeting dear friends, and the delights of Christian society at home, he agreed, but said after a while, 'I believe that I like work best.' Indeed, when at home in 1856, after the first joy of meeting his relatives, they began to feel that he was theirs no longer. His whole heart was in his work. The last six months in Bassein, a kind of restlessness took possession of him. Although evidently not in full strength, and suffering from local troubles, yet his desire to work became a passion, and he undertook more than he had ever attempted before. I felt that he was killing himself, and besought him with tears to moderate his labors; but it seemed as though he could not. Perhaps he had a premonition that his time was short. In England he once remarked, that probably his work had shortened his life by ten years; but he seemed to think that it was worth the sacrifice.

"He was attached to the Karens with a deep and undying love; and yet that affection never led him to seek popularity among them, or to flatter them, or to refrain from telling them the whole truth, if they ought to know it, in the plainest manner. He knew their faults so well, and felt them so deeply, and often spoke of them so plainly, that I sometimes wondered how he could still have such unwearied patience with them. The Karens would hardly have endured his plain speaking if they had not felt his deep and true affection for them.

"One characteristic of Mr. Beecher's, which must have struck all those at all intimately acquainted with him, was his perfect truthfulness. He hated exaggeration, and rather underrated than overrated his own work, or suffering, or success. Indeed, he criticised rather severely some who spoke eloquently of the sufferings and privations of missionary life, never allowing that they were worth mentioning. His exactness led him to enjoy and value statistics, and he delighted in making them out himself.[1] He had many accounts to keep,—with the society, the school, the Karens, and with the government for 'grants-in-aid;' and he kept them all clear and unconfused. He was a good business-man,—could build a house better and cheaper than most men, and would always buy and sell at the right time, greatly to the advantage of the school and mission. In a word, he was a strong man, one to be trusted and relied upon, not one who would easily change or waver. He was also eminently disinterested and unselfish in all the relations of life. Of what he was as a husband and father I hardly dare to speak."

{ Footnote: [1] To Mr. Beecher the readers of this volume are chiefly indebted for the full and instructive statistical information herein contained. }

During the later years of his life Mr. Beecher's spirit was much softened; and before his death, we are told that every trace of bitterness was obliterated. He referred in affectionate terms to the brethren of the Missionary Union, and especially to his old friend and associate, Mr. Abbott. He died, as we all would die, at peace with all the world. He rests well: his work abideth.

On the west wall of the spacious and beautiful Memorial Hall in Bassein may be seen two marble tablets side by side, as the two brethren and companions in labor would wish them to be. The one is sacred to the memory of E. L. Abbott. The other bears this inscription, imperfect, in that it contains no mention of the American Baptist Free Mission Society, to which he was so true:—

Self-Support

Sacred to the Memory of
JOHN SIDNEY BEECHER

[Name and title in Karen.]

Missionary of the American Baptist Missionary Union
And, by the help of God, the Founder of the
Bassein Sgau Karen Normal and Industrial Institute.

Born in Hinesburg, Vt., U.S.A., Feb. 19, 1820;
Arrived in Sandoway, Burma, December, 1847;
Opened this Institution in 1860;
Died in Plymouth, Eng., Oct. 22, 1866.

His is the distinguished honor of establishing
The first Christian School in Burma on
The basis of indigenous support.
The Karen Christians of Bassein will not suffer
His name, or the Institution which he founded,
To perish.

[In Karen] May his work ever flourish!

CHAPTER XVII.

1867.

"Christians are God's people, begotten of his Spirit, obedient to him, enkindled by his fire. To be near the Bridegroom is their very life: his blood is their glory. Before the majesty of the betrothed of God, kingly crowns grow pale: a hut to them becomes a palace. Sufferings under which heroes would pine are gladly borne by loving hearts which have grown strong through the cross."—COUNT VON ZINZENDORF, *the Moravian.*

We have seen that the Karens were so full of zeal and courage in 1857-58, that they were ready themselves to undertake the support of an additional teacher from America. No less conscious of needing more teachers, they were not long in finding that there was a limit to their pecuniary ability. They now call upon American Christians to send them a suitable man or men to carry on the work to a higher stage of advancement. A few words on the subject thus suggested seem to be called for.

So great is the poverty of Asiatic Christians, and so great is the consequent disparity between their mode of living, and the living which is absolutely necessary for the preservation of a white foreigner's health and strength in their country and climate, that we should deem it most unwise to ask or permit them to contribute to the support of American missionaries, although the missionary's whole time and strength be used for their benefit. To ask a native, who lives in a hut on five dollars a month, or less, to bear his share of the support of his own native pastor, and, in addition, to contribute to the support of his missionary, who lives in a house which would be to him a palace, on fifty dollars a month, which would be to him the height of luxury, would be unreasonable, and most unhappy in its effects every way. Self-respect would constrain a missionary, in accepting native support, to bring down his living as nearly as possible to the native level, although it might involve the loss of health and years of usefulness.

But we urge more especially, that, *to do the native Christians and the heathen the greatest amount of good, the missionary must be quite independent of native support.* Paul refused personal gifts and personal support from all his converts, save those in Philippi, although they belonged to nations wealthier and more civilized, probably, than his own, in order that the Gentiles everywhere might know that he sought "not yours, but you." (See 1 Cor. ix. 12, 15, 18; 2 Cor. xii. 14; 2 Thess. iii. 8, 9, and elsewhere.) So John, in his Third Epistle: "For His name's sake they went forth, taking nothing of the Gentiles." For any missionary to violate this principle, and make a gain in any way of the people whom he goes to elevate and save, is disastrous to his influence and usefulness. Develop the principle of self-support, by all means, to the utmost; but let American churches look to the support of their own missionary representatives.

Despairing of adequate help from the Free Mission Society, the Bassein pastors united in the following letter to the A. B. M. Union. It was sent through Mr. Douglass, in March, 1866, after its contents had been made known to Mr. Beecher.

BASSEIN, BURMA.
To our beloved brethren in America, pastors, elders, and all disciples of Christ:—

We, pastors and Christians of Bassein, send a Christian greeting. May the grace of God abide with you! Dear brethren, we desire to tell you a little of our present condition. We cannot forget the great grace brought to us by you formerly. We constantly remember the time when teacher Abbott first came to us. His coming caused us great joy. From the death of our beloved teacher until now, we have never been so happy and steadfast as before, and in some things we have retrograded. *First*, the schools in town and in the villages have diminished: in some of the villages, schools have long ceased to exist. *Secondly*, the number of men willing to go and preach to the heathen has decreased. *Thirdly*, conversions from among the heathen do not increase: they have nearly stopped. *Fourthly*, the love of the disciples generally to the Saviour is less, and they appear not to have the same pleasure in serving him as formerly; thus they seem retrograding year by year.

Beloved brethren, this state of things is very hard for us. We Karens do not understand; we cannot devise; we have no power; we are a feeble people, and have as yet little strength to do for ourselves. We wish therefore to ask you a few questions:—

What are teacher Abbott's two sons doing? How are they living? How employed? Are they not worthy to do the Lord's work? We have hoped they would remember the work their father left here. We express our wish in this matter, but we cannot bring it to pass of ourselves. It must be decided as you think best for us. Teacher Beecher says he cannot remain long among us, but a new teacher will come to take his place. We feel that one missionary is not enough for Bassein. We need two or three American teachers all the time. We want one man to teach English, one man to teach the Bible and other books in Karen, and one man to have the superintendence of the churches. One man cannot supply our necessity: possibly two might do. But, dear brethren, our wants are so great, we cannot provide for them all, unaided by you. We are still weak, and there is much poverty among us. We therefore implore your help.

The churches in Bassein have many things to do for themselves. They have the Home Mission Society to support, and the English Institute for young men and women. They also have the schools in their villages to support, besides their own pastors. These things we must do; and, as we cannot do all that ought to be done, we write to tell you, dear brethren, and pray you to remember us, and send us help. When you have received this our letter, and considered it, we beg you to be patient, and inform us whether you will try and send us one or two missionaries or not.

May the blessing of our Lord Jesus Christ be with you all! Amen.

(Signed)
MYAT KEH.   TOOTHAH.   MAU YAY.   TOHLO.   PO KWAY.

The falling-off in the schools, to which the pastors allude, must have been in comparison with what was done in the first years after Mr. Beecher's return to Bassein from America, not in comparison with what was done in Mr. Abbott's time, when, from the untoward circumstances, very little indeed could be done in that line. The decline in spirituality should have been attributed mainly to the prosperity and the worldly cares which followed the irregularity, the losses, and, to some extent, the license, of the war. The fact was, also, that Mr. Beecher at last found himself simply overborne by the magnitude of his work. He had said again and again that the work in his field required the full time and strength of three men. He was a strong man, and he had literally used himself up in the vain struggle to overtake the various tasks that pressed upon him. True as most of this letter was, and not uncalled for, the reading of it, in his prostrate condition, must have added to his pain. To have delayed the writing a few weeks would have been more merciful, and none the less effectual.

Aside from communicating with the sons of Mr. Abbott, no action was taken by the Executive Committee until after news of the departure of Mr. Beecher from Burma had been received. It then being settled that neither of the young men referred to was prepared to respond favorably to the call of the Karens, Secretary Warren wrote to the pastors, assuring them of the warm interest of the Missionary Union in the Bassein Christians, and suggesting the name of Rev. D. A. W. Smith of the theological seminary, as a man well able to supply their needs. By the same mail a letter was sent to Mr. Smith, opening the way for him to go to Bassein, in case he should feel inclined. The very day before this letter arrived, however, it had been arranged, provisionally, that Mr. Thomas, who was on the eve of embarking for the United States, in broken health, should try the effect of a change to Bassein, Mr. Smith supplying his place in Henthada. Mr. Thomas was already well known and loved by the people of Bassein; and he soon received cordial letters from the Karens, inviting him thither. That this deferring of the homeward voyage would cost the mission his valuable life was far from the thoughts of his friends; but so it proved. The arrangement gave general satisfaction. One of the leading brethren in Rangoon wrote at the time: —

"A noble band of Christians they are at Bassein, and they need look no farther for a man adapted to them. It is the hand of the Lord reinstating the Missionary Union in its own field. We have great reason to rejoice in the present harmony prevailing among all the missionaries of this field."

Mr. Thomas reached Bassein the last of February, 1867. Mr. and Mrs. Scott were occupying the mission-house and compound owned by the Free Mission Society. A new dwelling-house must be built before the rains; and Mr. Thomas, though much debilitated, set about the task promptly. The site selected was on the Free Mission property, at a convenient distance from the chapel and school-buildings. To avoid complications of ownership, the materials and some money gathered by the Karens for a house for Mr. Scott were made over to Mr. Thomas; and the balance necessary, furnished by the Union, was to be regarded as advance rent, the house to belong to the Karens, when the accumulated rents should amount to a sum equal to that put into the house by the Union. A harmonious division of the work assigned to Dr. Scott the superintendence of the English school, in which he was succeeding finely, and to Mr. Thomas the care of the churches.

The statistics of the Sgau churches for 1866, the last year of Mr. Beecher's connection with the mission, footed up, — churches, 52; baptisms, 209; pastors (ordained), 12; unordained pastors and preachers, 72; communicants, 5,658. Total contributions for religious and educational purposes, Rs. 17,549. The Pwo statistics for the same year show 17 churches, 74 baptisms, 631 communicants, 5 ordained pastors, 23 preachers, and the total contributions and expenditures, Rs. 3,282.

Mr. Thomas's letters from Bassein this year give us a clear idea both of the field as he found it, and of the nature of his closing labors on earth:—

"BASSEIN, *Feb. 28, 1867.*—Having passed beyond the Henthada field, I spent a day at Kwengyah, the seat of the first Bassein church, and tried to arouse them from their spiritual stupor. Towards night we started for our boat, nearly a mile from the chapel, followed by a large number of the disciples and by nine candidates for baptism. On reaching the river, we had worship, and then, in the presence of many heathen Burmans, I baptized these, re-entered my boat, and hastened to the next church.

"Friday was spent with the large church in M'gayl'hah. I attended an early prayer-meeting, visited young converts and old members at a distance of three miles, preached at eleven, A.M., at noon baptized five, communion in the afternoon, and left, to sleep five miles farther down, at Pohdau. As the pastor was unwell, we did not hold meetings here, but pressed on early the next morning to Hseat-thah and Shankweng, where are more than two hundred disciples. There I spent Saturday and Sunday. 'The word of God was precious.' Sunday noon I baptized fifteen happy converts in the Bassein River,—a beautiful baptistery.

"In all the above places the simple preaching of one, two, or three sermons, was but a small part of the labor to be done: hence I reached the city weary and worn, yet not abating 'a jot of heart or hope.' Now with my whole heart I entreat the dear people of God in America to pray, 'O Lord, revive thy work' in Bassein."

"*March 29.*—Soon after arriving in Bassein, I started southward, to visit churches that were in a bad condition. I visited six, all that there are on the river in that direction. I was very kindly received in every place, and found many who seemed like true children of God. March 13 we went to the association. Messrs. Scott and Thomas with their families were there, and Brother Van Meter, and a very good representation from the churches. We spent four days and five nights preaching, praying, devising, and directing in reference to the interests of these churches."

The letter closes thus:—

"The schools are prosperous. I do not think there is any widespread error in Bassein; but I am deeply impressed with the conviction that there is a very low state of piety. We need a revival here. Plead with the Saviour that he may again 'visit his plantation.' Let our united cry be, 'O Lord, revive thy work' in Bassein!"

Mr. Scott writes to the "American Baptist:"—

"The twenty-fourth annual meeting was held with the Lehkoo church. A large number of pastors and delegates were present, though a few of the churches were not represented. Some of the Karens came in on elephants. The stately march of seven or eight of these huge animals through the streets of the little village, to and from the thickets where they sought their food, was quite a sight to us. The meetings, four each day, were all well attended. Hundreds flocked to the daily sunrise prayer-meetings, in striking contrast to the few who usually find their way to similar meetings at home. The spirit of believing prayer seemed to be in the hearts of many.

"Brother Thomas presided throughout the meetings in a very interesting way. Sermons were preached by brethren Thomas, Dahbu, Kwee Beh, and Poo Goung. An obituary notice of Brother Beecher, testifying to the value of his labors, was adopted, and ordered to be printed with the minutes. Pastor Dahbu, one of Brother Beecher's pupils at Sandoway, was appointed to prepare a letter of sympathy to Sister Beecher and her fatherless little daughters.[1] A desire to send the gospel to the regions beyond was evinced by the adoption of a resolution to support three men in the Henthada district, if fit men could be found; also to aid two of the Bassein evangelists in Prome. A collection of eighty-five rupees was given in aid of [Sahpo, who has recently returned to Bassein from Henthada, where he had been laboring faithfully for several years]. The question of the continuance of the English school was discussed.

When the vote was taken, nearly the whole audience voted affirmatively, by rising to their feet. On Lord's Day afternoon, the Lord's Supper was observed with the Lehkoo church."

{ Footnote: [1] This letter pledged pecuniary assistance from the Bassein churches, if needed. }

July 24 Mr. Thomas writes, that since they moved into their new house, on the 6th of June, Mrs. Thomas's health had been much better. He adds,—

"We have been passing through sad scenes. The wife of Sahnay was buried yesterday. Do you recognize the name Sahnay? He is the man whom Mr. Beecher sent to America to be educated, now head master of the Anglo-Karen school [on this compound]. His wife, Nau Pyoo Mah, only spoke Karen. She belonged to a fine family, and was an earnest, consistent Christian. We all feel our loss most deeply. There are too few such women left. On hearing that many heathen Burmans were expected [at the funeral], I sent for Brother Crawley, reminding him that there might be a good opportunity to preach the gospel. He came. Our large chapel was filled, and there were not less than a hundred Burmans. So, after the reading of Scripture-selections in Karen, Brother Crawley made one of his most appropriate and effective addresses in Burmese, from the words, 'That ye sorrow not, even as others which have no hope.' While he spoke of the hope we have of the dying believer, they listened attentively, and only began to be restive as he pictured the condition of those without hope. The heathen listen, and are interested; but they return to their unholy ways. Whatever may be the results of this address, I am very deeply impressed with the great privilege of thus preaching the gospel to the heathen. Oh that many of the young brethren just about to enter upon life's duties may decide to tell these heathen of Jesus!"

During the rains Mr. Thomas was teaching in the vernacular department three hours a day, besides preaching, and attending to the innumerable calls from the jungle villages. Moreover, he was hard at work, often until late at night, in writing and revising hymns for the new edition of the Karen hymn-book, then passing through the press. Not a few of his Karen hymns will live, and exert their quickening influence, so long as the Karen language is used. Besides all this, and the finishing of his house, he was preparing copy for the Karen "Morning Star," which he edited for many years. He also published at this time two excellent tracts, on "Family Worship" and "Revivals of Religion." No wonder that he writes to a correspondent, Aug. 30, "Really I am too weary to write much now, and have no time to do so."

In October he writes to a friend in Rangoon that the attendance at the Ministerial Conference was very large. The subject of discontinuing the English school was again under discussion. If we mistake not, Mr. Thomas himself was in favor of its discontinuance, and pressed the subject somewhat. Mrs. Scott had been obliged to leave the country on account of serious ill health, and there was a prospect that her husband would have to follow her before long. The school was dismissed for six weeks; but it was finally settled that it should be carried on, and that a single lady from America should be obtained, if possible, to assist in that department. At the fullest session Mr. Thomas introduced a resolution to this effect: "As the Burma Baptist Missionary Convention is of the same faith and order with ourselves, we put our minds at one with them" ("pah p'thah t'plerhau dau au"). There followed an hour of warm discussion. Sahnay led the opposition. Mr. Thomas spoke much, he writes, giving all the light he could on the objections raised, the principal one seeming to be the fear that some time the convention might even introduce life-memberships. Finally the subject was wisely dropped, without taking a vote. Evil seeds of distrust had been sown, even in that early day, which would yield their bitter fruit in that otherwise fair field for many a long year.

We give two more characteristic extracts from Mr. Thomas's letters to the secretary:—

"*Aug. 10.*—Last evening the mail came in, and we got accounts of your meetings at Chicago. Many things astonish us nowadays, but nothing more than the growth of the West in America. In Chicago there is evidently something besides a vast city and numerous men and women; these we have on this side of the globe: but there is *moral power*. We rejoice that perfect unanimity prevailed in the missionary meetings; yet I feel the need of something still better,—a tender, melting sense of God's presence. Peter could walk on the water while he kept lowly, and while his eye was fixed on Jesus.

"*Nov. 24.*—The rainy season passed away much as it has seventeen other times since I have been in Burma. Only this season I have had more anxiety about the churches. The care of them and the station-work, with instruction in the vernacular school, nearly all the preaching in Sgau Karen, preaching once a month in English, together with editorial duties, have kept me busy, nay, crushed me almost to the earth."

Owing to the mortal disease which was upon him, though he knew it not, Mr. Thomas turned back from Rangoon, quite unable to reach the convention at Maulmain. For medicine, he again resorts to travel among the jungle churches. He writes:—

"*Dec. 24, 1867.*—On my return from Rangoon, I commenced my preparations for work among the Karens. The country was not dry enough for me to travel safely until the first of this month. Having returned to the city for a few days, I hasten to give a few particulars in regard to my tour. From them the reader may infer the general state of things now existing in Bassein.

"I visited twelve different churches. In some of them my stay was brief; but in others, circumstances required me to prolong it. To the most of the twelve, I came ten years ago. In some, say in three of the twelve, I can see a very decided improvement; in other places there has been no improvement; while in a few, deterioration is to be plainly seen.

"The church in Shan Yuah is in a very undesirable state; but, as I can go there easily, I propose to visit the place later, when I can spend a longer time. Hence I did not call the disciples in from their distant fields. At evening, however, I preached to a good congregation from John xv. 8, urging the people to bring forth fruit, much fruit; e.g., support their pastor, instruct their children, and other things in which I knew them to be deficient.

"Thence we proceeded to Wetsoo, on the east side of the river, some twenty miles from the city. In this place we spent three days. Here are about one hundred disciples, who seem to be true believers; yet they are divided, one half adhering to the preacher established there, while the other half, only two miles distant, have put up one of their own number as their pastor. This preacher is a very modest, intelligent, sincere-appearing man.[1] While there were no outbreaking sins to be dealt with, there was a want of vigor and of general intelligence. But both branches would be deemed worthy Christians in any part of the world, and yet they were hopelessly divided. Last March I spent a day and night here. We urged them to be united under one preacher, but that union is impossible. Hence, after much prayer and consultation, the Wetsoo church agreed to become two bands. They seemed relieved when they found they could do this, and to love each other better than ever before.

{ Footnote: [1] We regret to say that Pahlo, the preacher referred to, was disfellowshipped at the association in 1882, for practising heathen enchantments. }

"Our work was very simple after we found that union could not be had. It was merely to form an additional church. There were no letters of dismission to be read. One church simply agreed to separate into two. Then, before the elders from neighboring churches and the missionary, they agreed to love and aid each other, to maintain the ordinances of the gospel, and to extend the blessings of Christ's kingdom in the world. Hence we all agreed that they were two real churches of Jesus. How simple, yet how mighty through God, is a church of Christ! We had the communion with both churches separately, but persons to join both were baptized by me at one place. It was a very solemn occasion. Four were accepted out of ten applicants.

"From Wetsoo, returning up stream a few miles, we entered a large river to the west, called Thandoay. On this river and its tributaries are many of our churches. We soon came into a beautiful country. The spurs of the Western Yoma range began to show themselves, — beautiful, gravelly hillocks, on which are thrifty gardens of pine-apples, shaded by jack and mango trees in great numbers. Here the people are not confined to rice-cultivation. Between the hills, paddy grows luxuriantly; but, should the rice-crop fail, these fruit-gardens still remain. It is a land richly blessed of Heaven.

"We first stopped at Hsen Leik, not because of any difficulty known to exist in the church, but, as this is the place for the association this year, I wished to see if all was likely to be in readiness, and if the time of meeting was understood. Here is Thahree, one of our most intelligent ordained men. There are pleasing signs of enterprise and Christian activity in this church. Improvement is very visible. I was here ten years ago, and spent a whole day in trying to unite this church, and to induce them to make choice of a pastor.

"From Thahree's church we proceeded up the stream ten miles, to one of the most disordered churches in the district,—the one in Gai-kalee [or Pee-neh-kweng]. It numbers a hundred and twenty-five members. Five years ago the pastor (unordained) was expelled from the church for open sin. Thus far all was in order. But here the difficulty began. A large party, mostly relatives of the pastor, were opposed to calling a new man. They said their old pastor, if he should repent, ought to be reinstated. But the majority prevailed. They called another man, restored the offender to church privileges, but opposed his becoming a preacher again. Upon this the friends of the offender withdrew a few miles, and proposed to become a new and separate church. In this condition I found them when I came to Bassein. Often have I urged them to return to their church relations, or else, by aid of a council of brethren, to form themselves into a new church with a man of untarnished character for pastor.

"But on reaching Gai-kalee all had to be talked over again. The names of all were still on the church list at Gai-kalee, yet for three years the disaffected had never reported themselves. Bad reports also were in circulation about many of the lost members. Our first work was to have the Gai-kalee church erase these to them lost

Self-Support

members. This was done understandingly, though perhaps it was now done for the first time in Burma. The church understood that they had cut off thirty members from all connection with them; that, if these members were ever admitted into any church, it must be on experience, much as candidates for baptism are received.

"Our next business was to go to the members thus cut off, and see what could be done with them. Having called the elders of the nearer churches, we went to Lahyo, where these irregular members reside. We found them in a beautiful place. They had built a small chapel, and on our arrival they received us with great cordiality. At first nothing would do but to acknowledge the once excluded preacher as their pastor. This we firmly resisted; and after preaching and praying, and a great deal of talking, all gave up their favorite, and agreed to do as their brethren thought they ought to do. They were willing to accept another man as pastor.

"Then we formed a kind of council of the elders in the vicinity, who knew all about these scattered members. Out of about thirty, fourteen were found without fault. These wished to be constituted into a new church. After questioning them as to their belief and future intentions, it was voted that they be a church of Christ in Lahyo. Then from among themselves was found a very worthy appearing man, Tookyau, who was unanimously chosen as their minister. A deacon was not ready just then; and the missionary told them that a church could exist without a deacon, at least until such officers are needed. Having thus formed a little church, and they having chosen their pastor, they proceeded to other business. Three candidates for baptism were accepted. Two more persons, whom no church had claimed for years, were received on experience. Then we all went to the baptismal waters; and then, for the first time in Lahyo, was celebrated the dying love of Christ.

"I was surprised to find that many heathen Karens reside near Lahyo, and Tookyau seems to be pleased to labor among these heathen. Who knows but this little one is to become a thousand? These twenty poor disciples cannot yet support their preacher; but I have just received the good news that God has put it into the heart of a sister in Milesburg, Penn., to send twenty-five dollars to be spent by me. This money shall be given to aid Tookyau to preach the gospel among the heathen in Lahyo.[1]

{ Footnote: [1] Rev. Ng'chee, the present pastor at Lahyo, in addition to the care of his little church, does regular, hard work among the heathen far and near, for which he receives from the Karen Home Mission Society pay enough to give himself and family a frugal support, without looking to Christians in America for help. }

"From Lahyo, we went on as far as we could before Sunday was upon us again. That was a precious sabbath. We spent it in two places quite near together. In Mohgoo, Rev. Shahshu is the ordained pastor. Their meeting-house is the very best I have yet seen in the jungles of Burma. There and in Taukoo it was very cheering to see stable, orderly, intelligent Christian men and women. The word of God has taken deep root in many villages. It will be sure to bear fruit to God's glory, and that for years to come. But we need a revival, oh, how much!

"The sabbath past, we again directed our course where our help was needed. Several members of the Hohlot church had been to me in town, complaining that three ordained men and several elders had decided that one of their members, an elder of the church, was guilty of immorality. This, they affirmed, was not so; and, to prove it, they declared that the church had not excluded said elder. On arrival, I found that nearly all the church believe the man guilty, but hardly dare to exclude him. They feared to act, and tried to hope that it was sufficient for a *quasi* council to act for them. We tried to make the church feel that they must take action at all hazards. I will not stop to tell how we passed up to the very end of the Thandoay River, trying to stir up other churches, until I reached another river to the north-west of Bassein, when, hearing that cholera was raging in town, I returned, fearing that the school might be scattered."

We quote most of the above letter, because it would be difficult to find a more graphic and truthful picture of missionary work as it goes on to-day among the Karens. We have heard it whispered that missionaries in foreign lands are prone to assume episcopal powers. That they are called upon to do the work of a bishop, in the New-Testament sense, on a far wider scale than pastors in America, and that they endeavor to fulfil the duties of that office in the fear of God, will not be denied. We have here a fair sample of their work in stimulating pastors and churches to activity, in healing divisions, promoting wholesome discipline, order, and orthodoxy in faith. Let the descriptions which Thomas and others have frankly given in our missionary publications be read critically. Where is the assumption of unscriptural authority? Let the particular fault be pointed out, and missionaries, we are sure, will not be slow to correct their errors. The letter which follows is the last that appeared in the "Magazine" from the pen of its lamented author.

BASSEIN, Jan. 8, 1868.

This second trip has been among the churches up the river to the north. Let me say a few words as to what I have seen and heard.

I have seen many professed Christians: but many of them have a wild, heathenish appearance; this is especially true of the women. The fact is, the members of these churches read but little. When I first reached Bassein last year, there were less than fifty Karen newspapers taken and read in Bassein, among six thousand Christians. Over three hundred are now taken, but they are read by a few only. There are but few Bibles in Bassein. I have already furnished one for every church in this district. A few private members have received the same great blessing. But this precious book looks too large for this people to undertake to read it. They are absorbed in their paddy-fields. They admire fine guns and fine cattle to cultivate their fields, but to read the word of God there is but little disposition. They do like to hear read the news items in the monthly paper; but, as they can get these from their pastors, they decline, as a body, to "take the paper" for themselves.

I have found schools, though just now not in operation, as it is harvest-time; but they are held mostly in buildings with no walls and but indifferent floors and roofs. All seems so cheerless, and so destitute of all that is adapted to interest children, that one is led to doubt if education can be maintained among any people in this way.

The women of this district are in a worse state than the men. They work in the fields with their husbands. They are careworn, with children clinging to them every moment in the day. No child can be left alone for a few moments, shut up, it may be, in a room, while the parents attend to household affairs. In these Karen houses there is no room into which to put children. They must be held by might and main to keep them from falling through the bamboo floors, or over the edges of the verandas, on which there are no railings. Hence women grow old while very young. They are destitute of nearly all the privileges enjoyed by women in New England. They seldom attend meeting, or only with a child or children too troublesome to admit of the mother hearing God's word. The missionary's wife is in the city; but not more than one Karen woman in a hundred ever goes to these good missionary women; and alas! there is no female missionary to go to them: all are away, or worn out with years of toil.

I have only written a few of the disheartening things which have pressed themselves upon my attention during the past two weeks. I am oppressed with a burden upon my soul,—a burden which no human hand has placed there, and which no hand but that of our gracious God can relieve. I bless God that I have been permitted to preach the gospel with such freedom here in Bassein, and to so many. Now my strength is nearly gone. But there must be hard, persevering, earnest preaching of the gospel here. There must be work done.

At last, like Beecher, Mr. Thomas awoke, too late, to the necessity of an immediate change. At the close of January he was in Rangoon, "a mere skeleton," and "too miserably unwell to write." Feb. 28 he penned a letter from Madras, which lies before us. From that port, onwards to Marseilles, he suffered agony almost from every revolution of the steamer's screw. In Paris he enjoyed a brief meeting with the Baptist brethren, and put himself under the care of an eminent physician for a few weeks; but he was very weak. In one of his last letters he writes:—

"Earth has lost in my eyes much of her charms; but, now that I am on my way home, I have a great desire to see all there. But there are purer, brighter scenes above, even if I fail to see those I so much love in America."

In his very last letter to Secretary Warren, dated London, May 8, he speaks a word for peace:—

"I want you and Dr. B——to be united; i.e., I want the two societies to become one, at least as far as Burma is concerned. This union would be the greatest thing you could do for Bassein. Please remember this, as you go to New York for the meetings.

"Yours in the gospel of Jesus,
"B. C. THOMAS."

Hastening on, he reached New York on the 8th of June, and died three days later, surrounded by sorrowing Christian friends and relatives.[1]

{ Footnote: [1] An obituary notice of Rev. B.C. Thomas may be found in the Missionary Magazine for September, 1868, p. 381. }

On his gravestone, in the cemetery at Newton Centre, Mass., these true words are inscribed:—

"He preached Christ; he trusted in Christ; he has gone to be with Christ."

May we do our work as well, and enter into our rest as peacefully, as did the warm-hearted, manly man, and devoted missionary, Benjamin Calley Thomas!

CHAPTER XVIII.

1868-1874.

"If India is ever to be evangelized, it must be by the voluntary efforts of her own sons, not by agents sustained by foreign money, and directed by foreign committees...Not invasion, but permanent occupation, is our object: that object can never be attained, *save by making the war support itself.*" — *Indian Evangelical Review*, April, 1874.

The manner in which the American Baptist Missionary Union finally obtained undivided possession of the Bassein field is worth recording. Soon after the departure of Mr. Thomas, Mr. Scott received instructions from his board, that, in case he should leave Bassein, he was to sell the property of the society to as good advantage as he could, or, if unable to sell, to make it over legally to Rev. Messrs. J. B. Vinton and R. M. Luther, their missionaries in Rangoon. Mr. Scott accordingly wrote to those brethren, giving them the first opportunity to buy the mission-compound, and proposing that one of them should remove to Bassein, and take charge of the school and mission, as he himself was about to return to the United States. Mr. Luther replied, on behalf of Mr. Vinton and himself, to the effect that they had not the funds wherewith to buy the property, nor was either of them at liberty to leave their work in Rangoon. They also suggested the purchase of the property by the Karens. A general meeting of the pastors and elders was accordingly called on the 11th of June, 1868. Mr. Douglass, who is our authority, was present at the meeting, by invitation. Mr. Scott, as agent of the Free Mission Society, offered to sell the entire property to the Karen Home Mission Society for twenty-six hundred rupees, a nominal price; that being the amount actually expended by the Free Mission Society on the dwelling-house and outbuildings of Mr. Beecher. This sum the Karens at first agreed to pay, on condition that Mr. Douglass would move into the house, and take temporary charge of the property and the school. This he declined to do. After five days of prayer and consultation, the pastors united in a request that Mr.

Douglass would purchase the property for the Missionary Union, and himself take the superintendence of the mission. We quote from his letter to Secretary Warren:—

"They said that they wished the Missionary Union to own the property, for two reasons. (1) If they were required now to raise the money to pay for the property, it would, for at least a year, so absorb their contributions, that their schools and home-mission work would greatly suffer; but,

"(2) They especially wished the Union to own the property as long as foreign teachers remained among them, as they would then be united and happy among themselves; while, if they owned the property, some might wish a teacher from one society, and some from another, and thus they might become divided. They said they feared to have teachers from two societies, lest they should not agree between themselves, and the Karens should be divided, some for one teacher, and some for the other."

It was finally arranged that Mr. Douglass would make the purchase in his own name, and at once offer the property to the Union, he, meanwhile, taking temporary charge. Mr. Scott's deed to Mr. Douglass is dated June 25, 1868. In closing the letter announcing his action to Dr. Warren, Mr. Douglass uses this language:—

"As the Sgau Karen churches in this district have from year to year, for the last twelve years, contributed more for schools and religious objects, furnished more students and candidates for the ministry, and sent out more missionaries, than all the other districts in Burma combined (I think this statement is strictly true), I doubt not that you will favorably regard the wish of these pastors, and accept the offer that I make to you of the property."

In a subsequent letter he says,—

"Another man is needed here, and another man these Karen pastors are determined to have, for the educational department...Look at what God is doing,—a people that were in pagan night, and did not know a letter of the alphabet thirty years ago, now laying hundreds and thousands of rupees at the feet of the missionary, and demanding a man to teach them, and fit them to work for God!"

The Executive Committee promptly authorized the purchase of the property, and the transfer was made to the Union by Mr. Douglass for the exact amount paid by him for it. From July until November, Mr. and Mrs. Douglass occupied the Beecher house, left vacant by the return of Mr. Scott to America. He divided his time and labors between the Burman and Karen departments, while his wife gave her time chiefly to teaching in the Karen school. In consequence of his over-exertion at this time, Mr. Douglass was much worn down, and in the following July he succumbed to an attack of bilious-fever, to the deep regret of his associates and many friends.[1]

{ Footnote: [1] For an account of Rev. J. L. Douglass's last sickness and death, see Missionary Magazine, November, 1869, p. 417. }

In November, 1868, a most interesting and profitable meeting of the Burma Baptist Missionary Convention was held in Bassein, on the Sgau Karen compound. The steamer *Pioneer* of Rangoon having been chartered for the occasion, there was a large attendance of missionaries and native delegates from abroad, as well as large delegations from the jungle villages of Bassein. The Karens contributed cheerfully and generously for the entertainment of their guests. The work in Bassein was duly reported with that of other districts. Not a few pastors and laymen of Bassein united with the visiting body as individuals; but, with cordiality of feeling increased somewhat, there was no general movement towards a formal union with the convention.

The question who should succeed the lamented Thomas in this important field, was uppermost in all minds. On the third day of the meeting the first telegram ever sent from the Rooms in Boston to the American Baptist missions in Asia gave answer. Seven words— "Carpenter transferred to Bassein, Smith to Rangoon"—produced a great calm in the minds of all, save the delegation of Henthada Karens, who were loath to lose their new teacher. As Mr. Carpenter had already received letters from Boston on the subject of a change of work, and an urgent invitation from the Bassein pastors[1] to become their leader, he was ready for immediate removal. His only experience in station-work had been gained in two vacations spent on the Maulmain Karen field; but, during his connection of five years and a half with the theological seminary in Rangoon, he had acquired the Karen language, and gained, also, a personal acquaintance with the younger Bassein pastors and a goodly company of the best educated young men in that district.

{ Footnote: [1] This letter breathes so excellent a spirit, that we give an exact translation:—

BASSEIN, Sept. 9, 1868.

May abundant blessing from God the Father, God the Son, and God the Holy Spirit, descend like the morning dew upon you and your household, dear teacher Carpenter! We the Karen churches in Bassein address you in these words:—

When we heard that it had pleased God to call home our dear teacher Thomas, who labored so hard among us, and cause him to rest from his spiritual conflict, and give him a shining crown of gold which will never fade, we were truly filled with grief. But since God saw it to be best thus, we the Bassein Karen churches consented to this act of the Divine Will. And now we are left like sheep without a shepherd, like lambs whose mother has died and left them. Moreover, when we came down to the city for consultation on various matters, we received our brother, teacher Sau Tay's letter, which said that he had heard that the Missionary Union had consulted about sending you to us to take up the unrusted sickle which teacher Thomas laid down, and reap the ripened harvest. Thereupon we greatly rejoiced. We the churches in Bassein took counsel together, and agreed with one heart that you should come and labor among us as teacher Thomas did.

Therefore, when you get this our letter, we hope that both you and *mama* Carpenter, with cheerful consent, and full of the love of God, will come and do God's work among us. Thus, when the convention meets in Bassein next November, we beseech you to come at once, and remain among us.

And you, dear teacher, having lived among Karens, know about them. We are weak and imperfect in wisdom. In order that we may grow more perfect in these respects, our strength is in you, that you will help us abundantly. For this reason, inasmuch as you love God, and like his work, with all your heart, we hope that he will be with you in every thing you do, and bless you in all. On that account we write you these words. In like manner, all of our brethren hope in you, and put their strength in you, that you will certainly come.

(Signed)
MYAT KEH, *Chairman,*
THAH DWAY, *Scribe,*
(*On behalf of all the Bassein churches*). }

Returning to Rangoon with the convention party for their household effects, the Carpenters again embarked, and reached their new home in Bassein Nov. 24. They were joined in a few days by Miss DeWolfe of the Nova-Scotia missionary society, who rendered valuable assistance in the school until her transfer to Henthada in 1870, and soon after by Miss I. Watson, who has served the school faithfully most of the years since.

Various duties pressed upon the young and inexperienced missionary. He wished first of all to make the acquaintance of his people in their homes, and thus to learn at once the geography of his field, and the circumstances and character of his widely scattered flock. The week following his arrival, therefore, he started on a tour to the southernmost group of churches. And, throughout the travelling season, every day that could be spared from the pressing work in town was spent in touring; the result being, that, before the end of April, forty-four of the churches were visited, besides scattered hamlets of Christians and heathen. Sermons were preached in every place, women's prayer-meetings revived, the schools and cases of discipline attended to, large numbers of Bibles, hymn-books, and school-books sold, and the people made to feel that they once more had a teacher and *mama* whom they could call their own. To the surprise of the new missionaries, it was found that not a few of the Christian villages even had never been visited by a white face before; and, with much to encourage, they could not be blind to the signs, in many places, of ignorance, superstition, and worldliness, that had impressed Mr. Thomas so painfully.

Mr. Beecher's description of the manner in which many of the pastors had entered upon their work will throw much light upon the condition of a field which has been sometimes spoken of by those ignorant of its real state as "a well-tilled garden."

"The remarkable manner in which many of the Bassein churches were first gathered, and their first pastors chosen, operates strongly against their ordination and against their present usefulness. When the gospel was first proclaimed among the Karens of this district, it was accepted in many places by whole families and whole communities, and that, too, immediately and almost implicitly. They were ready to begin to worship the true God before they could properly be taught how to call upon his name. Educated preachers were nowhere to be found. In this extremity, each community selected from its own number the elder whom they thought best fitted to conduct their religious services. He was brought to the missionary, taught a few weeks or months how to read, if he had not previously learned, then the first principles of faith in Christ, the necessity of abandoning all heathen practices, and how to perform the duties incumbent upon pastors. He was furnished with a Testament, a hymn-book, and a few catechisms, and duly commissioned to the ministerial office. It was the best and only thing that could be done at the time, and these men have done an important work. If they could have been satisfied to serve the brief period they were really needed, all would have been well. One-fifth, however, of the pastors of this mission, are still composed of this class, who remain incorrigibly illiterate, superstitious, and seriously obstructive. They can never be worthy of ordination; and, being well supported by church-members who are their own relatives, they cannot be made to feel that it would be for the interest of the cause for them to resign, and allow some of the many educated young preachers to take their places.

"It will be seen from these statements, that the appointment and dismissal of native pastors is very seldom in this mission dependent upon the will of the missionary. Nowhere in the world are Baptist churches more fully or more provokingly independent in all their church polity. They are free enough in seeking the advice and aid of the missionary, and just as free in neglecting it, or setting it aside. But this is, on the whole, much more cause of rejoicing than of regret: they will learn all the sooner how to govern and provide for themselves." — *Missionary Magazine*, July, 1866, p. 253.

There was indeed a great and difficult work of discipline to be done in Bassein; and that work must begin, if possible, among the pastors. The ordained pastors and a considerable number of those unordained were stanch Christian men, and intelligent enough to know, that so long as immorality and superstitious rites were practised by a number of the pastors, with little attempt at concealment even, there could be no hope of improvement in the Christian communities at large. On those faithful pastors, and on the promised presence and help of the great Head of the church, was the missionary's sole reliance.

In his first northern tour the new missionary found in one of the largest churches an uneducated boy of sixteen, the son of the late pastor, duly installed in the pastor's office by vote of the church, the church virtually without an instructor or guide, and on the down grade to destruction. Two days of hard work with individuals and with the assembled church, in expounding the indispensable scriptural qualifications of a pastor, resulted in the reconsideration of their action, and in the appointment to the pastorate of an old seminary student, a very suitable man, nominated by themselves. The subsequent peace and prosperity of the church at Mee-thwaydike abundantly proves the wisdom of their action.

Before the close of 1870 three of the older unordained pastors were clearly convicted of practising heathen enchantments, or of permitting them to be practised, in cases of sickness in their families, or in their herds, and were duly disfellowshipped, and set aside from the ministry. Another man, in middle life, was convicted of drunkenness, of sabbath-breaking, and of threatening the life of one of his deacons. He, also, was set aside by the unanimous vote of thirty-nine of his fellow ministers. Another elderly man was set aside for forgery and other grave reasons. Two others, men of ability and wide influence, were commonly reported to be guilty of adultery, and by this and other offences to have lost the "good report of those without."

As the first of these cases (that of Pah Yeh, for many years the unordained pastor of the church in Shankweng) has been commented upon unfavorably in this country by those who have heard only the offender's side of the story, we will give a brief *résumé* of the case, which may be easily verified by the records of the council on file in Bassein. It is safe to say, that, while the best pastors felt the need of action, no action whatever would have been taken but for the missionary. The case, therefore, may be another illustration of the supposed stretch of authority exercised by missionaries in foreign lands. Let the masters of Israel read, and then tell us how far the theory of church independence is to be carried in heathen lands, when truth and righteousness, ay, and the very existence of the church itself, are imperilled; also, whether Paul's interference with the independence of the church in Corinth (1 Cor. v.) was placed on record simply to show what an apostle might do on occasion, but a missionary, held responsible by all the world, and, as he believes, by the Saviour himself, for the good morals and Christian character of the churches under his oversight, may never do.

As in a well-known case in Pittsburg, Penn., and as in the majority of cases in heathen lands, where pastors are guilty of moral delinquency, action did not originate with the church. It was not until the pastor's conduct through a series of years had become a public scandal, that other pastors in the association, feeling that the cause of Christianity, and the character of the Christian ministry, were suffering serious reproach, brought the matter to the notice of the missionary. At his request, therefore, and with the consent of the church, a council, composed of twelve ordained pastors, sixteen unordained pastors, and five lay elders from abroad, with the missionary, assembled in Shankweng, Dec. 7, 1870.[1] The brethren were hospitably received, and kindly treated by the church throughout their stay. The accused was present, with his friends and one of his alleged paramours; and every opportunity was given for a full and fair hearing. Probably no council of native Christians was ever held in Burma of equal numbers, or weight of character, none in which more time or pains were taken to arrive at the whole truth and a just decision. Ten long sessions were held in the course of three days. Many witnesses were examined; and all the evidence and the arguments offered on both sides were carefully weighed, and a *unanimous* decision was reached. While there was not a doubt, probably, in the mind of any member of the council, that an adulterous connection existed during the trading-tour of three or four months in Upper Burma, which Pah Yeh made with a woman of doubtful character, with whom, as he confessed, he lived on the most intimate terms during the whole time, while his relations to another (a Burman) woman at an earlier period had been the occasion of grave scandal, the finding of the council was simply this: (1) That Pah Yeh had left his church for months together to engage in trade; (2) That on these expeditions he had habitually broken the sabbath; (3) That he had been guilty of gross improprieties, amounting to a strong presumption of adultery. For these reasons, he being no longer of good report before the world, the council recommended his exclusion from the church, and the withdrawal from him of fellowship as a minister of Christ.

{ Footnote: [1] For the opinion formed by Rev. B. C. Thomas of this church and its pastor in 1857, see p. 276. }

Will it be believed, that notwithstanding all the evidence, and the decision and the entreaties of the council, a large minority of the church, composed mostly of his relatives, determined to adhere to Pah Yeh still; and adhere to him they have, up to the present time. It is our painful duty to add, that, if it had not been for aid and comfort extended at another mission-station to the delinquent pastor and the ill-advised faction which followed him, their repentance, and return to duty, might probably have been secured. As it was, the repeated letters and visits both of committees and of missionaries were in vain. A majority of the church, with a nephew of Pah Yeh for pastor, continued in the fellowship of the association; but the minority stubbornly adhered to their old leader. Unfortunately it has been found in more than one mission, that there is quite as much danger that the principle of non-interference will be violated by adherents of the same society as by those of rival societies, and that the ruin resulting from such interference may be even more irreparable.

The other case, exactly similar in its nature, but occurring later, took a different turn. The church (really the pastor) refused in insulting terms to receive a council, or to have any thing to do with one. A committee was sent to visit the church, and induce them to change this decision, but in vain. The facts being known to all the pastors, the only thing that could be done was done at the meeting of the association in Mohgoo, March, 1871. The pastors present, resolving themselves into a council, unanimously withdrew from Shway Byu the hand of fellowship, basing their action on 1 Tim. iii. 2, 7; and the church was advised to seek a new pastor. This they would not do. The year following, Shway Byu was called to his last account. It was then hoped that the church would return to their duty; but, instead of doing so, they received as pastor Moung Coompany (referred to p. 309), a confessed adulterer, and fugitive from debts; since which time, under the fostering influences alluded to in the previous paragraph, the last state of that church has been worse than the first. After five or six years of patient effort and waiting, the name of the church was finally stricken from the roll of the association in 1876. A few of its members have united with neighboring churches, but the main body keep up their worship; and Coompany, having received ordination at the hands of Pah Yeh and two or three laymen, administers the ordinances to his own church and to that in Shankweng.[1] The end is not yet; but that these and other most difficult and painful cases of discipline were justified and approved by the great body of pastors and church-members throughout the district, is proved conclusively by their harmonious and enthusiastic following-out of the plans of their new leader, at the cost of great sacrifices, through a long series of years.

{ Footnote: [1] Although it is in accordance with Old-Testament and apostolic precedent, we publish the above facts with reluctance and pain, actuated by the hope that a wider knowledge of the trials that beset missionary work in every land may lead to wider and more intelligent sympathy, and especially to a more scrupulous observance on mission-fields of the vital principle of non-interference. }

In addition to the need of discipline, there had been for several years a falling-off in the number of men available for home-mission work. At the first meeting of the Ministerial Conference after Mr. Carpenter's arrival, in May, 1869, only two men presented themselves as candidates for that service. It had come to pass that nearly all of the contributions were being divided up among the pastors of the smaller churches, the larger allowances going generally to the men who would "put on the poorest mouth." When the subject was fairly presented to the brethren, it seemed reasonable to them, that, while a church of five or six families could not ordinarily support their pastor, the very fewness of their numbers afforded a reason why they need not take up all of his time. The pastor of such a flock, for example, might give to each of his families as much care as the pastor of a flock three times as large could give to his, and do it in one half of the time, perhaps, leaving the other half free for labor among the heathen, for which the Home Mission Society would gladly give him fair remuneration. The following minute was discussed, therefore, and finally adopted unanimously, and placed upon record at the meeting six months later. The result proved that the measure was a long step in the right direction.

"This is not an eleemosynary society, to assist (1) feeble churches because they are feeble, or (2) poor ministers because they are poor. It is a *missionary* society, to help on the work of evangelizing Bassein; and it aims to do this by sending out (1) its own special agents, or (2) by 'helping those who help themselves,' i.e., feeble churches that are willing to grow strong by enlightening others (the rule of the Eastern Turkey mission was here quoted from the 'Missionary Herald'), and by assisting poor but faithful ministers, by giving them a money equivalent for evangelical work actually done among the heathen or scattered disciples. The very inability of their churches to support them is evidence that the disciples are few, and hence that the preacher has time for outside labor: therefore

"Resolved, That henceforth we cannot, as a rule, help any church in which there are not signs of healthy growth in Christian graces and activity, if not in numbers. Nor will money be paid to any preacher, whether local or itinerant, who does not present a written and accurate report of missionary work performed among the destitute, Christians or heathen, Sgaus, Pwos, or Burmans; and the amount paid will in all cases be proportioned to the amount of labor bestowed."

Considerable school-work had been done since 1858, mainly by Karen assistants, and yet only an impression had been made upon the dense mass of ignorance in the Bassein churches. In 1868-69, the year of Mr. Carpenter's arrival, a majority of the adult church-members were returned as unable to read or write; and of the readers, the less said about the amount of their reading and understanding, the pleasanter for the author and his readers. It should be said, however, that, at that time, 209 copies only of the Karen Scriptures (Bibles and New Testaments) were found in the hands of 5,988 church-members. Under the stimulus of a grant from government of from fifteen hundred to two thousand rupees a year in aid of their jungle schools, the number of pupils had risen to 1,321; but what were these among a Christian population of school-going age of not less than six thousand? And what would the bare learning to read avail, if the practice of reading was to be dropped at the end of from three to twelve months of schooling?

The missionary could not disconnect the signs of rampant superstition from the prevailing ignorance. On the one hand, all the native missionaries had gone out from the schools, such as they were. In the several churches, also, the degree of benevolence and of the missionary spirit was exactly proportional to the high or low grade of the village school. On the other, the outbreaking immorality and heathenism were in the villages where ignorance prevailed from the parsonage throughout the parish. He could not forget that the third generation of Christians, from the great ingathering under Abbott, was now coming on to the stage. While God had mercifully given special grace to the first generation, to make up for their involuntary ignorance, was it not sheer presumption to count on a continuance of that special grace to the second and third generations, when the ordinary means for the improvement of minds and hearts, God's most sacred trust to his children, were neglected? It seemed to him worse than useless to go on baptizing, and founding churches, leaving the disciples with indifferent schools, and with Bibles closed and unread.

If possible, a fresh impulse must be given to the jungle schools; and, with increased numbers in the town school, there must be an increase in thoroughness, and an extension in the courses of study. As one means of effecting the first object, twenty-seven of his old pupils from the seminary in Rangoon, and three young women, were provided with places, and set at work teaching during their long vacation in 1869, in addition to the force of teachers regularly employed. The number of pupils in the association quickly rose to 2,057, a number not since equalled, we are sorry to say. By combined effort the number of Bibles within the limits of the association was increased in two years to 321, and of New Testaments to 815, mostly by purchase for cash;[1] while the number of church-members able to read was brought up in the same time to 3,735, and the number unable to read was reduced to 2,554,—a report of progress only which left numerous and high mountains yet to be removed.

{ Footnote: [1] Up to Dec. 31, 1871, Mr. Carpenter had received for Scriptures and books sold in Bassein cash to the amount of Rs. 8,098-6-10. Besides the sales in town, the mission-boat always carried a box of Bibles and other books for sale, wherever it went. The sales might have been increased, no doubt, by the employment of special colportors; but it was thought that the increased expense would outweigh the advantage. }

To the town school, Mrs. Carpenter in charge of the new female department and in the vernacular, assisted by Misses Watson and DeWolfe in the English department, would give their invaluable assistance. The Thomas house, not needed at the time for a dwelling, could be easily adapted to the purposes of a general chapel, and schoolrooms for the English department. The school-buildings, erected by Mr. Beecher ten years before under great difficulties, had now reached a condition of dilapidation and ruin. All of them, moreover, and the two mission-houses as well, being covered with thatch, and connected by low, thatched passage-ways, the whole would be swept by fire in half an hour, if a fire should break out at any point. It was like living in a powder-magazine, with smokers all around. Preparations for permanent and more commodious school-buildings must be begun at once; and, if possible, the heavy bills must be paid without calling upon the over-burdened society in America.

Twenty days after the arrival of the new teacher in Bassein, the pastors came together, at his request, for consultation. Plans had been drawn for their inspection, — one for laying out the compound anew, dispersing the native buildings somewhat, and arranging for a park of fruit-trees in the centre, so as to give the place the aspect of a model Karen village; the other for the erection of fourteen substantial cottage dormitories and teachers' houses, each twenty-seven feet square, with teak roof and walls. The labor of grading and laying out the compound would be performed by the pupils without cost in money; but the buildings projected would cost about six thousand rupees, and the missionary quietly proposed that the pastors should then and there pledge their churches to raise the amount within the ensuing three years.

The changes proposed, and the plan of the buildings, the pastors had already heartily indorsed; but they were evidently taken aback by the idea that they were to raise the money from their people. After a little delay, J. P. Sahnay, the head teacher in the English school, educated in America, arose, and said that the buildings were just what the school needed and must have; but the teacher, being new to Bassein, was unaware, probably, of the great poverty of the Karens. "Why," said he, "there is not one of these pastors here to-day who has a rupee in his bag [quite true probably. — ED.]; yet the teacher asks them to raise six thousand rupees from their people, who are as poor as they are. There is a great deal of money in America. Cannot the teacher get the money more easily from there?" To Sahnay's credit, it should be said that this was the last occasion on which he ever hung back, or seemed to oppose the plans of the missionary in charge. He became a thorough convert to the doctrine of self-help for his people; and he gave freely, after a time, of his money and of his influence, up to the time of his lamented death, nine years later. In reply to this suggestion, which expressed the desire of every Karen in the room, and in the district too, for that matter, the burdens of the American Christians growing out of the late war were spoken of, and plans set forth by which the poorest of the people could make special offerings for this object, to the amount of at least a rupee each in three years. The result was that the pastors gave the pledge with some hesitation; and the work of reconstruction and enlargement begun that day has not yet ceased, although the six thousand rupees has been raised and expended more than ten times over.

It was pleasant indeed to see how the interest and the courage of that dear people grew, as the work progressed from stage to stage. That very season, before the rains, three nice cottages were completed, and the debt contracted at the outset fully discharged. The next year four more were finished and paid for, and the third year seven, making the full number required; and considerable timber, etc., was on hand for further operations. Instead of the six thousand rupees which they had pledged with trembling, they had paid in over eight thousand; and they were ready to go on with preparations for a new girls' school-building, which was much needed.

Marking the quick response to every effort made for their improvement, and the unrivalled advantages of Bassein as a location for the higher Karen schools, Mr. Carpenter, ignorant of any previous movement in that direction, addressed a letter to his revered friend and late senior associate, the Rev. Dr. Binney, dated Oct. 4, 1869, in which he strongly advised the transfer of the Karen Theological Seminary from Rangoon to Bassein. The reasons urged were briefly these: that, as more than half of the teachers and pupils in the seminary were from Bassein,[1] that place would be more accessible, and really more central to the major part of the constituency of the seminary, than any other; that the seminary would exert a more powerful indirect influence for good upon the large circle of churches in Bassein than it could hope to do anywhere else; that it would have sympathy and pecuniary assistance from those churches to a far greater extent than it could expect to receive elsewhere; finally, that Bassein is the place of all others for a successful preparatory vernacular and English school in connection with the seminary. Knowing as we now do the position which Dr. Binney had taken with reference to previous attempts to move the seminary westward, it is evident that but one answer could come from him. His reply, which lies before us, is brief, but characteristically kind:—

"Respecting the removal of the school to Bassein, I am not surprised that the subject should occur to you. Before driving a stake in Rangoon, I fully canvassed that point in connection with Henthada and Maulmain. I knew that Bassein had the points you mention strongly in its favor. Beecher wished it might be in Bassein."

{ Footnote: [1] In 1869 Bassein alone had fifty-five young men studying in the Karen Theological Seminary, and thirteen preachers at work in the Toungoo and Prome districts. }

Then he goes on to give as the determining reasons for his decision the expressed wish of the Executive Committee, and the fact that Rangoon is the metropolis of British Burma, and more central than any other station. In closing his remarks on this subject, he adds,—

"Still, it may be a question yet, especially respecting general education. Respecting that school [since called a 'college'], though it should be general [i.e., for all the stations], I do not feel so certain that it should be in Rangoon, especially while so many of the pupils would be mere children. It is a matter for grave thought."

In a letter written a month later he says,—

"Press your English school hard. Make it, as far as you can, a specialty. Have only a select number that continue after the first year. One year is enough to indicate whether a boy or girl had better be retained in that [department of the] school or not."

To increase and strengthen the tide of benevolence in the churches, the duty of giving liberally and systematically was pressed upon the pastors as a body. At the regular meeting of the Conference, in October, 1870, after a citation of "blind Johannes'" argument from the "Missionary Herald," all of the pastors, and, not long after, the assistant teachers in the Institute, with hardly an exception, signed a written agreement to give to the cause of the Lord not less than one-tenth of all their income. This agreement was faithfully observed for ten years; and to this self-sacrificing example of that rare company of men is to be attributed, in no small degree, our subsequent success in raising large sums of money from a comparatively poor people.

Another important work kept in mind was that of seeking out and ordaining suitable men as pastors and evangelists. It was a work that could not be hastened faster than men suitably qualified and tested were supplied. At the meeting of the association in Kyootoo, in 1870, four were ordained at the request of their respective churches, who have since been true pillars in the spiritual temple; viz., Deeloo, Pohtoo, Too Po, and Toomway. The year after, at Mohgoo, Thah-yway and Poo Goung were ordained, — the latter as an evangelist, for which office he had special qualifications; making twenty-two ordained ministers then laboring in connection with the Sgau Karen churches of Bassein. Other worthy pastors were invited to present themselves as candidates, but were hindered by excessive modesty.

At the two associations last named, special efforts were made to bring the Bassein churches into thorough sympathy with the Burma Baptist Missionary Convention, in order that, with other advantages, their zeal for foreign missions might find therein freer vent and more generous scope. It was thought that we had succeeded. Resolutions of sympathy and active co-operation were passed with apparent unanimity and cordiality; but, two or three years later, complications arose which dashed these hopes for a time.

Meanwhile, notwithstanding the trying cases of discipline, and the heavy drafts on their liberality, the ordinary blessing of the Spirit upon the Word preached in much weakness by the native brethren and their missionary, was not withheld. The number of baptisms among the Sgau churches for the four years ending February, 1872, was 1,125,—an annual average of 281, to an average of 231 for the eleven years previous. The number of itinerants in the home-field, under the regular pay of the Home Mission Society, was not quite up to the average of former years perhaps; but a considerably larger amount than usual of unpaid, voluntary work had been done by the settled pastors and lay-elders.

Prematurely, after only three years and a half had been spent in this most interesting and engrossing work, Mr. and Mrs. Carpenter found themselves obliged to leave Bassein for temporary rest and change in the United States. As in the case of his predecessors, long marches on the feverish Arakan coast, night-watches, and heavy responsibilities and anxieties, had thus quickly reduced the missionary from a state of vigorous health to one of invalidism; while the health of his efficient and devoted companion was seriously impaired. Secretary Warren had written, early in 1869:—

"One thing the Committee want,—hold the Karens together, and hold them to us, even if you must give them another man to be associated with you. We shall look for a young man, and, if you desire it, send him on at the earliest day possible."

Such was the weight of the load, that the new incumbent speedily sought the relief which had been promised. He wrote for the second man again and again. At the association, in March, 1870, the Karens unanimously invited the Rev. Melvin Jameson, recently arrived in Bassein, under appointment to the Burman department, to become their missionary with Mr. Carpenter. Permission was granted by the Executive Committee to make this change, but Mr. Jameson's decision was "to hammer away at the Burman rock."

It was not until near the close of January, 1872, that Rev. H. M. Hopkinson, a graduate of Colby University and Newton Institution, reached Bassein with Mrs. Hopkinson. The Carpenters, on their way to the United States, met them in Rangoon, and gave them such information and advice as they could, in a brief day or two, at another place than Bassein itself. Mr. Hopkinson was a man of piety and ability. He found Misses Watson and Norris, J. P. Sahnay, and a well-trained corps of native teachers, ready to work with him in the school, and a noble band of pastors and preachers ready to work with him in the district; but he labored under great disadvantages. To place any man fresh from home in tropical Burma, with not a word of the new language at his command, and to roll upon him from the first day of his arrival the burdens that necessarily devolve upon the missionary in Bassein, is cruel, as well as most impolitic. He also had to struggle from the outset with ill health in his family and in his own person. During the three years of his incumbency, if nothing new or startling was attempted, it is creditable enough that there was no disaster anywhere, and no falling off, but a small increase both in the number of baptisms and in the amount of the annual contributions. He continued on the field until 1875, when he was obliged, by continued and increasing ill health, to return with his family to America. Miss Norris (later Mrs. Armstrong of the Nova-Scotia Society) had early left Bassein for another field; while Miss A. L. Stevens of Illinois, who had joined the school in 1872, was obliged after one year to return home, on account of serious disease. Both were ladies of rare qualifications for the work. Their places were filled after a time by others, who will be noticed in the next chapter.

Meanwhile, what of the Pwo department? Mr. Van Meter's labors among that interesting but somewhat unstable people had been abundant and not unfruitful. He gives the following abstract of his work for the year 1867: —

"I have given almost my entire time and effort to jungle labor, having gone out every month of the year, in all thirty-two times. The number of visits made [to villages], at some places repeated several times, is 80. The whole number of miles travelled is 2,341, on foot 343 (barefoot about 50), all in direct missionary work in the Bassein district. The greatest distance of round trip has been 200 miles. Baptized, 45.

"I have preached or conducted religious exercises about five hundred times, usually three times, and occasionally as often as five times, in one day. During these visits I am constantly distributing books (for pay where they are able to pay), establishing schools, prescribing for the sick, in some cases where another day's neglect might have been serious, if not fatal. At the same time I have endeavored to instruct them as to the care of their houses, themselves, and their children; matters, perhaps, which to some would appear of a trifling nature, but really affecting their health and comfort to a great degree. Especially have I had to call attention to the severity of the tasks too often imposed on the women. The gospel for woman is still a great need among the Karens. I consider nothing beneath my attention that affects their welfare."

Mr. Van Meter's ideas of jungle travel, outfit, etc., as given in the Magazine for January, 1868 (p. 18), would not, probably, be fully accepted by all; but his ideas and methods are at least worth reading and considering by all missionaries. Miss S. J. Higby joined the mission in June, 1868, and soon began to do excellent and much-needed work in the Pwo school. The statistics of this branch of the mission for 1868 are as follows:—

"Churches, 19; baptized, 33; church-members, 767; nominal Christians, 727; total Christian community, 1,494. Preachers, 52; ordained, 6. Pupils in town school, 67; in twelve village schools, 237; total, 304. Total contributions and expenditures, Rs. 2,582. Books sold, Rs. 663. 'Burman Messengers,' for the most part taken and paid for by the people, 220."

In October Mr. Van Meter wrote of the formation of the nineteenth Pwo church in Bassein, and added,—

"During no one year have more been reported of those who have forsaken their heathen rites and relatives, and of those who have pledged themselves to become Christians. At Pantanau I baptized six."

During the month of June, 1869, he was laid aside with a bad leg and a head affection, accompanied with deafness. In July he watched with Mr. Douglass through his long last illness, taking his turn, alternate nights, with Mr. Carpenter. His health suffered perceptibly under the strain. A little later he found that he must leave Burma; and by making short stages, by the overland route, he finally reached New York, but so reduced in strength that he could not rally. He died in Mottville, N.Y., Aug. 18, 1870, only a few weeks after landing.[1]

{ Footnote: [1] An appropriate notice of Rev. H. L. Van Meter's life and labors may be found in the Missionary Magazine, October, 1870, p. 370. }

His excellent wife, Mrs. Helen L. (Hooker) Van Meter, remained in charge of the mission for a little more than one year. She exerted herself to keep up the work. A few of the weaker churches, set off by her husband a little prematurely perhaps, she recommended to re-unite with the mother-churches from which they had been taken, thus reducing the number of churches, but adding to their strength. Her varied and heavy cares proved too much for her; and she, too, died after a painful illness, on the 27th of August, 1871, the last survivor of the three missionary couples who were associated in labor at Sandoway in the early time.

Rev. Sabin T. Goodell and wife came to the relief of Miss Higby in the following March. He took hold of the work with such vigor and discretion as to gain the regard and confidence of the Pwo Christians in an unusual degree. To earnest piety, Mr. Goodell added good executive ability, and tact in teaching. He had just completed the translation and publication of "Stilson's Arithmetic" in Pwo Karen, he had secured from the churches under his care three or four thousand rupees for the erection of a substantial school dormitory, and was moving on strongly in all kinds of mission-work, when he, too, was called away after a distressing illness, Nov. 16, 1877, at the early age of forty-one.[1] Miss C. H. Rand, coming from Maulmain, had joined the Bassein Pwo Mission in 1876. Mrs. Goodell returning to the United States in 1878, Miss Rand continued alone in the work for some months. In May, 1879, she was united in marriage to the Rev. J. T. Elwell, in whose charge the Pwo mission remains at the date of this writing.

{ Footnote: [1] Rev. Dr. Jameson's interesting obituary can be found in the Missionary Magazine for March, 1878, p. 88. }

The remarkable mortality in the Bassein mission is exhibited in the following table:—

E. L. Abbott	died 1854,	aged 45 years,	1 month,	10 days.
J. S. Beecher	" 1866	" 46	" 8 months,	3 "
B. C. Thomas	" 1868	" 48	" 2 "	9 "
J. L. Douglass	" 1869	" 46	" 5 "	15 "
H. L. Van Meter	" 1870	" 45	" 10 "	27 "
Mrs. Van Meter	" 1871	" 46	" 4 "	8 "
W. M. Scott	" 1872	" 43 "		(about.)
S. T. Goodell	" 1877	" 41	" 5 "	24 "

Besides the above, there were Mrs. Abbott, the first Mrs. Beecher, and the first Mrs. Douglass, who died early, also the gifted Maria C. Manning; while others have been driven home prematurely by disease. The missionaries who have lived longest in Bassein are confident, that, for the tropics, it is unusually healthy. The opinion of the heathen is, that witchcraft alone will account for the mortality. We believe, on the contrary, that overwork, and excess of care, are the true explanation. When the duties of all pastorates at home, or the management of all railway lines, or the burdens of all college presidents, are equally heavy and wearing, we may assume that all positions in our foreign mission-field are equally onerous, but not before. Until the work of the Sgau Karen mission in Bassein is subdivided between two or three men, it will continue to be heavier than the work of any other mission-post in Burma, and the certainty that the missionary in charge will prematurely break down and return, or break down and die, will continue. Is it right or necessary that such an alternative should exist, when the second man so often asked for by the Karens and their overburdened teachers would probably do away with it?

More than fifty years ago Dr. Judson united with his missionary associates in the following prayer:—

"Have mercy on the theological seminaries, and hasten the time when one-half of all who yearly enter the ministry shall be taken by thine Holy Spirit, and *driven* into the wilderness, feeling a sweet necessity laid upon them, and the precious love of Christ and of souls constraining them."

O ye young men now dedicating the strength and richness of your lives to Christ's work! cast not your eyes on the high places in Zion, nor seek for the pleasant places near at hand; look away yonder to that "thin red line," now advancing, now retreating, in the forefront of the battle in pagan lands. If you have no pity for the worn and wasted standard-bearers falling there, at least let the deep organ-tones of your ascending Lord, the Crucified, sounding down the ages, bidding you "Go, disciple all nations," arouse you to duty; and let the accompaniment to that divine voice, the low wail of eight hundred millions of heathen perishing in their sins, without hope, and without God, lend wings to your feet and a holy unction to the glad tidings which you bear. For Christ and the heathen's sake volunteer for the work abroad!

CHAPTER XIX.

1875-1880.

"Human nature remaining, as it is in the best of men, imperfect in its judgments and imperfectly sanctified, and trained towards perfection, as our regenerated human nature is trained by the Master, by trial, by burden-bearing, by debate, and even by harsh collisions with the imperfections of others, including our true brethren, we need not wonder at a partial and transitory dissonance, or even at broad divergences, of opinion and feeling. Such collisions and the consequent thwarting of endeavor must be expected and accepted, often hailed even, as indispensable to progress, and as preparatory to our final union in fuller light." —*Missionary Magazine*, 1855, p. 158.

One more attempt to make Bassein the seat of an advanced school is now added to the many which have preceded. Mr. Carpenter returned to Burma early in April, 1874, as president of the Rangoon Baptist College, so called, an institution then recently opened in response to the united request of the Karen missionaries. The missionaries to other races had not joined in the request; and it was generally understood that the school was to be mainly, if not exclusively, for the benefit of the Karens.[1] To his great disappointment, Mr. Carpenter found, on his arrival, serious differences of view, and dissatisfaction with the location which had been selected. He also found little evidence of a disposition to sink differences in order to promote the growth of that which was hoped to be a college in embryo. Coming back to Rangoon as he left it in 1868, with little thought of the grave moral and pecuniary disadvantages of the metropolis as a place for training jungle youth for humble, self-denying work in the jungles and mountains, he, nevertheless, could not avoid contrasting his new surroundings in a great city, cut off from all Karen support and from almost all intercourse with the people to whom his life was devoted, with those which he had so recently left in Bassein. He could not escape the conviction, that a momentous mistake had been made by the Executive Committee in locating the college there, and by himself in accepting the charge of it. He was expected to go on at once, and expend twenty-five thousand rupees of Christ's money in erecting a school edifice in a place where he now saw clearly, or believed that he saw, that the money would be worse than thrown away; for every rupee expended would tend to perpetuate the evil and the waste. He could not shake off the conviction, that, before a rupee had been spent upon buildings, there was yet time for reconsideration. As the responsibility of the enterprise rested immediately upon himself, he could not conscientiously do otherwise than communicate his change of views to the Committee in Boston, to Rev. Dr. Binney, his predecessor in office, and to all of the Karen missionaries in Burma. This he did on the 13th of May. He also visited Bassein the same week, to learn what offers the Christian Karens of that district would make, in case the Executive Committee should consent to remove the college thither. The leading pastors promptly promised all that he asked;[2] viz., twenty thousand rupees in cash towards the college-building fund, and the contribution, year by year, of rice sufficient for the use of all pupils, from whatsoever quarter they might come.

{ Footnote: [1] The recent throwing open of the College to pupils of all races and creeds, without distinction, seems to be unacceptable thus far to the Karens. Nor would it have been agreed to, probably, by the Karen missionaries of a former generation. Mr. Abbott wrote as follows on the subject of a seminary for the Karens, Sept. 17, 1838; and, so far as we know, his views remained unchanged to the time of his death:—

"A professor in the Burman seminary can never at the same time be a professor of a Karen seminary,—*no, never*. If any thing is ever done to prepare the young men of the Karen jungles to preach the gospel of God's dear Son, it must be done by a man *expressly, exclusively appointed to that work by the Board*; and the quicker they appoint their man, the better. As regards the qualifications of such a man, all I have to say is, that the Board should appoint just such a man as they would appoint over a theological seminary in the United States...

"Such an institution must be *decidedly and distinctively Karen*, not only as regards its professor, but its native language. It will never do to make it a part, or parcel, or department, of a Burman institution; because that would frustrate the whole plan. As regards the importance of establishing a Karen literature, I will now say nothing; as no doubt the Board have heard much on that subject. Such an institution must be not only Karen as to its literature, but as to its location. I can never (with my present views) send the Karen young men of this vicinity to a Burman institution; although every thing else but the location be decidedly Karen, so far as Karens are concerned. Where the Burman theological seminary will be eventually located is doubtful, as the brethren are not agreed. But, at whatever place, let the Karen theological seminary be somewhere else. In this view I shall be sustained by every Karen missionary.

"There is not a subject within the scope of the Board's observation and effort of more importance than this, nor one which has stronger claims on their immediate attention and immediate action."

If it is not thought best to insist upon whites and blacks attending the same schools in the South, is it more judicious and right to denounce Karen Christians, and warn them to beware of the condemnation of the Jews, because they decline to send their children to a school for all races? It is to be presumed that the Executive Committee will at least hold to their resolution of November, 1876: "The Executive Committee have no desire to restrict the freedom of the Christian Karens in selecting schools for their children at any of the stations, provided their children...are supported by the Karens themselves, without additional expense to the Union."

[2] We have in this connection a capital illustration of Karen character and methods. In the two public meetings that were held on this subject, in the English schoolhouse built by Mr. Beecher, the missionary in charge strongly opposed the plan set forth by Mr. Carpenter. After considerable friendly discussion, the veteran Myat Keh arose on behalf of the pastors, and delivered himself of this parable:—

"We Karens are in the position of a weak, sickly lad, whose father advises him to eat some dried fish, while his mother forbids his doing so. First, let our parents agree between themselves in this matter, then we shall know what to say and do about it."

As the desired agreement seemed to be impracticable, Mr. Carpenter, though fully convinced of what the independent choice of the Karens would be, withdrew his proposition, without asking for any definite pledges, trying to be content with the general expression of favor which they had given. Immediately after the adjournment, however, without his solicitation, and entirely without his knowledge, the pastors got together by themselves, talked the whole matter over again, decided that the plan was desirable and feasible, so far as they were concerned, and agreed each to raise his proportion of the twenty thousand rupees, if the college could be moved. They also wrote a formal letter to the Missionary Union, asking that the change of location might be made. Rev. Po Kway and Choot, then the devoted and efficient steward of the school, and a deacon of the Institute Church, waylaid Mr. Carpenter on his way to the Rangoon steamer, and communicated to him their action, with strong assurances of cordial and unanimous co-operation.—C. H. C.}

GIRLS' SCHOOLHOUSE, BASSEIN, BUILT 1875

The statement prepared by Mr. Carpenter went the rounds in Burma: but with the exception of the missionary in Maulmain, and, later, of the one in charge at Henthada, the Karen missionaries as a body, and the Burman missionaries as well, opposed the change; and many of them were not slow to say that the fulfilment of the Bassein pledge was impossible. The Executive Committee, accordingly, decided the question in the negative. Mr. Carpenter, convinced that he could do more to advance the interests of higher education among the Karens as a people in Bassein, without the college and without pecuniary aid from America, than he could do in Rangoon at the head of the college, backed by the treasury of the Missionary Union, resigned his position, and early in March, 1875, was again in the midst of his loving and trustful people,—the very people who had loved and reverenced Abbott as a father,—the people who had stood by Beecher through thick and thin.

It will be remembered, perhaps, that the school in Bassein differed essentially from the college in Rangoon, in that it was emphatically of indigenous growth, and in no sense an exotic. It was the child of an intense desire and of a settled purpose, on the part of the Karens of that district, to secure for their children and their children's children the benefits of a Christian education, the higher, the better to their liking. It was the child of their prayers, fed and clothed from its birth by their own unstinted bounty. In March, 1860, at the association in Naupeheh, Mau Yay had given expression to the convictions of the Karen leaders thus:—

"DEAR BRETHREN,—It is now several years since we became Christians. Each passing month and year should have seen an improvement in the schools for our children: nevertheless, whether we look at the school in town, or at those in our jungle villages, nothing is complete. Let it be so no longer, brethren; for a Christian education is the foundation of every thing good. Your committee, therefore, have resolved that nothing should be allowed to hinder any girl or young woman, any boy or young man, who wants to get an education. Moreover, if any are so stupid as not to desire one, let their parents and pastors take them in hand. Moreover, let the churches help orphans and the children of poor or heathen parents to the utmost of their ability. As to the contributions for the town school, we judge that every disciple should give half a basket of paddy and four annas [twelve cents] in money before the end of March every year."

At this very time, while Mr. Beecher—holding, with many others, that an English education was not desirable for Karens—had repeatedly declined their proposals to establish an English department in the town school, the pastors were laying plans and collecting money to establish an English school of their own at Kohsoo. Finding how determined they were, Mr. Beecher wisely yielded to their wishes, and accepted their liberal offers. His expenditures would be trebled. War was on the eve of breaking out in America, and he could look for no aid from that quarter. In this juncture the Karens must bear their own burdens, and nobly did they come up to the work. For the year 1861-62 they brought in, for buildings and the current expenses of the school, Rs. 2,427 and 1,168 baskets of paddy, and the association voted to assess the churches on the scale of Rs. 3,000 and 1,500 baskets of paddy annually. Their contributions continued for a long time on this generous scale, and were at length much increased. The government, indeed, came to the relief of the school in 1863-64, with an annual grant of Rs. 1,500; but it came out of the heavy taxes paid by Karen cultivators. This aid was increased in 1869 to Rs. 2,000, to Rs. 2,500 in 1876, and still later to Rs. 3,000, to match the improvement of the school and the largely increased gifts of the Karens; but from America, for the six years preceding Mr. Beecher's departure, his accounts show that less than a hundred and thirty rupees were received for the school, an average of less than one dollar a month. In like manner it can be shown, that from the beginning until now, *including the cost of land and buildings,* wages of native teachers, pupils' board, and all current expenses save the salaries of American teachers, less than five per cent of the expenditures has come from private friends, churches, and societies in America.

Widely different was the plan on which the Rangoon Baptist College was conceived. Widely different had been, and must ever be, its mode of existence and growth, if growth there could be in the uncongenial soil where it was planted. Is it remarkable that one who had inherited, with the field of Abbott and Beecher, somewhat of their spirit and ideas, should find himself, to his own surprise, unable to abandon the goodly foundation which they had laid on the Karen rock, in order to enter a structure costlier, perhaps, but reared with American silver, and, as he judged, upon the sand?

At Awahbeik, Thursday evening, March 18, 1875, the association unanimously voted to raise Rs. 20,000 within four years for the erection of a spacious and substantial chapel and school-building for the male department. The resolution was passed with far less doubt and hesitation than the one to raise Rs. 6,000 in December, 1868. They had begun to find their strength. Mr. Hopkinson having obtained the posts for the girls' school-building, projected in 1871, work was begun upon it directly after the association. Forty strong men from Kohsoo, Mohgoo, and two other villages, came in to raise the heavy iron-wood posts. The hard and dangerous job was finished late in the evening of the second day, when, after a hearty hymn of praise, the dusty, tired men bowed upon the turf in the moonlight, and dedicated the house there begun to the Christian education of the future wives and mothers of the Karen people. The building was formally dedicated, after its completion, on the 10th of October following. Dedicatory prayers were offered by both Myat Keh and Po Kway: the sermon was by the missionary. It was a two-storied structure of teak and iron-wood, fifty-four feet by thirty-six, with a driveway and upper veranda-room on the front, twenty-one feet by eighteen. The roof was of teak. The rooms were painted throughout, and furnished with desks and seats from Chicago; the latter being the gift of the Woman's Baptist Missionary Society. In consideration of having the upper story finished off ultimately for the occupation of the ladies of that society, they also contributed Rs. 1,980 towards the cost of the building; and afterwards, when it was made over to their use, they met the cost of inside partitions, doors, etc., for that story, which brought up their entire contribution to a little less than half of the whole cost of the structure.

The school, meantime, was constantly growing in numbers and in efficiency. Nowhere in Burma was the happy effect of "woman's helping hand" more plainly visible than here. Misses Baldwin (later Mrs. Dr. Cross), Walling (Mrs. Dr. Jameson), Batson (Mrs. Price),

Manning, and McAllister, with Miss Watson, who has been already mentioned, contributed very largely to make the school what it was. Besides these of American birth, Yahbah Tohlo, Moung Tway, and Dr. Boganau, returning from schools in the United States, and Sandwah,[1] Taynau, Toolay, Rev. Shway Gah, Maukeh, Pahhah,[1] Nyahgeh, Thah-too-oo,[1] and others, sons of the soil, and of the schools of Bassein itself, did good service in teaching and in the equally important out-door work of the Normal and Industrial Institute. The number of pupils increased from year to year until it reached two hundred and fifty; and the director of public instruction with the government inspectors have ranked the school from that time to the present, sometimes as the model school of the province, and always as one of the first. While it was in advance of other Karen schools,[2] very few of its classes ever passed beyond the middle (grammar) school standard; and the limit of its scholastic ambition was to graduate classes fitted to pass the "entrance examination" fixed by the Calcutta University. In a word, while bearing the name given by its founder, Mr. Beecher, the school aimed to do thoroughly the work of a New-England academy *plus* a comprehensive course of Bible study; and well manned as it was by the woman's societies, with experienced teachers of good education, it was fairly well able to do that work.

{ Footnote: [1] These three energetic, well-trained men are now serving their people under government, as deputy inspectors of Karen schools.

[2] As to secular studies, we presume that the remark is true of all the schools of our mission in Burma (see Appendix C). As to sacred studies the theological seminary would stand first, of course. }

During the year 1876 a two-story L, one hundred feet by twenty-seven, was added to the rear of the girls' schoolhouse,—the upper rooms to be used as dormitories for the girls; the lower rooms, for weaving, storage, etc. The cost of this building was given by an old friend of the mission, resident in Burma. Moreover, much of the timber, and all of the choice iron-wood posts, for the projected Memorial Hall, were collected from the forests, fifty miles or more distant, and conveyed to the building-site. On the 23d of August, at four, P.M., ground was broken for grading the site of the new hall.

Ez. ii. 68—iii. 13 was read by Shway Gah. After a hymn sung by the school, and remarks with a financial statement from Mr. Carpenter, prayer was offered by Rev. J. P. Sahnay, the pastor of the Institute Church.[1] The ladies, and the native teachers of the school, then lifted each a spadeful of earth; and the hard work of removing the top soil, and grading up with laterite, was delegated to the young men and boys of the Institute. At the close of the year we were sending off Bogalay, our first missionary to the Kakhyens of Bhamo; the "Thomas House" had been torn down, and taken to another site to make room for the Memorial Hall; the Chinese contractor was beginning to hew and smooth the posts of the latter; we had taken delivery of a hundred and forty thousand teak shingles from Maulmain, and the building-fund had been brought up to ten thousand six hundred rupees.

{ Footnote: [1] This was one of the last public services performed by this excellent Karen brother. For a brief memorial sketch of his life and character, see Missionary Magazine, April, 1877, p. 97. }

The year 1877 was one of great anxiety and of the severest labor. To add to his legitimate cares, the missionary had been compelled to enter upon a difficult and most unwelcome course with reference to the chief civil authority in Bassein. Nowhere in the world, probably, is there a class of officials more highly paid, or, as a class, possessed of higher qualifications for their responsible duties, than the officials of the British Government in India. There are among them not a few who combine with the highest ability and training the beautiful characteristics of an inward Christian life. British Burma owes much to the administrative power of chiefs like Sir A. P. Phayre and Sir A. Eden, and not less, certainly, to the Christian wisdom, combined with rare general ability, of an Aitchison, a Thompson, and a Bernard. It is the exception, however, that proves the rule. In an interior district, at rare intervals, officers have been known to do what they could on British soil to reproduce the tyranny of the old Burman rule.

It would be easy to fill half of this volume with well accredited facts of what the native subjects of her Majesty had to endure about this time in the Bassein district,—forced labor exacted wholesale over wide tracts of territory; the compelling of all persons of the humbler classes to kneel, in the great man's presence, on the street, or wherever they might chance to meet him; many cases of personal violence done to innocent men by the magistrate's own hands (or feet); Karen Christians obliged in repeated instances to violate the Christian sabbath, and also to contribute for the celebration of heathen festivals, etc. Matters reached such a pitch, that an appeal was made to the highest authorities in May, 1876. This was followed by the wanton wrecking of one of our Karen chapels (in Tohkwau) by the orders of the officer in question and in his own presence; by persistent endeavors to prevent our obtaining the timber necessary for our extensive buildings, on which we had paid advances, and to which we had a legal right; and, finally, by fostering a vexatious criminal charge brought against the missionary, on the alleged ground of "wrongfully confining" one of his pupils nearly a year before. The subject was referred by the chief commissioner to the viceroy of India for orders. An informal and by no means an exhaustive inquiry was held in August, 1876; but it was not until the middle of April, 1877, that the decision of the Indian Government was made known.[1] The delinquent was reduced in rank, and removed to a distant station.[2] In consequence, a sense of relief, and thankfulness for partial justice even, pervaded all classes of native society in Bassein.

{ Footnote: [1] However strangely it may sound to American ears, it is a fact that no inquiry whatever was made into the charge of cruel treatment of the natives, and no fair opportunity was given to the injured persons to present their testimony. No compensation was ever offered for the chapel destroyed; and, in the letter announcing the judgment to the framer of the charges, no weight whatever was given to any thing brought forward by the missionary. It was made to appear that the decision was grounded solely upon a fact confessed by the gentleman himself, that, contrary to the rules, he had accepted a loan of a few hundred rupees from one of his native subordinates. So much for official pride and class-feeling, not to speak of the gross disregard of the rights of the poor and helpless. It may not be out of place to add in a footnote, that the missionary himself was under police *surveillance*, and the name of every visitor to his house was reported to the magistrate daily, for months. The members of his family, as well as himself, were not surprised to find themselves "sent to Coventry" for a still longer period, by all save two or three stanch English friends. — C. H. CARPENTER.

[2] He has since retired from government service. }

On the 5th of February the last of the one hundred and sixteen heavy iron-wood posts of the Memorial Hall was raised, with the English and American flags waving at the top, fifty-six feet from the ground. The roof was completed on the 15th of May, just as the annual rains began. By a great effort the building-fund had been brought up to Rs. 22,850 at the close of the year, but it had been necessary to spend large sums for material and on subsidiary buildings. We had re-erected the "Thomas House" as a boys' dormitory, a hundred feet by twenty-seven, with a carpenter's shop, a turning-room, and a small book-bindery below: we had completed also a very substantial granary of thirty-five hundred baskets' capacity, to receive the rice contributed by the churches. Sheds for grinding and pounding out the school rice were annexed, above which was a dormitory for boys, seventy-two feet by twenty-seven. The rains, moreover, had been very late in coming; and in July and August the district was visited by floods of unprecedented height and continuance. It was feared that the rice-crop would be a total failure throughout Lower Burma. The seedlings were killed, and had to be reset twice and three times. At the same time a cry of deepest distress came from the Telugu Christians across the bay. We might ourselves be in the midst of famine within six months; but an appeal was prepared in Karen, and sent to every one of the churches. As two or three years before, in a time of scarcity in Toungoo, a thousand rupees were cheerfully raised for their needy Karen brethren, so now an equal amount was promptly brought in by the churches, and sent to Rev. Mr. Clough and his associates, for distribution among the suffering Telugus.

In March two more missionaries had been sent, with Rev. Messrs. Cushing and Lyon, to the Kakhyens beyond Bhamo. In October two others volunteered for the same self-denying and perilous work. The Home Mission treasury was empty: what would the pastors do? We shall not soon forget old Mau Yay's reply, "Is the teacher afraid to lend three hundred rupees to the Lord?" Koteh and his companion were at once sent forward with the wife and infant son of S'peh, who was already at his grand work on the mountain peaks overlooking China; and the debt assumed by the pastors was discharged in a few weeks.

On the 31st of December we were five thousand rupees in debt for building, and still we were driving the work as fast as thirty carpenters and sawyers could do it. We had formed the purpose, with God's blessing, to dedicate the principal building May 16, 1878, as the "Ko Thahbyu Memorial Hall." That day would be the fiftieth anniversary of the baptism by Boardman, in Tavoy, of the first Karen convert to Christianity. Ko Thahbyu, afterwards so zealous and successful in missionary labor as to be called "the Karen apostle," was a Bassein man: his widow and son were still living among us, worthy members of the church in Kaukau Pgah. The first jubilee that the poor, once degraded, devil-worshipping Karen ever had, ought to be worthily celebrated.

God was better to us than our fears, better even than our most sanguine hopes. One-third only of the villages lost their crop, for the third year in succession. Two-thirds of the Christian villages, those in the lower part of the district, owing to most favorable latter rains, made a bumper crop; and, most unexpectedly of all, paddy was bringing nearly double the ordinary price. Never before, not even in the year of the great Bengal famine, had the Karens in the fortunate part of the district received nearly so much money for their grain.

At the annual meeting of the association in March, 1878, it was voted, in view of the exigency, to make a second, supplementary effort, and, by a special contribution of two rupees and a half per member, bring the building-fund up to forty thousand rupees before May 16, in order that the memorial building might be dedicated without a debt. The two months following were crowded with blessings and the hardest kind of work for every member of the Bassein mission. It was the hottest of hot seasons, but there was no flinching. The devoted pastors again took hold of the work of collection with fresh zeal and an invincible determination to succeed. It is needless to say, that as a body they themselves gave to the very extent of their resources. An enthusiasm for giving seemed to fall

401

upon the people. On the day of dedication, our building-fund, which we had set at the modest figure of Rs. 20,000, had reached the sum of Rs. 42,342-3-0. The debt was extinguished. There was an abundance of material on hand, and over Rs. 8,000 in cash,—considerably more than enough to complete the Memorial Hall and two or three smaller buildings then under way. The Karen contributions alone during the five months previous had added Rs. 17,139 to the building-fund. For years we had been humming, "In some way or other the Lord will provide." Faith was now changed to sight; and for two days we had such a jubilee as the Jews may have kept, at the other southern corner of the continent, in Solomon or Zerubbabel's day.

At the solemn services Rev. C. Bennett and wife, for fifty years most useful and esteemed members of the Burman mission; the earnest and devoted Mrs. Thomas, who but a few years before had a happy home on the very spot now dedicated to the work of Christian education; and Rev. M. Jameson and wife of the Burman Department, with the members of the Karen mission in Bassein itself,—all assisted by their presence, and some of them by valuable papers, reminiscences, or exhortations. Rev. D. A. W. Smith of the seminary in Rangoon contributed an inspiring Karen hymn. Last, but not least in importance, were the Karen pastors, especially the veterans Mau Yay, Myat Keh, Po Kway, and Shway Bo,—all of whom were prepared for their work and ordained by Abbott himself,—Shway Bau, Tohlo, Dahbu, Pohtoo, and Deeloo, Kyoukkeh from Toungoo, and Rev. Sau Tay from the Karen Theological Seminary in Rangoon, together with the widow and son of Ko Thahbyu himself, and hundreds of others, of high and low degree, from almost all parts of Karendom. To all it was an occasion of deep and thrilling interest. The addresses of Myat Keh, Tohlo, and Shway Bau; the papers read by Mrs. Thomas, Mr. Bennett, Mr. Carpenter, and Sau Tay; the sermon by Poo Goung; and the dedicatory prayer by Mau Yay,—all were worthy of the occasion, and produced a deep impression; while the discussion of the twin-questions, "During the next fifty years what would the Karens have God do for them, and what would the Lord have them do for him?" led many, it was hoped, to fresh and deeper consecration to the divine service.

KO THAHBYU MEMORIAL HALL, PAID FOR BY THE BASSEIN
KARENS, DEDICATED MAY 16, 1878

The building was not finished at the time of the dedication; but a
brief description of it as it was finished shortly after (see engraving)
will not be out of place. Its general form is that of the letter H less the
bottom half of the left leg: in other words, it consists of a main
building with three wings; two projecting on the north, and one,
containing the driveway and front entrance, with tower attached, on
the south. In the centre of the main building is a chapel for the united
worship of all departments on Sundays and at morning prayers. The
audience-room is sixty-six feet and a half by thirty-eight. The floor
slants on three sides towards the platform, which is in the middle of
the south side. Verandas ten feet broad on the north and south sides,
and galleries of the same width on the east and west, add largely to
the capacity of this place of worship. A rich teak entablature runs the
whole width of the audience-room over the east gallery; and upon it
is carved in large Karen letters, "Behold the Lamb of God, which
taketh away the sin of the world." Over the west gallery is inscribed
in uniform style, from Deuteronomy, "These words which I
command thee this day,...thou shalt teach them diligently unto thy
children." On the west wall, side by side with the marble tablet to
Mr. Beecher, already described, hangs its counterpart, with this
inscription:—

"Sacred to the memory of
ELISHA LITCHFIELD ABBOTT.

[In Karen] Father-teacher Abbott.

"Missionary of the American Baptist
Missionary Union, and under God the
Founder of the Bassein Karen Mission.
Born in Cazenovia, N.Y., U.S.A., Oct. 23, 1809;
Arrived in Maulmain, Burma, 1836;
First tour to Kyootoo, Bassein, Dec. 23, 1837;
Died in Fulton, N.Y., U.S.A., Dec. 3, 1854.

"He was enabled to establish fifty Christian
Churches among the heathen, in which
Self-support was wisely practised
From the beginning. His name will ever live
In the traditions of the Bassein Karens
As that of a hero, and their beloved
Spiritual father."

[In Karen] We loved him very much.

The chapel contains also one of J. Estey & Co.'s best missionary organs, the gift of the generous makers. The iron-framed settees in the chapel, and the excellent desks and seats throughout the building (sufficient to accommodate three hundred pupils), are of Chicago make, and were the gift of L. D. Carpenter of Seymour, Ind., and another friend.

The east end of the main building, with its two wings, all two stories, is for the study and recitation rooms of the English department. It comprises one schoolroom thirty-eight feet by twenty-eight and a half, three lecture and class rooms twenty-eight feet and a half by nineteen, and three rooms nineteen feet square, besides much good veranda room. The west end of the main building, with its one wing, is used by the vernacular department. It has one large schoolroom thirty-eight feet by twenty-eight and a half, five rooms twenty-eight feet and a half by nineteen (one of which is occupied by the library), and one room nineteen feet square, besides available room on the verandas.

The south front of the Memorial Hall measures 134 feet; the east, including the tower, 131 feet; and the west, 104 feet. The tower on the south-east corner is four stories, or sixty feet from the ground to the top of the gilded Greek cross. A fine-toned bell presented by "The Fort-holders" of the First Baptist Church Sunday school, New York City, swings in the belfry. The building was thoroughly painted throughout by the students, at the cost of the material only. Most fortunately, the acoustics of the chapel, and the ventilation of the whole building, prove to be all that can be desired. A two-story covered gallery, 350 feet long, connects the Hall with the mission-house and the girls' school; thus saving the teachers and pupils from all exposure to sun and rain in passing to and fro, and the ladies from much fatigue in going up and down stairs.

At the association held in Singoo-gyee, March, 1879, Rev. Mr. Smith, president of the Karen Theological Seminary, was present by invitation, and gave valuable aid in the deliberations of the body. The work of providing the school with ample buildings having been completed, there being also no token manifest of exhaustion on the part of pastors or people, the project of raising fifty thousand rupees to be the nucleus of an endowment for the school, under the name of the "E. L. Abbott Endowment Fund," was discussed. Mr. Smith also wished to know what terms the Bassein Karens would offer, in case the Missionary Union should see fit to remove the theological school to Bassein. A conference was held with the pastors, all of whom were anxious to do every thing in their power to effect an arrangement which they had so long desired. The association finally voted unanimously, and the leading pastors and elders signed a formal pledge for transmission to Boston, to raise five thousand rupees at least, for the erection of a dwelling-house for Mr. Smith; to give for the use of the seminary the seven cottages on the western side of the compound, of which the cost value was not less than five thousand rupees; the free use of the western half of the Memorial Hall, so long as Mr. Smith and his teachers would be responsible for the management of the vernacular department of the Institute; and all the rice needed year by year for the consumption of the pupils of the seminary. It was also voted unanimously to raise within seven years the proposed endowment of fifty thousand rupees, and ten thousand rupees for a small hospital, doctor's house, etc., besides the ten thousand rupees for Mr. Smith's house, and for dormitories to take the place of the buildings to be transferred to the Theological Seminary, in case it should be removed to the Sgau compound in Bassein.

This munificent offer, made in the best of faith, and from no selfish or narrow motives, the Executive Committee were unable to accept in the face of probable opposition from many missionaries. If there were any ground to hope that the offer would be favorably considered, it would doubtless be renewed, and the pledge, like all the pledges of that noble people, would be more than redeemed. Meanwhile the work of raising the endowment goes on. Serious opposition to the endowment-plan was raised, in one quarter at least, where there should have been the heartiest co-operation; but the work went on. Over Rs. 31,000 had been paid in, before ill health again obliged Mr. and Mrs. Carpenter, in November, 1880, to leave Burma. Of this endowment-fund raised by the Karens, $15,066.66 are now safely invested in this country, under the control of the Missionary Union, for twenty years; and the accruing interest, undiminished, is forwarded semi-annually to Bassein for the support of the Institute.

Rev. C. A. Nichols, a graduate of the college and seminary at Hamilton, N.Y., arrived in Bassein with Mrs. Nichols in December, 1879. Under his direction, with the continuance of the divine blessing, the work will not cease to progress. A telegram of a single word, "ten," recently received from him, indicates the purpose of the pastors and the trustees of the Institute to raise and forward $10,000 more towards the endowment this year. May the God of Abraham speed him and them in all their works of faith and patience until the blessed consummation!

To sum up. Since 1868 the Sgau Karen Christians of Bassein alone have contributed Rs. 82,511-14-5 (equivalent, at the rates of exchange current during the period, to $36,564.96) for the erection of permanent buildings, and for the permanent endowment of their Normal and Industrial Institute. There have been no fairs, grab-bags, or ingenious devices of any kind, to lure away their money without their feeling it. That amount has been given out and out, in cash, besides thousands of rupees' worth of gratuitous labor, in addition to all their heavy contributions for the support of the gospel, for the current expenses of the Institute, and their own village schools. In the exercise of a beautiful confidence in the Christian honor and love of their American brethren, this large sum has been either expended on the property of the A. B. M. Union in Bassein.[1] or intrusted to the treasurer of the Union in Boston for investment. Missionary friends and others in Burma have also given within the last twelve years, for the endowment of this school, for permanent school-buildings and furniture, Rs. 53,649-7-4; making a grand total of Rs. 136,161-5-9 permanently invested thus far in this indigenous school enterprise. To this may be added Rs. 4,153-5, given by the Woman's Baptist Missionary Society (mostly to provide accommodations for their missionary ladies) and by private friends in America, and the "Mark Carpenter Scholarship Fund" of $4,000.

{ Footnote: [1] Of late, incited, perhaps, by the example of the Karen Home Mission Society in Rangoon, there has been an increasing desire, on the part of many pastors and laymen in Bassein, to own the valuable property in Bassein in their own name. The writer has not been in favor of yielding to this desire heretofore, although it will doubtless be brought about naturally and easily in the course of time. To hold the property, a Karen Society would have to be formed, and legally incorporated; and the consent of the government to the transfer of the land granted by it to the Free Mission Society would have to be obtained. In the present immature stage of Karen character and social development, differences of view, and practical difficulties of management, would be likely to arise, which would make the possession and control of the mission-compound by them unprofitable and unwise.

In view, however, of the fact that the Christian Karens have expended not less than fifty thousand rupees on this property to less than five thousand expended by the Union, the writer did urge the Executive Committee strongly, to give to the Karen pastors a formal "refusal" of the property, binding themselves and their successors to give the Sgau Karen Baptists of Bassein the right of first purchase, at a price not greater than the actual cost to the Union of the property, whenever the society may think it wise to dispose of the same.

It seems, however, that this suggestion was not heeded, and that an excellent letter (referred to in the Missionary Magazine, July, 1883, p. 203), filled with kind assurances and Christian counsel, was sent, but *not* through the missionary who made the application. It seems to the writer that this refusal to meet a generous and trusting people half way will some day have to be reconsidered. }

To keep up such a scale of giving through so long a term of years, *without allowing their Christian work to flag in any particular*; to do it, as that dear people did, in the face of opposition from without, and finally from within also; in the face of the dismission of four entire churches with their pastors to join the Rangoon association, and of the emigration of not less than five hundred adult members of other churches to the limits of the same association; in the face of the defection of two other large churches through the influence of corrupt pastors; in the face of unusual ravages by pestilence; in the face of the loss of the greater part of their cattle by murrain, of the oft-repeated loss of their crops by floods; in the face of increased taxation, and, for a time, of positive oppression, and the disfavor of their rulers,—was nothing less, surely, than a marked triumph of that divine grace which enriches "in every thing unto all liberality," and works, through the saints, "thanksgiving to God." To Him who increases "the fruits of righteousness" be all the praise!

We close this record of the mingled trials and blessings of forty years' labor in a remote corner of the Lord's vineyard with two instructive tables, which will receive, we trust, the careful attention of all thoughtful readers, although consigned to the Appendix. The first table shows the gradual growth of the Bassein churches, Sgau and Pwo, in numbers, benevolence, etc., from 1857 to 1879 inclusive. The second contains the amounts given by the several Sgau Karen churches of Bassein for the permanent buildings and endowment of their school from 1868 to 1880,—the churches being arranged, not according to the aggregate amounts given, church by church, but according to the average given per member; the smaller churches thus having as good a chance for precedence as the larger,—and also the donations of each church to ordinary and special objects for the jubilee year 1879.

As our readers may be interested to know how the annual contributions set forth in the Appendix are distributed between the various objects, we introduce a short table on the opposite page.

Classified Table of Contributions, Bassein Sgau Karen Churches, 1870-79.

OBJECT.	1870.	1871.	1872.	1873.	1874.	1875.	1876.	1877.	1878.	1879.
	Rupees.	Rupees.	Rupees.	Rupees.	Rupees.	Rupees.	Rupees.	Rupees.	Rupees.	Rupees.
Support of pastors (cash and paddy) .	5,257	5,247	6,165	7,036	7,647	6,887	6,040	7,806	12,117	13,014
Missions, home and foreign (in part) .	1,008	811	903	936	749	746	710	1,049	1,581	1,394
Building and repairing village chapels,	1,685	2,218	2,401	2,402	3,612	5,372	2,789	2,703	2,418	5,853
Village school-teachers	1,849	2,205	2,083	2,290	2,256	2,434	2,017	1,621	2,472	2,687
Books, religious and school (in part) .	2,112	472	425	729	846	1,127	2,182	1,694	2,728	2,634
Town school, in cash and kind . . .	2,340	2,080	1,099	1,841	2,672	3,460	3,049	5,224	6,870	6,378
For buildings and endowment of do. .	1,521	980	1,013	652	333	3,625	5,767	10,127	13,631	23,679
Miscellaneous objects	2,044	277	4,429	4,557	6,176	4,263	5,249	6,307	5,800	5,471
Total rupees	18,746	15,191	19,510	20,476	23,991	27,954	29,612	36,131	47,917	61,578
Average contribution per member . .	Rs. 3-0-1	Rs. 2-7-0	Rs. 3-3-6	Rs. 3-5-0	Rs. 3-10-0	Rs. 4-4-3	Rs. 4-9-3	Rs. 5-8-0	Rs. 7-3-11	Rs. 9-1-4

Classified Table of Contributions, Bassein Sgau Karen Churches,
1870-79

If an inquiry is raised as to the condition in life of these generous native Christians, we reply that ninety-nine hundredths of the laity are ordinary lowland rice-cultivators. Not one of them owns the field which he tills. The high taxes which they pay may be regarded as of the nature of rent paid to the Empress of India, who is the legal proprietor of all ungranted lands in Burma. The charge varies, according to the quality of the soil, from Rs. 1-8 to Rs. 3-4 per acre annually for all land under cultivation. To this, a cess of ten per cent on all tax-bills is added for roads, police, education, etc. Then there is the house-tax of Rs. 5 for every married man under sixty (not a school-teacher, or minister of religion), and Rs. 2-8 for every bachelor; besides the export duty on their rice, and a small duty on most imported goods, which amount to a pretty high indirect tax. They are not, however, impoverished, like the people of Bengal, by *zemindars*. There is no fictitious landed nobility here to stand between the people and the government, fattening on the life-blood of the poor. Lord Cornwallis, whose name is somewhat familiar to Americans, created such a class for unhappy Bengal; but Burma escaped him.

The Bassein Karens are hard workers; and as their district is troubled with an excess of water, rather than the reverse, they are, as a class, undoubtedly more prosperous than the corresponding classes in India. Still, they are poor. Their standard of comfort is low, and they have very little property. A few cattle, a house or hut that counts for nothing, a single change of clothing, a heavy knife or two, a few baskets and other utensils of his own manufacture, a hymn-book or a New Testament, perhaps a gun (it may be the gun without the hymn-book), are all that you will find in the possession of the ordinary Karen householder. Their prosperity is merely relative compared with their own estate under the Burman rule, or that of others in the lowest depths of poverty. Such as it is, their prosperity is not often enhanced by high prices received for their crops in consequence of famines in India. Many of the cultivators accept advances early in the year, to be paid back in kind at harvest, at the very lowest rates. Those who are more fore-handed almost always sell directly from the threshing-floor, both to meet the demands of the tax-gatherer and to save the trouble of storing. The rise in prices, when it comes, takes place after the bulk of the crop is out of the hands of the cultivator; and the profits of India's misfortune are generally reaped by speculators and middlemen. The year 1878 was a marked exception to this rule.

Money is plentier, no doubt, among the natives of Burma than it is among the natives of India; but in comparing wages, contributions, etc., the great difference in the cost of living should always be considered. A common cooly in some of the Madras ports is glad to work for four or six cents a day, and that suffices for his daily necessities. The same man in Burma could easily earn from twenty-live to fifty cents, according to the season; but, if his family were with him, he would require to spend nearly the whole of it to live upon. The prices of all things, not excepting rice even, are far higher in Burma than on the opposite coast of the bay.

While we would not be so bold as to proffer advice to any, a lesson from our experience may possibly be of interest or value to some of our readers; and so we give it. Our experience in Bassein, then, teaches, that, to enlist native Christians heartily in benevolent enterprises, the following things are at least highly desirable: —

(1) The enterprise selected should be of such a nature as to attract them, as well as to commend itself to their Christian hearts and their sober judgment. The Bassein Karens have been eager for Christian education from the first; but that which animated and sustained them throughout this arduous undertaking was the conviction that what they were doing was for the advancement of the kingdom of God and the moral and temporal elevation of their own children. The doctrine of Christian stewardship has been freely preached among them, to the poorest as well as to the richest. The duty, rather the privilege, of giving *out of their living*, if necessary, has been inculcated on all.

411

(2) It is hardly necessary to say that they should have a leader who is strictly responsible, and able to keep accounts. He must also secure their perfect confidence by enlightening them as to his plans at every stage, and by reporting to them frequently the exact sums which he has received and spent, from whom he has received, and for what the money has been spent. The author has always taken great pains to have a well-matured plan prepared in advance, and to talk over his plans, and exhibit his drawings, to as many of the leading men as possible; to keep a small ledger, in which there is a separate account with every one of the seventy odd churches, so that he could answer exactly, at a moment's notice, any inquiry as to the amounts given by any church or leading individual; also to have all his accounts balanced from time to time, and thoroughly audited, and compared with the vouchers, by competent Karens, as well as by fellow-missionaries; and, moreover, to give at all the general meetings of the pastors and people, at least three times a year, a clear and exact abstract of all receipts and expenditures, showing the precise balances on hand, or the deficits to be made up. In a word, he has constantly endeavored to treat the work as *their* work for God, and to hold himself as *their agent and servant for the efficient carrying out of the common design.*

(3) The work once resolved upon, it should be pressed, even in advance of the receipt of contributions. Show the people that you trust their pledges. Like children, they are best taught by "object-lessons." They will best understand and appreciate your plans by seeing them wrought out in brick and wood before their eyes. The work once well begun, the desire and determination of pastors and people to complete it will grow with every stroke of the hammer. If we had waited until twenty thousand rupees had been secured, before beginning operations, instead of dedicating the building at the end of the third year, we should have waited at least ten years before breaking ground; and, before the people would have intrusted a new and untried man with such an accumulation of money to lie dormant, he might have waited till he was gray. That is not the way in which heathen temples and pagodas are built. Such a policy, excellent as it may be for the West, is not in accordance with the genius of Asiatic peoples. The more the writer has ventured in the

Lord's work in Burma, the more he has received. He would therefore earnestly recommend a trial of this method by other missionaries.

(4) "Many a little makes a mickle." Our people being so poor, with no wealthy class to lean upon, their strength lay in their numbers, and unanimity of feeling and purpose. From the beginning, our aim was to enlist in the effort every church, and every member of each church with their children, so far as possible. While the native assistants in town, under the direct control of the missionary, gave largely and cheerfully for the buildings and endowment, month by month, by far the larger share of the credit for our success should be given, under God, to the devoted native pastors. With a single temporary exception, not one of these sixty-five men ever receives a rupee from America, or is beholden to the missionary for temporal assistance of any kind. Of course the missionary's influence over them is very different from what it would be if he had some thousands of rupees of foreign money to dispense among them annually. As a body, they are truly humble men; and yet the writer would not know where to look for manlier men. Their influence over their own people is great. Their mutual regard, their confidence in each other, and their delicate respect for each other's feelings, are touching to behold, and have no little to do, probably, with their efficiency. A small volume might be filled with an account of their sacrifices.

The church at Kaukau Pgah, which heads the list of the jungle churches, is by no means rich, even for a Karen church. It is composed largely of the poorest people; but Rev. Dahbu, their noble pastor, is a man of resource and boundless faith. Of the Rs. 4,289-6 brought in by them for our buildings and the endowment, it is safe to say that the pastor himself contributed more than any four, perhaps more than any six, of his members. Some of the younger men, pastors of the smallest churches, have shown a spirit of self-sacrifice and devotion rarely equalled. Shway Louk, one of our old seminary graduates, receives from his church a salary of just forty dollars a year in money, and about forty bushels of cleaned rice. He has raised from his own people $751 for the permanent buildings and endowment of the school. Ng'Chee, also one of our old

413

seminary pupils, receives from his little church of twenty-nine members twenty dollars a year only, and no rice. This would mean simple starvation, but for the fact that he receives about the same amount from the Home Mission Society for his earnest labors among the heathen. He, too, has brought in for the school-buildings and endowment $162. Shway Chee and his gentle wife, graduates of the Karen Theological Seminary and the Bassein girls' school respectively, eke out a scanty living on $15.45 in money, and forty baskets of cleaned rice. Under his leading, the little church of twenty-seven members has contributed $140 for the special object under consideration. The little church at Th'byeelat, the remotest of all our churches, has but twenty members on the roll; yet the good old elder, one of Abbott's men, has brought in $116 for the Institute buildings and endowment.

The Hsen Leik church has given Rs. 1,660 for the Memorial Hall and Abbott Fund: of this the pastor, Rev. Thahree, formerly Mr. Abbott's personal attendant for years, gave, with his children, Rs. 72 at one time, besides generous sums before and since. The Kyootoo church raised Rs. 2,630. Their pastor, Mau Yay, has been already referred to as the oldest of our pastors, and the first man to learn to read Karen in all Bassein. He is a gigantic man for a Karen, but as gentle as a child. At the time of the English attack on Bassein, his life was sought by the Burmans; and it is said that the cross on which he was to be hung was actually constructed. His zeal in all good enterprises is unbounded. Notwithstanding the complete destruction of their crops by floods, three years in succession, the Yaygyau church raised Rs. 1,408. Their pastor, old Nahpay, never recovered fully from the tortures inflicted upon him by the cruel Burmans. Up to the time of his death, in 1880, his limbs were still distorted, and he suffered greatly from rheumatic pains. In October, 1877, when it was certain that their crop was again destroyed beyond hope, the old man surprised me one day by coming in with Rs. 50-5 for the Telugu famine. I remonstrated with him, and told him that his people had no more rice for the year to come than the Telugus. I knew that the old man and his people were poverty-stricken and suffering, while intelligence had come, that, owing mainly to the unbounded generosity of the people of England, the crisis in Madras was passed.

I proposed to him to take back a part or all of the money, and use it as he thought best; but he would not listen to it. "We think that the Lord will not forget us. He has destroyed the rice, but not the fish. We shall get on in some way." These cases are selected almost at random. Where nearly all have done nobly, to single out any may almost seem to be invidious. The best of it all is, that the elect ones in Bassein have no thought of stopping in this course of giving. Where can we look for brighter examples of sacrifice and devotion on the part of whole communities in Christian America?

In the very crisis of affairs, two months or so before the Jubilee, the writer proposed to send out some of his assistant teachers to aid a few of the pastors in raising their quotas; but hardly one of them was willing to have an "agent" to help them to do their own work. They said it would make them too much ashamed. Of course there are close-fisted, if not miserly, men, even among the Karens. One of the pastors told me of his unfailing device in such cases. He would go with one or two of his deacons, and quietly labor with the brother all day. Very little would be said directly of the real errand. Perhaps the man would disappear, and go to his work. If an apology was offered, it was readily accepted. They were in no haste. They had come to make him a good long visit. They would sleep with him that night, and have a long, earnest talk about "the kingdom of God." A second night was rarely necessary. The next morning, after family prayers, he was generally ready to meet their wishes.

We would urge the importance, finally, of enlisting the aid of the native Christians, at the earliest possible day, in all departments of mission expenditure, save only the personal support of the foreign teacher. The school-buildings and houses of worship on the mission-compound in town should *not* be excepted. No matter how small and insignificant the amount they give at first, let them have an opportunity to help. It is only thus that they can become accustomed to the idea of bearing all of their own burdens; and they will never cease to creep in weakness, unless they are encouraged to stand erect, and walk. Strength and assurance come with the repeated use of limbs and will. "Sow an act, and you reap a habit; sow a habit, and you reap a character; sow a character, and you reap a destiny."

CHAPTER XX.

1881-1887.

"I believe that He who was once crowned with thorns shall yet be crowned with many crowns."—PRESIDENT MARK HOPKINS.

"All nations shall call Him blessed. Blessed be the Lord God, the God of Israel, who only doeth wondrous things. Blessed be his glorious name forever: and let the whole earth be filled with his glory. Amen, and Amen."—DAVID, *the son of Jesse.*

The fulfilment of the prophecy waits upon the lethargy and unbelief of God's people in Christian lands. Oh for the dawning of that day of power in which all Christians, north, south, east, and west, the world around, shall be "willing"!

As the impregnable position assumed by the pioneer Bassein missionaries from thirty to forty years ago has been still further fortified by events recorded in the later chapters, it may be well to sum up the wisdom of the pioneers, and the experience gained by their successors. Briefly, the principles by which the work in Bassein has been uniformly shaped, from the outset to the present time, are these:—

(*a*) "While all Christians, women and children as well as men, are bidden to bear a part in the direct work of evangelization, it is a grave question whether God calls to exclusively religious labor a larger proportion of his church in any land than can be supported, as well as the average membership live, from local sources. The command, "Go ye into all the world," etc., undoubtedly requires the personal service of a far greater number of the ablest men than have as yet responded; but it does *not* (in our judgment) include for Christians at home the duty of subsidizing foreign churches, or of affording regular support to any of the converts who may be made.

(*b*) It is certain that the mere fact of a foreign missionary dispensing considerable sums of foreign money from month to month mars his influence.

(*c*) It is deleterious to the native preacher himself, and to the native church, to receive foreign aid.

(*d*) It puts the native preacher in a false light before the heathen, and seriously diminishes his usefulness.

(*e*) The apostle Paul suffered neither in character nor influence from making tents, elsewhere than in Philippi; nor will the native preacher thus suffer, if, in default of a comfortable support from his own brethren, he ekes out the supply of his necessities, like the Baptist ministry of a former generation in America, by the labor of his own hands or brain for a portion of his time.

In 1841 Mr. Abbott asked, for his great and most difficult work, Rs. 1,500. He was allowed but Rs. 1,000 ($454) for every thing outside of his own support. Notwithstanding this hard treatment, he and his mission got on fairly well; while the small Burman missions in Arakan, each of which received the same amount, and from which he asked for the aid of a few hundred rupees in vain, have long been practically extinct. The worst result of the lavish expenditure of home funds in mission-work is not so much the waste, as we deem it, of Christ's money, as the permanent weakening and emasculation of hundreds of young Christian communities. That destructive influence the Sgau Karen churches of Bassein have wholly escaped, thank God!

On the whole, the prospects of the Bassein Karen mission, though not unclouded, are bright. The hands are too few, but the work is in good hands. May God speed the time when "the little one shall become a thousand, and the small one a strong nation," and when, "from the rising of the sun even unto the going-down of the same," the Lord's name "shall be great among the Gentiles"! What foreign missionary does not long for the day when his peculiar vocation shall be gone,—the day in which the churches in lands now heathen shall be both competent and willing to manage all of their affairs, and to assume all of their Christian responsibilities, — the day when he may be released from the labor and cares which now almost crush him to the earth, — the day when he may be left free, either to spend his declining years in the home-land, amid the scenes of his youth, drinking in the healthful air of his native hills, or, girding himself for fresh conquests, to pass on with a force of his late disciples to the yet unevangelized regions beyond? What of the night, watchman? What signs of promise herald that glad day when we may leave Burma to the care of its own converted peoples, assured that its future and theirs will be bright with the presence and all-sufficient aid of the Redeemer King?

From the facts set forth in the preceding chapters, it is evident, we think, that many long steps towards pecuniary independence have already been taken in Bassein; but, before complete moral and intellectual independence are achieved, it is equally evident, we think, that many more long steps must be taken. Note this patent fact. Whenever the numerous native missionaries of Bassein have been well led by their American brethren, as in Bassein itself, in Toungoo, Prome, and Bhamo, they have done yeoman service, and have been efficient factors, in the work of saving the lost. Note another fact, equally patent. Thus far, in almost every instance in which they have attempted independent missions, as in Upper Burma in 1859, towards Zimmay in 1863, later in the Meklong Valley of Siam, and, shall we add, beyond Zimmay to Lakon in 1881, their efforts have well-nigh come to naught. Long journeys have been made successfully; money for the journeys has been forthcoming, and abundant enthusiasm at the start: but of the home-coming, and of the spiritual results, what can we say?

We have looked also with regret at their weakness in the presence of wrong-doing. If the offender were a Karen of standing and influence, or a man likely to be a dangerous enemy, or even if he were but one of the same family or clan, whom they felt bound, as by secret oaths, to screen from justice, how often have they silently endured his presence in the church or in the ministry, instead of openly rebuking the wrong, and taking scriptural steps for the excision, or the discipline, of the offender! These and other marked weaknesses of character must be overcome before the Karen churches will be truly independent, and able to walk erect, without support, superior to fear, and in danger of no deserved reproach.

Like a young person, a young nation or people must pass through that period when the puffing-up of a little knowledge, and the lack of confirmed strength and confidence, lead to a somewhat unpleasant sensitiveness. The Karens seem to be approaching that stage. They are losing a little of their old docility, they are seeking new avenues to fortune and power; some of them are casting about for leaders of their own race; and perhaps a few would-be leaders are casting about for constituencies. All this is to be expected, and it indicates that the Karen Christians must be treated with more than ordinary gentleness and forbearance until they have had time to attain to that higher stage of mingled humility and self-respect which follows deeper knowledge and hard-won success. May God help and bless them always! With their antecedents and the divine favor which has hitherto rested upon them, they cannot go far wrong; and the day of complete independence, which they and we alike long for, will surely come.

But what of this desired independence when that happy day arrives? Not a few friends of missions have congratulated themselves on the fact that one of the stations in Assam, in the absence of a missionary, has been left for a few years to the management of a native brother. This may have been the best arrangement possible under the circumstances: but the appointment of any native brother by the Missionary Union to the place and rank, as it were, of an American missionary; the regular support of that brother by the Union on a salary much larger than he could hope to receive from a congregation of his own people; the regular payment into his hands of considerable sums of mission-money for disbursement among the other native assistants, thus giving to him a prestige and power that is dangerous to his own character, and as foreign to Assamese ideas as it is to the polity of the New Testament,—this, we say, cannot be the true independence that we are looking for. Is it a small step even, in the direction of that independence? No. Complete pecuniary independence must come first.

Then native leaders must arise, — God's men, "full of faith and of the Holy Ghost;" sons of Burma; not Americanized Karens, but Karens of the Karens; men so pre-eminent in goodness and greatness, that these qualities shall be recognized by their fellow-Christians, who will gladly call them, trust them, and support them, in preference to leaders of any other race, though they come bringing their own support. Such men are wanting now. Their time has not yet come. The educational conditions are still deficient, but they will be made complete. Schools higher and better than any that now exist in all that land will arise, and men of the requisite natural qualities will be forthcoming. Some of the first generation of pastors came short, only by their utter lack of school-privileges. Men like Tway Po and Po Kway among the dead, and men like Myat Keh and Mau Yay, who are permitted still to linger among the living, had all of the natural qualifications of leadership. They had, besides, the grace of God in their hearts in large measure, and, not least, that rare meekness and humility which seem to be so sadly deficient in many of the younger men of the schools.

The Karens are not a decaying people: they are rapidly increasing in numbers.[1] Their mental powers are not on the wane, neither is there any evidence that in spiritual things the grace of God has deserted them; and yet it is a problem where the God-ordained leaders for whom we look and pray are to come from. Among the younger men, our own loved pupils, we see but few who give promise of being to the next generation what the men we have named, and others, have been to the present generation and the last.

{ Footnote: [1] Between August, 1872, and February, 1881, the census says that the Karens of British Burma increased from 331,706 to 518,294, an increment of *fifty-six per cent*. This increase is due, not to immigration, but to fertility. The ratio of increase for the Burmans in the same period was thirty-one per cent only, and they were aided by a large immigration from Upper Burma. The increase in the entire population of the Bassein district is over forty-four per cent, and to this increase the Karens contributed their full share. If the race should continue to multiply in this ratio for forty years to come, there would be over three millions of Karens in British Burma alone. }

Our schools are not what they ought to be. Says President Eliot of Harvard, "A good school is not a grand building, or a set of nice furniture, or a series of text-books selected by the committee, or a programme of studies made up by the superintendent; and all of these things put together, though each were the best of its kind, would not make a good school; for a good school is a man or a woman." Under God the great want of the Karen people to-day is some man or men of commanding intellect, of high training, and absolute devotion, who shall do for the choice youth of the rising generation what Arnold of Rugby and Wayland in Providence did for the young men whom they first drew to their schools, and then moulded to be leaders of thought and action for communities and nations. If such men are to be found, let them know their opportunity, and let them go forth, secure of personal support from the home-land, but looking confidently for the means they need for their work among a grateful people. Let the Karen school or schools of the future be created, not out of nothing, but chiefly from the offerings called forth from a people responsive above most others to the slightest touch of loving and masterful devotion. Let the common schools be improved, and let them reach all, not one-fourth or one-sixth only, of the children. Let us keep striving until the family altar shall be naturalized in Karen homes, and until there shall be some show, at least, of family discipline. Let us strive to infuse a deeper and more genuine love for God's Word and for all useful books. Let us draw out more and more the missionary spirit of that missions-loving people, and systematize and stimulate their efforts in behalf of the perishing. And let us continually wait upon God for his begetting and his anointing grace. Then we may hope to see in due time a prosperous and enlightened people, rejoicing in that happy combination of natural gifts, grace, and culture, which shall mark the new era of complete independence for the Karen churches, and fit them for the highest and broadest usefulness.

If there were evidence of a gradual, even though it were but a slow, throwing-off of the monetary shackles which cramp and enfeeble the development of native churches in some other fields, there would be less occasion for the lessons which this historical sketch enforces. One of the most dangerous features of the subsidizing system, which Mr. Abbott so vigorously attacks in Chap. VII., is its tendency to perpetuate its evil influences. While there has been some gratifying advance, the fact should be recognized, abroad and at home, that the mission which he singled out in 1848 as the special object of his criticism still continues to be the most expensive of all the Baptist missions in Burma, while, for the amount of labor and money bestowed, it appears to have been rather below the average in fruitfulness. Another field in which the pioneer missionaries began their labors on the healthful principle of self-support has drawn, under the later management, increasingly heavy sums from the home churches, until now it is numbered among the most expensive of our missions. Too many other missions are lapsing deeper and deeper into the slough of dependence on foreign bounty.

The Missionary Union as a whole, instead of being free to advance into new fields for the enlightenment of those who still sit in utter darkness, finds its resources subjected to a constant strain to supply the ever increasing demands from the old fields. However important and needful other branches of Christian work may be, most Christian people will agree that the chief work of an evangelical missionary society should be the maintenance in heathen lands of men from the home-land who are called of God to preach the everlasting gospel. The number of men actually engaged in this work on foreign shores at any given time may be taken as a fair measure of the amount of work done in this the main line of the society's operations.

A careful study of the treasurer's reports of the A. B. M. Union year by year since 1840 shows, that, for the ten years 1840 to 1849 inclusive, an average of 33 6/10 American male missionaries were maintained in Asia, Africa, and Europe, including, with preaching missionaries, schoolmen, translators, printers, and new men learning the language. Dividing the gross expenditure for all purposes by the number of men on the field, we find the average expenditure to be $2,425.48 per man. From 1850 to 1859, an average of 36 1/10 men were supported on the field at an average expenditure, for all purposes, of $3,070.39. From 1860 to 1869, an average of 31 6/10 men were kept on the field at an average expenditure per man of $4,389.15. From 1870 to 1879 there was an average of 43 4/10 men, and an average expenditure of $5,336.35. From 1880 to 1883, notwithstanding the restoration of our currency to a gold basis, with an increased average of 54 1/4 men, there was a gross expenditure of $5,322.80 per man. A part of this increased expenditure is due to an increase of salaries paid to missionaries on account of the increased cost of living in the East; a part is due to the sending-forth of so many worthy and efficient single women: but a careful analysis shows that neither one nor both of these together will account for the great discrepancy that exists between the expenditures of 1840 and 1883. To a large extent the increase is due to the largely increased sums expended upon native schools and native helpers. Taking at random the report for 1880-81 for a sample, we deduct the amount of "collections on the field," and the amount of annuities paid to donors of permanent funds, and we have left $275,079.99 for expenditure. Of this total, we find that twenty-one per cent only ($60,030.90) was paid for the support of male missionaries and their families on the field; about seven per cent was paid for the support of thirty-eight single lady missionaries, mostly employed as teachers in the schools; eight per cent, as nearly as we can reckon, was spent upon mission compounds, chapels, school and dwelling houses, of which half, perhaps, should be added to the cost of supporting mission-families on the field; a trifle over seven per cent was paid for the outfit and passage of missionaries, male and female; about four per cent was paid in allowances to missionaries at home on furlough; eleven per cent was used for home expenses proper, including officers' salaries, publications, etc.; while, as nearly as we can reckon, $78,593.45, or twenty-eight per cent of the whole, went for "schools and mission-work," of which nine-tenths, probably, was used in the support of native pupils, or natives engaged in teaching their countrymen or in preaching to them; about ten per cent, also, was sent in aid of native work in Europe and Africa, while about five per cent was appropriated for Scriptures and printing. It is safe to say, that at some stations from two to six times more money from America is now spent than was spent in them by the fathers thirty years ago.[1] More than one of our own Baptist missions might be named which were begun on sound, economical, self-supporting principles by the fathers, but which are now being weakened by the free expenditure of money given by the Sunday schools and churches of this land. Far less money for "station-work," so called, ten times more money for the support of earnest and devoted missionaries to be sent forth from America to reap the whitening harvests in a hundred fields both new and old, should be our rule of action.

{ Footnote: [1] Over forty thousand dollars in specific donations were given last year, through the A. B. M. Union and the auxiliary Woman's Societies, for the support of native preachers, "Bible-readers," pupils, and schools, in addition to large appropriations from those societies for the same objects. (Specific donations for the support of missionaries, for the Children's Home at Newton Centre, for Bible-work, and some other minor objects, are not included in the above statement.) If all of our missions would come up to the position which has been consistently maintained since 1854 by the mission whose story is here told, this large sum, with a large proportion of the present appropriations for "mission-work" and schools, might be at once devoted to the establishment of new missions and the re-enforcement of old ones. The saving made by the hearty adoption of the self-supporting principle would suffice, even with no increase of giving from Christians at home, to enlarge the force of American missionaries on the field nearly if not quite one-half. }

The doctrine of this book, and, we fear, the examples set by Bassein, are not welcome in some quarters; and yet the prevalence of these principles everywhere in our missions is vital to true and lasting success. What can be done to correct the evil referred to? what to convince the most unbelieving and unwilling minds? We reply, after long reflection, that the most direct way to promote self-support throughout Burma is to give to that principle its fullest development and its completest success *in Bassein itself*. It is not only the American missionaries in Bassein (to the Burmans, as well as to the Karens) who are the strongest advocates of the doctrine. Listen to Kyoukkeh[1] and Klehpo, away on the Toungoo mountains; listen to the scores—shall it not be in the future the hundreds?—of men trained in the Bassein schools, eye-witnesses of the benign effects of consecrated enterprise and beneficence on that wide circle of churches, using their influence to reproduce what they have seen, in all parts of Burma and in the adjacent lands. The strongest argument that we can put into the mouths of these and other men who agree with them, the strongest appeal that we can make to backward missions, is to secure the largest and completest success of this principle on the field of its earliest victories in Burma. What, then, is lacking there to-day?

{ Footnote: [1] See Rev. A. Bunker's report of an address "of unusual fire and force" on this subject by Kyoukkeh, Missionary Magazine, June, 1870, p. 171. }

What is lacking in Bassein? Go with me to Great Plains, which once blossomed as the garden of the Lord (pp. 89, 173). Many of the descendants of Wahdee's flock are still there; the fruit-trees which he planted still feed the dwellers by the sea: but the candlestick has been removed, the church is extinct. Drunkenness and licentious revels have taken the place of sober industry and hymns of praise. Buffalo, M'gay-hmau, To-kwau, Layloo, Shankweng, and Wah-klaulot are not much better off. A dozen others are honey-combed with impoverishing, soul-destroying superstitions. Always weak by reason of the unconverted element admitted at the beginning, they are steadily going backward and downward. Half of the churches are comparatively strong; but many things need to be set in order, even in them: and the half-light of the morning should be superseded by the full light of God's day. The dead and dying churches want only to be let alone; but the great desire and the greatest need of the living, self-sacrificing churches and pastors is, and has been for thirty years, *a vernacular Bible school in Bassein itself*.[1]

{ Footnote: [1] See pp. 284, 311, 325, 326, 341, 350, and elsewhere in this volume. }

The simple fact is, that Bassein has been heavily handicapped from the time of the first great ingathering in 1844 until now. Her very numbers, and the weight of the interests involved, have been in the way of her pastors receiving that careful instruction which was essential to the spiritual prosperity of the mission. Said Abbott, "I deem it absolutely essential that I see all these men *together* once in the year. Even were I permitted to visit Burma, and go from church to church through the whole land, I should still deem it essential to have an annual association of pastors,...and to have them all together for several weeks, perhaps months...They cannot go to Maulmain...They have no libraries" (p. 152). Dr. Stevens can call his Burman preachers around him every rains for careful and systematic study of the Bible doctrines and church history. Dr. Cross and Messrs. Bunker and Crumb in Toungoo can and do give hours of solid work to teaching the Bible and other studies every day during the rains. The Karen missionaries at most of the other stations can do the same for their preachers and young men, but the man at Bassein is utterly unable to do any thing of the kind. His time and strength are absolutely used up on other more importunate objects and in the work of superintendence. True, he has the help of one or more ladies from America, and several good native assistants; but it is vain to think that these will supply the lack of his own personal instruction and influence. Abbott, in his annual meetings with the preachers at Ong Khyoung, exerted a mighty influence, the effects of which are still visible. But Abbott's men are fast passing away. For twenty years or more but little has been attempted in the way of personal teaching of the pastors and candidates for the ministry by the missionary in Bassein; and, unless something is done to supply this pressing necessity speedily, still greater declension may be expected.

The compiler of this volume returned to America, at the close of 1880, broken down in health, but charged by the Bassein pastors with an important mission, —a mission that has waited hitherto upon the completion of this history, and the restoration, in some measure, of his strength. At the meeting of the Pastor's Conference, held in

Bassein, May 26, 1880, the following resolutions were unanimously adopted, and signed by nearly if not quite all who were present: —

"*Resolved*, 1. That, without one American missionary devoted exclusively to the work of teaching and conducting a Bible-school in the vernacular languages, the system of schools in Bassein is utterly incomplete, and unable to do for us and for the heathen that which must be done continuously for generations to come, if Christianity is ever to be extended and developed properly in this great district and the regions beyond: therefore

"*Resolved*, 2. That we earnestly desire teacher Carpenter, during his approaching sojourn in America, to secure the services of such a teacher, and an endowment of forty thousand dollars for his support and for the partial support of the school.

"*Resolved*, 3. That, for our part, we hereby pledge ourselves and our churches, in good faith, to build a suitable house for the missionary teacher aforesaid, at a cost of not less than five thousand rupees; to furnish the school with all needed permanent buildings, and to give rice (paddy) year by year, amply sufficient for the sustenance of all pupils who may resort to the school.

(Signed)

"Rev.	MAU YAY.	Preacher	TOO-KYAU.
"	MYAT KEH	"	AY-SHAH.
"	TOHLO.	"	N'KAY.
"	DAHBU	"	SOO-KOH.
"	YOH PO.	"	SHWAY CHEE.
"	THAHREE.	"	KOHKOH.
"	TOHTAH	"	MAU LOOGYEE.
"	POHTOO.	Teacher	NG'THAY.
"	POO GOUNG.	"	YAHBAH.
"	PAHOO	"	BOGANAU, M.D.
"	MYAT KOUNG.	"	NYAHGEH.
"	TOOLAT.	"	THAHTOO-OO.
"	THAHDWAY	"	MAU SHWAY TOO.
"	SHWAY GAH.	"	NAHGOO.
"	TAYNAU.	"	PAHAH."

This money is wanted, not for the support of native preachers, not to feed and clothe the youth of Bassein, not for buildings and land even, but for the support of one additional American teacher in Bassein, if not two. It is easily within the power of a few of the many wealthy Baptists of the Northern States to grant the urgent request of the leading pastors and laymen of Bassein by furnishing a moderate endowment for this most important object. The numerous friends and admirers of E. L. Abbott alone might do it, and thus complete for all time, so far as pecuniary aid from America is concerned, the work which he so grandly began. Shall it be done? By thus subdividing the work, the apparent necessity for the one man to kill himself will be obviated; the work may be done with a thoroughness hitherto impossible; new influences potent for good may be brought to bear upon that field of vast capabilities; and the reproach which has so long rested upon American Baptists, of making inadequate provision for the removal of the ignorance and superstition so long rampant in that field, will be taken away.

To one who has been intimately connected with the Bassein mission for fifteen years, the new stage to which the work should be speedily advanced unfolds itself in these forms: —

(1) Having established the proposed Bible-school, we would call in as many of the pastors as possible, every rains, for special courses of study adapted to their wants. Either provision should be made for their families on the school-compound, or they should be allowed to return to them on Saturdays. Their pulpits would be supplied, in their absence, by the village school-teacher, who is generally, in effect, a licensed preacher. In this way twenty or thirty of the unordained pastors might, without doubt, be speedily fitted to assume the full responsibilities of the pastoral office, and a vast deal of quickening and uplifting influence might be brought to bear through the pastors on the entire district.

(2) The entire native Christian population of Bassein should be resolved into a Christian education society. This plan is already being set on foot by Mr. Nichols. Certificates of life-membership have been prepared. Any Christian Karen may become a life-

member of the new society by the payment of twenty rupees in instalments or at one time, or a life patron of the Institute by the immediate payment of a hundred rupees. A main object is, of course, to secure an endowment for the Institute, but not for that only. If the people grasp the new idea with their former enthusiasm, the "Abbott Fund" will equal a hundred thousand rupees within five years, and it will go on increasing as the churches receive new accessions. The income of such an amount would more than suffice for the wants of the Institute, and we could go on and rear "academies" in local centres like Singoo-gyee, Merpahk'mah, Hsen Leik, Naupeheh, Lehkoo, M'gayl'hah, P'nahtheng, Parakhyoung, and others. Grants from the endowment income, of from two to four hundred rupees yearly, would enable the liberal churches above named to employ two competent teachers the year round. If, in addition, we should be in a position to release those villages from all responsibility of supplying the town-school with rice, we believe that they would go on, and make provision for the entertainment of pupils from other villages. Thus we should have a system of "feeders" for the Institute, and there would be a great gain in general intelligence. We should hope, also, ultimately to aid the common village-schools.

But more especially our object in this educational movement would be to enlist the minds and hearts of all the people for the Christian education of all their children, girls as well as boys, up to the point where they can not only read and write, but think for themselves, and communicate their thoughts to others. While Bassein has sent forth scores of men like Rev. Sau Tay, Rev. Shway Noo, and Taytay, teachers in the theological seminary; Rev. Thanbyah in the Rangoon College; Rev. Myat Thah, assistant to Rev. D. L. Brayton in the translation of the Pwo Karen Bible; Revs. Thahmway, Shway Nyo, Mau Kyah, Kwee Beh, and Shway Do, pastors in the Rangoon association; Rev. Toowah in Henthada; Rev. Pahgau in Prome; Bogalay in Tavoy; a goodly company already referred to in Toungoo; and, best of all, nine foreign missionaries now at work (some of them with wives trained in the Bassein Karen girls' school) on the Kakhyen Mountains, and on the upper waters of the Salween, far beyond British territory; while it has been in the past, and ought to be still more in the future, the great hive from which preachers and teachers go forth to all parts of the land,—the fact remains, that, in educational matters, Bassein is very, very backward.

REV. MAUKEH, HIS WIFE, AND SHWAY GYAU, BASSEIN
MISSIONARIES TO THE KAKHYENS

(3) Steps should soon be taken towards an arrangement which shall do for these churches what "the Sustentation Fund" is doing for the free churches of Scotland. The "pice-a-week" collection, already started, if systematized, and devoted by the churches generally to the objects now proposed, could easily be made to yield from six thousand to eight thousand rupees yearly. A moiety of this sum would be sufficient, if carefully distributed, to bring up the salaries of all approved pastors to not less than a hundred rupees in cash and seventy-five baskets of paddy for each family annually. How would brotherly love increase, and comfort, with no degrading sense of dependence on foreign bounty! The other half would enable us at once to double or treble our expenditure on foreign mission-work. The fields opening so auspiciously on the borders of China and in Northern Siam could be occupied in strong force, and an avenue

thus be opened to the gospel, and to the energies and faith of our most zealous and enterprising young ministers. Nor should we relax our efforts in this direction until every Christian in Bassein is warmly enlisted in missionary work.

(4) We have long had it in mind to institute each season, after harvest, a series of what may be called "revival meetings" in convenient jungle centres, in the hope of calling down upon this people, who seem to be rather unsusceptible to emotion, a more than ordinary measure of the Holy Spirit's power. A meeting of days, devoted exclusively to prayer and the exhibition of divine truth in its more pungent forms, would be something new in Bassein; and, if wisely and prayerfully followed up, we believe that great good might be accomplished.

Without the addition of the vernacular Bible-school to the agencies already existing, no great increase in efficiency can be looked for. The machinery already existing in Bassein is more than enough to task the powers of one man to the utmost, though he were of the ablest. Nor have we failed, we believe, to make the largest use possible of the abundant supply of native talent available at this station. The obvious deficiency is that pointed out so often from Beecher's day to the present,—more American brain and heart to teach God's Word, to devise plans, and, not least, to stimulate and direct the great store of life and energy that lies dormant in that circle of ninety self-supporting, but, alas, for the most part, self-contained and self-satisfied churches. With the addition asked for to the teaching and executive force of the mission, and friction watchfully excluded, the effectiveness of the mission in all its departments should be doubled. The work would be systematized more thoroughly, and a large increase of power and of precious result would be secured. Shall the boon asked for be denied? What field has yielded a richer harvest from the seed sown and the labor bestowed upon it? Does any field now open to the Missionary Union give brighter promise of vigorous growth and abundant fruitage from roots within itself than this? If so, where is it?

The Bassein jubilee properly falls at Christmas-tide, 1887. The fiftieth anniversary of Abbott's first visit to Kyootoo will doubtless be observed with becoming solemnities. Shall it also be observed with fulness of joy? Before that year of grace, with its hallowed associations and precious memories, comes around, the Bible-school, with the help of God and his people in America, maybe in full operation; the "Abbott Endowment Fund," raised by Karens, may be brought up to fifty thousand dollars; the present preparatory school may be enlarged, and elevated to a higher and a secure position; the girls' school may have taken on completer form and fulness of strength; half a dozen academies may be working efficiently at as many convenient points in the district; a full hundred common schools, in the charge of well-qualified masters and mistresses, may be doing their no less important work in as many Christian villages. In all these schools there may be not less than four thousand boys and girls, young men and maidens, in daily attendance. The number of living, growing churches in the district shall have surpassed a round hundred; the members in full communion, a myriad. Fifty, sixty, ordained pastors, and a hundred licensed preachers, shall see to it, that, with regular ministrations of the word to all Christians, not a heathen Karen family in all the district fails to receive the offer of salvation at least yearly, while a thousand miles away, among the robber-haunts of the Kakhyens, and in the realms of despotic Laos princes, a score or two at least of humble, faithful sons of redeemed Bassein, shall be found proclaiming Christ and him crucified, the only Saviour of lost men.

When we survey the past, what God has wrought from such feeble beginnings, the souls that have been born again, the workmen that have there received training; as we look forth upon those churches, and see that their faith in the school and in the missions of their own planning, and their willingness to sacrifice in this glorious cause, are, if possible, greater than ever; as we look out upon the heathen, and see village after village, and tribe after tribe, calling for teachers to lead them into the way of light and life,—our hearts swell with courage and hope. Surely, with all the imperfections and failures, this is a vine of God's own planting. To his name be praises everlasting! And may he incline all who read this record to test the methods which have secured his favor in such glorious results! "God loveth the cheerful giver" indeed; but he loveth best him who is judicious as well as cheerful in his giving. Why should we not help first those who desire Christian instruction, and are striving to help themselves? May the Spirit of truth help us all to see "eye to eye"!

Finally, O ye Christians of great Christian America! absorbed in your farms, your merchandise, your stocks, your families, and in responding to the claims of "society," ye who are engrossed with the architecture of your churches, the music, the sermons, and all the proprieties and elegancies of public worship in these modern days, know ye that the populations of the Pagan world, sixteen times more numerous than the entire population of your own enlightened land, are perishing for lack of the gospel which you can give them, to your own unspeakable advantage. They, God's men and women, for whom our Lord and Saviour died, are going down to the starless, eternal night of the idolater and the devil-worshipper, with no hope. Your Karen allies on heathen shores are in the forefront of the battle, eager for service, but half-armed and un-disciplined. They cry for arms; they cry for leaders. Is not Jesus Christ your King? Has he not laid this great work upon you? Awake! The King's business requires haste. *"How shall they call on Him in whom they have not believed? and how shall they believe in him of whom they have not heard? and how shall they hear without a preacher? and how shall they preach except they be sent?"*

"Shall we whose souls are lighted
With wisdom from on high, —
Shall we, to men benighted,
The lamp of life deny?
Salvation, oh, salvation!
The joyful sound proclaim,
Till earth's remotest nation
Has learned Messiah's name."

433

APPENDIX A.—Table showing the Growth of the Bassein Churches.

APPENDIX A.

Statistics showing the growth of the Bassein Karen Churches, 1857–79.

YEAR.	No. of Churches.	No. of Ordained Pastors.	No. Unordained Pastors and Preachers.	Adult Baptisms.	No. of Pupils in Schools.	Whole No. of Church-Members.	Total Contributions, Religious and Educational.	Average per Member.
							Rs.	Rs. A.
1857	52	8	. .	265	820	5,345	6,785	1–4
1858	52	9	. .	151	304	5,578	6,074	1–2
1859	55	9	. .	298	665	5,479	8,400	1–8
1860	56	9	. .	194	735	5,591	9,586	1–12
1861	61	10	. .	274	1,002	5,776	10,004	1–13
1862	64	10	77	244	874	5,926	9,518	1–10
1863	64	15	89	196	1,070	6,015	10,702	1–12
1864	67	15	92	373	1,006	6,172	14,060	2–4
1865	69	17	94	283	1,183	6,289	20,666	3–4
1866	70	18	93	276	1,118	6,374	16,443	2–9
1867*	58	14	. .	281	1,175	5,862	15,338	2–10
1868*	58	14	60	263	1,321	5,988	16,283	2–12
1869*	59	20	76	363	2,057	6,109	19,361	3–2
1870*	61	21	71	267	1,818	6,201	18,746	3–0
1871*	64	19	78	232	1,616	6,219	15,191	2–7
1872	81	27	100	379	2,071	6,814	20,879	3–1
1873	82	26	103	260	1,942	6,922	23,575	3–6
1874	83	31	92	356	1,833	7,403	23,822	3–3
1875	80	31	94	320	1,993	7,207	31,400	4–6
1876	81	31	87	277	1,884	7,314	33,006	4–8
1877	83	30	92	407	1,544	7,464	39,525	5–5
1878	88	30	93	395	1,858	7,562	53,572	7–1
1879	92	31	99	365	1,998	7,818	68,327	8–12

* Pwo Karen statistics not included from 1867 to 1871 inclusive.

APPENDIX B.—Table.—Contributions of the Churches.

412   *APPENDIX.*

APPENDIX B.

Contributions of the Bassein Sgau Karen Churches.

NUMBER.	CHURCH.	PASTOR.	Members in 1879.	SPECIAL FROM 1868 TO 1880.		ORDINARY AND SPECIAL FOR '79.	
				For Buildings and Endowment of the B.S.K.N. and L. Institute.	Average Member, per	For Support of Pastors, Chapels, Schools, etc. and Endowm't.	Average Member, per
				Rs. A.	Rs. A. P.	Rs.	Rs. A. P.
1	Institute church . .	Rev. Shway Gah . .	53	2,303– 1	43– 7– 3	805	15– 3– 0
2	Kaukau P'gah . . .	" Dahbu . . .	182	4,280– 6	23– 9– 0	3,111	17– 1– 6
3	Shan Yuah	" Pohtoo . . .	146	3,179– 0	21–12– 4	1,983	13– 9– 4
4	Thoungyee	" Toolah . . .	84	1,681– 5	20– 0– 9	765	9– 1– 9
5	Para Khyoung. . .	" Deeloo . . .	240	4,613–15	19– 3– 7	3,049	12–11– 3
6	Hohlot	Shway Louk . . .	87	1,652– 3	18–15–10	713	8– 3– 2
7	Naupeheh	Rev. Tohlo	168	3,164– 4	18– 7– 7	1,799	10–11– 4
8	Ng'kwah	Too-au	73	1,335– 0	18– 1– 0	836	11– 2– 4
9	Kyootoo	Rev. Mau Yay . .	153	2,620– 8	17– 2 11	1,094	7– 2– 5
10	Kohsoo	" Myat Keh . .	175	2,997– 9	17– 2– 1	2,028	11– 9– 5
11	Singoogyee	" Baugyee . . .	154	2,469– 8	16– 0– 6	1,055	6–13– 7
12	Kahb'lah	" Th'dah[1] . . .	61	931– 5	15– 4– 3	607	9–15– 2
13	Adalouk	" Toomyat[1] . .	43	609–14	14– 2–11	491	11– 6– 8
14	Yuahplau	Pohnahpay[1] . . .	71	977– 8	13–12– 2	849	11–15– 3
15	Singoung	N'kay.	88	1,194– 0	13– 9– 1	623	7– 1– 3
16	Dehtberpler . . .	Thahlootoo	27	363– 8	13– 7– 5	247	9– 2– 4
17	Zouayahgyun . . .	Pahlo[2]	43	563– 9	13– 1– 8	264	6– 2– 3
18	P'heeloo	Rev. Tohtah[1] . . .	90	1,154–12	12–13– 3	719	7–15–10
19	Th'byaylah. . . .	Sahyay	20	255– 0	12–12– 0	158	7–14– 5
20	Taukoo	Deedah[1]	85	1,049– 8	12– 5– 5	479	5–10– 2
21	Lahyo	Rev. Ng'Chee . . .	29	357– 6	12– 5– 0	191	6– 9– 5
22	Kaulah	" Myatsoh . . .	49	590– 0	12– 3– 7	370	7– 8– 9
23	Kyangahdouk . . .	" Toomway . .	91	1,107– 0	12– 2– 7	635	6–15– 7
24	Mohgoo	Maupay	197	2,336–15	11–13– 9	1,021	5– 2–11

[1] Deceased.   [2] Fallen.

APPENDIX B.— *Continued.*

Number.	Church.	Pastor.	Members in 1879.	Special from 1808 to 1880. For Buildings and Endowment of the K. S. K. N. and I. Institute.	per Average Member.	Ordinary and Special for '79. For Support of Pastors, Chapels, Schools, etc. and Endowment.	per Average Member.
				Rs. A.	Rs. A. P.	Rs.	Rs. A. P.
25	Awahbeik	Rev. S'Bleh . . .	85	1,020- 8	11-12- 4	625	7- 5- 8
26	Kwengyah, 2 . . .	Shway Chee . . .	27	398- 0	11- 6- 6	299	11- 1- 2
27	Kyun Khyoung . .	Rev. Thahdway . .	155	1,660- 4	10-11- 4	1,562	10- 1- 3
28	Penehkweng . . .	" Pahoo¹ . . .	80	949-11	10-10- 8	602	6-12- 3
29	Taupausoh	Beekoh	101	1,641- 4	10- 4-11	1,014	10- 0- 7
30	P'uahtheng	Rev. Po Kway¹ . .	183	1,855- 5	10- 2- 2	2,232	12- 3- 2
31	Sinleik	" Thahree . . .	165	1,660- 0	10- 1- 0	2,538	15-11-11
32	Kindat	Shwaymyee . . .	45	450- 0	10- 0- 0	234	5- 2- 2
33	Khyoungbyah . . .	Shwaylin²	58	572- 6	9-13-10	246	4- 3-10
34	Teelaypeng	Tookyau	50	564- 0	9- 8-11	322	5- 7- 2
35	Singoo	Shway Poo. . . .	87	827- 8	9- 8- 2	502	3- 7- 6
36	Thahbubau	Shway Byu. . . .	62	571- 4	9- 3- 5	867	13-15- 9
37	M'gayl'hah	Rev. Too Po . . .	133	1,195- 3	8-15- 9	1,291	9- 0- 6
38	Merpahk'mah . . .	" Thahyway¹. .	223	2,087-12	8-15- 4	1,880	8- 1- 1
39	Th'hauser	Toothah	22	193- 8	8-12- 8	77	3- 8- 0
40	Lehkoo	Rev. Poo Goung . .	143	1,115- 4	8- 0- 7	580	4- 0-11
41	Kyootah	" Myatsoh . . .	118	930- 8	7-14- 2	238	2- 0- 2
42	Tahtaseng	Toombau	54	425- 0	7-13-11	610	11- 4- 9
43	Sahprah	Sau Kay.	117	914- 8	7-12- 3	626	5- 5- 7
44	T'kau	Pohlin	18	131- 0	7- 4- 5	135	7- 8- 0
45	Dallah Thounggyee.	Rev. Tahloo . . .	80	571- 6	7- 2- 3	915	11- 7- 0
46	Mwayzah	Shway Gyah . . .	47	330- 2	7- 0- 4	181	3-13- 7
47	Meethwaydike. . .	Rev. Thahtooau . .	134	997- 0	6-15-10	690	5- 2- 5
48	Danoo Khyoung . .	Kweeyoh	108	742- 8	6-14- 0	729	6-12- 0
49	Kaunee	Mau Loogyee . . .	66	449-12	6-13- 0	415	6- 4- 7

¹ Deceased.   ² Fallen.

APPENDIX B.— *Concluded.*

Number	Church.	Pastor.	Members in 1879.	SPECIAL FROM 1863 TO 1880. For Buildings and Endowment of the B. S. K. N. and L. Institute.	per Average Member.	ORDINARY AND SPECIAL FOR '79. For Support of Pastors, Chapels, Schools, etc., and Endowments.	per Average Member.
				Rs. A.	Rs. A. P.	Rs.	Rs. A. P.
50	Kyauk'rer	Sahdoo	107	709- 4	6-10- 0	920	4-15- 0
51	Hseatgyee	Sau Ng'too	64	407- 7	6- 5-10	375	5-13- 9
52	Shankweng. . . .	Pahyeh¹	52	312- 2	6- 9- 0	Not in	fellowship.
53	Tauk'loh	Thahchoo	30	230- 0	5-14- 4	570	14- 9-10
54	Wetsoo	Mau Ko	86	467- 2	5- 6-11	337	3-14- 8
55	Mahgon	Rev. Yohpo . . .	57	307- 0	5- 6- 2	309	6- 7- 7
56	Layloo	Shway Au	100	516- 0	5- 2- 6	231	2- 5- 0
57	Yaygyau	Rev. Nahpay² . . .	274	1,497- 8	5- 2- 2	587	2- 2- 3
58	Taukahlat	Mau Oo	99	486- 5	4-11- 7	254	2- 9- 0
59	Kwaydoukkhyoung.	Rev. Myat Koung .	74	342- 0	4- 9-11	390	5- 4- 4
60	Kwengyah, 1 . . .	. . . .	65	262- 7	4- 0- 7	No return.	
61	Kyedaukweng. . .	Shway So	140	562- 0	4- 0- 2	303	2- 2- 7
62	Winkabah	Shway Nee	72	282-10	3-14- 9	226	3- 4- 5
63	Tohkwau	Thahlweh	57	290- 4	3-10- 8	113	2- 0- 0
64	Ong Khyoung . . .	Maudau	105	384- 4	3-10- 6	254	2- 6- 8
65	Nyohmau	Shway Bau	180	657-10	3- 7- 8	686	3-10- 1
66	Tanthonbeng . . .	Kahpeh	67	191- 0	2-15- 6	258	3-13- 7
67	Seingtoekweng . .	Keekoh	171	430- 3	2- 8- 0	356	2- 1- 4
68	Kwengthah	Ayshah	45	97- 0	2- 2- 6	80	1-12- 5
69	Buffalo	. . . .	31	39- 7	1- 4- 4	No return.	
70	Khyenggön. . . .	. . . .	20	29- 4	1- 0- 2	No return.	
71	Gonmeng	. . . .	37	17- 0	0- 7- 4	No return.	

¹ Fallen.   ² Deceased.

N. B. — Twelve *pies* make one *anna ;* sixteen *annas*, one rupee. The rupee, at par of exchange, is nearly equivalent to 45¼ cents United-States money. Owing to the fall in value of all silver currencies, the value of the Indian rupee at present is about 41 cents.

APPENDIX C.

TESTIMONIALS TO THE EXCELLENCE OF THE BASSEIN KAREN NORMAL AND INDUSTRIAL INSTITUTE.

Hon. Sir Ashley Eden, then Chief Commissioner of British Burma, since Lieutenant-Governor of Bengal, and member of the Council for India, after spending several hours in the school (Sept. 2, 1871), wrote officially as follows:—

"I may safely say, that I have seldom paid a visit to any school from which I derived more satisfaction and pleasure. The proficiency of these Karen children in geography, arithmetic, and geometry, was extraordinary, and reflects the highest credit upon those by whom they have been taught. I had not time to hear the classes go through their course of study in any subjects except those I have mentioned. The singing was remarkably good...No doubt, in the course of time the training of a large number of Karen children will leaven the mass of the Karen population."

In September, 1873, Bishop Milman of Calcutta wrote as follows in the Visitor's Book of the Institute:—

"I had much pleasure in visiting the Sgau Karen Institute, under the charge of the Rev. Mr. Hopkinson. I cannot, from ignorance of the language, judge with any certainty; but, as far as I could follow, the pupils seemed well taught. The answers were quickly given, and apparently with accuracy: the tone and manner of the school seemed very good. The English taught was good, as far as it went. It is pleasant to see these Christian schools, and to consider what general progress in the district they indicate. I am sorry that I have not time to write more fully.

(Signed)
"R. CALCUTTA,
"Bishop and Metropolitan."

Mr. Rivers Thompson, C.S.I., Chief Commissioner of British Burma, and later a member of the Supreme Government in Calcutta, made a personal donation of two hundred rupees to the school, and wrote as follows, Aug. 24, 1875:—

"I visited the Sgau Karen school this day, accompanied by Capt. and Mrs. Wells. The different classes were examined before me in English reading, the Scriptures, arithmetic, geography, and the elements of physiology, with a success which gave me a very pleasant surprise.

"I wish to record, what I took the opportunity of expressing verbally at the close of the examination, that the government is largely indebted to Mr. and Mrs. Carpenter and their coadjutors for the work they have undertaken in the education and advancement of these tribes. It is a very noble work, looked at merely for its secular advantages; but it has higher aims, and will, I have no doubt, under God's blessing, bear rich fruit yet for the good of the district and the country generally...

"The Institution well deserves the grant-in-aid which it receives from government."

The next chief commissioner, Mr. C. U. Aitchison, C.S.I., now Lieutenant-Governor of the North-West Provinces, with a handsome donation, wrote as follows, July 6, 1878:—

"The visit which I paid to this school yesterday afforded me the most sincere pleasure. I had often heard of the school before I came to Burma, but was not prepared to find it so large, so efficient, so thoroughly well managed in every respect. The importance of the work, both secular and missionary, which is being quietly and efficiently done by Mr. and Mrs. Carpenter and their staff of teachers, cannot be overestimated. They are laboring in a field which the government cannot by its educational establishment overtake; and their efforts for the education and elevation of the Karen tribes deserve the cordial acknowledgments of all interested in the welfare of this province. Those more competent to estimate with precision the educational results than I am have recorded opinions most favorable to the school and the methods of teaching adopted in it. For myself, I will say, that the pupils in the various classes examined acquitted themselves in reading, spelling, arithmetic, and geography, better than in any of the schools I have yet seen in Rangoon, or elsewhere in Burma. In writing English to dictation, the pupils were not so strong.[1] I heartily wish Mr. and Mrs. Carpenter Godspeed in their noble work."

{ Footnote: [1] Owing to a lack of time, Mr. Aitchison was unable to examine the two highest classes. — C. H. C. }

Bishop Titcomb wrote as follows on the same day: —

"The Bishop of Rangoon, who accompanied the Chief Commissioner in his visit to this Normal School, has the sincerest pleasure in stating his full concurrence with every word written upon the preceding page. The bishop left the Institution lifting up his heart in praise to God for the noble and successful work of missionary education conducted by the American brethren, and begs to assure them, that, so long as he is spared to the diocese upon which he has entered, their labors will always have both his sympathy and admiration.

(Signed)
"J. H., RANGOON."

Mr. M. H. Ferrars, Senior Inspector of Schools, had officiated as Director of Public Instruction for one year. On the 14th of August, 1879, he wrote thus: —

"In the Departmental Annual Report, 1877-78, I designated the Bassein Sgau Karen school the model school of the province, both as regards aims and attainments. In this its relative position it has not been disturbed, nor do I perceive much prospect of its being so. A record of the absolute position of the school, however, is desirable, and would have been provided by the provincial examinations, but for the circumstances of many pupils having held back, for reasons of their own, and of the pupils not being trained throughout the year with almost the sole aim of these examinations in view. In my tour of 1879-80 I am applying tests of a more incisive kind even than the provincial examinations, and of a character as uniform as theirs. The results obtained at all schools will be compared at the close of the year. The 'imponderables' will find no place in this comparison. And in this comparison, as far as my tour has extended, the Sgau Karen Normal School is as far ahead of the others which I have examined as it is ahead of them in those respects where sentiment and opinion have a more legitimate scope."

On the 29th of the same month Mr. Ferrars wrote again: —

"The results I obtained in the Rangoon Government High School were a little lower than at Mr. — —'s school, of which your school is about one class in advance. Your school is accordingly head and shoulders above all the schools of the province."

Mr. Aitchison wrote again, Sept. 14, 1879: —

"I have again had the pleasure of a visit to the Sgau Karen Institution, and am not surprised to find it maintains its well-established reputation. I examined the ninth, fourth, and first classes. The performances in all were very creditable, particularly those of the fourth class in geography and arithmetic, and the first class in algebra, arithmetic, and the elements of botany. The Institution fully merits the commendation bestowed on it by the Inspector of Schools. I am very glad to see the spacious hall completed, and in full use. The building has been almost entirely constructed by contributions from the Karens, and bears strong testimony to their appreciation of the Christian education afforded. Mr. Carpenter and his staff of efficient and devoted teachers are doing a noble work in which I again wish them God-speed."

Mr. P. Hordern, for many years the efficient Director of Public Instruction in British Burma, wrote, Nov. 29, 1879: —

"It is nearly four years since my last visit to this school; and, comparing its present condition with that in which I found it in 1876, material and satisfactory progress is evident in every direction. The first sign of the school's prosperity, is seen in the handsome buildings which have been completed since my last visit. The existence of these buildings,—among the finest school-buildings in the province,—which have been erected mainly by the munificence of the Karen villagers, is a most gratifying proof of the popular appreciation of the work which the school is doing. It is also abundantly evident that the facilities for school-work thus given have been, and are being, used to the best advantage. Mr. and Mrs. Carpenter are supported by a very efficient staff of teachers, both native and American; and the thoroughness of the work done is seen in every class.

"I remember the ready response given by the managers a few years ago to the desire of the government, that the study of the Burmese language should be encouraged in Karen schools, and I have been much struck by the progress made in this direction. The familiarity with the language shown throughout the school is at once a novelty in Karen schools, and evidence both of hearty co-operation with the Education Department, and of careful and diligent teaching. The English language is no less carefully and successfully taught.

"The first class showed a fair knowledge of algebra, and in arithmetic a high standard is reached. My examination was necessarily limited, but was enough to enable me fully to confirm the favorable judgment passed by inspecting-officers and other visitors, and to satisfy me that the school has not stood still, but has steadily progressed during the past four years.

"Tested by the newly prescribed standards, the school will, I anticipate, hold a high place; and I should hope that a class or department may be formed to prepare pupils for the university entrance examination. It is very desirable that the Karens should be tested by the same standards as their Burmese fellow-countrymen, and the way for such competition has been admirably prepared in this school."

Mr. C. Bernard, the late Chief Commissioner, and long a member of the Supreme Government in Calcutta (a nephew of the late Lord Lawrence), visited the school Aug. 18, 1880, and sent, with the following minute, a personal donation of two hundred rupees: —

"I have been much surprised and delighted with what I have seen to-day at the Karen Institute, and at what I have heard regarding the sixty-four Christian Karen villages in the interior connected with the Rev. Mr. Carpenter's mission. I was allowed to examine and test the work of most of the classes, to see all the schoolrooms; dormitories, dining-rooms, and other arrangements. On the whole, it is quite the most complete thing of its kind I have seen in British India. The progress of the higher classes in English, geography, arithmetic, and in penmanship, was very satisfactory. Scriptural knowledge is, as it always ought to be at a missionary school, well taught and fairly understood. Saving the three American ladies who have given their lives and talents to Karen mission-work, all the teachers are Karens, and all are Christians.

"It is pleasant to hear that some thirty or forty village schools in Christian Karen villages are dependencies of and offshoots from this Institution, and also to learn that the American missionaries have got the Karens to adopt and act upon the Western principle of self-help.

"Mr. and Mrs. Carpenter and their fellow-workers, and the native pastors and elders of the Karen mission, are to be congratulated on the great and successful work they are doing. From the government point of view, their work and its results are full of promise for the future of the Karen race in British Burma. I have been glad to see that my predecessors, and many public officers of different grades and departments, have given their hearty sympathy to the Bassein Karen Mission Institute."

The present Chief Commissioner, C. H. Crosthwaite, Esq., visited the Institute, July 4, 1883, and left on record the following: —

"I have not seen any thing in India which gave me so hopeful a view of the possible future of the people as this school has done. I have heard much of what the American Baptist Mission have done in Burma, but I do not think any one who has not seen this establishment can appreciate the results of this mission. It has manifestly raised the Karens, and placed them on a distinctly higher stage of civilization. I consider the government of India is deeply indebted to the American Baptist Mission for their work. They have succeeded, where we utterly failed, in winning and civilizing this timid and formerly oppressed race. I have no doubt that their present success is only a beginning, and that we shall see these Christian Karens progressing, and forming a very valuable element in the population of British Burma. I hope and believe they will gradually attract and influence their wilder brethren in the hills.

"One of the best characteristics of the Institution, and that which promises best for its permanence, is that it is self-supporting. This shows the value the Karens place on it, and it is not likely that it will meet with less support when every Karen village shall be full of men and women educated in it.

"Of the singing I need say nothing. Every one has heard of Karen singing, and we were delighted with it. I am very much obliged to Mr. Nichols for allowing us to hear it, and for his kindness in showing us all over the Institution. If I remain in Burma, I shall certainly visit the school again."

Further quotations are needless; but it should be added, that the above are a few only out of scores of favorable notices and reports of the Bassein Sgau Karen Institute.

INDEX.

Witchcraft,

Yahbah, Moung,
Yohpo, Rev.,
"Young Chief" (Shway Weing),

Lightning Source UK Ltd.
Milton Keynes UK
UKHW010637230721
387648UK00001B/6